Neural Mechanisms in Behavior

A *Texas Symposium*

Edited by Dennis McFadden

With contributions by
H. B. Barlow, R. M. Boynton,
E. V. Evarts, E. R. Kandel,
F. Ratliff, J. E. Rose,
and R. F. Thompson

With 151 Figures

Springer-Verlag
New York   Heidelberg   Berlin

DENNIS McFADDEN
Department of Psychology
University of Texas at Austin
Austin, Texas 78712, USA

Library of Congress Cataloging in Publication Data
Main entry under title:
Neural mechanisms in behavior.
    Sponsored by the Dept. of Psychology of the University
of Texas at Austin.
    Includes index.
    1. Neuropsychology—Congresses. I. McFadden,
Dennis. II. Texas. University at Austin. Dept. of
Psychology.
QP360.N49   1980   152   79-25314

9 8 7 6 5 4 3 2 1

ISBN 0-387-90468-9 Springer-Verlag New York Heidelberg Berlin
ISBN 3-540-90468-9 Springer-Verlag Berlin Heidelberg New York

Preface

This book is the product of a two-day symposium held at the University of Texas, Austin, in March 1978. There was double motivation for our hosting a symposium on neural mechanisms in behavior. The 1977–1978 academic year marked both the 50th anniversary of the Department of Psychology at Texas and the 30th anniversary of the famous Hixon Symposium organized by the longest serving member of the department, LLOYD JEFFRESS. PHILIP GOUGH, then chairman of the department, suggested that the department celebrate these two historic events, and honor itself in the process, by holding the first of a series of symposia on topics in experimental psychology. Approval and initial funding for this enterprise came from ROBERT KING, then Dean of Social and Behavioral Sciences; additional funds were provided by the Program in Cognitive Science of the Sloan Foundation. Proceeds from the sale of this volume will all pass into a fund to help support subsequent symposia and volumes.

At 50 we are clearly a young department, even for a psychology department, but psychology was at least nominally present from the beginning of The University of Texas in 1883. Then, courses in psychology were offered in the School of Philosophy and had wonderful titles, such as "Mental Science (Strictly Speaking)." In 1898, the first experimental psychology course was offered. (Or at least it was intended to be offered; the catalog indicated that it was contingent upon the availability of necessary equipment. I suppose there have always been purchasing problems.) In 1915 psychology moved up to share a title of an administrative unit as the School of Philosophy became the School of Philosophy and Psychology. In 1925 the same unit became a department, and in 1927 the Department of Psychology became an independent unit.

The faculty of the first department consisted of one professor, three associate professors, and two instructors (the University's faculty numbered 111). One of the associate professors was LLOYD JEFFRESS, who had come the previous year (as an instructor) after completing his degree under WARNER BROWN at Berkeley. His intent was to stay one year and move on, but he abandoned that plan and ended up staying and teaching 52 years. One must hedge a little bit on this statistic, for they were not 52 *consecutive* years —he missed one in the middle, 1947–48, which he spent as a visiting professor in biology at Cal Tech in Pasadena. One purpose of this sabbatical was to organize a symposium on cerebral mechanisms in behavior to be supported by the Hixon Fund. This fund was established from the estate of Frank P. Hixon in order to "support scientific endeavor which offers promise of increased understanding of human behavior." One of the members of the committee established to administer this fund was Lloyd's boyhood friend, LINUS PAULING, and it was from a Sunday afternoon conversation Lloyd and Linus had about possible neural mechanisms of memory that the idea for a symposium sprang.

Lloyd was able to attract a very impressive array of people as participants. Papers were given by JOHN VON NEUMANN, WARREN MCCULLOCH, R. LORENTE DE NO, KARL LASHLEY, HEINRICH KLÜVER, WOLFGANG KOHLER, and WARD HALSTEAD, but also in attendance and active as discussants were the likes of RALPH GERARD, DONALD LINDSLEY, PAUL WEISS, and C. A. G. WIERSMA, not to mention Jeffress and Pauling. That the mean IQ was very high is clear, but perhaps the small standard deviation is even more impressive than the large mean.

As you can imagine with a group such as this, the conversation sparkled, and the excitement and tension still come through today, even in the edited version that was published [L. A. Jeffress (ed.), *Cerebral mechanisms in behavior*. New York: Wiley, 1951].* As a consequence, the book still makes for fascinating reading. In one section, von Neumann challenges McCulloch after McCulloch asserts that memory simply cannot be a matter of reverberating circuits because during coma and sleep *all* neural ac-

* Reprinted as: L. A. Jeffress (ed.), Cerebral mechanisms in behavior: The Hixon symposium. Hafner Press, 1967.

tivity ceases, yet memories are retained after arousal. Von Neumann wants to know what the evidence for this cessation of *all* neural activity is, and McCulloch says something to the effect that he can turn the gain on his amplifiers all the way up and still cannot see anything. Von Neumann persists. He wants to know whether that really means *all* neural channels are silent or whether the problem is one of instrumentation, and somehow McCulloch eludes this attack and finesses the whole issue. In another place, Linus Pauling asks in all seriousness how *big* a memory might be. And the marvelous part is that his question is multiple choice! Is it between 2 and 10 Å, between 10 and 40 Å, or from 40 to 500 Å? Of course, the question was not an idle one. For him, different implications followed from the different answers. I think my point is made; it is simply that the book still offers the student of the brain some fascinating reading, and I recommend it to all who have not read it or who have not read it recently.

In their wide-ranging discussions, the participants in the Hixon Symposium touched on nearly every active research area in experimental psychology today—sensory processes, neural coding, learning and memory, attention, arousal, sleep, motor control, language, reading, etc. Our hope in organizing this symposium was to update those discussions and, further, to attempt to uncover those research topics that will be actively pursued 20 and 30 years from now. In accord with these goals, we invited participants whose interests or specialities covered all, or at least most, of those topics touched on in the Hixon Symposium, and I believe our success rivals Dr. Jeffress's 30 years ago.

Each participant spoke for about an hour, after which there was a discussion period. A longer discussion period followed the last talk on the second day. These discussions were tape recorded and transcribed. I edited the transcription for disfluencies and redundancies and then copies were sent to the participants for comments. I requested that they restrict their editing to matters of substance and that they try to preserve the flavor of the spoken English whenever possible. All cooperated fully in this. The majority of the changes made were clearly motivated by a desire to ensure the reader's understanding. In most instances this was accomplished only by rearranging words and phrases; sometimes rearrangement was accompanied by the addition of supplementary information. However, the essence of the questions and answers was never altered intentionally either by the participants or by me. Unfortunately, the eye is less

accepting than the ear. I was forced to delete some phrases
and comments that convey much meaning and information
when heard but that cannot be adequately punctuated, emphasized, or inflected in print and only serve to disrupt
smooth reading. The loss is primarily in mood—I believe
the relaxed informality of the discussions still comes through,
but when heard unedited, they seem much more lively and
spontaneous than does the edited text. I suppose this loss
is inevitable, but I regret it nevertheless.

Obviously, I have had much help prior to and during the
symposium, and in the preparation of the manuscript for
publication. Primary among these has been JUDITH SEARCY,
who has aided at every turn and as usual has done most of
the real work. ED PASANEN, JOE and JULIE KEARNEY, TED
LANGFORD, MIKE DOMJAN, and TERESA TICE gave needed
help at critical points. JOEY WALKER cleaned up the finan-
cial confusion that somehow followed me like a wake. Finally,
I want to thank the symposium's participants for their cheer-
ful cooperation at every stage of the project.

Austin, Texas   DENNIS MCFADDEN
Spring 1980

Table of Contents

Symposium participants. *Front row:* Floyd Ratliff, Jerzy Rose, Eric Kandel.
Back row: Dennis McFadden (moderator), Robert Boynton, Edward Evarts,
Richard Thompson, Philip Gough (chairman of Psychology department),
Horace Barlow.

List of Contributors

JERZY E. ROSE
The Laboratory of Neurophysiology, University of Wisconsin, Madison, Madison, Wisconsin 53706, USA

ROBERT M. BOYNTON
Department of Psychology, University of California, San Diego, La Jolla, California 92093, USA

FLOYD RATLIFF
Professor of Biophysics and Physiological Psychology, Rockefeller University, 1230 York Avenue, New York, N.Y. 10021, USA

HORACE B. BARLOW
Kenneth Craik Laboratory, Department of Physiology, Cambridge, CB2 3EG, England

RICHARD F. THOMPSON
Department of Psychobiology, University of California, Irvine, California 92644, USA

EDWARD V. EVARTS
Laboratory of Neurophysiology, National Institute of Mental Health, 9000 Rockville Pike, Bethesda, Maryland 20014, USA

ERIC R. KANDEL
Department of Physiology, College of Physicians and Surgeons, Columbia University, 168th St. and Broadway, New York, N.Y. 10032, USA

CHAPTER 1

Neural Correlates of Some Psychoacoustic Experiences

Jerzy E. Rose

It is altogether fitting and proper that in celebration of the achievements of Dr. Jeffress I present several sets of neurophysiological data that seem relevant to the understanding of some psychoacoustic experiences in humans. Our data concern (1) monaural cochlear masking, (2) combination tones, (3) the relation of threshold to tone duration, and (4) pitch of complex sounds and, just possibly, consonance of musical intervals.

I shall restrict myself to results obtained by our Wisconsin group on single auditory nerve fibers of the squirrel monkey and on single neurons located in the anteroventral cochlear nucleus of the cat. Our research team has varied over a period of years and I am but one member of the team. The other members have been Dr. J.E. Hind, the permanent member of the group; Dr. D.J. Anderson; Dr. J.F. Brugge; Dr. M.M. Gibson; Dr. L.M. Kitzes; and Dr. G.F. Smoorenburg. Each of them has been instrumental in the success of the various joint enterprises. I wish also to thank especially Dr. Gibson for her invaluable help in analyzing some of the data that are used in this publication.

1 Introductory Observations

Before I present the appropriate evidence it is useful to recall that auditory nerve fibers and a large class of cells located in the anteroventral cochlear nucleus have similar discharge characteristics (Rose, Hind, Anderson, & Brugge, 1971; Rose, Kitzes, Gibson, & Hind, 1974). Therefore, it is often of great advantage to record from an anteroventral cell rather than from a nerve fiber, because an electrode remains commonly for many hours in contact with a cell, whereas contact with a nerve fiber is usually of short duration. In the presentation to follow, unless otherwise stated, a finding reported on an auditory nerve fiber holds true also for an anteroventral neuron of the mentioned class, and vice versa.

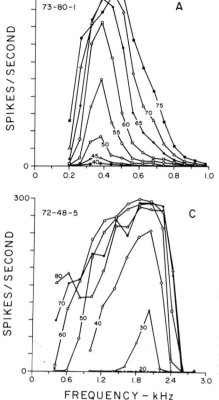

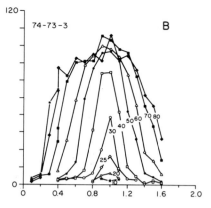

Figure 1.1. Pure-tone response areas in the form of isointensity contours for three neurons. Sound-pressure level (SPL) in decibels re 0.0002 dyne/cm² is indicated for each curve. Abscissa: frequency in kHz. Ordinate: discharge rate. Tone duration: 5 sec. Neurons located in the anteroventral cochlear nucleus. (Modified from Gibson, Hind, Kitzes, & Rose, 1977—with permission.) (Copyright by Academic Press Inc. (London) Ltd.)

Figure 1.1 shows the response areas of three single neurons. Stimulus frequency is plotted on the abscissa. The ordinate shows the discharge rate. Each response area is defined by a series of isointensity contours. The numbers indicate the stimulus level in decibels. For each response area there is a frequency, called the best or characteristic frequency, that is the optimal stimulus in terms of the discharge rate. This best frequency is 380 Hz in Figure 1.1A, 1,000 Hz in Figure 1.1B, and 2,000 Hz in Figure 1.1C. When the stimulus level is raised, the effective frequency band broadens systematically. It usually broadens predominantly toward higher frequencies when the best frequency is quite low, more or less symmetrically about the best frequency when the latter is about 500–1,000 Hz, and the effective frequency band tends to broaden predominantly toward lower frequencies when the best frequency is higher than about 2,000 Hz.

I shall not discuss here the mechanisms that are responsible for such findings except to state that the best frequency indicates, as it were, that locus on the cochlear partition at which the mechanical disturbance, caused by a given frequency, is maximal. For the purpose at hand, the important conclusions are that the effective frequency band is, within limits, a function of stimulus level, and that at any level the effective band is restricted to a smaller or larger segment of the frequency spectrum in which the animal is known to hear.

It is obvious from the graphs that there are many frequency–intensity combinations which yield the same discharge rate. One may perhaps infer that if the discharge rate is the same the information transmitted is altogether equivalent. This, however, is not the case, at least not when the neuron responds to low-frequency stimuli. Figure 1.2 shows the response area of a neuron whose best frequency is 380 Hz. The effective frequency band broadens as the stimulus intensity is raised. At 65 dB sound-pressure level (SPL) the effective band ranges from less than 200 Hz to about 700 Hz. It will be noticed that at this stimulus level the frequencies between about 300 Hz and 540 Hz cause similar discharge rates. Let us examine the fine time structure of the response for each frequency that has produced a substantial number of spikes at 65 dB SPL. One way to do this is to measure successive intervals between discharges throughout tone presentation and to plot the duration against the number of interspike intervals.

Figure 1.3 presents such plots for neuron 73-80-2. The abscissa shows the duration of the intervals in milliseconds, each bin being 100 μsec. The ordinate indicates the number of intervals per bin. Dots below the abscissa indicate integral multiples of the period for each frequency employed. In every histogram, the interspike interval distribution is sharply polymodal. Each modal population is approximately normal. The modal peaks tend to coincide with the integral multiples of the stimulus period. Discharges occur preferentially during a segment of the stimulus cycle; they are locked to the cycle of the stimulating frequency. We term such a discharge pattern a *phase-locked response*.

If the discharges are phase locked at any intensity level, they remain phase locked at all effective sound-pressure levels. Figure 1.4 provides evidence for this statement. The neuron responds to its best frequency of

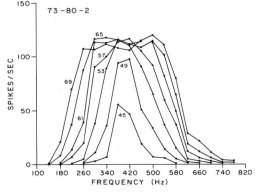

Figure 1.2. Isointensity contours for neuron 73-80-2. Abscissa: frequency in Hz. Ordinate: discharge rate. Tone duration: 5 sec. Other data for this neuron are shown in Figure 1.3. Location: anteroventral cochlear nucleus. (From unpublished material of Gibson, Hind, Kitzes, & Rose.)

73 - 80 - 2

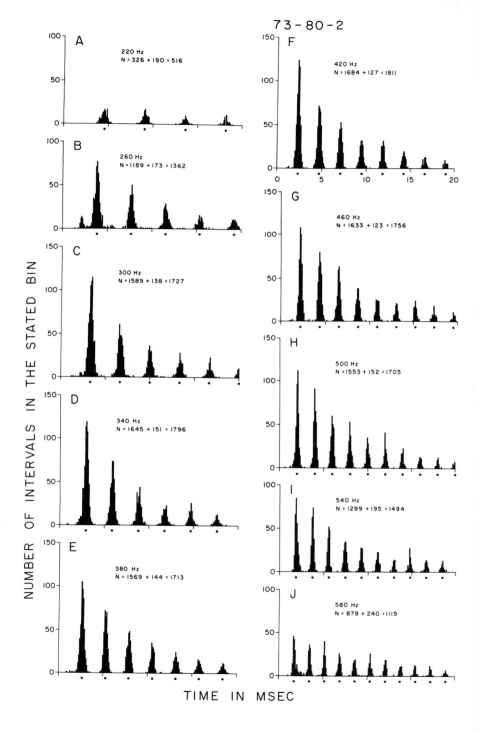

NUMBER OF INTERVALS IN THE STATED BIN

TIME IN MSEC

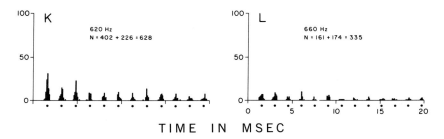

◀ **Figure 1.3.** Neuron 73-80-2. Periodic distributions of interspike intervals when pure tones of different frequencies activate the neuron. Stimulus frequency in Hz is indicated in each graph. Intensity of all stimuli: 65 dB SPL. Stimulus duration: 5 sec. Responses to three stimuli constitute the sample upon which each histogram is based. Abscissa: time in milliseconds; each bin = 100 μsec. Dots below the abscissa indicate integral multiples of the period for each frequency employed. Ordinate: number of interspike intervals in the bin. N = number of interspike intervals in the sample. N is given as two numbers. The first indicates the number of plotted intervals; the second is the number of intervals whose values exceeded the maximal value of the abscissa. (From unpublished material of Gibson, Hind, Kitzes, & Rose.)

1,111 Hz at various intensity levels. The discharges are phase locked from near threshold level at 20 dB to a level as high as 90 dB SPL.

How high can the stimulating frequency be and still cause a phase-locked response? Figure 1.5C shows that the discharges can be obviously locked to the cycle of 2,000 Hz, although, presumably because of the refractory period of the neuron, the first two modal peaks deviate from the expected values. However, as the stimulating frequency is further increased, the locking becomes less precise and gradually the phenomenon disappears altogether. It is therefore desirable to devise some measure of the degree of synchrony of the discharges with the cycle of the stimulus. To do so, we prepare a *period histogram*. To obtain this display we time each discharge, as it occurs during tone presentation, relative to the stimulus period. That is to say, the timing counter is reset after each stimulus period and all discharges are plotted as if they had occurred during *one* stimulus cycle. The abscissa of the period histogram is therefore equal to the period of the stimulating frequency. If the discharges are locked to some segment of the stimulus cycle, they group within this segment as shown in Figure 1.6A; if no such relation is present, the histogram is flat (Fig. 1.6B). Once a period histogram has been obtained, there are several ways to calculate the degree of synchronization. I shall mention here only one measure, which we term the *coefficient of synchronization*. The coefficient is calculated by counting the number of spikes in the most effective half of the stimulus cycle and expressing this number as a percentage of the total spike count. The coefficient is 100% if all discharges occur within a half-cycle of the stimulus; it is 50% if the discharges are distrib-

6

J.E. Rose

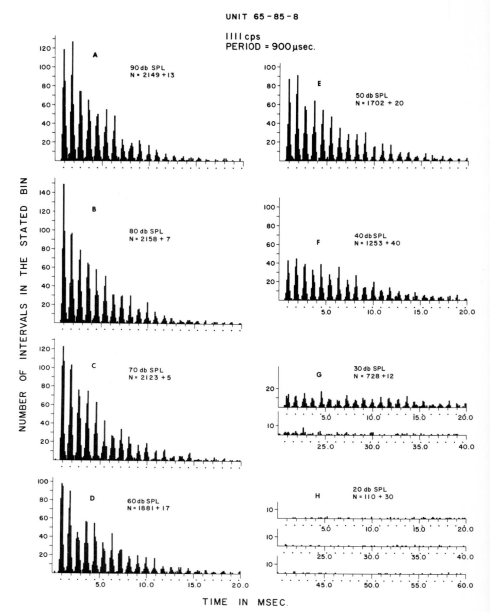

Figure 1.4. Auditory nerve fiber 65-85-8. Periodic interspike interval distributions at different intensities (A–H) of the stimulus. Stimulus: best frequency tone. Each histogram is based on responses obtained in 50 trials. Tone duration: 200 msec. Repetition rate: two per second. Spontaneous activity: six per second. Abscissa: time in milliseconds; each bin = 100 μsec. Abscissa covers 20 msec in (A)–(F), 40 msec in (G), and 60 msec in (H). Other legends as in Figure 1.3. (From Rose, Brugge, Anderson, & Hind, 1967.)

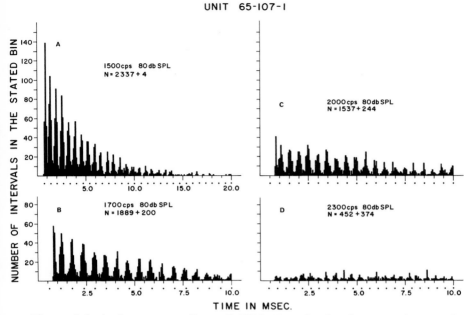

UNIT 65-107-1

Figure 1.5. Auditory nerve fiber 65-107-1. Periodic distributions of interspike intervals for four tones (A–D) of different frequencies. Abscissa: time in milliseconds; each bin = 100 μsec in (A), and 50 μsec in (B)–(D). Other legends as in Figure 1.3. (From Rose, Brugge, Anderson, & Hind, 1968.)

uted uniformly throughout the entire stimulus cycle and there is no relation to phase at all.

Figure 1.7 illustrates the relation between stimulus frequency and the coefficient of synchronization. Such plots can be constructed only if the neuron responds well to both the lower and the higher frequencies. The curve is fairly representative. The coefficient of synchronization is usually 90%–100% for low frequencies. Typically, it starts to diminish for

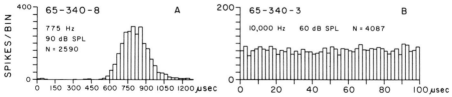

Figure 1.6. Period histograms for two auditory nerve fibers. (A) Stimulus: 775 Hz, period: 1,290 μsec. Abscissa = time up to 1,290 μsec; each bin = 30 μsec. Ordinate: number of spikes per bin. Discharges occur preferentially during half of the stimulus cycle. Phase-locked response. (B) Stimulus: 10,000 Hz; period: 100 μsec. Abscissa = time up to 100 μsec; each bin = 2 μsec. The discharges occur seemingly at random during a stimulus cycle; the period histogram is flat. (From unpublished material of Anderson, Brugge, Hind & Rose.)

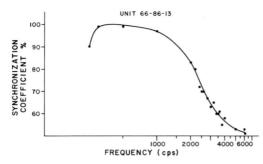

Figure 1.7. Relation between stimulus frequency and the degree of synchronization for auditory nerve fiber 66-86-13. Best frequency: 6,000 Hz. Abscissa: stimulus frequency. All stimuli 90–100 dB SPL. Ordinate: value of the synchronization coefficient. See text for further explanations. (From Rose et al., 1968.)

frequencies above about 1,500–2,000 Hz, and there is usually no significant synchronization for frequencies above 4,000 Hz.

Considering all the results, the following can be stated as regards the response of the neuron to a sustained low-frequency pure tone. All auditory nerve fibers and a large (but not the entire) population of anteroventral neurons produce a phase-locked response. Whereas the position of a given frequency within the response area of the neuron and the stimulus level determine the discharge rate, it is the frequency of the stimulus, and that frequency alone, which determines the fine time structure of the response.

A simple way to account for phase locking is to assume that the hair cells are activated only by unidirectional elevations of the cochlear partition. If this were so, it would be obvious why only a portion of the cycle is an effective stimulus.

Whether the time structure of the response is relevant to perception of low frequencies is not known. If one assumes that it is, certain psychoacoustic experiences may be accounted for, as I shall point out later (see section 5). However, for the considerations in the next section it is immaterial how tone sensation arises. What matters is that the fine time structure of the response is frequency specific. Hence, if an unknown low frequency is applied, it is possible to determine from the interspike interval histograms what the actual stimulating frequency was.

2   Monaural Masking at the Level of Single Neurons

I have just asserted that the time structure of the response to a pure tone of low frequency is frequency specific. It is therefore of special interest to examine what the time structure of the response may be when two low-frequency tones are presented simultaneously to the ear. Figures 1.8–1.10 show three sets of data concerning the same auditory nerve fiber. Best frequency of the neuron is 1,000 Hz. For data in Fig. 1.8 a 1,000-Hz, 40-dB SPL stimulus (f_2) is held constant. A response to f_2 alone is shown in A. In the column on the left, responses to a 200-Hz tone (f_1) are shown

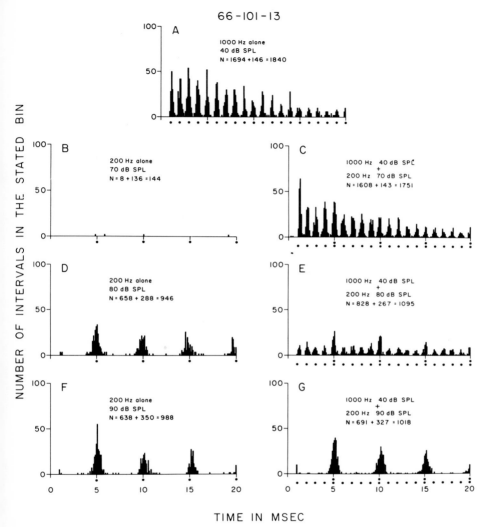

Figure 1.8. Interspike interval distributions showing masking of a tone by another tone. (A) Invariant tone at 1,000 Hz (best frequency), 40 dB SPL. Variant tone: 200 Hz. Column on left shows responses to 200-Hz tone alone at the indicated SPLs. Column on right shows responses to both tones presented simultaneously. Note that the time structure of the response is that of the 1,000-Hz tone in (C), and that of the 200-Hz tone in (G). In the right-hand column responses to two stimuli constitute the sample upon which the histogram is based. In the left-hand column the histograms are based on responses to one stimulus but the spike numbers were multiplied by 2 in order to make the numbers in both columns directly comparable. Dots below abscissa indicate integral multiples of the period for each component tone. Tone duration: 8 sec throughout. Other arrangements as in Figure 1.3. Auditory nerve fiber 66-101-13. (From unpublished material of Anderson, Brugge, Hind, & Rose.)

at three different sound-pressure levels. The column on the right depicts
responses when both tones are presented simultaneously. The response
to combined stimuli shows no influence of f_1 when f_1 is at 70 dB SPL (Figure 1.8C). However, f_1 alone at 70 dB SPL is barely above threshold (Figure 1.8B). Both f_1 and f_2 are effective in the response to combined tones
when f_1 is at 80 dB SPL (Figure 1.8E); and there is no significant influence of f_2 on the response to combined stimuli when f_1 is at 90 dB SPL
(Figure 1.8G). The time structure of the response changed drastically,
because the discharges in Figure 1.8G are locked only to the cycle of f_1.
The neuron responds as if f_2 had not been present in the stimulus; *the
1,000-Hz tone can be said to have been effectively masked*.

Figure 1.9 illustrates data when f_2 is held constant at 1,000 Hz, 40 dB
SPL, and the second tone (f_1) is 400 Hz at three different sound-pressure
levels. In the response to both tones, the discharges are locked to the
cycle of f_2 when f_1 is at 60 dB SPL (B) even though there is a vigorous

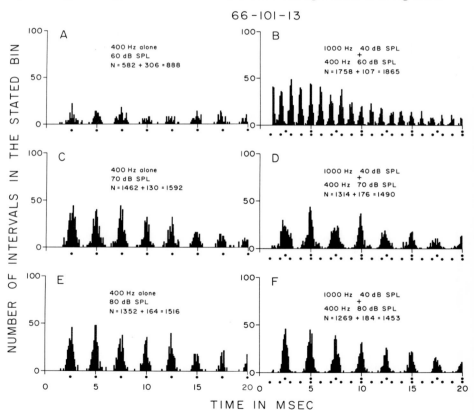

Figure 1.9. Same neuron and similar data as in Figure 1.8. Invariant tone:
1,000 Hz at 40 dB SPL (see Figure 1.8A). Variant tone: 400 Hz at indicated SPLs.
All arrangements as in Figure 1.8. (From unpublished material of Anderson,
Brugge, Hind, & Rose.)

response when f_1 is presented alone (A). At this level of f_1 it is f_1 that is masked by f_2. When the SPL of f_1 is raised to 70 dB, both f_1 and f_2 seem effective in the response to combined stimuli, although f_1 is dominant (D); when f_1 is at 80 dB SPL the discharges in the combined response are locked only to the cycle of the 400-Hz tone; the 1,000-Hz tone is again masked (F).

In Figure 1.10 the invariant tone is 600 Hz (f_1) at 100 dB SPL. The second tone is the best frequency at 1,000 Hz (f_2). When both tones are pre-

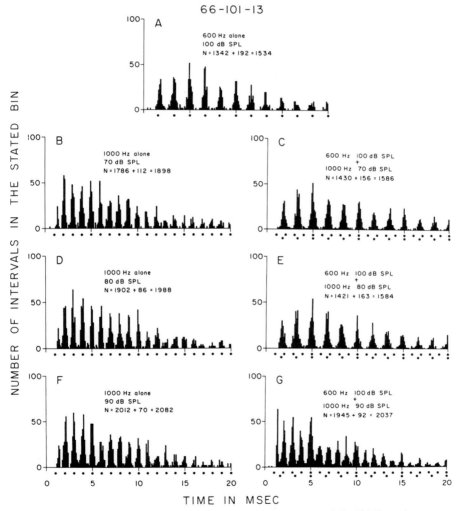

Figure 1.10. Same neuron and similar data as in Figure 1.8. (A) Invariant tone at 600 Hz, 100 dB SPL. Variant tone: 1,000 Hz at indicated SPLs. Other arrangements as in Figure 1.8. (From unpublished material of Anderson, Brugge, Hind, & Rose.)

sented, the discharges in the combined response are locked to the cycle of 600 Hz when f_2 is at 70 and 80 dB SPL; the 1,000-Hz tone is masked. When the level of f_2 is raised to 90 dB the discharges become locked to the cycle of the 1,000-Hz tone; the 600-Hz tone is masked.

Figures 1.8–1.10 suggest that the change in the time structure of the response occurs with fairly small increments in sound-pressure level of the masking sound once both tones interact. The spike counts produced by various stimulus combinations are of interest. When stimulus levels are moderate or high and one or the other tone dominates the time structure of the response, the discharge rate produced by the two-tone combination is similar to that provoked by the dominant component when it is acting alone. The important point is that, for stimuli well above threshold, there is, in the combined response, no significant summation of the respective spike counts produced by the two components when they are acting alone. This fact must be taken into account when considering the mechanism of masking, as pointed out by Hind, Anderson, Brugge, & Rose (1967).

The findings presented are typical and may be summarized as follows. The time structure of the response to two tones is always in one of three modes: The discharges are locked either to the cycle of one tone, to the cycle of the second tone, or, finally, to various extents to the cycles of both tones. Which mode prevails is a function of the respective sound-pressure levels. Hence, in a two-tone combination, either component may act as a masker or as a masked stimulus. The only restriction is that both tones must lie within the response area of the neuron.

The data are best understood if one assumes that masking occurs when the stimulating waveform, which arises along the cochlear partition at the locus connected with a given neuron, becomes dominated by the masking stimulus. We have argued elsewhere that the dominant tone actually damps the amplitude of the masked sound (Rose et al., 1974). If this be so, it follows that when successfully masked, the masked stimulus does not enter the waveform of the tonal combination with sufficient amplitude to affect significantly the combined stimulating waveform. It appears then that it is the stimulus, rather than the response, which is masked, and in a suitable masking situation a masked response does not arise at all because the appropriate stimulus component is below threshold.

It is reasonable to conclude that the time structure of the response reveals whether the information transmitted concerns the one, or the other, or both components of the stimulus. If the information pertains only to one of the components, the second component is "inaudible" to the neuron.

The behavior of single neurons responding to low-frequency tones parallels the psychoacoustic experience in humans. The basic psychoacoustic set of observations concerning monaural masking of a tone by another tone is that a tone which is audible when presented alone becomes inaudible, that is, masked, when a second tone of suitable frequency and intensity is added to it. The masked tone becomes again audible if its sound-pressure level is appropriately increased. It may be added that low-frequency tones are more effective maskers, for a human observer, than are tones of high frequency. It is also known that the intensity differential between the masker and the masked tone tends to be larger the further apart along the frequency scale are the two tones. It is noteworthy that such findings are to be expected from consideration of the response areas of single neurons. However, I shall not elaborate here on these details.

3 Responses of Single Neurons to Some Combination Tones that Are Lower than the Lower Primary

Another set of neurophysiological data that seems relevant to psychoacoustic experience concerns the origin of combination tones. It was discovered in the 18th century by Sorge, Romieu, and Tartini that when two tones are presented simultaneously, a human observer may often hear a third tone, even though no such tone is present in the stimulus. Tones of this kind are known as combination tones. It is likely that not all combination tones are generated by the same mechanism. The subgroup I shall be concerned with in this section consists of combination tones that are lower than the lower primary. As pointed out by various workers, these combination tones are perceived by human subjects as if they were tones actually delivered to the ear. They beat with tones of slightly different frequencies; they can be masked; they can be canceled by tones of the appropriate frequency, stimulus level, and phase. The combination tones most frequently heard are the difference tone ($f_2 - f_1$) and the cubic difference tone ($2f_1 - f_2$).

How such combination tones arise was not understood for a long time. Helmholtz was the first to propose that they are the result of nonlinear distortion in the transmission apparatus of the ear. This view is widely held nowadays, although the place where the distortion originates is thought to be not the middle ear, as originally suggested by Helmholtz, but the inner ear.

Difference tones and cubic difference tones have been shown to activate auditory nerve fibers (Goldstein & Kiang, 1968; Nomoto, Suga, & Katsuki, 1964). Observations by Smoorenburg et al. (1976) pertain to responses of neurons in the anteroventral cochlear nucleus in the cat. Because the subject is rather complex, I shall not give a detailed summary of this investigation. Instead, I shall limit myself to the presentation of two leading findings. The first is that anteroventral neurons commonly respond to a variety of combination tones. The second concerns the locus of origin of the disturbance that is responsible for the combination tone, and the propagation of this disturbance along the cochlear partition.

Neurophysiological studies of the response to combination tones are in some aspects simpler than are studies on human subjects. Because single neurons respond only to a restricted range of frequencies, it is usually an easy task to select both primaries in such a way that *neither* excites the neuron when presented alone; that is to say, both primaries lie outside the response area of the neuron. If now, a simultaneous presentation of both primaries causes a response at the appropriate combination frequency, the produced discharge rate can be taken as evidence that the neuron indeed responds to a given combination tone. It is, of course, critical that the combination-tone frequency falls within the pure-tone response area of the neuron, for otherwise the neuron is not aroused.

Figure 1.11 illustrates data from one experiment. The plot on the left shows the pure-tone response area of neuron 72-126-1 in the familiar form of isointensity contours for five sound-pressure levels. The contours are irregular at higher sound-pressure levels, but it is obvious that the best frequency is 1.0 kHz and that the neuron is not aroused by frequencies higher than about 1.8 kHz. We now select f_1 primary at 3.0 kHz and 65 dB SPL and we shall maintain this primary constant; f_2 will be augmented in 200-Hz steps. The sound-pressure level will be successively 45, 55, 65, 75, and 85 dB. With f_1 constant we will evaluate the discharge rate produced as a function of f_2. Two distributions are apparent in the graphs on the right. The peak of the first occurs when f_2 is at 4.0 kHz, the peak of the second when f_2 is at 5.0 kHz. The peak at 4.0 kHz corresponds to a combination tone $f_2 - f_1$ of 1.0 kHz (4.0 kHz − 3.0 kHz = 1.0 kHz); the peak at 5.0 kHz corresponds to the combination tone $2f_1 - f_2$ of 1.0 kHz (2 × 3.0 kHz − 5.0 kHz = 1.0 kHz). Note that the response is maximal when the combination frequency coincides with the best frequency of the neuron, regardless of the level of f_2. However, a number of other combination frequencies are effective and they outline the combination-tone response areas for $f_2 - f_1$ and $2f_1 - f_2$. Therefore, for example, f_2 at 3.8 kHz and 4.2 kHz yield combination-tone frequencies ($f_2 - f_1$) at 0.8 kHz and 1.2 kHz, respectively.

The most commonly encountered combination tones in our material are $f_2 - f_1$ and $2f_1 - f_2$. However, there is evidence that a number of combination tones of the general form of $f_1 - n(f_2 - f_1)$, where n is a small integer, can be produced in the ear.

Figure 1.12 shows the pure-tone response area for neuron 72-332-3. The best frequency of the neuron is 5.1 kHz; the upper effective frequency is about 5.7 kHz. When the lower primary (f_1) is held constant at 7.8 kHz, changing f_2 in small steps produces several distributions of discharge rates, each outlining a combination-tone response area (Figure 1.13). The most prominent is the area for the lowest member of the group, that is for $2f_1 - f_2$. However, response areas for combination frequencies $3f_1 - 2f_2$ as well as for $4f_1 - 3f_2$ are also evident. Moreover, re-

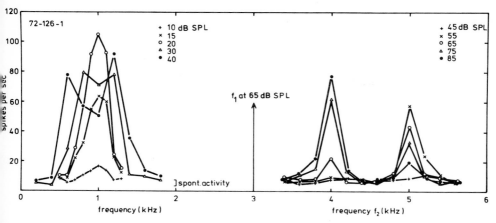

Figure 1.11. Leftside: Pure-tone response area for neuron 72-126-1 at five sound-pressure levels. Rightside: Response of the neuron to two tones presented simultaneously; f_1 component is fixed at 3.0 kHz, 65 dB SPL; f_2 component varies as indicated. Graphs plot the discharge rate as a function of f_2 for five sound-pressure levels of f_2. Stimulus duration: 10 sec. Location: anteroventral cochlear nucleus. (From Smoorenburg, Gibson, Kitzes, Rose, & Hind, 1976.)

sponses to still higher order combination frequencies are indicated in the graph, although their evaluation is difficult because their combination-tone response areas overlap.

The combination-tone response area for $2f_1 - f_2$ is wider than are the response areas for the higher order combination tones. This is because the combination-tone areas are plotted as a function of f_2. If combination-tone response areas are plotted as a function of the combination fre-

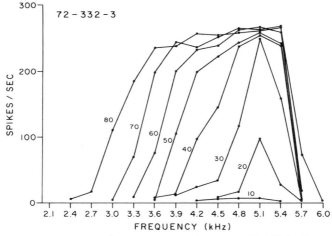

Figure 1.12. Pure-tone response area for anteroventral neuron 72-332-3. Tone duration: 5 sec. (From unpublished material of Gibson, Hind, Kitzes, Rose, & Smoorenburg.)

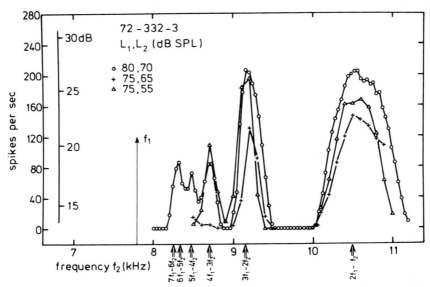

Figure 1.13. Combination tone response areas for neuron 72-332-3, whose pure-tone response area is shown in Figure 1.12. The f_1 component is fixed at 7.8 kHz; f_2 varies as indicated. Sound-pressure levels of the primaries (L_1 and L_2) are indicated by different symbols in the graph. Arrows below abscissa point to those values of f_2 for which the respective combination frequency is equal to the best frequency (5,100 Hz) of the neuron. The decibel scale parallel to the ordinate indicates the sound-pressure level of the best frequency tone that produced the spike rate shown on the ordinate. Stimulus duration: 5 sec. (From Smoorenburg et al., 1976.)

quency $f_1 - n(f_2 - f_1)$ the areas are n times as wide. Plotted in this way the different combination-tone areas are of similar width.

Figures 1.14 and 1.15 provide data that permit some inferences as to the place of origin of the difference tone $f_2 - f_1$. Figure 1.14 illustrates the pure-tone response area of neuron 72-227-3. The best frequency is 450 Hz. The upper effective frequency is close to 1,200 Hz. Figure 1.15 shows the difference-tone response areas $(f_2 - f_1)$ of this neuron for seven different values of f_1. Numbers above the arrows indicate the actual frequencies of the lower primary for each spike distribution. The frequency of the higher primary (f_2) varies as indicated. The arrows point to those values of f_2 for which the difference tone coincides with the best frequency of the neuron. The sound-pressure levels of the stimuli are given in the legend. Seven combination-tone response areas, comparable in width, are in evidence. Each distribution is centered about the combination frequency of 450 Hz, which is the best frequency of the neuron. The effective band of the combination-tone frequencies extends from less than 200 Hz to about 1,200 Hz. Clearly, when the frequencies of the primaries are higher than the upper effective frequency in the pure-tone re-

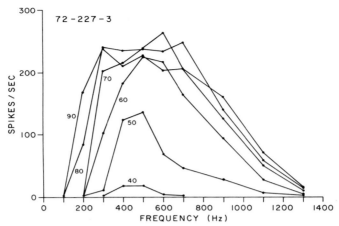

Figure 1.14. Pure-tone response area for anteroventral neuron 72-227-3. Tone duration: 10 sec. (Modified from Smoorenburg et al., 1976.)

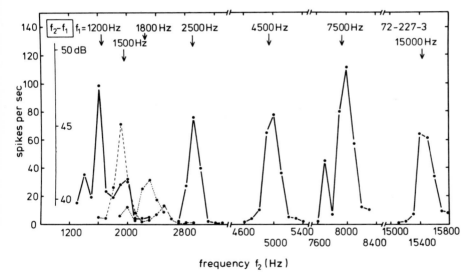

Figure 1.15. Combination tone response areas for neuron 72-227-3, whose pure-tone response area is shown in Figure 1.14. Combination tone $f_2 - f_1$ as a function of f_2 for seven values of f_1. Stimulus parameters for the seven curves from left to right: $f_1 = 1{,}200$ Hz, $L_1, L_2 = 60{,}60$ dB; $f_1 = 1{,}500$ Hz, $L_1, L_2 = 80{,}80$ dB; $f_1 = 1{,}800$ Hz, $L_1, L_2 = 70{,}70$ dB; $f_2 = 2{,}500$ Hz, $L_1, L_2 = 80{,}70$ dB; $f_1 = 4{,}500$ Hz, $L_1, L_2 = 94{,}84$ dB; $f_1 = 7{,}500$ Hz, $L_1, L_2 = 80{,}80$ dB; $f_1 = 15{,}000$ Hz, $L_1, L_2 = 70{,}80$ dB. Arrows indicate those values of f_2 for which the combination frequency coincides with the best frequency (450 Hz) of the neuron. Stimulus duration: 10 sec. (From Smoorenburg et al., 1976.)

sponse area of the neuron, similar combination-tone areas are generated regardless of the position of the appropriate primaries along the frequency scale.

It seems permissible to infer from the data that the mechanical disturbance responsible for the difference tone arises at those loci on the cochlear partition at which the primaries normally act. The disturbance is then propagated from the point of origin toward the apex of the cochlea and activates the neuron in apparently the same way as does the disturbance that is actually caused by an external tonal stimulus.

There is a remarkable agreement between the findings on single neurons and the psychoacoustic experience in humans. Broadly speaking, the same combination tones seem to arise in human and cat, the most prominent in either case being the difference tone and the cubic difference tone. The neural data imply that the combination tones lower than the lower primary behave as if such tones were actually delivered to the ear. It has been already stressed that the psychoacoustic data suggest the same conclusion.

4   Relation of Threshold to Tone Duration in the Response of Single Neurons

Recent work on the latency of the initial spike produced by neurons located in the anteroventral and in the anterior portion of the posteroventral cochlear nuclei has yielded new information on the relation of discharge threshold to the duration of the tonal signal (Kitzes, Gibson, Rose, & Hind, 1978).

It has been known for some time that the threshold for detection of a tonal stimulus becomes lower, for a human observer, when the duration of the signal is increased. The relation is remarkable both because the threshold shift is substantial and because the relation holds out to relatively long durations of the signal.

Figure 1.16 shows the measurements of Blodgett, Jeffress, and Taylor (1958) made some 20 years ago; shown are the masked thresholds of tonal pulses in a number of different interaural listening conditions. Threshold becomes lower by about 20 dB as the signal (500 Hz) increases in duration from 5 to 500 msec. Although the slopes of the individual curves differ somewhat, the central observation is that the duration–intensity reciprocity holds for stimuli of different configurations. Hence it is instructive to average the appropriate data. Plomp and Bouman (1959) did these calculations and the result is shown in Figure 1.17.

The facts that the threshold is lower the longer the tone duration and that the effective tone duration can be surprisingly long have led some workers to suggest that a long-lasting temporal integration in the higher

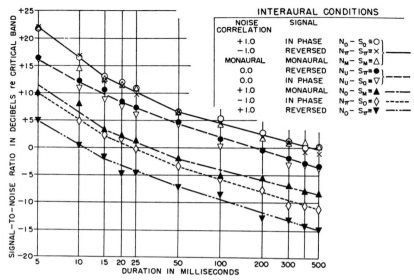

Figure 1.16. Masked threshold v. signal duration for different interaural conditions. (Signal: 500 Hz) N, noise; S, signal. (From Blodgett et al., 1958.)

auditory centers must be postulated to take place before a signal is recognized. According to our findings, however, a relation of threshold to tone duration of approximately the same magnitude as observed in humans is already demonstrable at the level of single neurons in the anteroventral cochlear nucleus. Therefore, it is not necessary to assume long integration times in the higher auditory centers to account for the threshold-tone duration relation.

Figure 1.18A shows the stimulus level of tonal bursts at best frequency (1.8 kHz) plotted against the discharge rate of the neuron and the latency

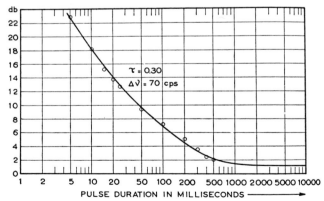

Figure 1.17. Threshold vs. duration of the tonal pulse for the averaged data of Blodgett et al. (1958). (From Plomp & Bouman, 1959.)

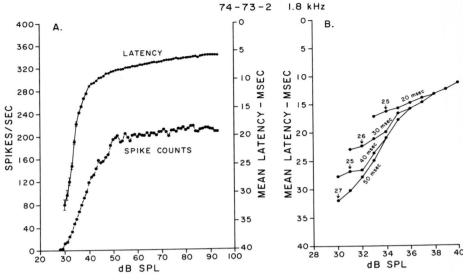

Figure 1.18. Neuron 74-73-2. (A) Discharge rate and mean latency of the first spike as a function of SPL for best frequency stimulus at 1.8 kHz. Tone duration: 50 msec. Rate: four per second. Each data point is based on 50 stimulus presentations. Standard error, if larger than 0.5 msec, indicated by a bar. (B) Part of the latency curve shown in (A) redrawn on an expanded decibel scale. Mean latency of the first spike and threshold intensity as a function of tone duration. Tone duration (sampling time) is consecutively 20, 30, 40, and 50 msec. Numbers at the base of the arrows indicate the number of effective trials in a sample of 50. Further explanations in text. (From Kitzes et al., 1978.)

of the first discharge. Each data point is based on 50 stimuli, each 50 msec in duration. The rise–fall time of the tone is 6 msec. The neuron is silent when not stimulated. Figure 1.18B shows the same data on an expanded decibel scale when the mean latency is successively plotted for stimulus durations of 20, 30, 40, and 50 msec, respectively. The mean latency of the first spike lengthens as the stimulus is made longer. Threshold is defined as that stimulus level at which 50% of the trials are effective. The arrows point to the number of effective trials out of 50 stimuli; for simplicity we will assume that 25 effective trials corresponds to threshold intensity. When the stimulus is 20 msec in duration, threshold is at 34 dB SPL; it is nearly at 32 dB for 30 msec duration, at 31 dB for 40 msec duration, and nearly at 30 dB SPL for a 50 msec long tonal signal. The threshold decreases therefore by 4 dB as the stimulus duration lengthens from 20 to 50 msec. This value is actually quite similar to the value obtained by Dr. Jeffress and his colleagues (Figures 1.16 and 1.17).

When the stimulus level is near threshold, the initial discharge of a neuron can occur at virtually any time during tone presentation (except for a short initial time segment). Neurons that are silent when not stimulated and whose discharges are locked to the stimulus cycle are particularly well suited for near-threshold studies because phase-locked discharge can be taken as presumptive evidence that the discharges are indeed evoked by the stimulus.

Figure 1.19 shows one such study. An anteroventral neuron is responding to a tone of 0.22 kHz. The tone duration is 220 msec. The number of initial spikes in 500 trials constitute a sample; a 40-dB stimulus caused only one spike in 100 trials. Consider first panel E where the stimulus is at 45 dB SPL. This level is somewhat above threshold because 364 trials out of 500 are effective in causing discharges. The plot shows the distribution of the latencies of the initial spikes. After a short initial time period nearly every stimulus cycle is effective at least once and the longest single latency of the initial spike is nearly equal to stimulus duration. It is tempting to infer that at levels still closer to threshold, the probability of spike occurrence is about the same for each potentially effective cycle throughout tone presentation.

The broad distribution of latencies of the initial discharge at near-threshold levels contrasts sharply with the results when the stimulus

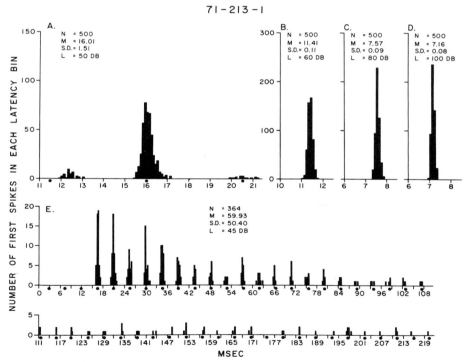

Figure 1.19. Latency of the initial discharges for neuron 71-213-1 responding to a 0.22-kHz tone. Tone duration: 220 msec. Rate: one per second. Initial discharges locked to the cycle of the stimulus. Each graph based on 500 stimulus presentations. Latency bin: 100 μsec in A–D, 300 μsec in E. Abscissa in E consists of two segments. (From Kitzes et al., 1978.)

becomes more intense. For example, for stimuli at 50 dB SPL (Figure 1.19A) the latencies of all initial spikes group about four modes (the fourth is not shown in Figure 1.19A because it consists of only three values); for still higher sound-pressure levels (Figure 1.19B–D) all initial discharges occur within one stimulus cycle. The mean latency of the initial spike is nearly 60 msec at 45 dB SPL but only 7.16 msec at 100 dB SPL. The reduction in the dispersion around the mean is still more instructive. Standard deviation is about 50 msec for the 45-dB condition; it is reduced to 0.08 msec when the stimulus is at 100 dB SPL.

The long latencies at threshold of the anteroventral neurons raise the question: Do such latencies arise in the anteroventral cochlear nucleus or do they result from the mode of activation of the primary neurons? No comparable latency data are available for the auditory nerve fibers. However, there is a fair amount of information on interspike intervals, and it suggests that the firing of a spiral neuron is a probabilistic event whose occurrence is a function of both the stimulus level and the stimulus duration.

Let me develop the argument on the basis of interspike interval data shown in Figure 1.4, where the response of an auditory nerve fiber to its best frequency tone is shown for eight sound-pressure levels. The plot was shown previously to demonstrate that locking of discharges to the stimulus cycle occurs at all effective stimulus levels. Now, I wish to call attention to the length of interspike intervals as a function of stimulus level. Stimuli are tonal bursts 200 msec in duration; responses to 50 bursts constitute a sample. N is given as two numbers. The first shows the number of plotted intervals; the second, the number of intervals that are longer than the time covered by the abscissa. For intense stimuli, short intervals are numerous and intervals longer than 10 msec are infrequent. In Figure 1.4A, for example, there are 2,162 interspike intervals but only 13 are longer than 20 msec. With a decrease of stimulus level, longer intervals become more numerous. As the total number of intervals decreases, the successive modes become more nearly equal in size. Near threshold (Figure 1.4H), there are only 140 intervals, and 30 of them are longer than 60 msec. They seem to occur with about equal probability for each stimulus cycle.

Observations on interspike intervals produced by auditory nerve fibers imply that any discharge near threshold is an event of low probability and that the chance of spike occurrence is, within limits, better the longer the waiting time. The evidence at hand indicates, then, that the dependence of threshold on tone duration is already demonstrable at the level of the cochlear nuclear complex. Moreover, it is probable that this relation is, in fact, the result of the way the hair cells set up the action potentials in the spiral neurons.

5 Responses of Single Neurons that May Pertain to Psychoacoustic Experiences if the Time Structure of the Response Is Germane to the Perception of Pitch

I have considered so far some possible neural correlates of several psychoacoustic experiences without any commitment as to how a tone sensation may arise. In this section, I shall present data that may pertain to psychoacoustic experience if it is assumed that cadence of discharges is in some way relevant to perception of a tonal signal. How sound such an assumption may be is a matter for conjecture.

There are several anatomical facts that support the idea that the time structure of the response is of functional significance. For example, out of the three major divisions of the cochlear nuclear complex, each of which is tonotopically organized and commands a full tonal spectrum (Rose, Galambos, & Hughes, 1959), it is only one class of cells in the anteroventral division that preserves, *fully*, the low-frequency phase information provided by the auditory nerve fibers. Many auditory nerve fibers terminate in special endings known as the endbulbs of Held. Endings of this type are unique to the auditory system and they occur in the cochlear nuclear complex only in the anteroventral division, which is—it may be mentioned—especially prominent in humans. The endbulbs form a calyx surrounding the nerve cell, suggesting formations of particularly secure synaptic arrangements. If such formations should serve to preserve timing information one would be inclined to believe that the discharge cadence is physiologically utilized. However, even if this is the case, it does not necessarily follow that it is the discharge cadence which underlies the perception of pitch. Nevertheless, an assumption that the time structure of the response is relevant to tone perception seems useful for interpreting some neural data.

I have previously asserted that when two tones are presented simultaneously, the time structure of the response corresponds either to one or to the other primary or indicates that the tones interact. Which mode prevails is a function of the respective sound-pressure levels of the primary tones. Phase relations of the primaries are also of great importance (Brugge, Anderson, Hind, & Rose, 1969) but I shall not be concerned with this problem here. Let us look more closely at the time structure of the response when two tones are locked to each other in a ratio of small integers to form a *complex periodic sound* and the tones interact.

However, before we do so, a methodological remark is in order. Because I shall present the results in the form of interspike intervals and period histograms, the construction of the latter requires a comment. When the response to a complex periodic sound is examined, the abscissa of the period histogram must obviously be equal to the period of the fun-

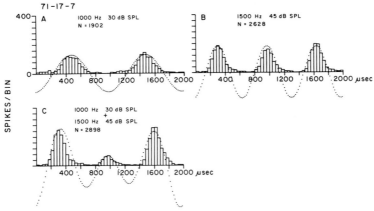

Figure 1.20. Construction of period histograms for responses to a complex periodic sound when two low-frequency tones are locked in a ratio of small integers. (A) 1,000-Hz tone presented alone; (B) 1,500-Hz tone presented alone; (C) 1,000-Hz and 1,500-Hz presented together. (From unpublished material of Gibson, Hind, Kitzes, & Rose.)

damental frequency of the complex sound. Therefore, all discharges are timed with respect to this period even when the component tones are presented alone. Figure 1.20 illustrates the results of such a procedure. A 1,000-Hz tone and a 1,500-Hz tone will be locked in a ratio of 2:3 to generate a complex periodic sound. The fundamental frequency is 500 Hz; its period is equal to 2,000 μsec. In Figure 1.20A the 1,000-Hz tone is presented alone. The abscissa is exactly twice the period of the tone. Responses group in two half-cycles as suggested by the matching sinusoid. The two distributions are expected to be equal in every respect. In Figure 1.20B the 1,500-Hz tone is presented alone. The abscissa is exactly three times the period of the tone. Three equal and equidistant distributions are expected. In Figure 1.20C a complex periodic sound is presented. The tones interact; the three distributions are not equal in height and their peaks are not equidistant. The envelope of the period histogram can be outlined by adding the two sinusoids shown in Figures 1.20A and B after suitable adjustment of their respective amplitudes and phase angles.

Figure 1.21 shows interspike intervals and period histograms for an au-

Figure 1.21. Interspike intervals and period histograms for auditory nerve fiber ▶ 67-92-6 responding to complex periodic sound. A tone of 800 Hz is locked to a tone of 1,200 Hz in a ratio of 2:3. The lower frequency tone is fixed at 80 dB SPL; the SPL of the higher frequency tone varies as indicated. Each sample is based on responses to two tonal presentations. Duration of each presentation: 10 sec. Period of complex sound = 2,500 μsec. Interspike interval histograms: abscissa, time in milliseconds, each bin = 100 μsec; ordinate: number of intervals in each bin. Period histograms: abscissa, time in microseconds, each bin = 100 μsec; ordinate: number of spikes per bin. See text for further explanations. (From Rose, Brugge, Anderson, & Hind, 1969.)

UNIT 67-92-6
TONE 1: 800 cps
TONE 2: 1200 cps
R = 2:3
A
TONE 1: 80 db SPL
TONE 2: 70 db SPL
N = 2238
SPIKES PER BIN
μSEC.
N = 2068 + 185
B
TONE 1: 80 db SPL
TONE 2: 75 db SPL
N = 2131
N = 1933 + 196
C
TONE 1: 80 db SPL
TONE 2: 80 db SPL
N = 2197
N = 2001 + 201
D
TONE 1: 80 db SPL
TONE 2: 85 db SPL
N = 2505
N = 2367 + 141
E
TONE 1: 80 db SPL
TONE 2: 90 db SPL
N = 2603
N = 2462 + 140
F
TONE 1: 80 db SPL
TONE 2: 95 db SPL
N = 3426
N = 3393 + 54
NUMBER OF INTERVALS IN THE STATED BIN
INTERSPIKE INTERVAL (MSEC)

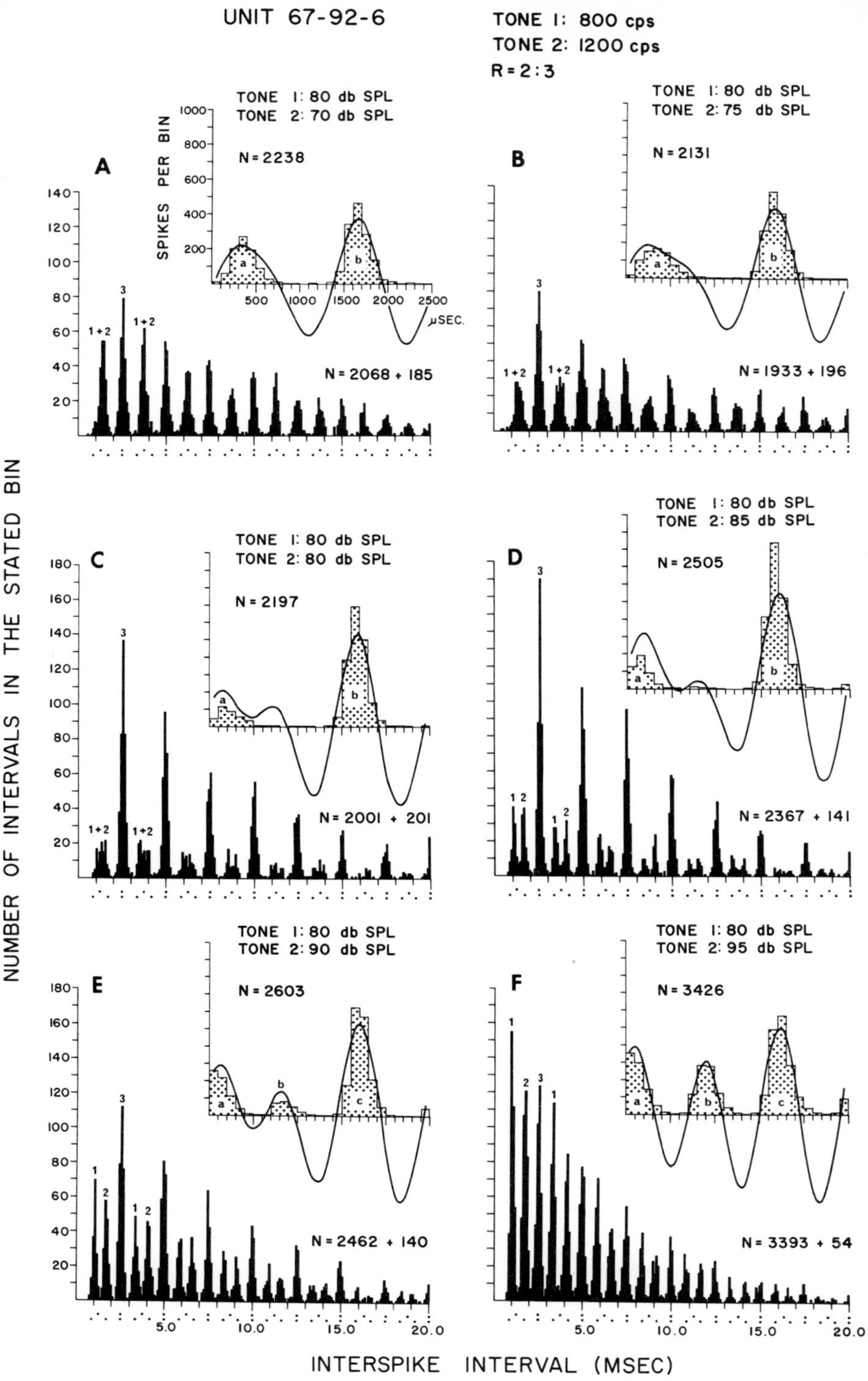

ditory nerve fiber when a complex periodic sound composed of an 800-Hz tone and a 1,200-Hz tone is delivered to the ear. The tones are locked in a ratio of 2:3. The fundamental is 400 Hz. The 800-Hz tone is always at 80 dB SPL; the sound-pressure level of the 1200-Hz tone is successively increased in 5-dB steps. In Figure 1.21A the 800-Hz tone is dominant because the discharges group mainly about integral multiples of the period of the lower frequency; the higher frequency tone is effectively masked. However, the uneven amplitudes of the two peaks in the period histogram indicate that the dominance of the lower frequency tone is not complete. In Figure 1.21F the higher frequency is dominant because discharges group about integral multiples of the period of the 1,200-Hz tone and the three peaks in the period histogram are nearly equidistant and nearly equal in height; the lower primary is largely masked. In Figure 1.21B–E the two tones interact strongly. Consider first the histogram in Figure 1.21D. In the period histogram there are only two major spike distributions designated as a and b. We shall characterize each by the mean value of each population. If a discharge occurs in a, the next discharge can occur either in a or in b, forming an a–a or an a–b interval, respectively. If the discharge occurs in b the next discharge can occur either in b or in a, forming a b–b or b–a interval. Therefore, there are four possible mean intervals: a–a, b–b, a–b, and b–a. Note that the b–a interval is measured by the distance of b to the end of the abscissa plus the distance from the point of origin to peak a because the abscissa in the period histogram can be thought of as a circle in which the last bin is adjacent to the first.

The mean intervals a–a and b–b must be equal because both measure the period of the fundamental, which here is 2,500 μsec. In contrast, the intervals a–b and b–a differ from the period of the fundamental and from the periods of either primary. Altogether there are three different mean interval values. The b–a intervals form mode 1 in the graph; the a–b intervals, mode 2; and a–a and b–b intervals, mode 3.

Two facts concerning intervals whose mean duration is equal to the period of the fundamental should be emphasized. First, such intervals occur regularly for any stimulus configuration. Second, they tend to be much more numerous than any other mean interval value, as long as the tones interact to a significant degree. For example, in Figure 1.21C and D, 72% and 66% of all intervals group, respectively, around the integral values of the period of the fundamental frequency.

We have defined previously the frequency that corresponds to the period of the complex sound as the major secondary tone (Rose et al., 1969). This tone is always the fundamental frequency. If the cadence of discharges is relevant to tone perception, one would expect a human observer to hear the fundamental tone when a complex periodic sound is presented regardless of whether or not the appropriate energy is present in the stimulus.

It is a common observation for humans that pitch of the complex sound is, in fact, usually judged to be that of the fundamental frequency. The neural data suggest one way such a phenomenon may arise.

Let us return to Figure 1.21D. As already stated, the mean durations of the b–a and a–b intervals (modes 1 and 2) differ from the period of the fundamental as well as from the periods of the primaries. What general statements can we make concerning such intervals?

First, we note that in contrast to the intervals that group around the integral multiples of the period of the fundamental frequency (mode 3), the mean durations of the intervals grouped in modes 1 and 2 are critically dependent on the sound-pressure levels (and phase relations) of the components. That this is so is clear from considerations of Figure 1.21A and F. In Figure 1.21A the phase-locked response pertains essentially to the 800-Hz tone, and in Figure 1.21F, to the 1,200-Hz stimulus. Because the frequency ratio is 2:3, every two consecutive modes in Figure 1.21A are replaced by three modes in Figure 1.21F. However, the mean duration of intervals in mode 3 is constant. Hence each mode labeled 1 + 2 in Figure 1.21A splits, as it were, into two modes whose separation increases progressively until all modes become nearly equidistant in Figure 1.21F. Figure 1.21B–E illustrates the orderly progression of this process as a function of sound-pressure level.

The first conclusion, therefore, is that if a complex periodic sound is presented and the two tones interact, there appears, besides intervals corresponding to the fundamental frequency, a family of interspike intervals whose mean duration varies systematically with stimulus configuration. I shall refer to such intervals as *odd intervals*. Elsewhere, the frequencies corresponding to odd intervals have been denoted as minor secondary tones (Rose et al., 1969).

How many populations with different mean values can occur for a given stimulus configuration? Obviously, this number is dependent on the number of peaks in the period histogram, whereas the amplitude and spacing of the peaks determine the frequency of occurrence and the actual duration of the intervals. Consider now that in response to a complex periodic sound the maximal number of peaks in the stimulating waveform and hence in the period histogram cannot be larger, although it can be smaller, than the number of peaks generated by the higher frequency component. The lower frequency component indicates the minimal number of peaks. If the higher frequency component is the denominator in the frequency ratio, it follows that the larger the denominator, the larger the maximal number of possible mean intervals; the maximal number of possible intervals increases as the second power of the denominator in the frequency ratio. For example, for a ratio of 1:2 there are at most four mean intervals and two of them are equal to the period of the fundamental; for a ratio of 2:3 there are at most nine intervals and three of them are equal to the period of the fundamental frequency. Actually, the number of distinctly different modes generated by the neuron is often very much smaller than predicted by this relationship. I shall not discuss

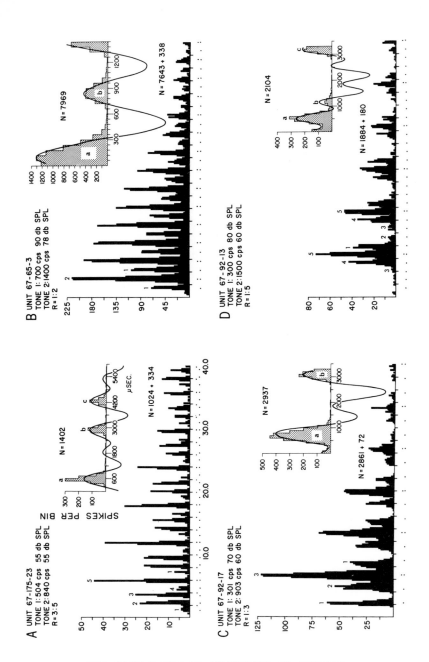

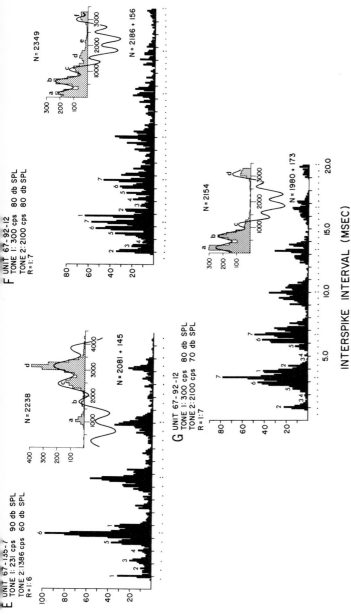

INTERSPIKE INTERVAL (MSEC)

Figure 1.22. Interspike interval histograms and period histograms for six auditory nerve fibers. Frequency and intensity of the component tones and the frequency ratio in which the tones are locked are indicated for each graph. Each histogram is based on responses to two stimulus presentations with the exception of (A), which is based on responses to four, and (B), which is based on responses to six stimulus presentations. Duration of each stimulus: 10 sec. Interspike interval histograms: abscissa, time in milliseconds, each bin = 200 μsec for (A), 100 μsec for (B)– (G); ordinate: number of intervals in each bin. Period histograms; abscissa, time in microseconds, each bin = 120 μsec for (A), 60 μsec for (B), and 100 μsec for (C)– (G); ordinate: number of different modes in interspike interval histograms is equal to the denominator in the frequency ratio. (From Rose et al., 1969.)

the reasons for this fact but merely shall state that the number of different modes is frequently equal to the denominator in the frequency ratio rather than to the second power of the denominator. In Figure 1.21E, for example, there are only three different modes even though there are three peaks in the period histogram. Figure 1.22 shows responses to complex periodic sounds for six neurons. The frequency ratio is 3:5 in Figure 1.22A, 1:2 in B, 1:3 in C, 1:5 in D, 1:6 in E, and 1:7 in F and G. For all ratios shown, the number of clearly different modes is equal to the denominator of the frequency ratio.

The point to be made is that a relation exists between frequency ratio and the number of different modes. The larger the denominator in the frequency ratio, the larger is the number of different odd intervals. Stated in different terms, the larger the denominator in the frequency ratio, the less regular is the discharge cadence.

What can be the physiological meaning of odd intervals? We can approach this problem in two ways, which are not mutually exclusive. First, we can recall that at least some of the minor secondary tones, defined by odd intervals, can be audible to humans as combination tones that are higher than the lower primary. Krueger (1900) described such tones, which he, following Stumpf, called intertones (Zwischentöne). We have discussed his findings in some detail elsewhere (Rose et al., 1969). The second approach is as follows. The neural data suggest a relationship between frequency ratio and cadence of discharges; psychoacoustic experiences indicate a relationship between frequency ratio and consonance of intervals. Can the cadence of discharges be relevant to consonance?

It was known even to Pythagoras, although he did not state it in these terms, that if the frequency ratio of two tones could be expressed by small integers, the tonal interval would be more consonant the smaller the integers. Figure 1.23 shows the table of Helmholtz in which various frequency ratios are ranked according to consonance. The consonance decreases as the denominator of the frequency ratio increases. Note also that for the same value of the denominator, the interval is ranked more consonant when the numerator is smaller. Not all authors would accept the ranking of Helmholtz; however, there is little doubt that a relationship exists between consonance and frequency ratio, at least when the tones are complex rather than simple tones.

Why consonance is associated with the ratios of small numbers is a question that has frequently been asked, even in antiquity, but still is not

1. Octave	.	.	.	1 : 2	
2. Twelfth	.	.	.	1 : 3	
3. Fifth	.	.	.	2 : 3	
4. Fourth	.	.	.	3 : 4	
5. Major Sixth	.	.	3 : 5	Figure 1.23. Ranking of musical
6. Major Third	.	.	4 : 5	intervals according to Helmholtz.
7. Minor Third	.	.	5 : 6	(From Helmholtz, 1954.)

yet answered satisfactorily. There are two, fundamentally different views on the relation of consonance to frequency ratio. One view holds that this relation arises solely as a consequence of learning and cultural conditioning of the observer; no neural mechanism in the cochlea or auditory nervous system is involved. The contrary and, I believe, more prevalent view is that consonance is a peculiar sensory experience that is independent of learning or knowledge of music and inherently different for different ratios. A compromise view is advocated by Terhardt (1974). He distinguishes between "psychoacoustic consonance," characterized by the absence of roughness, and tonal consonance, which plays a basic role in tonal music and which, he believes, is the result of learning.

If cadence of discharges were relevant to tone perception, one could infer that the less regular the cadence, the harsher or rougher or more dissonant the sensory experience. If this were true, the neural data would predict a relation between consonance and the frequency ratio because, in response to a complex periodic sound, the smaller the numbers in the frequency ratio the more regular is the discharge cadence. Therefore, our neural data can be taken to support a frequency-ratio theory of consonance.

Galileo (1638/1974), who formulated such a theory more than three centuries ago, was perhaps less in error than is usually supposed when he stated:

> I say that the length of strings is not the direct and immediate reason behind the forms of musical intervals, nor is their tension, nor their thickness, but rather, the ratio of the numbers of vibrations and impacts of air waves that go to strike our eardrum, which likewise vibrates according to the same measure of times. This point established, we may perhaps assign a very congruous reason why it comes about that among sounds differing in pitch, some pairs are received in our sensorium with great delight, others with less, and some strike us with great irritation; we may thus arrive at the reason behind perfect consonances, and imperfect, and dissonances. The irritation from the latter is born, I believe, of the discordant pulsations of two different tones that strike on our eardrums all out of proportion; and very harsh indeed will be the dissonances whose times of vibration are incommensurables. . . . Those pairs of sounds will be consonant, and heard with pleasure, which strike the eardrum with good order; this requires first that the impacts made within the same period are commensurable in number, so that the cartilage of the eardrum need not be in perpetual torment of bending in two different ways to accept and obey ever-discordant beatings. Hence the first and most welcome consonance is the octave, in which for every impact that the lower string delivers to the eardrum, the higher gives two, and both go to strike unitedly in alternate vibrations of the high string, so that one-half of the total number of impacts agree in beating together. (p. 104)

6   Closing Remarks

It can be assumed a priori that any psychoacoustic experience depends on the nature of the cochlear output and on the way this information is transmitted, transformed, and organized in the higher auditory centers. I have been concerned only with neural studies of the cochlear output. It is apparent, I believe, that in the squirrel monkey and cat the behavior of single auditory nerve fibers and single anteroventral cells predicts important features of several psychoacoustic experiences in humans. This fact is remarkable because it implies that the functional organization of the cochlea is basically similar in humans and other mammals, and because some classical psychoacoustic observations concerning masking, combination tones, dependence of threshold on tone duration, and possibly even the pitch of complex sounds and the consonance of musical intervals seem to reflect primarily the different ways the cochlea originates information for different stimulus configurations rather than the ways in which this information is handled in the higher auditory centers.

References

Blodgett, H.C., Jeffress, L.A., & Taylor, R.W. Relation of masked threshold to signal duration for various interaural phase combinations. *American Journal of Psychology*, 1958, *71*, 283–290.

Brugge, J.F., Anderson, D.J., Hind, J.E., & Rose, J.E. Time structure of discharges in single auditory nerve fibers of the squirrel monkey in response to complex periodic sounds. *Journal of Neurophysiology*, 1969, *32*, 386–401.

Galileo Galilei. *Two new sciences including centers of gravity and force of percussion*. Stillman Drake, trans. Madison: University of Wisconsin Press, 1974. (Originally published in 1638.)

Gibson, M.M., Hind, J.E., Kitzes, L.M., & Rose, J.E. Estimation of traveling wave parameters from the response properties of cat AVCN neurons. In E.F. Evans & J.P. Wilson (Eds.), *Psychophysics and physiology of hearing*. London: Academic Press, 1977.

Goldstein, J.L., & Kiang, N.Y.-S. Neural correlates of the aural combination tone $2f_1 - f_2$. *IEEE Proceedings*, 1968, *56*, 981–992.

Helmholtz, H.L.F. *On the sensations of tone as a physiological basis of the theory of music* (2nd ed.). [A.J. Ellis, trans.; from the 3rd (1870) and 4th (1877) German eds.] New York: Dover Publications, 1954.

Hind, J.E., Anderson, D.J., Brugge, J.F., & Rose, J.E. Coding of information pertaining to paired low-frequency tones in single auditory nerve fibers of the squirrel monkey. *Journal of Neurophysiology*, 1967, *30*, 794–816.

Kitzes, L.M., Gibson, M.M., Rose, J.E., & Hind, J.E. Initial discharge latency and threshold considerations for some neurons in the cochlear nuclear complex of the cat. *Journal of Neurophysiology*, 1978, *41*, 1165–1182.

Krueger, F. Beobachtugen an Zweiklängen. *Philosophische Studien*, 1900, *16*, 307–379; 568–664.

Nomoto, M., Suga, N., & Katsuki, Y. Discharge pattern and inhibition of primary auditory nerve fibers in the monkey. *Journal of Neurophysiology*, 1964, 27, 768–787.

Plomp, R., & Bouman, M.A. Relation between hearing threshold and duration for tone pulses. *Journal of the Acoustical Society of America*, 1959, 31, 749–758.

Rose, J.E., Brugge, J.F., Anderson, D.J., & Hind, J.E. Phase-locked responses to low-frequency tones in single auditory nerve fibers of the squirrel monkey. *Journal of Neurophysiology*, 1967, 30, 769–793.

Rose, J.E., Brugge, J.F., Anderson, D.J., & Hind, J.E. Patterns of activity in single auditory nerve fibers of the squirrel monkey. In A.V.S. DeReuck and J. Knight (Eds.), *Hearing mechanisms in vertebrates*, Ciba Symposium, London: Churchill, 1968.

Rose, J.E., Brugge, J.F., Anderson, D.J., & Hind, J.E. Some possible neural correlates of combination tones. *Journal of Neurophysiology*, 1969, 32, 402–423.

Rose, J.E., Galambos, R., & Hughes, J.R. Microelectrode studies of the cochlear nuclei of the cat. *Bulletin of the Johns Hopkins Hospital*, 1959, 104, 211–251.

Rose, J.E., Hind, J.E., Anderson, D.J., & Brugge, J.F. Some effects of stimulus intensity on response of auditory nerve fibers in the squirrel monkey. *Journal of Neurophysiology*, 1971, 34, 685–699.

Rose, J.E., Kitzes, L.M., Gibson, M.M., & Hind, J.E. Observations on phase-sensitive neurons of anteroventral cochlear nucleus of the cat: Nonlinearity of the cochlear output. *Journal of Neurophysiology*, 1974, 37, 218–253.

Smoorenburg, G.F., Gibson, M.M., Kitzes, L.M., Rose, J.E., & Hind, J.E. Correlates of combination tones observed in the response of neurons in the anteroventral cochlear nucleus of the cat. *Journal of the Acoustical Society of America*, 1976, 59, 945–962.

Terhardt, E. Pitch, consonance and harmony. *Journal of the Acoustical Society of America*, 1974, 55, 1061–1069.

Discussion

Dr. McFadden: I have a question which really can't be answered at this time but which will be answered as the symposium progresses, and it's simply whether any of the other speakers are going to give us examples like those Dr. Rose gave us today, and has shown us in the past, of firing rate sometimes being really rather an uninteresting aspect of the neural activity. He has, here, in talking about some of the masking data, and in previous times has published figures showing that drastic changes in the pattern of firing—in the periodicity of the activity—can be realized by various stimulus manipulations with very little change in firing rate. The implication is strong that if, in fact, that neuron is communicating anything to the higher nervous centers about whatever it is—the detectability of the tone if it's a masking situation, or the detectability of some combination tone if it's some kind of periodicity situation—it cannot be doing it via firing rate. I am curious if in the visual system or elsewhere we'll see other examples of pattern of firing being an important aspect of neural activity.

I also have something more specific as a question. You hinted at today, and have spoken about in the past, the fact that when two tones are presented, one can, by proper analysis—the process of folding—appreciate that there are present periodicities other than those associated with the two primary components. You showed us that today in the slides at the end, and you've shown it in the past. So, one might think about the neurophysiological basis for some combination tones as being in the periodicity of the firing. You've also shown us, in the early part today, that when one presents two tones, that nonlinearities in the basilar-membrane mechanics produce activity at a lower frequency, at a different place on the membrane, so that additional neurons are being exposed to activity in addition to those that are concerned with the two primaries. What we have, then, is the potential for two types of combination tone to result. That is, there is a periodicity basis for combination tones when it's in the firing pattern itself at the "correct" location on the basilar membrane, and there is also what you might call a place form of combination tone where a different set of neural elements is activated due to the nonlinearity of the system. The question is, how do you think about the relationships between these two forms of combination tones?

Dr. Rose: I don't have a ready answer to your question, but I think that there are indeed two groups of combination tones which should be distinguished from each other, for different mechanisms are presumably involved in their generation. The best known combination tones are lower than the lower primary. They are heard as tones corresponding to such frequencies as $f_2 - f_1$, $2f_1 - f_2$, $3f_1 - 2f_2$, and so on. There is, I believe, little doubt that this class of combination tones is due to distortion products that arise in the inner ear even at low stimulus levels. Another class of combination tones is in evidence when the listener perceives pitches that do not correspond to stimulus frequencies present in the stimulus. Combination tones of this kind were first heard by musicians a long time ago, but the mechanism of their origin is still in doubt. Neurophysiological evidence suggests that pitches corresponding, for example, to the missing fundamental could be expected to arise and be heard by a human observer, even if no distortion were present, provided that the time structure of the neural response is relevant for perception. And we do not know this; there is no evidence that it is, other than the behavior. As for myself, I think that we should abandon the notion that we must choose one of the two theories which are opposed to each other, a frequency theory and a place theory. I think both of them are short sighted; the auditory system does not work on the basis of a single code. Depending on the region you are studying, you have evidence for either a time or a place code. I think Dr. Jeffress was entirely correct in suggesting many years ago that at some levels a place code is a neurophysiological necessity. In the cortex, for instance, there is no sustained discharge, there are no such beautiful discharge patterns as are obtained in the auditory nerve fiber or in some other low auditory centers. Somehow time has been converted into place. I think the two theories are not contradictory but complementary. We need not pose the question either/or, as has been customary in psychoacoustics for a century. The authors are divided into two groups. One group points out with glee the difficulties of the frequency theory, the other with equal zeal the inadequacy of the place theory. I think that in the cochlea you can clearly see both place and time coding. It takes activity at a certain place on the cochlear partition for the neuron to be aroused by a given frequency band. No other place will do; and this is in harmony with place theory. On the other hand, the evidence is, I think, very strong that the time structure of the response is of significance. At least at this level, the response lives up to every requirement of frequency theory. Within the frequency band to which the neuron responds, the neuron does not differentiate between the effective frequencies in terms of place; it differentiates in terms of time, since it is the stimulus frequency and the stimulus frequency alone that determines the time structure of the response.

Dr. Boynton: I'd like to make a comment that is related to Dr. McFadden's question about whether a similar type of encoding of information in terms of the pattern of nerve discharge applies also to the visual system. I'm sure Horace Barlow or Floyd Ratliff or others could follow up on this. Horace Barlow's colleague at Cambridge, Giles Brindley, in his second edition of *The Physiology of the Retina and the Visual Pathway*, claims to have surveyed the entirety of the literature on vision up until 1970, and states that if anything has been omitted from his book, it has been done deliberately. Therefore I like to refer to his book. He specifically discusses this issue and comes to the conclusion that he can find no evidence that any such temporal patterning is important for carrying visual information. If we accept this as true—and perhaps we won't want to, but just for the moment let's do it—we could speculate a bit about why there should be such a difference between the visual and the auditory systems. Discussing this gets ahead of the subject a little bit for I think one or two of the points that I'm going to make in my talk will bear upon this, but I would like to throw out the following speculation: I think the difference might very well have something to do with the very different nature of the physical stimuli that are appropriate for the two senses. If we consider for a moment, for example, the way in which information about frequency versus intensity is encoded in the two cases, we have to realize that in the auditory instance a single molecule of atmosphere beating itself against the eardrum cannot, in and of itself, very well carry any information about the frequency of atmospheric disturbance in terms of which the auditory message is so importantly conveyed. But in the case of vision, it is now very well accepted that it's quite appropriate to talk about the frequency of light or, if you wish, its reciprocal, the wavelength of a single photon—a photon of light being the adequate stimulus for vision. Therefore, it seems to me that any possibility of trying to unscramble, at the level of a single neural unit, the meaning of the message vis-à-vis frequency versus intensity is lost right away at the initial detection event in

the case of vision, in a way that perhaps it is not in the case of audition.
Dr. Barlow: I think the possibility that there is some fine structure in the
responses in the visual system is certainly something that should always
be in one's mind. However, in practice, if you look at the discharges in
the visual system, the regular feature is the mean rate over rather a long
time interval—something on the order of a tenth of a second or ten milliseconds or somewhere between the two—and you can't find anything to
correlate the finer structure with. I think that's the basis for believing that
if you look at the mean frequency you are looking at the right thing.
However, it's certainly a point always worth bearing in mind, especially
when the mean frequency doesn't seem to carry the information you
expect it to.

Can I just make another comment about hearing? It seems to me that
the problem with hearing, or with designing an ear, is that you have a
rapidly fluctuating sound pressure where fluctuations occurring over time
differences of the order of microseconds are very important, and the
structure on that scale is important, but you have to translate that down
to things varying with a time scale that is behaviorally important. It is no
use getting a temporal structure that changes much more often than you
can react behaviorally. You've got to express the result in things which
are invariant over periods of the order of tenths of a second or so, whereas
the input is coming in events with a fine structure in microseconds. That,
of course, is why the transition to a frequency representation is a way of
doing this. You do a Fourier analysis over that kind of time scale and so
you get things that are not varying more rapidly than the animal can itself
handle. I don't know if I've got that idea across at all, but if you do look at
hearing in that way you come to regard the whole of the hearing organ as
a way of getting structure over time intervals of the order of a tenth of a
second. The cochlea is a fast way of doing this because you make a temporary store of the sound and look for structure within that store. It's a
time delay to get a temporary pattern of the whole sound over the recent
past. You cannot do the whole job in one stage, so you have to look for
structure in the neural messages that get into the brain and here, I
imagine, is where the anteroventral nucleus comes in. Of course, the
very important thing that I have not yet mentioned is the lateralization of
sound, which depends on time differences of a very short duration and
which must be carried by the impulse train. There's no way of doing that
peripherally as far as I know. So, it seems to me that the nervous system is
forced, in the case of hearing, to use the fine structure of the neural discharge but it is not forced to do so in the case of the eye.
Dr. Rose: I think that your comment is very pertinent. I am impressed by
the differential between the number of receptors required in vision and
the number of auditory receptors. There are about 124 million photoreceptors in the human retina but only 100 inner hair cells per millimeter of
length in the human organ of Corti. This density is almost invariant in
different mammalian species. So, there are altogether about 3,500 inner

hair cells in the human cochlea and about three times as many outer hair cells. (Whether the outer hair cells act similarily to the inners is now being hotly debated.) In any case, there is no way but to reutilize the same hair cell in order to obtain any reasonable sensitivity. I have amused myself by calculating what difference it would make if you consider the cilia on the hair cell as being the sensitivity units. You improve the sensitivity estimate but, of course, we do not know what the sensitivity unit is.

Dr. McFadden: It's too bad the cilia are all glued together.

Dr. Barlow: I am a little sensitive about talking about this with people who specialize in hearing, but you have to take account of the fact that there is very much more information in the visual image and the ratio of the bandwidths for video and audio in television gives some impression of how very much more actual information there is in the visual image than there is in the acoustic message.

CHAPTER 2

Design for an Eye

Robert M. Boynton

1 Introduction

A A Theological View of Vision: William Paley, 1802

> Were there no example in the world of contrivance, except that of the *eye*, it would be alone sufficient to support the conclusion which we draw from it, as to the necessity of an intelligent creator.

These words were written 176 years ago at Oxford by a British theologian and natural philosopher, William Paley (reprinted 1845, p. 60) who enjoyed an impressive grasp of what was then known about man considered as a machine. His motivation to master and disseminate such material related to his certain conviction, illustrated by the passage above, that the existence of elegant biologic machinery affords the clearest possible evidence of God's design and handiwork. Paley confronts his readers with enough examples of such ingenious engineering to fill 400 pages; in addition to vision, he appeals to mechanisms of audition, botany, comparative anatomy, and vascular hemodynamics. I will mention some of his visual examples.

Paley described the eye as an optical instrument. He was fully aware of the single most important discovery ever made about vertebrate vision— already by then some 200 years old—that an optical image is formed upon the retina at the back of the eye. Because photographic cameras were not yet available to be compared (as now) with eyeballs, Paley used the telescope as his analogy. In discussing the arrangement of the six extraocular muscles of each eye, he revealed a special enchantment with the superior oblique, a muscle that manages to turn the eye to the required extent in the downward and outward direction by threading itself through a cartilaginous natural pulley (Figure 2.1). Paley quite correctly considered the pupil as a mechanism for extending the range of intensities over which the eye could otherwise function. The eyelids were appre-

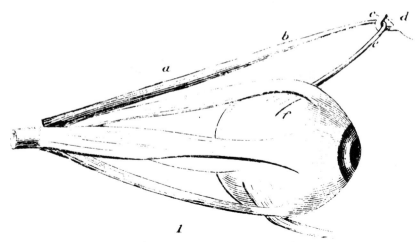

Figure 2.1. An example of an anatomical illustration from the collected works of William Paley (1845).

ciated also as devices to spread tears in order to lubricate the cornea, as well as to shield the front surface of the eye, the remainder of which was regarded as still more fully protected, as indeed it is, within the fatty depths of the bony orbit.

B   Some Nineteenth-Century Developments

Although one must agree with Paley that the visual mechanisms he accurately describes are excellent examples of the marvels of nature, so little was understood about vision in 1800 that the machinery known to him seems almost simpleminded in comparison with what has been discovered since. For example, in the 1800s, after the compound microscope had been perfected, Max Schultze observed the rods and cones; by the end of the century S.R. Cajal, author of the neuron doctrine (Cajal, 1893), had investigated the retinal neurons and glial cells. Also in the 19th century, Hermann von Helmholtz (1924) made his monumental contributions to physiological optics, too numerous to summarize here, of such enduring value that his work is still being reprinted. About 100 years ago, Franz Boll (1877/1977) observed the bleaching of sehrot (visual red) in the frog retina, work soon augmented by monumental photochemical studies by Willy Kühne (1879/1977) at Heidelberg. In midcentury, James Clerk Maxwell (1855) laid the foundations of colorimetry, and later he developed his famous equations, which by the turn into the present century would help enable the powerful conception of light as a form of electromagnetic energy.

C   The First Half of the Twentieth Century

Despite the impressive advances of the 19th century, only a little was
known about vision even by the year 1900. The light microscope had revealed, especially in the hands of Cajal, the five kinds of nerve cells of the
retina (see Figure 2.2) but it told only a little about their connections and
revealed nothing certain of their function. It was generally believed that
electric currents were delivered to the brain, through the fibers of the
optic nerve, in the same way that electricity is transmitted along a telephone wire.

   By 1925 the invention of the vacuum-tube amplifier served to open the
modern era of electrophysiology. In the 1930s, Hartline and Graham
(1932), by shredding the optic nerve of *Limulus*, were the first to record
from single neural units in the visual system. They were able to confirm
that the all-or-none law applied to vision, and that a relation similar to
Fechner's law could be discerned in the nearly linear relation between
spike frequency and log intensity, which Adrian had earlier observed in
the mass discharge of sensory nerves. The chemical investigations of
George Wald and H.J.A. Dartnall revealed the ubiquitousness and essential similarity of all visual photopigments.[1] By 1950, despite these and

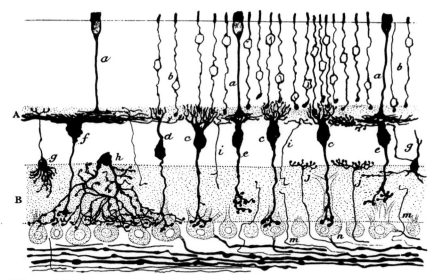

Figure 2.2. An example of the beautiful 19th-century anatomical drawings of
the retina as seen in the microscope by Cajal. This is a section of the retina of an
adult dog. In his illustration, *a* and *b* are cones and rods; *c*, *d*, *e*, and *f* are bipolar
cells; *n* is the cell body of a ganglion cell; and the lateral processes at the bottom
are ganglion cell axons (optic nerve fibers). (From Cajal, 1893; reproduced from
R.W. Rodieck. W.H. Freeman and Co. Copyright © 1973.)

---

[1] An excellent summary of Wald's contribution to this topic exists in his Nobel Prize address
(Wald, 1968). Dartnall's work (1962) is beautifully summarized in Volume 2 of the first edition of *The Eye*, edited by Hugh Davson.

other advances, some false notions had become widely accepted. It was, for example, incorrectly assumed that photoreceptors, like optic nerve fibers, generated spikes. Another erroneous conception was that the visual cortex provides a passive display of the retinal image, an idea based on the earlier discovery of a kind of topological double play, from retina to lateral geniculate to visual cortex.

Color vision is my favorite subject, one which therefore will receive particular emphasis in this paper. By 1950 nothing was directly known about the physiology of color, except for some preliminary records obtained by the famous Swedish physiologist Ragnar Granit (1947/1963), which he was not able to interpret very well. However, it is of interest to note that psychophysics, leading the way as this approach sometimes does, had by then fairly well confirmed that Thomas Young's (1802) speculations about the trichromacy of human color vision were essentially correct.

D   Recent History

Among the totally unpredicted discoveries of the past quarter century are the following examples. It has been learned that vertebrate photoreceptors are maximally active in the dark and least so in the brightest light. Moreover, these initial signals of vision, far from being all-or-none spikes, are instead slow, graded potentials (Arden, 1976). More recently, it has been discovered that photoreceptors do not function in the isolated way that any reasonable theory about visual acuity would seem to demand. Instead, they communicate electrically by specialized gap junctions and thereby share one another's currents; also, they are interconnected synaptically by way of horizontal cells, as first shown by Baylor, Fuortes, and O'Bryan (1971). These conceptions, first suggested by the more detailed knowledge of anatomy made possible by electron microscopy, have been verified in some species by electrophysiological procedures.

None of these new insights, nor many others that might be mentioned, could have been achieved without spectacular advances in experimental procedures. To illustrate, I recall two occasions when the presentation of a slide depicting a new technical achievement inspired an audience to erupt into spontaneous applause. The first was on June 12, 1969, at the University of Rochester, when Akimichi Kaneko, a member of Tomita's group from Tokyo, displayed a glowing bipolar cell (Figure 2.3) which had been injected with procion yellow, a fluorescent dye of very low molecular weight found capable of infiltrating even the smallest processes of the impaled cell, without spilling into the surrounding medium (Kaneko, 1970). Of special importance, injection had been made through the same micropipette with which intracellular electrophysiological records had just previously been made. For the first time, a positive identification of exactly which cell had contributed to the electrical record was possible.

Another occasion when applause broke out was on April 27, 1977, at a meeting of the Association for Research in Vision and Ophthalmology

Figure 2.3. The glowing element is a bipolar cell, injected with a procion yellow dye following recordings made through the same micropipette that impaled the cell both for electrical recording and dye injection. (The original was in color.) (Photograph furnished by A. Kaneko of the Keio University School of Medicine.)

(ARVO), when Denis Baylor of Stanford University showed us a suction electrode (Figure 2.4) developed in his laboratory, by means of which a single rod, too small to withstand electrode penetration, could be swallowed up, so to speak, permitting its isolated activity to be studied without destroying it.[2]

E   The Return of William Paley: Design or Evolution?

The advances just described have surely been surprising ones, as I think that anyone of my generation, who has had the opportunity to observe these events of the past 30 years in real time, will agree. Imagine the im-

---

[2] I am deeply indebted to Professors Kaneko and Baylor for furnishing me with copies of their original slides, reproduced here with their permission. Dr. Baylor's presentation was part of an ARVO symposium honoring the 70th birthday of Professor Wald (Baylor, 1977). Dr. Kaneko's slide was displayed at the Fifth Annual Symposium of the Center for Visual Science at Rochester, New York.

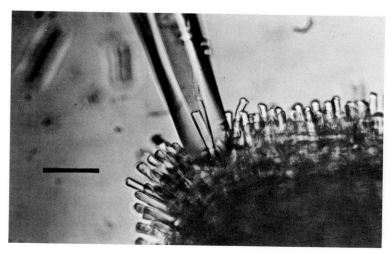

Figure 2.4. "Under infra-red light an outer segment (of a toad) is sucked into a close-fitting pipette and current monitored with a current-to-voltage transducer holding the interior of the pipette at a selected potential. Light flashes induce slow outward photocurrents." Calibration mark = 50 μm. (Quotation from 1977 ARVO abstract by D. Baylor, p. 98, who furnished this photograph, the original of which was in color.)

pact of this new information upon a resurrected William Paley. He anticipated none of it, of course, any more than we can predict the discoveries of the centuries stretching ahead of us. Paley's reaction nevertheless seems predictable—he would perceive this new knowledge as further evidence of the handiwork of God.

Suppose, however, that we were to fill him in on certain other advances, not strictly of a visual nature, but nevertheless related to the issue at hand. The theory of evolution, the most important unifying concept in the history of biology, was, after all, developed while Paley was away. This was also the period that gave birth to the science of genetics. At first the gene was merely an abstract and speculative concept, analogous in some ways to the three different kinds of "sensitive filaments" that Thomas Young had earlier imagined as necessary to explain color vision. Today the gene has a chemical reality, and although much remains to be learned about exactly how genes are arranged in human chromosomes and of the specific processes that they control, it now seems impossible to deny the basic genetic conception. We also now attempt to visualize, over an almost incredible span of time, the combinatorial possibilities afforded in sexual reproduction, enhanced by mutations and differential probabilities of survival in a competitive world and these ideas now seem sufficient to explain the development of progressively better biologic machinery, perhaps even a human eye.

If Paley were alive today, I believe he would be inclined to accept the idea of evolution. However, he would see it as a further revelation of the cleverness of the divine manufacturing process. Perhaps, he might suggest, the "Great Designer" needs feedback to refine his products, just as humans do. We know that the initial design of man-made machines and instruments is usually imperfect. A sophisticated product results only after many years of interaction between design and evolution, in which feedback plays an essential role.

To illustrate this, I compare in Figure 2.5 a modern single-lens reflex camera with a collector's item that I own, a 1909 Kodak. I present these

Figure 2.5. Each of these photographs was taken with the other camera. A 1-diopter lens was placed inside the fixed-focus box camera to permit photographing the modern camera at a distance of 1 m.

pictures also to suggest that, despite many improvements and embellishments, the basic principles of photography, like those of vision, remain unchanged. (To illustrate this, each photograph has been taken with the other camera.)

F   The Search for Eidola

In the most global terms, the overall purpose of the device called an eye is to permit sensory action at a distance, that is, to allow the virtually instantaneous appreciation of the size, location, color, movement, and meaning of objects that are located remotely from us. We will get nowhere in the design process if we regard these objects naively, as having a physical existence that differs little from how they are perceived.

We wish to design a device that will permit the remote apperception of an object, for example a tree. If we regard the "tree" as a stimulus for vision, we are immediately faced with a conundrum because we then have no explanation of how it manages to cross the intervening distance to stimulate us. Like the Greek philosopher Epicurus (see Ronchi, 1970, p. 27), we might suppose that there exist husklike replicas of the tree, called eidola, capable of being freed from its surface, pried loose by the action of light, enabling each eidolon to dart into our eyes. We would need to learn whether each element of the object had the holographic property of conveying the whole. This would be a useful property because eidola could then be small enough to pass through the pupil of the

Figure 2.6. Eidola theory to explain how images of objects enter the eye (shrinking version).

eye. However, the fact that the partial interposition of one object before another obscures only a portion of the first would necessarily lead to the rejection of that hypothesis.

Alternatively, as illustrated in Figure 2.6, it might be supposed that all features of an eidolon shrink proportionally as it moves toward the eye, finally permitting it to enter. If the latter concept were correct, essential tasks of empirical visual science today would be to extract eidola from the surfaces of things, in order to study the forces that caused them to shrink. Because it is the shrunken eidola that stimulate the eye, we would want to examine them microscopically, spin them in a centrifuge, bombard them with X-rays, or perhaps even build a mile-long "eidolatron" with which to blow them apart. The visual physiologist would of course search for the eidola detectors, most likely to be located (according to ancient tradition) in the lens of the eye. These notions are neither stupid nor bizarre—not if one believes in eidola.

2   The Importance of Light

A   Although We Cannot See It, Let There Be Light

The Greeks knew a bit about light, and it was obvious to them, even as to a child, that light is somehow necessary for vision. Light, however, is curious and difficult stuff, whose investigation has characterized some important, intricate, and controversial chapters in the history of physics (Ronchi, 1970; Sarbra, 1967). From the standpoint of a psychologist, one of the most intriguing facts about light is that we ordinarily cannot see it. This idea is extremely important, so let me say it again: *We do not see light*.

A few examples will help to clarify what I mean by this. Light beams are invisible in a vacuum, where the most potent laser beam imaginable could pass laterally in front of an eye, a scant millimeter from the cornea, and there would be no awareness of it. We see beams of light in a smoky room only because of what scatters out of the beam; the beam itself is not available to us. We do not see the light from the sun that illuminates the earth; instead we perceive forms and objects whose properties are visually known to us only by way of the light they reflect. However, we do not see this reflected light, either; we see objects. Yet without viewing the sky, we can tell the difference between a sunny and a cloudy day. A poet would even say that he sees the world "bathed" in light, and we seem to agree, although to say this is to make an inference, however immediate and possibly unlearned it may be. We are unable to have any direct view of illumination.

To build an eye, its design must incorporate a reactivity to light. Although we know this to be true, suppose we lacked this information and therefore had to retreat to a more primitive level to initiate the design process. Because we cannot see the light, why then should we even believe that it exists?

B   Why We Should Believe in Light

We should believe that light exists because there is a consistent body of physical data and theory showing that it does (Ditchburn, 1976; Kurşunoğlu, 1974). All highly developed sciences produce theories that lead to applications. Inventions based upon optical theory are much too numerous, and they work entirely too well, for us to believe that they have been designed on false premises.

The present conceptualization of light nevertheless constitutes relatively new and important knowledge, long sought and hard won, which not too long ago seemed impossible to achieve. For example, the *Encyclopedia Britannica* in 1792 stated (Henderson, 1970, p. 1), "It is obvious . . . that whatever side we take concerning the nature of light, many, indeed almost all of the circumstances concerning it are incomprehensible, and beyond the reach of human understanding." By 1929, despite the enormous advances of physics in the late 19th and early 20th centuries, the *Brittanica* does not sound much more hopeful:

> It might perhaps be expected that we should begin by saying what light 'really' is, and should then develop its characters from such a starting point; but this procedure is not possible, since light is essentially more primitive than any of the things in terms of which we might try to explain it.

Yet in 1968 Gerald Feinberg, writing in a special issue of *Scientific American* concerned with light, could say:

> At present the photon theory gives us an accurate description of all we know about light. The notion that light is fundamentally just another kind of matter is likely to persist in any future theory. The idea is the distinctive contribution of twentieth century physicists to the understanding of light, and it is one of which we can well be proud. (p. 59)

As philosophers of science have argued, there may be no universal truth or ultimate reality of a form accessible to scientific inquiry. Karl Popper (1959), for example, says (p. 59), "Theories are nets cast to catch what we call 'the world': to rationalize, to explain, and to master it. We endeavour to make the mesh ever finer and finer." As we try to catch the world, in this sense, it tends to elude us and even to change its character. This has happened with the study of light; the resolution that Feinberg seems happy with has resulted, I think, from the discovery that all of the wavelike properties of light seem to reside within the individual photons. These should then be conceived as vibrating, as they travel forward at the speed of light, in orthogonal planes and at a frequency that determines the wavelength of each cycle of vibration.

Popper also states (p. 47) that

> *there can be no ultimate statements in science:* there can be no state-
> ments in science which cannot be tested, and therefore none which
> cannot in principle be refuted, by falsifying some of the conclusions
> which can be deduced from them.

Finally, (p. 46)

> No matter how intense a feeling of conviction it may be, it can never
> justify a statement. Thus I can be utterly convinced of the truth of a
> statement; certain of the evidence of my perceptions; overwhelmed by
> the intensity of my experience: every doubt may seem to me absurd.
> But does this afford the slightest reason for science to accept my state-
> ment? Can any statement be justified by the fact that K.R.P. is utterly
> convinced of its truth? The answer is, "No"; and any other answer
> would be incompatible with the idea of scientific objectivity.

Although I disagree not at all with Popper's ideas, it has nevertheless
been my observation that the best scientists seem to have an unusual
faith in an absolute truth, and a conviction that, in a set of conflicting
theories, if each is testable (as it must be to belong properly in the system
of science) all but one will ultimately fail. The physics of light has
received the concerted attention of some of the best scientific brains in
history; such men as Maxwell, Einstein, Bohr, and the rest, and has produced a concept of light that seems right to Feinberg and, for the lesser
amount that it is worth, also to me. If the probable truth of theories could
be established on a ratio scale, where the best theory that we have in psychology were arbitrarily given unit value, I think the present physical theory of light would be worth at least a five. There can be no doubt that
light, whatever it may be, is what intervenes between what we see and
what we are. The photon theory is as close to a valid conception of light
as we can get, at least for now. Students of visual perception who choose
to ignore what actually stimulates the eye, do so at their own great peril.

C   The World of Physics versus the World of Perception

You may immediately protest that the world of subjective perception is
equally real as that of physics, yet it disagrees violently with the idea of a
universe replete with weird particles assembled into atoms and molecules
of various sorts, vibrating away in mostly empty space. I cannot resonate
to this objection. Excepting dreams and hallucinations, there is a physical
basis for all that we see, but the subjective reality that emerges need not
seem to all creatures as it seems to us. Neither is there any requirement
that all humans should see the world in exactly the same way: Indeed, we
know this requirement is not met. The single example of color-blind
humans is sufficient to make the point.

What we see is to an important extent a matter of what we are able to
discriminate with the naked eye. If things too small to see could only be

made large enough, then we could see what they are, as for example in the case of these rods and cones (Figure 2.7) that have been revealed by scanning electron microscopy. Although photons, by means of which we see, cannot reveal this structure to us, even with optical magnification, such failure must not be taken as evidence that rods and cones are not really there.

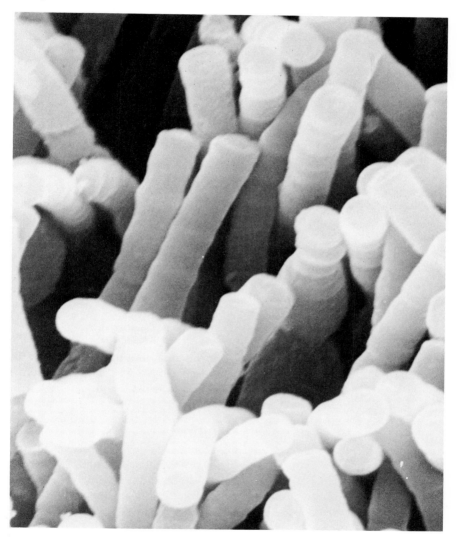

Figure 2.7. Rods and a cone of a human retina as revealed by scanning electron microscopy. Normally, the rod outer segments, which are mostly what show in this picture, are parallel. Here, they have been deliberately discombobulated in order to expose the outer segment of a cone, which is shown just to the right of center. (Photograph furnished by Dr. G. Wickham).

Likewise, take the case of our planet, as it has now been seen from outer space. Suppose that this is all that you, a moonperson, had ever seen, but that by some indirect procedure—perhaps some gargantuan version of lunar X-ray cystallography—someone claimed to have discovered the structure of, say, the buildings on Manhattan Island. If you were to reject that description as unreasonable, merely because it disagreed with your raw perception, you would simply be wrong. You should be implored to leave the moon and to descend toward earth in order to view the buildings from an altitude of 5,000 ft. This would reveal the structure of Manhattan Island to your vision in a way that is analogous to seeing the rods and cones in the electron micrograph.

The problem of perception is to understand how and why we perceive reality at the particular level that we do. The more restricted problem to which I address myself is, how do we design an eye capable of accomplishing this? We cannot explain this level of perceived reality in terms of itself, because we cannot use reality so conceived as the input to the machine we wish to design. In other words, what we are capable of seeing cannot bridge the space between ourselves and what we do see. We need instead a way of describing the stimulus in a manner that enables us to understand what actually does bridge the gap, using concepts that do not depend directly upon human perception. What physical scientists have provided is exactly what we require: a description of reality that transcends human perception, and that presumably would still be valid even if all humans and other perceiving organisms were wiped off the face of the earth this minute. We must accept the idea of an invisible light as providing the stimulus for vision.

D   Why Light Is Best for Vision

We can begin now in earnest to ask how we may design a system that will permit such perception to occur. Although I have a primary interest in color, a critical ground rule is that the design must not interfere with a function of vision that is more important than the perception of color, namely the determination of spatial location and the resolution of fine detail. Therefore we must consider spatial vision first.

There are many forms of energy from which to choose. After considering various alternatives, we would reject some entirely, set others aside for other senses to use, and select light as the form of energy to utilize for visual purposes because of a number of desirable properties that it seems to possess. (1) It is copiously available in the daytime and is seldom totally absent, even at night. (2) Light travels through the atmosphere relatively unhindered and in reasonably straight lines. (3) Its speed is so great that "travel time" is negligible for terrestrial purposes. (4) Light interacts with the molecules of many surfaces in such a manner as to be partially absorbed and partially reflected, thus rendering the surfaces opaque and providing the primary physical basis for the perception of surface qualities, including color. Because objects are usually not transparent to light, the cues that are critically important for figure–ground perception are made available. (5) Light is potentially eternal; photons can last forever. Ancient quanta from distant stars lose none of their capacity to stimulate the eye.

Consider the consequences if some of these advantageous properties of light did not obtain. If light always followed a curved path, instead of doing so only under the extreme conditions capable of bending light rays, mirages would become commonplace. For example, if light traveled as slowly as sound, we would seriously misjudge the location of objects that moved relative to those that did not. To illustrate this, we wanted to make a double exposure taken from a vantage point a half-mile distant from Interstate 5 near Del Mar, California. Sound travels about 1,100 ft/sec; a half-mile is roughly twice this distance, so two brief exposures separated by just over 2 sec would do the job. You can imagine the result: The mountains and the road would remain fixed and the moving vehicles would be depicted twice, separated by several car lengths. Because we could not find a camera to make double exposures, we instead had the bright idea of using a single exposure of about 2 sec, with the expectation that the moving vehicles would turn into streaks. The result is more interesting than the expected picture would have been: It shows what vision would be like if the physiological time frames were 2.5 secs long rather than the 100 msec or so that they are. Interstate 5, midday on a weekend, appeared utterly devoid of perceptible traffic!

In addition to the desirable properties just enumerated, we will find that light can be utilized in a biological organ of reasonable size, in a manner that will permit the critically important inference of the direction from which the photons came, thereby providing knowledge of the location and detailed structure of remote objects.

3   The Detection of Light

A   The Ubiquity of Visual Photopigments

Not all electomagnetic radiation possesses the desirable properties just enumerated, especially if the problem of detecting it is added, as it must be, to the list of design requirements. Some wavelengths are not sufficiently available in nature. If the known principles of ocular design were used, long wavelengths would require scaling the eye to enormous dimensions as illustrated by the model cones in Figure 2.8 once used by Brian O'Brien (1951), who hung them out a window of the Institute of Optics in Rochester to study an analog of the Stiles–Crawford effect using 3.2-cm waves of electromagnetic radiation from a distant source.

Figure 2.8. Model polystyrene foam cones studied by O'Brien (1951). The photograph has been slightly retouched to show the ends of the structures more clearly.

Receptors of this size would require an eyeball roughly a mile in diameter to house them. Very short wavelengths, including X-rays, reflect poorly from objects and are not significantly refracted by optical media; to build a biological device to detect the direction of their travel might turn out to be impossible. From the standpoint of both environment and eye, the use of electromagnetic radiation in the wavelength range between about 400 and 750 nm seems to be an optimal choice for vision.

Even under optimal conditions, the job of detecting photons is a formidable one. In the early days of optics, the eye was the only photon detector available. Photographic emulsions provided the first breakthrough, but in order to make daguerrotypes, for example, an exposure of several minutes was required. Thermopiles and other nonselective radiation detectors followed, and then came photocells, photomultipliers, television pickup tubes, and photodiodes. Most of these man-made devices are bulky, and their nonorganic molecular structure would make them unsuitable for an eye.

The biological solution to the light-detection problem is so universal in seeing creatures that it is profitable to assume that no alternative solution exists. To design a photon detector suitable for an eye, one evidently must use a visual photopigment very much like rhodopsin. The molecules of this stuff react to the absorption of light by the isomerization and dissociation of their chromophores, giving up enough energy in the process somehow to initiate a visual signal. Such a molecule is small, which is surely a desirable property. It reacts usefully and well to light. However, it suffers from a very serious disadvantage. It is very unlikely to absorb light in the first place.

B   On the Insensitivity of Photopigment Molecules to Light

The probability that a single molecule of photopigment will absorb a photon, even when that photon is in the immediate vicinity, is in fact almost vanishingly small. This problem of photon ineffectiveness seems related to the fact that photons contain very little energy. Pirenne (1948, p. 78), in the following delightful way, points up the astonishing sensitivity of the eye that is nevertheless achieved. "The mechanical energy of a pea falling from a height of one inch would, if transformed into luminous energy, be sufficient to give a faint impression of light to every man that ever lived."

Rough numbers will suffice to give an idea of how improbable it is that a photopigment molecule will absorb a photon. It is known that, if about 10 photons are absorbed in the dark-adapted eye in response to a small and brief flash, a visual sensation will probably result (Hecht, Shlaer, & Pirenne, 1942). For purely optical reasons it is not possible to concentrate this light within a group of receptors numbering fewer than about 10. By psychophysical experiment it is well established that it makes no difference where, within such a group of receptors, the photons are absorbed. Each receptor is estimated to contain about 40 million molecules of photopigment in its outer segment (Wald, Brown, & Gibbons, 1963), so there are approximately 400 million photopigment molecules in 10 cones. Therefore, even if all incident photons were absorbed in one or another of these molecules, the probability that any particular molecule would do the absorbing is 10 divided by 400 million, or about one in 40 million. The true odds are even longer than this, because even at the wavelength of maximum spectral sensitivity, no more than about 20% of the incident photons are absorbed, which reduces the chances that any individual molecule will absorb a photon to only about one in 200 million. It seems that a very improbable resonance must take place between the vibrations of a photon and those of the atoms which comprise a photopigment molecule before an absorption will take place.

The result of this calculation has anticipated the essential nature of the solution to the problem of photopigment insensitivity: This is to place huge numbers of molecules inside each receptor, arranged in a manner that favors their encounter with photons, thereby building up the proba-

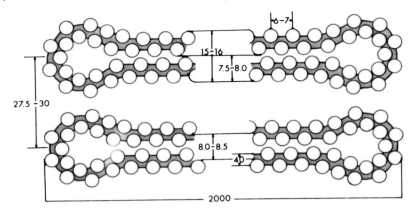

Figure 2.9. Model proposed by Vanderkooi and Sundaralingham to show how the visual pigment (circles) and lipid (shaded area) are positioned in rod disks. The middle area (not shown) is about 50 times as long as the flanking segments. (From Rodieck, 1973, p. 106.)

bility that absorption will occur *somewhere* in the receptor (see Figure 2.9). In addition, it is necessary that the receptor should produce a signal even if only one photon is absorbed, no matter in which of its 40 million molecules the photon is captured. Finally, we will do well to interconnect the receptors so that they can assist one another in the production of signals of sufficient stability and magnitude to be worth transmitting to the next stage of retinal processing.

C   The Problem of Registering Direction

Given all these problems and limitations, how do we build an eye to absorb photons, while keeping in mind also the essential requirement of spatial vision, which is the registration of direction? At first blush it may seem possible to create a particle of stuff capable of registering directly, somehow, the direction of incidence of a photon that strikes it. This simply will not work because we are dealing with molecules that are barely capable of registering even the *fact* of photon incidence, let alone the direction of their arrival; to add the requirement of directional registration to the signal produced by an activated photopigment molecule is out of the question. To stand any probability whatever of being stimulated, the molecule must reduce its signaling capability to the simplest possible binary level: It must state within each sampling period either that a photon has been absorbed or that one has not; it cannot tell anything about where the photon came from.

Looking ahead to color vision, it is worth noting also that directional information is not all that is lost; so also is information about the wavelength of the photon.

4   The Registration of Direction

A   Some Less than Optimal Solutions

Just because an individual photopigment molecule loses track of direction, it does not follow that there is no way to recover such information. One way to do so is to locate the molecule so that it is impossible for photons to reach it unless they arrive along some particular path. We could do this with a parallel array of soda straws, blackened inside so that only axial photons stand much of a chance of passing through without being absorbed. This is essentially the principle utilized in the compound eyes of many creatures, including houseflies and *Limuli*. However, blackened tubes would be terribly inefficient; instead, the ommatidia of compound eyes are optically quite complicated. Each one accepts photons over a range of angles, but with a stable probability, which varies as a function of direction (see Figure 2.10). Given the reactions of many such elements, each with a slightly different orientation, it is the job of the beast's visual nervous system to figure out, as best it can, the direction from which a stream of photons has arrived (see Figure 2.11). If only a very few photons arrive, calculation cannot be made with much precision, but at high intensities the probabilities translate into stable amounts and the calculation becomes relatively precise.

Another solution might be to concentrate an enormous quantity of photopigment into a restricted space, and then to wave just a single black-

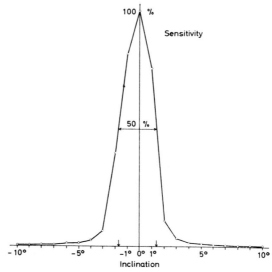

Figure 2.10. Directional sensitivity of an ommatidium of the blowfly. Sensitivity is shown as a function of the angle of incidence of the stimulating light beam. (From Burkhardt, de la Motte, & Seitz, 1966).

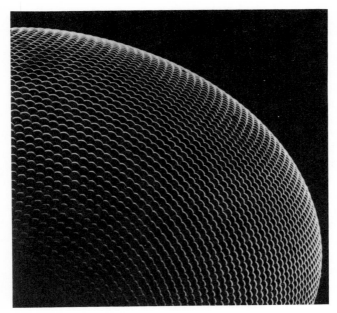

Figure 2.11. Magnified appearance of the eye of the ordinary housefly, show-ing the highly regular way in which the orientation of each ommatidium varies across its surface. (Reprinted by permission of Schocken Books Inc. from Mag-nifications by David Scharf. Copyright © 1977 by David Scharf.)

ened tube at the environment. If the motion were programmed in a pre-dictable way, and if the nervous system had a good enough clock, it would know where the light came from in terms of *when* a signal was ini-tiated. However, such a biological clock is unlikely, and we would want to abandon this scheme anyway as requiring a too vigorously moving part, which would wear out quickly if it scanned the world at the very high rates required for adequate temporal resolution. We might be able to find a way around this problem, but even so, our ultimate conclusion would be that this is a better plan for television than for human perception. Other implausible or impractical schemes might follow, only to be re-jected for one reason or another.

B   The Optimal Solution

Eventually we hit upon a better plan, probably the optimal one. With scanning ruled out, we look again at the compound eye and note that it translates directional information—the flight path of an arriving photon—into spatial information, in the form of which ommatidium is most likely to be activated. The optimal plan has in common with this the translation of photon direction into retinal location, but otherwise it differs greatly from it, especially because the direction of the photon as it strikes the photoreceptor does not encode information about directions in visual space. The solution is not obvious. It is in fact so nonintuitive that, despite a curiosity about vertebrate vision as old as recorded history, and the existence of some considerable knowledge about optics and of the gross anatomy of the eye known since antiquity, it was not until 1605 that Kepler finally figured out what the Great Designer had done.

In attempting the design ourselves, we might stumble upon it in the following way. Instead of putting the array of photodetectors on the outside of the eye, we decide to put them inside. Perhaps this way we can use smaller, more delicate, more finely tuned receiving elements. Again, we make it a firm requirement that *which* receptor receives a photon must depend somehow upon from *where* in space that photon has come. One way to do this, known to Alhazen in 1066, would be to place a pinhole at the surface of an eye filled with air. This would serve to constrain the arrival of photons in the desired manner, as shown in Figure 2.12(a).

At first this seems to be a good scheme, but we quickly discover that it wastes far too much light. Whereas the compound eye has a large convex surface to receive light, so that most of the photons arriving at the eye are able to enter one ommatidium or another, our pinhole eye can see only by means of the very tiny amount of light that is able to pass through the hole. We try next to enlarge the pinhole (Figure 2.12b) only to discover that light from a point in space now falls on too many receptors.

The solution that we eventually achieve is a wild one. We place a curved surface over the enlarged pinhole—let us call it a cornea—and fill the eye with a water medium that slows the flight of the incident photons by about a third. The additional delay is of no consequence, but associated with it is an abrupt and precise alteration of the direction of the flight path of each photon as it moves from air into the eye at the optical interface represented by the curved cornea (Figure 2.12c). We speculate:

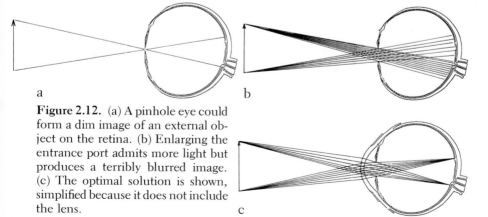

a

b

Figure 2.12. (a) A pinhole eye could form a dim image of an external object on the retina. (b) Enlarging the entrance port admits more light but produces a terribly blurred image. (c) The optimal solution is shown, simplified because it does not include the lens.

c

Figure 2.13. Simulation of blur caused by defocusing the eye by 0.39 diopter. The road sign was located 15.2 m from the camera, which was focused at that distance for the bottom picture (taken through 50-mm lens at $f/4.5$, corresponding to a pupillary diameter of 5 mm for an eye of that f number). For the top photograph the camera was improperly focused at a distance of only 2.2 m. Under that condition, the increased distance between the lens and film plane of the camera corresponds to 0.39 diopter of excess optical power (myopia) for an object at the distance of the road sign. For an eye of focal length 22.79 mm, this optical error would correspond to an image shift along the optical axis of only 0.2 mm.

Might it be possible to shape the cornea so that all photons originating from a single point in space arrived at a single point on the retina? Also, could the cornea be shaped so that, if we were to move the point in space in a plane lateral to the line of sight, the point on the retina would also move laterally and in proportion?

This is a very tall order; it would take a Great Designer indeed to work it all out. At first blush the whole idea seems preposterous, if only because the precision of the relations that are required to keep the focused light at the proper plane of the retina seems unattainable. (One needs to have traced a few rays to have a proper feeling for this.) Relative to the length of the eye, the curvature of the cornea must be of just the right sort; relative to the curvature of the cornea, the eyeball must be of just the right length. For example, Figure 2.13, bottom, shows what the world looks like to a human whose eye is of the right size relative to its corneal curvature; above, is illustrated the effect of increasing the length of the eye by 0.2 millimeter, less than 1% of the length of the eye.

There are even worse problems, which we will not deal with in detail but which should at least be mentioned. The eye must grow with the developing creature. Is it really feasible to keep these relations in an appropriate register throughout the developmental process? Moreover, what do we do about points in space that are located closer to the eye, when we discover that their photons are insufficiently refracted to converge properly upon the retina? How do we produce, biologically, an interface that is smooth within a quarter of a wavelength of light? How do we keep the structure from collapsing? Can we do all this, and still have the eye mobile? A priori, to build such an eye seems about as impossible as anything that one can imagine. If we did not know that such image-forming eyes existed, why would we ever believe that they could?

5   The Registration of Color

A   We Are All Color-Blind

The evidence that there are conditions where all of us are color-blind is available to anyone willing to pay attention to what he sees by the light of the quarter moon. I refer to the total color-blindness of rod vision, and I shall return to that subject shortly.

The evidence for a more limited color-blindness of a second kind is not so readily available; it exists in the form of inferences from laboratory observations of a sort that were begun more than a hundred years ago by Maxwell (1855), who dealt in a quantitative way with a subject long known to artists but little understood by them: color mixture. Even at high levels of lighting, where the cones are operating, we are all color-blind in the sense that there exist for us pairs of physically different stimuli that nevertheless look alike. The most extreme example of this so-called chromatic metamerism is a white, produced by an equal-energy spectrum, that can be matched by superimposing highly saturated red, green, and blue spectral primaries.

However, we are, of course, far from totally color-blind. We easily enough discern the colors of various objects in daily life, and when two surfaces are placed close together, their colors are very unlikely to look exactly the same. Indeed, even when the two samples are intended to be of the same color, as with paints, tiles, or fabrics manufactured at different times, the eye has an embarrassing ability to recognize a small physical difference between them as a difference in perceived color. By extrapolation from experiments on just-noticeable color differences, it has been estimated that we can discriminate at least 100,000 different colors in side-by-side comparisons.

Dichromats are not totally color-blind either. They can discriminate many colors as different, but not so many as normal subjects. Their problem is believed related to the lack of one of the three kinds of normal cone photopigments, whose spectral sensitivities are shown in Figure 2.14. For those of us having normal color perception, the ability to discriminate between physically different pairs of stimuli could surely be improved by introducing a hypothetical fourth type of pigment, providing that it were properly housed and the type of cone containing it were appropriately connected to more central stages; and in principle we could add a fifth type, or however many would be required to convert the eye into a biological high-resolution spectrophotometer, capable of discerning as different any two spectral distributions of light that are not *physically* identical.

Relative to such a chromatic ideal, perhaps we are color-blind for the following reasons:

1. If it were possible to construct much more narrowly tuned photopigments, the rejection of all but a narrow spectral bandwidth would dramatically decrease the sensitivity of each receptor to light. Very narrow spectral tuning of receptors for color would in this sense be

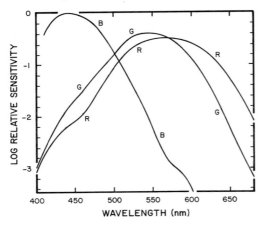

Figure 2.14. The spectral sensitivities of human R, G, and B cones plotted on a logarithmic ordinate, using data furnished by Walraven (1974). These curves are based upon a substantial body of psychophysical evidence and are consistent with objective measurements.

analogous to the pinhole solution for spatial vision: Both procedures would be far too wasteful of light.[3]

2. It apparently is not possible to evolve a photopigment whose resonance with incident vibrating photons is much more sharply tuned than what is described by the action spectrum of rhodopsin.

3. For good spatial vision we cannot afford to have a retina that is functionally riddled with holes, as it would be if many of the receptors were totally blind — and narrowly tuned receptors would be in response to an unbalanced spectrum.

B   Of What Use Is Color Vision?

Unless there is some clear visual advantage to be achieved, there is no point in designing an eye to see color. There are advantages, however, and these appear to be twofold. The first — and in my opinion the most important — is that color enables us to discern a property of objects that has survival value for us. One aspect of this property is relative. For example, it is possible to choose uniforms for two competing football teams whose colors, though dramatically different as seen by the fans in the stands or as reproduced by color television, prove indistinguishable on black and white TV. This illustrates that color enables us to distinguish between objects of two classes that otherwise would be confused; what the colors are does not matter very much. Many times, though, we need to recognize the "true" colors of things, which means seeing color relative to some kind of internal representation. We require a stable and reproducible sensation of color, one that is associated with a surface even in the face of substantial changes in illumination and surrounds. Arbitrary assignment of color to two classes of bananas would not enable us to tell the ripe ones, and we would like the ripe ones to look ripe, whether viewed indoors under incandescent light or taken outside to be seen by the light of the sun.

The second benefit of color relates to an aspect of the more primary function of vision, which is the perception of contour. Color differences sometimes permit contours to be perceived that otherwise would be invisible; we may for example discern a red ball lying in green grass that might not be visible to a dichromat.

Color has other benefits for us of course. Colors undeniably have aesthetic value; few of us would wish to be deprived of the extra beauty with which color enriches our lives. Like odors, colors seldom seem neutral. They please us or they do not; they tend to energize or subdue; they seem warm or cold. Such affective properties of color are of great concern to

---

[3] This is what Thomas Young implied when, in 1802, he said: " it is almost impossible to conceive each sensitive point of the retina to contain an infinite number of particles, each capable of vibrating in perfect unison with every possible undulation." He went on to suggest that "each sensitive filament of the nerve may consist of three portions, one for each principal colour." This was the first clear statement of a trichromatic theory of vision.

artists, fashion designers, architects, and interior decorators, but they have not yielded very much as yet to scientific examination.

C   Why Color Vision Is Photopic

At low levels of illumination it is necessary that the resources of human vision be mobilized with one overriding objective: sensitivity. A degree of spatial vision must also be preserved by rods but this must be compromised, for it is better to see an object indistinctly than, in a vain effort to discern its fine details, to miss seeing it altogether. Consider a 10° field of light that is centered 10° from the point of fixation. Switch on this light, at an intensity that is about twice the absolute dark-adapted threshold. After a brief delay of less than 100 msec, the light will be seen. Yet under these conditions there is so little light that an average rod must wait for about 60 seconds before it absorbs its first photon, and an average molecule must wait 33 weeks.[4] Receptive fields must therefore be made very large, so that the combined effects of excitation from just a few rods anywhere within the field can be summed in order to provide a signal reliable and large enough to register beyond the initial receptor stage. At these low levels, no advantage would accrue from providing rods with more than one kind of photopigment, because the degree of summation that is required for rod vision would not easily permit the system to react differentially to signals coming from the two or more classes of rods. Adding a second pigment would only serve to broaden the absorption spectrum of the group of rods in the receptive field, adding to the problem of chromatic aberration (discussed in Section 5,D) and complicating the design of the system without providing sufficient compensating benefit.

As the illumination level is raised, the number of photons available to the receptors increases in proportion. The eye must be able to function over an extremely large dynamic range. At the threshold for cones, where color perception just begins to come in, each cone absorbs about one photon per second. At a level corresponding to poor interior illumination, where color vision is fairly good but not yet optimal, each cone absorbs about 1,000 photons each second. The response level of each cone fluctuates because it is related, during each sampling period, to the product of two probabilities: (1) the probability that a photon will travel in the neighborhood of a receptor and (2) the probability that such a passing photon will be absorbed by that receptor. As intensity increases, meaning that more photons are delivered to the eye, the variance of the response

---

[4] If one rod must wait 60 sec to absorb a photon, the probability that any particular molecule will absorb it is 1 in 40,000,000 or 2.5×10^{-8}. To raise this probability to 0.5, then $0.5/(2.5 \times 10^{-8})$ 1-min sampling periods (20,000,000) would be required. The remainder of the calculation:

$$20,000,000 \text{ min} \times (1 \text{ hr}/60 \text{ min}) \times (1 \text{ day}/24 \text{ hr}) \times (1 \text{ week}/7 \text{ days}) = 33 \text{ weeks}$$

magnitude of the receptor becomes less relative to its mean, and a more reliable signal is established (Rose, 1948).

Beyond about 3,000 absorptions per cone per second, which is a level of comfortable and essentially optimal chromatic vision, the task of the system includes dealing with photic excess rather than insufficiency. Various adaptive mechanisms come into play and the excess is utilized in a positive way to further improve both the spatial and temporal resolving power of the system. As examples, it is found that the crispness of cone responses to an impulse input is enhanced (Baylor & Hodgkin, 1974), and that a reorganization of the visual pathways occurs where the inhibitory surrounds of receptive fields exert a progressively more powerful effect as intensity is increased.

Only at photopic levels are there sufficient numbers of photons available so that the visual system can afford the luxury of color vision, which therefore seems to be a bonus to be utilized and enjoyed only when the more basic requirements of adequate sensitivity and good spatial resolution have been met.

D   The Chromatic Aberration of the Eye

The amount of refraction that occurs at an optical interface, including the corneal surface dividing the eyeball from air, depends upon the wavelength of the light. An optical system designed to provide a good image of longwave (red) light will have excessive optical power for shortwave (blue) light; the rays cross in front of the image plane and provide a blur circle behind.

It is possible to correct for this problem in man-made optical systems but it is not easy to do so; multiple elements must be used, made of different kinds of glass, and some of these elements include concave surfaces. The design of the eye includes no correction at all for chromatic aberration, leading to about two diopters more optical power for light at 400 than at 750 nm (Bennett & Francis, 1962, p. 128). This means that if the eye is accommodated for red light at optical infinity, a violet light must be brought to within 50 cm of the eye in order to be in optimal focus.[5]

We may speculate that, given the other design requirements of the eye and the difficulty of evolving optical elements of the varying curvatures and refractive indices necessary to correct for chromatic aberration, na-

---

[5] The demonstration that was used in the oral presentation cannot be reproduced in a book. A slide showing some experimental data with a large number of points was divided into two portions by means of blue and red Wratten filters. The red portion, which otherwise would have projected much brighter than the blue, was backed with some neutral filtering to make them nearly equal in brightness. At a long viewing distance, the red points and lettering looked sharp and clear; the blue ones fuzzy and out of focus. No alteration of the focus of the projector will improve the appearance of the blue portion. At a viewing distance of 50 cm from the screen, the blue portion appears sharp, equivalent to the red part (2 diopters of accommodation of the eye would be needed for the latter).

ture simply gave up trying to meet this requirement. Yet we do not experience chromatic fringes in ordinary vision. The reason that we do not is related in part to central mechanisms, such as those implied by the adaption experiments of I. Kohler (1964), and in part attributable to mechanisms in the retina to be described shortly.

E   Schemes to See Color that Do Not Quite Work

How can we utilize the extra photons of photopic vision in order to see color? To minimize chromatic aberration we would want the absorption band for wavelength to be as narrow as possible; to accomplish this we might be tempted to equip each cone with the same photopigment and design a mechanism in which to locate that pigment which can tell the wavelength of the absorbed photon. Because I have already belabored at great length the impossibility of doing this, let us pass on to the scheme that Thomas Young correctly visualized, without having much evidence for it, nearly 180 years ago.

The solution manifests itself in the presence of three different classes of cones that I shall call R, G, and B (Figure 2.14). These differ by containing three different photopigments whose absorption curves are shifted along the wavelength scale relative to one another.

It has already been established why we cannot settle for an infinitude of cone types, each with an infinitely narrow spectral sensitivity. However, why should we settle for just three types of cones instead of, say, four? Consider the nature of reflecting surfaces. The basis for perceiving their colors lies in their diffuse spectral reflectance curves, which show the amount of light that is returned from them as a function of wavelength. A common characteristic of most such curves that are found in nature is that they do not have sharp changes in slope. They tend instead to wiggle along through the spectrum in a rather gradual fashion. To analyze the structure of curves with sharp peaks and deep valleys, one requires many narrow sampling windows along the wavelength scale. Gentle curves, such as these, require fewer. Apparently three are sufficient.

If we accept that three is the proper number, the next question to ask is: How should these be spaced across the visible spectrum in order to extract the maximum color information from environmental surfaces? An attempt to answer this question could be made by playing the following game. Take a large number of real-life reflectance curves—a good ecological sample—and integrate each one with the spectrum of sunlight. This will show the spectral distribution of radiance that reaches the eye. Take three pigments, each with the rhodopsin type of spectral absorption curve, and begin by setting their peaks at arbitrary places, say 350, 500, and 750 nm. Derive an index of differential absorption for the three pigments, assuming that these have been irradiated in turn by all of the stimuli of the ecological sample. Such an index might be the average of R/G, G/R, and R/B. Sum the index for the computations based upon all of the samples and store that value. Then, with two of the peak wavelengths unchanged, vary the third one a bit, recompute, and determine whether the value of the differential absorption index has increased or decreased. Continue until an optimal wavelength is found and then start manipulating the peak wavelength of the second pigment. Do the same with the third and then go back again to the first and continue until there is no further improvement in the discrimination index. One could think of more sophisticated multidimensional scaling methods, but I hope I have communicated the general idea. By this means, an optimal placement of the three pigment peaks could be determined.

In fact this exercise would lead to an incorrect answer, because the assumption concerning the comparison procedures for the relative outputs of the three types of cones is too simple. Unless we want to go back and redesign the optics of the eye, we must also complicate the design further in order to deal properly with the problem of chromatic aberration.

Figure 2.15 is from an experiment designed to illustrate the effect of eliminating the contribution of the blue-sensitive cones to spatial vision. The result is an improvement of image quality, caused by a reduction of the effects of chromatic aberration in the eye. Not shown here, but also studied, is a similar result that is produced by shifting the peak of the red-sensitive cone (the one at the right) from 565 nm to 640 nm, so that the curves overlap much less than in Figure 2.15. Some of the details of that experiment, which was carried out by David R. Williams for the purposes of this paper, are given in the Appendix to this contribution.

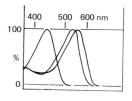

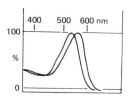

Figure 2.15. Results of an experiment designed to simulate the effects of chromatic aberration on retinal image quality. In the top picture, the blue-sensitive cones are assumed to contribute to spatial vision, whereas in the bottom picture they do not. See Appendix for details of the experiment.

F   A Scheme to See Color that Apparently Does Work

Two problems arise from what we have just done. First, is it possible, with the R and G curves lying so close together, for them to mediate a high level of color discrimination that is based upon their relative levels of activation? Second, by throwing out the B cones, we have created a dichromatic eye. Is there a way to restore trichromacy without reintroducing the problem of severe chromatic aberration?

Both answers are affirmative. In the face of such overlapping sensitivities, the solution to the problem of preserving good red–green discrimination is to take a difference signal between the outputs of the R and G cones and to do it without delay. The electrophysiological evidence now available indicates that for cold-blooded creatures, at least, this has already happened at the horizontal-cell level; in these animals, as well as in primates, horizontal cells interconnect synaptically with cones. In fish and turtles the signals generated by many horizontal cells reveal opponent color responses showing that such processing does in fact occur (MacNichol & Svaetichin, 1958). These opponent signals are subsequently converted to variable spike frequencies, which in primates are first revealed at the ganglion cells of the retina as either an upward or a downward modulation of a resting level of spike frequency, with the direction of change depending upon the wavelength of the stimulating light (DeValois, 1973).

How do we get the B cones back into the system without upsetting this scheme? In my laboratory we have recently learned the following. (1) If two stimuli, presented as contiguous half fields, are seen as identical by both R and G cones but differently by B cones, no contour is formed at their junction and the fields seem to "melt" together. (2) By separating two such fields a little, the color difference perceived between them is significantly enhanced (Boynton, Hayhoe, & MacLeod, 1977). We call this a "positive gap effect" and contrast it with the more common negative effect of field separation that has long been known for luminance discrimination. The B cones have an action spectrum whose peak is quite distant from those of the other two types. This is good from the standpoint of color discrimination, but it is a potential disaster for spatial vision because of chromatic aberration. The solution is to give the B cones essentially no role to play in spatial vision. The melting borders show that B cones do not mediate contour. The gap effect implies that R and G cones stake out the territory of vision and simultaneously provide some important chromatic information. It is then the business of B cones to fill in blueness within these boundaries.

For this purpose, relatively few B cones are necessary, because their outputs can be pooled to enhance their collective sensitivity, much in the manner of rods. All available evidence indicates that there are indeed relatively few B cones in the retina and perhaps none in the foveal region, where spatial vision is most acute. Therefore, it seems that most of the photons that are absorbed in the fovea are captured by either R or G cones and that the blue dimension of color experience is filled in by diverting for this purpose only a trivial fraction of the photons.

6   Summary

The problem of perception is to understand how and why we are able to see objects in the particular way that we do. There is no longer anything mysterious about what puts us in visual contact with remote objects: It is light. Although few people would deny this, it has proved easy to fall into the trap of considering objects as we perceive them as if they were themselves the "stimuli" for the perceptual processes that we are trying to explain. To do so is circular and nonproductive.

The design of the human eye is impressively subtle. There are many features about it, only some of which have been discussed here, that can serve to make this general point. Although the eyes of various creatures differ in many ways, the ubiquitous nature of their photopigments suggests that there is only one way to solve the problem of light detection in living creatures, and that is to utilize these pigments. When considered at a molecular level, such pigments are found to be very insensitive to light. This problem is solved for vertebrate vision by evolving specialized structures, the photoreceptors, that contain huge numbers of such molecules arranged so as to maximize the chance that at least one of them will catch a photon. In a short exposure, even at high photopic levels, most of them nevertheless will fail to do so.

Given these limitations, it is not possible for a photopigment molecule, if it registers the absorption of a photon, to issue a signal that also tells where the photon came from, or how fast it was vibrating. In the human eye the related problems of spatial and chromatic vision are ingeniously solved by the use of image-forming optics that are of very high precision except that they apparently cannot be corrected for chromatic aberration. The retinal image is dissected by rods and three types of cones. One type of cone seems to be exclusively concerned with color, whereas the other two kinds serve double duty by participating in spatial as well as color vision.

Whether the human eye has been produced by the Great Designer, by the process of evolution, or in some other way, it is difficult not to agree with William Paley that the eye appears to reveal a superb and sophisticated design, one that renders it capable of rapidly extracting a very high level of spatial and chromatic information from patterns of light in the environment. This paper has stressed the physics of light and the function of the eye as an optical device. Were I to continue to discuss the anatomy and physiology of vision, even at the level that these are known today, many more features of elegant design could be revealed, all of which show that the seemingly simple act of vision requires the most sophisticated biological instrumentation of any device in the entire world. There is reason to believe that the visual science of tomorrow will continue to reveal such mechanisms, and that more of them remain to be discovered than those that fill our textbooks and journals today.

Acknowledgments. Support of the author's research by NIH Grant EY-01541 is gratefully acknowledged. I thank David R. Williams for his assistance with the illustrations.

Appendix

The purpose of the following experiment was to illustrate the effect of chromatic aberration upon image quality in the human eye, as a function of (a) the number of assumed types of cone receptors and (b) the location of their spectral sensitivities in the spectrum.

The Dartnall nomogram (*British Medical Bulletin*, 1953, 9, 24) was used to specify the shapes of the cone sensitivity curves, which were slid along a frequency axis without change of shape in order to locate the peaks of their spectral sensitivities at 440, 540, 565, and 640 nm. It was tacitly assumed that the channels of the visual system concerned with pattern vision receive a linearly summated input from the cones. Four conditions were examined, where the contributing cones were assumed to have peak spectral sensitivities at the following wavelengths (in nm):

   A. 540, 565
   B. 540, 640
   C. 440, 540, 565
   D. 440, 540, 640

Each summated curve for these four conditions was divided into 10 equal-area segments, for which a mean chromatic aberration value [using data of Wald and Griffin (*Journal of the Optical Society of America*, 1947, 35, 187) and Bedford and Wyszecki (*Journal of the Optical Society of America*, 1957, 47, 564)] was computed for each wavelength interval. For example, for Condition D, the first interval includes 385–410 nm, for which the chromatic aberration to be simulated is − 1.81 diopters; for the tenth interval (running from 601 to 714 nm) the aberration value is + 0.30 diopter.

Using Tri-X film, photographs were taken of the scene of Figure 2.15 with the camera defocused in turn to simulate the chromatic aberration of each spectral band. The 10 exposures were superimposed without film advancement. In each case, mean aberration was converted into a distance setting at which the camera lens (55-mm focal length) would produce an equivalent blur. The individual exposures were of 1/30 sec with a 1.0 log unit filter in front of the camera. (Without the filter, this duration yielded a proper single-shot exposure.) An aperture of $f/3.8$, was used throughout, to simulate an eye with a 6-mm pupil.

Control experiments showed that when exposures were ordered from least to most defocus, the resulting image quality was superior to that obtained when the opposite order was used. This result shows that early exposures contribute more than late ones. To compensate for this effect, exposures were made in the order 1, 10, 2, 9, 3, 8, 4, 7, 5, 6 (ranks from least to most defocus). An asymmetrical blurring occurred in all resulting prints, showing that the lens was not exactly perpendicular to the film plane. This reduced the quality of all photographs.

As a follow-up check, the six possible pairs of photographs resulting from Conditions A–D were shown twice each to four members of the departmental staff. The photograph resulting from Condition A was preferred to the others on 91% of trials; Condition D was never preferred to Condition A.

References

Arden, G.B. The retina—Neurophysiology. In H. Davson (Ed.), *The eye* (2nd ed.). New York: Academic Press, 1976.

Baylor, D.A. Noise and signals in the retinal pathways. *Investigative Ophthalmology and Visual Science*, (Supplement 1977), 97.

Baylor, D.A., Fuortes, M.G., & O'Bryan, P.M. Receptive fields of cones in the retina of the turtle. *Journal of Physiology*, 1971, *214*, 265–294.

Baylor, D.A., & Hodgkin, A.L. Changes in the time scale and sensitivity in turtle photoreceptors. *Journal of Physiology*, 1974, *242*, 729–758.

Bennett, A.G., & Francis, J.L. The eye as an optical system. In H. Davson (Ed.), *The eye* (1st ed.). New York: Academic Press, 1962.

Boll, F. On the anatomy and physiology of the frog retina. (Ruth Hubbard, trans.) *Vision Research*, 1977, *17*, 1249–1265. (Originally published in 1877.)

Boynton, R.M., Hayhoe, M.M., & MacLeod, D.I.A. The gap effect: Chromatic and achromatic visual discrimination as affected by field separation. *Optica Acta*, 1977, *24*, 159–177.

Burkhardt, D., de la Motte, I., & Seitz, G. Physiological optics of the compound eye of the blow fly. In C.G. Berhard (Ed.), *The functional organization of the compound eye*. New York: Pergamon Press, 1966.

Cajal, S.R. La rétine des vertébrés. *La Cellule*, 1893, *9*, 17–257.

Cajal, S.R. The vertebrate retina. In R.W. Rodieck *The vertebrate retina* (Appendix I). (D. Maguire and R.W. Rodieck, trans.) San Francisco: Freeman, 1973.

Dartnall, H.J.A. In H. Davson (Ed.), *The eye* (Vol. 1) (1st ed.). New York: Academic Press, 1962.

De Valois, R.L. Central mechanisms of color vision. In R. Jung (Ed.), *Handbook of sensory physiology* (*Vol. VII, Part 3*). New York: Springer, 1973.

Ditchburn, R.W. *Light* (3rd ed.). London: Academic Press, 1976.

Feinberg, G. Light. *Scientific American*, 1968, *219*, 50–59.

Granit, R. *Sensory mechanisms of the retina*. New York: Hafner Publishing Company, 1963. (Originally published in 1947.)

Hartline, H.K., & Graham, C.H. Nerve impulses from single receptors in the eye. *Journal of Cellular and Comparative Physiology*, 1932, *1*, 277–295.

Hecht, S., Shlaer, S., & Pirenne, M. Energy, quanta, and vision. *Journal of General Physiology*, 1942, *25*, 819–840.

Helmholtz, H. von. *Physiological optics* (3 vols.). J.P.C. Southall (Ed.) Rochester, New York: Optical Society of America, 1924.

Henderson, S.T. *Daylight and its spectrum.* New York: American Elsevier, 1970.

Kaneko, A. Physiological and morphological identification of horizontal, bipolar, and amacrine cells in goldfish retina. *Journal of Physiology,* 1970, 207, 623–633.

Kohler, I. *The formation and transformation of the perceptual world.* (H. Fiss, trans.) New York: International University Press, 1964.

Kühne, W. Chemical processes in the retina. (G. Wald, R. Hubbard, trans., with the help of Helene Hoffman.) *Vision Research,* 1977, 17, 1269–1316. (Originally published in 1879.)

Kurşunoğlu, B. Quantum theory. In R.M. Bencanson (Ed.), *The encyclopedia of physics* (2nd ed.). New York: Van Nostrand and Reinhold, 1974.

MacNichol, E.F., Jr., & Svaetichin, G. Electric responses from the isolated retinas of fishes. *American Journal of Ophthalmology,* 1958, 46, 26–40.

Maxwell, J.C. Experiments on colour, as perceived by the eye, with remarks on colour-blindness. *Transactions of the Royal Society of Edinburgh,* 1855, 21, 275–298.

O'Brien, B. Vision and resolution in the central retina. *Journal of the Optical Society of America,* 1951, 12, 882–894.

Paley, W. Natural theology. In J. Paxton (Ed.), *The works of William Paley, D.D.* (Vol. IV). London: Thomas Tegg, 1845.

Pirenne, M.H. *Vision and the eye.* London: Chapman and Hall, 1948.

Popper, K. *The logic of scientific discovery.* New York: Basic Books, 1959.

Rodieck, R.W. *The vertebrate retina.* San Francisco: Freeman, 1973.

Ronchi, V. *The nature of light: An historical survey.* (V. Barocas, trans.) Cambridge, Mass. Harvard University Press, 1970.

Rose, A. The sensitivity performance of the human eye on an absolute scale. *Journal of the Optical Society of America,* 1948, 38, 196–208.

Sarbra, I. *Theories of light from Descartes to Newton.* London: Oldbourne Book Co., 1967.

Scharf. D. *Magnifications.* New York: Schocken Books, 1977.

Wald, G. Molecular basis of visual excitation. *Science,* 1968, 162, 230–239.

Wald, G., Brown, P.K., & Gibbons, I.R. The problem of visual excitation. *Journal of the Optical Society of America,* 1963, 52, 20–35.

Walraven, P.L. A closer look at the tritanopic convergence point. *Vision Research,* 1974, 14, 1339–1343.

Young, T. On the theory of light and colours. *Philosophical Transactions,* 1802, 12–48.

Discussion

Dr. Ratliff: I would like to say just a couple of things about philosophical points. One concerns the comments on the reality of the photon and current knowledge of light. This knowledge is continually evolving, unfortunately, and the situation is, I think, a little less stable and a little less certain than Bob might have wished to imply in his remarks. I remember not too many years ago I complained that I didn't know whether physicists thought there were 16 or 17 fundamental particles. I stopped counting then and I don't know how many particles the physicists now think there are, but there is, clearly, a continuous evolution of what the physicist conceives of as the real world and, to coin a phrase, we mustn't lose sight of that either. There are also conflicts between current theories. For example, I don't think the conflict between particle and wave theory has yet been resolved to everyone's satisfaction—it may have been resolved to some people's satisfaction but not to mine.

I would also like to make a brief comment on Bob's remarks having to do with objectivity. It is true that we can divorce physical knowledge from experience and perception to a considerable extent. Certainly whatever knowledge is due to any particular sense organ that we might have can be transcended by using another sense organ. Any knowledge that's peculiar to a particular observer can be transcended by turning to another observer or experimenter, but whatever there may be in our experience that all senses share in common and all observers share in common cannot be divorced from that common experience.

"Photons are forever" sounds like the title of a paperback love story or something, but are photons really forever? If there's any truth to the notion of the red shift or Doppler shift (the displacement toward longer wavelengths for light coming from great distances) some photons may not remain within the visible range forever.

A short comment on the compound eye. These seem like rather crude eyes when compared with the enormous sophistication of the vertebrate eye, but it's interesting that physicists working on solar light collectors in the currently popular field of solar energy have recently devised some very efficient nontracking collectors (this is work done by Roland Winston and his colleagues at Chicago) and it turns out that these collectors have almost exactly the same shape as the crystalline cone of the *Limulus* ommatidium. I don't know why *Limulus* would need any such thing at the moment, but maybe the Creator is thinking of something for the future. After all, *Limulus* has been around for 300 million years and maybe the Creator is looking ahead to future developments some 200 or 300 million years from now.

Concerning the contribution of the so-called blue cones, it's interesting that in a mathematical analysis of the contributions of the red, green, and blue cones, so-called, to the opponent cells, Israel Abramov and Michael Levine have found that the blue system seems not to interact with the red and green system very much, at least in early stages. However, according to their interpretation, there is a large amount of interaction between red and green systems. This may have some relation to your ideas about the red and green cones having to do with detection of contours and the blue only being a filling-in mechanism.

Dr. Boynton: Could I respond briefly to two or three of these points? I don't disagree at all with most of what Floyd has said. With respect to the concept of the photon, I think that visual science took almost a quantum leap ahead, if I may use the expression, around the time of the famous experiment by Hecht, Shlaer, and Pirenne (and some work by Ernst Baumgardt which really antedated that a bit), when people first started to think about the stimulus for vision in terms of photons. I think that for most purposes this is a very powerful way to regard light, but I certainly don't disagree with you that the development of physical theory, no less than that of psychological theory, is a continuing process and that there are still problems.

With respect to Floyd's comment near the end about the interaction between the red–green opponent channels and the yellow–blue channels, I think that he makes a very interesting point. I can make one additional contribution to that, based on the demonstrations that I brought along. If you have the capacity for varying the vergence of the two eyes without any external stimulus to guide it, you can superimpose the yellow streak from one eye with the squiggly outline from the other, and the filling-in process does not work at all under those circumstances. All you get is rivalry, and there is no cooperation. This doesn't prove that the interactions that we see monocularly do occur in the retina, but it certainly shows that they could. And I think they probably do.

Dr. Barlow: I have one comment about the sensitivity of the eye. It is always being boosted as being very sensitive, but you have to remember that one quantum is really quite a big package of energy, and it's all absorbed in a single tiny cell, whereas the ear can, I believe, detect about 1/10 that amount of energy. In that case, it's not all concentrated in one cell but spread out over quite a long length of the basilar membrane, so that for once the ear is considerably one up on the eye.

CHAPTER 3

Form and Function: Linear and Nonlinear Analyses of Neural Networks in the Visual System

Floyd Ratliff

Like is known only by like.
Adage of the ancient Ionian School

1 Introduction

Form and function are closely related in the visual system. For example, if a retinal network responds acutely to certain fine detail in the spatial pattern of a visual stimulus, then there must be some comparable fine detail within the structure of the network. Otherwise, the pattern could not be resolved. Also, if a network responds selectively to some particular orientation of a stimulus, then there must be some comparable orientation of the form of the network. Otherwise, the direction could not be sensed. Similarly, if a network responds faithfully to some regular temporal modulation of the stimulus, then there must be some comparable modulus in the temporal characteristics of the network. Otherwise, the variations in time could not be followed. In a very real sense, "like is known only by like."

Frequently many such relations between form and function are found in one and the same neural network. Furthermore, the several relations are seldom independent; they may interact with or depend upon one another. For example, resolution of a spatial pattern may vary with orientation of that pattern and also depend strongly upon its temporal modulation. One of the major shortcomings in the study of the visual system is that for one reason or another—usually limitations in technique—we focus our attention on the part processes and thereby overlook how they interact with one another and how they are integrated into the behavior of the whole. Moreover, when we do take a more organic or holistic approach, we are sometimes surprised by what we find. As Mark Twain's Huckleberry Finn put it in his remarks about the widow Douglas' cooking:

> When you got to the table you couldn't go right to eating, but you had to wait for the widow to tuck down her head and grumble a little over the victuals, though there warn't really anything the matter with

them. That is, nothing only everything was cooked by itself. In a barrel of odds and ends it is different; things get mixed up, and the juice
kind of swaps around, and the things go better.

The situation is similar in the visual system: "things get mixed up, and
the juice kind of swaps around, and the things go better." The problem is
not that something mysterious is going on and that in some inexplicable
way the whole is greater (or less) than the sum of its parts. Instead, the
problem is simply that we do not fully understand the properties of the
parts and how they are integrated into the whole. One of the major difficulties in the way of our reaching such an understanding is the enormous
complexity of the integrative action of the nervous system. This is probably the reason intuition and insight have played such important roles in
the study of the visual system so far. Indeed, many qualitative and impressionistic accounts of neural function have had, and still do have,
great value. Sooner or later, however—if we are ever to achieve an understanding of the psychophysiological bases of vision—we must come to
grips with the problem of form and function in all its complexity, and the
complexity is so great that one cannot fully comprehend it without the
aid of some systematic mode of thought. Mathematics offers one such
mode.

In those branches of the neurosciences that focus on information processing, applied mathematics is playing an increasingly important role.
The main purpose of this paper is to survey some of these applications in
recent studies of neural networks in the visual system. One aim is simply
didactic—to inform others about some recent developments in one particular highly specialized field. Another aim is boldly prophetic—to as-
sess these recent developments and to attempt to see a short distance into
the future.

A deep understanding of the mathematical foundations of classical
Fourier analysis and of the more complex Wiener analysis is not required
to grasp the essentials of linear and nonlinear analyses of neural networks. The essence of such studies may be illustrated by graphic examples of stimulus–response relationships. These concrete examples may
require some thought to understand, but they require little or no special
training in abstract mathematics beyond ordinary arithmetic. For the
benefit of the nonspecialist, this survey is presented entirely in terms of
such examples. For those who wish to pursue the subject to greater depth
and in greater detail, a brief mathematical account is appended and numerous references to comprehensive reviews and to reports of recent experiments are cited.

The foundation for an exact mathematical approach to the study of
the neural mechanisms of vision was laid nearly half a century ago. At
that time, H. Keffer Hartline, a physiologist, and Clarence H. Graham, a
psychologist, collaborated in a study in which they succeeded, for the
first time ever, in recording and quantifying the discharge of trains of dis-

Figure 3.1. Horseshoe crabs (on a Japanese postage stamp). There are at least three living species, *Tachypleus tridentatus* (Inland Sea of Japan), *Carcinoscorpius* (South China Sea), and *Limulus polyphemus* (Atlantic coast of North America). The compound eye (about 1 cm long—roughly the size and shape of a split pinto bean) is clearly visible on the ophthalmic ridge of the carapace (in adults, about 25 cm wide).

crete impulses by single neurons in the visual system. This pioneering work (Hartline & Graham, 1932) on the optic nerve of the compound lateral eye of the lowly horseshoe crab (Figure 3.1) opened up what was destined to become an enormous field of research. Today there must be hundreds, perhaps thousands, of investigators in vision research who routinely record data from single neurons. For it is now relatively easy to record electrical activity of almost any kind from single cells of almost any type at almost any level in the visual system—from retina to brain—in practically any species that happens to be at hand. As a result, raw data abound in great quantities, but a full understanding of any set of them is rare. Indeed, the problem we face today is not so much how to collect quantitative data but what to do with the collection once we have it—how to analyze it, how to interpret it, and how to integrate it all into a meaningful whole.

2   Excitation and Inhibition

The theoretical basis of our present understanding of the integrative action of the visual system may be traced back to the beginning of the 19th century, and perhaps even beyond. Important ideas about the interaction and integration of opposed influences in the retina—based mainly on visual phenomena such as brightness contrast and color contrast— were advanced long ago by well-known figures such as the German poet, Goethe; the French chemist, Chevreul; the Austrian physicist, Mach; and the German physiologist, Hering (for reviews see Ratliff, 1965, 1976, and 1977a,b). However, physiological confirmation of these early ideas and insights awaited the development of techniques for cell-by-cell analyses of retinal function. Several lines of supporting evidence appeared in the very first studies carried out by Hartline and Graham when they alone were working in the field. Two are central to the mathematical analyses presented in this essay. The first was in their original study (Hartline & Graham, 1932). It is simple, but fundamental:

> The higher the intensity of a small spot of light focussed on a single photoreceptor unit, the higher the rate of discharge of impulses in its optic nerve fiber (see Figure 3.2).

In research carried out a few years later (still in the 1930s, but not published until the 1940s) Hartline noticed that if he turned on the room lights during such an experiment, the rate of discharge of impulses slowed. When parts of the eye near the photoreceptor unit under observation were shaded from the room lights, however, the rate of discharge increased (Hartline, 1949)[1]. Therefore, the second fundamental finding was:

> The rate of discharge of impulses by a photoreceptor unit is slowed by illumination of other photoreceptor units nearby it (see Figure 3.2).

These two findings revealed the functional building blocks of the visual system: the opposed influences of excitation and inhibition.

Analogous interactions among opposed influences at one level or another in the human visual system are presumed to result in the familiar brightness–contrast effects. Such effects may be created easily and seen at once simply by cutting out two identical pieces of gray paper and placing them on different backgrounds—one on a white piece of paper, the other on a black piece. If the positions of the two gray pieces are inter-

---

[1] It was a quirk of fate that this lateral inhibition was not observed in the early studies. Hartline and Graham (1932) did record from several optic nerve fibers simultaneously and compared responses of single fibers with responses of several fibers. Unfortunately, because of limitations of their apparatus, they illuminated several photoreceptor units simply by defocusing (and thus enlarging) the small spot originally focused on a single unit. The resulting decrease in intensity with increase in area of the spot of light resulted in an expected slowing of the rate of discharge. The slight additional slowing resulting from weak lateral inhibition was not noticed.

Later Graham (1932) conducted experiments designed specifically to reveal excitatory interactions in the retina. In this work Graham followed the lead of Adrian and Matthews (1928), who had successfully measured interactions in the retina of the eel by observing changes in the latent period from the onset of the stimulus to the onset of the response of the whole optic nerve. It was most unfortunate that Graham chose the latent period as his measure. In his experiments all excitation was synchronous and because of the relatively long delay from excitation to inhibition (see Figure 3.7) there was no inhibitory effect on the short latent period of the initial excitatory response. Graham concluded (correctly) that there was no significant excitatory interaction. However, because of the design of the experiment, he failed to observe the subsequent inhibitory interaction that *did* take place after the initial excitatory response.

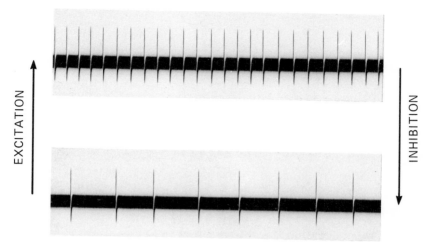

EXCITATION

INHIBITION

Figure 3.2. Two records of optic nerve impulses discharged over a 1 sec period by a single photoreceptor unit (ommatidium) in the retina of the compound eye of *Limulus*. Increasing the intensity of the light on the receptor unit increases the rate of discharge (excitation); conversely, decreasing the intensity decreases the rate. Increasing the area and/or intensity of illumination of neighboring receptor units slows the rate of discharge (inhibition). One record is set above the other for ease of comparison; both actually have the same baseline, and only the change in rate of discharge is significant. (Records courtesy H.K. Hartline.)

changed, the brightness contrast exerted on each changes accordingly. Paper cutouts in the familiar yin and yang pattern (Figure 3.3) do double duty because this form of the pattern has the interesting property that it is at one and the same time a symbol of interaction of opposed influences and an example of the phenomenon of interaction itself. A somewhat more "scientific" demonstration of the same effect is shown in Figure 3.4, in which two physically identical bars contrasted with the peaks and

Figure 3.3. Simultaneous brightness contrast on a yin and yang pattern. The two grey spots were cut from a folded piece of uniformly grey paper and are physically identical.

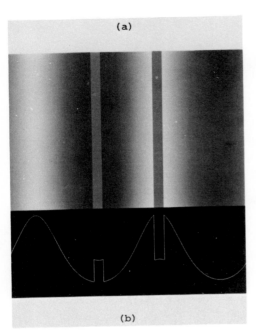

Figure 3.4. (a) Simultaneous brightness contrast of two bars on a spatial sinusoid. (b) Physical distribution of illumination (white line). The two grey bars are physically identical (except for the slight curvatures at their tops, which result from displacement downward from a peak at the sinusoid in one case and displacement upward from a trough of the sinusoid in the other case). (From Colas-Baudelaire, 1973.)

troughs of a one-dimensional sinusoidal distribution of illumination appear to be of very different brightness.

There are countless other well-known examples of brightness contrast and color contrast that are also presumed to result from the interplay of excitation and inhibition. Many of these effects are generally regarded as "illusions" or "aberrations." However, the point I wish to emphasize is that the very same kinds of interactions that are thought to underlie these effects are probably the physiological bases of most major aspects of "normal" vision, too. Our attention is drawn to the so-called illusions simply because they generally involve some easy comparison (as in Figures 3.3 and 3.4) by means of which the effect can be readily discerned. However —to cite just one example—we are hardly aware of the gradual processes of normal light and dark adaptation (in which spatial interactions almost certainly play an important role as a part of a gain-control mechanism) unless we adapt one eye and not the other so that a direct comparison can be made.

3 Spatial and Temporal Organization

The particular function (or functions) that excitatory and inhibitory interactions may serve depends upon the particular form that they take. Hartline (1949) found that in the retina of *Limulus* these opposed influences are spatially organized in the now familiar excitatory-center, inhibitory-surround configuration. There is an obvious similarity to the center–

Figure 3.5. One dimension of the excitatory center and inhibitory surround of a neural network near the center of the compound eye of *Limulus*. The abscissa is marked in intervals between ommatidia (photoreceptor units). (Data from Dodge & Kaplan, 1975; also see Barlow, 1969.)

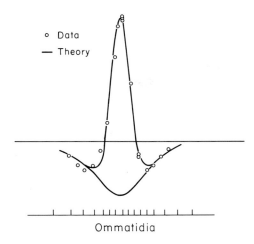

Ommatidia

surround organization of vertebrate retinal ganglion cells that was discovered some years later by Barlow (1953) in the frog and by Kuffler (1953) in the cat. However, *Limulus* is much simpler. Figure 3.5 shows recent measurements by Dodge and Kaplan (1975) across one dimension of the *Limulus* inhibitory network. The distribution of the influences may be regarded (approximately) as the superposition of a narrow, positive Gaussian curve and a broad, negative Gaussian. The three-dimensional appearance would be given (approximately) by rotating the curve in Figure 3.5 about its center. (Actually, the inhibitory field in the *Limulus* retina is slightly elliptical, with the major and minor axes in about the same ratio as the major and minor axes of the eye). The resulting solid would resemble a tall-crowned Mexican sombrero with a turned-up brim. The essential features of the form are an excitatory center that is relatively strong but narrow and an inhibitory surround that is relatively weak but broad. Well-known effects of such a distribution of excitation and inhibition (in the steady state) are the maxima and minima produced in the response to a step pattern (Figure 3.6). These are somewhat analogous to familiar border-contrast effects and Mach bands in human vision.

The distribution of excitation and inhibition in time is similar to the distribution in space, except that it is asymmetrical. The distribution is asymmetrical because excitation causes inhibition and because time proceeds forward only.[2] In fact, there is quite a significant delay between the discharge of impulses by one photoreceptor unit and the inhibition of impulses discharged by another (Figure 3.7). We now know that the inhibitory potential produced in one photoreceptor unit by an impulse discharged by another has a peculiar biphasic form—an immediate brief excitatory depolarization is followed by a longer, more pronounced inhib-

---

[2] Under certain special conditions one can observe an apparent "backward inhibition" (Ratliff, Hartline, & Miller, 1963).

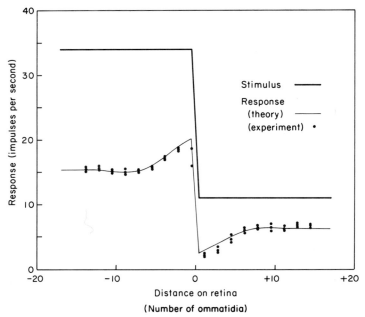

Figure 3.6. Response of an optic nerve fiber in the compound eye of *Limulus* to a step pattern of illumination. (Redrawn after Barlow & Quarles, 1975.)

itory hyperpolarization as shown in Figure 3.7C. Therefore the delay. One effect of this delay is that reponses to step increments and decrements of excitation in one part of the eye are followed shortly by responses of similar form but of opposite sign (inhibition) in neighboring parts of the eye (Figure 3.8).

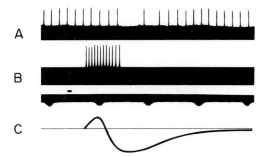

Figure 3.7. Transient inhibition of the discharge of impulses from a steadily illuminated receptor unit (A) by a burst of impulses discharged from a nearby receptor unit (B) in response to a 0.01-sec flash of light (signaled by black dot in the white band just above 0.2-sec time marks). (Records from Hartline, Ratliff, & Miller, 1961.) (C) shows the approximate form of the biphasic inhibitory potential. (Redrawn after Knight, Toyoda, & Dodge, 1970.)

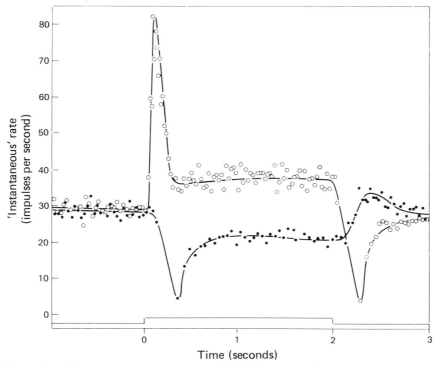

Figure 3.8. Simultaneous excitatory and inhibitory transients in the responses of neighboring ommatidia in the lateral eye of *Limulus*. One, represented by filled circles, was illuminated steadily throughout the period shown. The other, along with some of its neighbors, had the steady level on it increased to a higher steady level at $t = 0$ and then reduced to the original steady level at $t = 2$. (From Ratliff, 1961.)

4   Some Questions about Function

The basic principles of the functional organization of the *Limulus* retina are simple and easy to understand: Light causes excitation where it falls on the retina and that excitation subsequently causes self-inhibition there and lateral inhibition in surrounding areas of the retina. The simple addition of the two opposed influences of excitation and inhibition at any point and at any time in the retina determines the response at that point and at that time. Practically everything that has been discovered about the functional organization of any and every visual system appears to be some variation on or elaboration of these fundamental principles. Their apparent simplicity is deceptive, however; seemingly minor changes in the balance of excitation and inhibition and in their spatial and temporal distributions may bring about major changes in the function of a network. Indeed, the simple integration of the opposed influences of excitation and inhibition distributed in various forms over space and time can (in principle, at least) give rise to an almost unlimited number of functions.

However, we must not be too hasty in deciding what those functions are and to what features of a stimulus a neural network may respond. For example: One might easily jump to the conclusion that this network in the *Limulus* eye is a "small bright spot detector" (if one were inclined to think in terms of "feature detectors"—which some of us are not). For it is true that, in the steady state, a small spot of light that just fills the excitatory center of the network is a much more effective stimulus (in the sense that it elicits a higher rate of discharge) than is a larger spot of the same intensity that not only fills the excitatory center but also overlaps some or all of the inhibitory surround.[3]

Suppose, however, that the intensity of the light varies in time. To make matters simple, assume that it is modulated sinusoidally at a fixed amplitude about some mean level. At a frequency of about one cycle per second (cps), or below, one will find that the amplitude of the corresponding sinusoidal variation in rate of discharge will be greater for the small spot of light than for the large spot (as might well be expected from the steady-state results). In the range of about 2–5 cps, however, the situation is reversed. The amplitude of the sinusoidal variation in rate of discharge is *larger* in response to modulation of the large spot, which produces both excitation and inhibition, than to modulation of the small spot, which produces excitation alone. Evidently there is some strong interaction between the spatial and the temporal aspects of the excitation and the inhibition. A full understanding of this seemingly paradoxical reversal of sensitivity requires more detailed knowledge of the forms and functions of some of the spatial and temporal dimensions of the network. Let us consider them first and then return to a further consideration of this reversal of sensitivity. When seen in the broader context of a more comprehensive quantitative account of the spatial and temporal interactions, the paradox vanishes.

5   Linear Analysis of the *Limulus* Retina

Although the *Limulus* eye is highly nonlinear overall, it is (mercifully) linear segmentally, or piecewise, to a good first approximation. Therefore, standard methods of studying linear systems may be applied to these linear segments. Early work has been reviewed in detail elsewhere (Dodge, Shapley, & Knight, 1970; Graham & Ratliff, 1974; Hartline & Ratliff, 1972; Ratliff, 1974; Ratliff, Knight, Dodge, & Hartline, 1974). For

---

[3] An increase in an area of illumination does not inevitably lead to an increase in the inhibition that area exerts on a particular photoreceptor unit. Under special conditions, with certain configurations of stimuli, increasing the area of illumination may cause inhibition of inhibition (disinhibition) and so lead to an increase in effective excitation (Hartline & Ratliff, 1957).

accounts of recent experimental work and the most recent form of our linear theory, combining both spatial and temporal influences, see Brodie, Knight, and Ratliff (1978a,b).

The basic organization of the *Limulus* retina may be represented by a simple schema drawn on a section of the retina as shown in Figure 3.9. (See also Brodie, Knight, & Ratliff, 1978a; Dodge, 1969). The diagram shows the principal functional parts of the network associated with just one of the (approximately) 1,000 photoreceptor units in this retina. Light incident on a photoreceptor unit causes the production of an intracellular voltage change (a depolarization). Changes of opposite sign in the intracellular potential (hyperpolarization) are induced by the processes of self- and lateral inhibition. These voltages sum to produce a net intracellular potential, which serves as the input to the impulse-generating mechanism. The impulse generator produces the train of nerve impulses that is the output of the retina and that is conveyed along the optic nerve to the optic lobe of the brain. These same nerve impulses also serve as input to the self- and lateral-inhibitory processes, which feed back into the retina.

Simply stated, in terms of linear addition and subtraction, the rate of discharge of impulses from a particular photoreceptor unit is determined by the strength of the excitatory (positive) influence produced by light falling directly on that receptor unit diminished by the sum of whatever inhibitory (negative) influences are exerted back on it by itself and by neighboring receptor units. The strengths of the self- and lateral-inhibitory influences are determined by the rates of discharge of impulses from that unit itself and from its neighbors. In the steady state, the interplay of excitation and inhibition in the *Limulus* retina may be described to good approximation by a set of simultaneous, piecewise or segmentally linear equations (see Appendix) in which are represented the several part processes shown in Figure 3.9 and in which the strengths of their various influences are expressed in terms of rate (Hartline & Ratliff, 1958).

With time-varying stimuli, the same schema shown in Figure 3.9 applies, but full account must be taken of the various time constants of the system. Assume that the stimuli cause all the photoreceptor units to discharge impulses at a rate that fluctuates about some mean operating level. Assume also that this operating level is such that all receptor units fire at a rate above their inhibitory thresholds. It is convenient then to define the input and output variables to indicate deviations from mean values (of light intensity on input, of impulse rate on output), rather than in terms of the absolute numerical magnitudes. With these conventions, let us consider the responses to stimuli that are fixed in space but that vary sinusoidally in time (Dodge, Knight, & Toyoda, 1968; Knight, 1973; Knight et al., 1970). If the system is linear, it will respond to such a sinusoidal input with a sinusoidal output (Figure 3.10).

Relative amplitude of response as a function of frequency and phase shift of response as a function of frequency yields the so-called transfer function of the system (Figure 3.11A). (In actual practice, a sample of about ten properly spaced frequencies is usually more than adequate—the

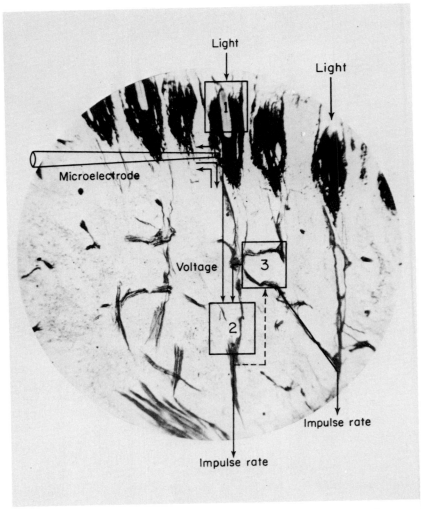

Figure 3.9. Schematic of the retina of a compound eye of *Limulus* superimposed on a stained section of the retina. At the top is a heavily stained row of ommatidia (photoreceptor units). Axons arise from the ommatidia and course downward, eventually coming together to form the optic nerve. Just below the ommatidia, the axons are connected by a lateral plexus of nerve fibers. Light incident on the receptors causes excitation (1), which leads to impulse generation (2). Inhibition (3) is exerted at or near the site of impulse generation. Self-inhibition (dashed lines, exact pathway unknown) is proportional to impulse rate in that axon itself. Lateral inhibition (mediated by the lateral plexus) is proportional to the rate of impulses in neighboring fibers. The microelectrode may be used to record excitatory and inhibitory influences directly from the receptor unit. Also, current may be passed through the electrode to excite or to inhibit the response of the receptor unit. Impulse rates are recorded by other electrodes (not shown) a few millimeters down the optic nerve. (From Ratliff et al., 1974.)

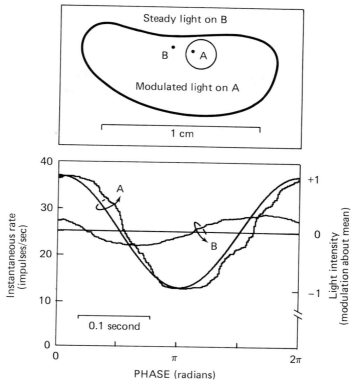

Figure 3.10. Above: Pattern of illumination for a typical two-nerve-fiber experiment. The outline of the compound lateral eye of *Limulus* is represented by the heavy line. Impulses were recorded from axons of the two receptor units represented by the black dots. The left one (B) was steadily illuminated. The right one (A) was illuminated, along with about 50 of its neighbors (as represented by the circle), with sinusoidally modulated light. Below: Responses to one full cycle of sinusoidal illumination at 3 cps. Light intensity on A (smooth curve) had peak-to-peak amplitude equal to 15% of the mean. The resulting instantaneous rate (ragged curve A) was nearly sinusoidal. The instantaneous rate of the steadily illuminated neighbor (ragged curve B) varied sinusoidally (at a lower amplitude and different phase—apparently leading the stimulus but actually lagging far behind) because of the lateral inhibition produced by the group A. (From Ratliff et al., 1974.)

functions are relatively smooth). The lateral inhibitory influences exerted on neighboring receptor units may be determined in the same way (Figure 3.11B) and expressed as a transfer function. Indeed, because the whole system is a concatenation of linear parts, each separate portion of the visual transduction will respond to sinusoidal inputs with sinusoidal outputs according to its own transfer function. Therefore, the so-called Hartline–Ratliff steady-state equations may be readily transformed to dynamic equations simply by substituting the appropriate transfer functions

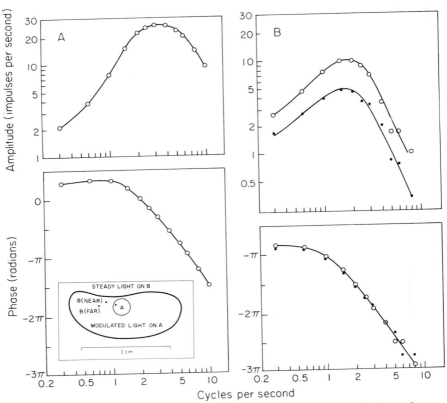

Figure 3.11. Effect of distance on amplitude (upper graphs) and phase (lower graphs) of excitatory and inhibitory responses. Inset, lower left, is the pattern of illumination in this three-fiber experiment. (A) The response of one selected member of the group on which the light was sinusoidally modulated (peak to peak: 15% of the mean). (B) The modulated responses of two neighbors (each separately and steadily illuminated) that resulted from inhibition by (A). The open circles represent the near neighbor; the filled circles represent the more distant neighbor. The amplitude at the greater distance is approximately one-half that at the lesser distance, but there is no significant phase shift with distance. (From Ratliff et al., 1974.)

for the corresponding static functions. (For a summary account see the Appendix; for details see: Brodie et al., 1978a,b; Ratliff et al., 1974).

6   On Tuning and Amplification

Let us now return to the problem outlined earlier: The relative sensitivity of the eye to sinusoidal modulation of small spots of light and of large spots of light at various frequencies. As was shown in Figure 3.7, a short and very intense flash on a receptor unit produced, after a short latent period, a fairly compact high-frequency burst of impulses. From the onset of this burst to the first perceptible inhibitory effect on a neighboring steadily illuminated receptor, however, there elapsed a period of about 150 msec or so—as would be expected from the biphasic shape of the inhibitory potential.

Such a delay literally tunes this neural network to particular temporal frequencies. It should be recalled that there is no phase shift of inhibition with distance (Figure 3.11). If the whole eye or a large area of it is illuminated synchronously with sinusoidally modulated light, then the greatest lateral-inhibitory influences on any particular receptor unit are all produced about 150 msec after the greatest excitation. This coincides approximately with a stimulus frequency whose half-cycle (time from peak of intensity to trough) is about 150 msec (a full cycle of about 300 msec), or a frequency of modulation of approximately 3 cps. The network is not sharply tuned because the inhibitory potential, although it is peaked, is spread out over considerable time.

One consequence of the delayed inhibition and the resultant tuning is that it leads to an amplification of the response (Ratliff, Knight, & Graham, 1969; Ratliff, Knight, Toyoda, & Hartline, 1967). That is, the peak-to-peak amplitude of the response at the best tuned frequency is greater with the inhibition than it is without it (Figure 3.12). The amplification

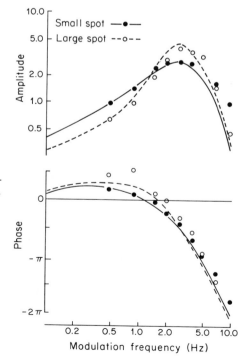

Figure 3.12. Tuning and amplification by lateral inhibition. Theoretical (solid line) and observed (solid circles) light-to-impulse-rate transfer function of a single receptor unit with no lateral inhibition (small spot). Theoretical (dashed line) and observed (open circles) transfer function for the same receptor unit with lateral inhibition (large spot). (Data from Ratliff et al., 1967; theoretical predictions from Knight et al., 1970.)

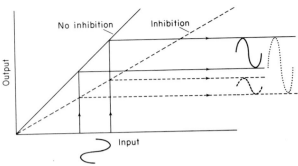

Figure 3.13. Theoretical steady-state input–output curves for a network with no inhibition (solid diagonal line) and with inhibition (dashed diagonal line). Calculated on the basis of these steady-state curves, the two outputs for a sinusoidally modulated input would not exceed the limits indicated by the pair of horizontal solid lines (solid curve, response with no inhibition) and the pair of horizontal dashed lines (dashed curve, response with inhibition). However, because of the delay to the maximum inhibitory influence (Figure 3.7) the inhibition can be effectively "turned off" at the peak and "turned on" at the trough at certain frequencies. Therefore, the two extremes—no inhibition and maximum inhibition—limit the amplitude of modulation of the response (dotted curve) and so the latter may be greater with inhibition than without inhibition. (From Ratliff et al., 1969.)

results because the "switching off" of the inhibition in the depolarizing phase of the inhibitory potential and the "switching on" of the inhibition during the hyperpolarizing phase of the potential results in a push–pull effect (Figure 3.13) on the response to those frequencies of stimulation to which the system is best tuned—that is, to those frequencies with periods approximately the same as the biphasic inhibitory potential. All this is in accordance with the adage "like is known only by like."

There is no question that this tuning and amplification results mainly from the time constants of the lateral inhibition. This can be demonstrated directly by exciting a photoreceptor unit with a small spot of light focused on it and inhibiting that same unit with a surrounding annulus of light on neighboring units. Sinusoidal modulation of the small spot of light alone will yield the usual transfer function for a single photoreceptor unit. Modulation of the spot and the annulus in synchrony will produce the expected tuning and amplification (as in Figure 3.12). If modulation of the surrounding annulus is increasingly delayed with respect to modulation of the spot, however, the amplification first increases and then decreases, the main peak shifts to lower frequencies, and higher order maxima and minima appear in the response. Phase is noticeably affected also. All these effects of artificial delay (Figure 3.14) are in accordance with the quantitative theory (Ratliff, Knight, & Milkman, 1970).

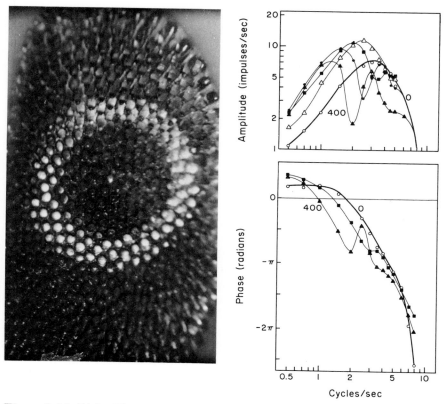

Figure 3.14. Right: The introduction of a substantial inhibitory time lag introduces considerable structure into the transfer function. An extremum in amplitude is found near any frequency where the excitatory phase differs from the total inhibitory phase (intrinsic plus lag) by a multiple of π radians. Consecutive maxima and minima arise as the inhibitory influence consecutively reinforces and opposes the excitatory influences. The larger the time lag, the smaller the frequency change needed to shift the inhibitory phase from opposition to reinforcement and back. Curves are shown for lag times increased by 100-msec increments from 0 through 400. Phase is shown for 0, 200, and 400 msec only. (From Ratliff et al., 1970.) Left: Pattern of illumination on compound eye of *Limulus* for study of delayed inhibition. Photograph taken from the rear of the cornea with the retina stripped away. The bright spots are the ends of the crystalline cones, which focus the light into the photoreceptor units. The discharge of impulses was recorded from the single brightly lit unit in the center of the eye. The surrounding annulus of illumination provided inhibition on that receptor. The intensity of the central spot and of the surrounding annulus were modulated sinusoidally, either in phase or with a phase lag introduced by delaying the modulation of the inhibitory annulus with respect to the excitatory center.

7   A Comment on Interplay between Theory and Experiment

The closer the coupling between theory and experiment, the more effective the aid each may provide the other. For instance, the first knowledge of the form of the lateral-inhibitory potential was derived from a Fourier analysis of the inhibitory system rather than from a direct electrophysiological measurement. The shape of the lateral-inhibitory transfer function indicated that the impulse function must be biphasic—a slight transient depolarization leading a longer and larger hyperpolarization. Later this deduction was verified by direct intracellular recordings of the inhibitory potential (Knight et al., 1970). The existence (and form) of the self-inhibitory potential was also deduced by mathematical analyses of data (Stevens, 1964) before it was observed by direct electrophysiological measurements (Purple, 1964; Purple & Dodge, 1965). Therefore, from a mathematical analysis of some of the behavior of a complex system, the form of essential underlying part processes can be determined.

This procedure can work in the opposite direction, too. Knowledge of part processes is often sufficient to predict previously unobserved behavior of the whole. For example, knowledge that the lateral inhibition in *Limulus* is mutual and recurrent enabled us to predict in advance of the actual experiments that disinhibition would occur under certain conditions (Hartline & Ratliff, 1957). Mere inspection of the biphasic shape of the lateral-inhibitory potential should have been sufficient for a qualitative prediction of all the main features of the "small spot–large spot" experiment (Figure 3.12), also. However, things did not turn out that way. The convergence of the two functions at high frequencies, the extent and direction of the divergence at low frequencies, and the location of peak tuning to intermediate frequencies were obvious and expected, but the amplification by inhibition in the intermediate ranges was not anticipated (Ratliff et al., 1967). Subsequently, however, when proper attention was paid to all details of the form of the inhibitory potential and exact calculations were made, the quantitative theory accurately accounted for all of the already observed effects and predicted accurately the effects of artificial delays that were not observed until later (Knight et al., 1970; Ratliff et al., 1969, 1970). This illustrates the advantage of an exact quantitative theory over one's intuition. Indeed, in more complex situations, in which many spatial, temporal, and spectral characteristics of stimuli vary simultaneously, one has little choice in the matter; comprehensive quantitative methods are essential.

8   The Spatial Domain

Measurements such as those in the "small spot–large spot" experiments described above span the whole range of temporal frequencies to which the network will respond. Therefore, they adequately characterize the re-

Stimulus Intensity
(spatial sinusoid)

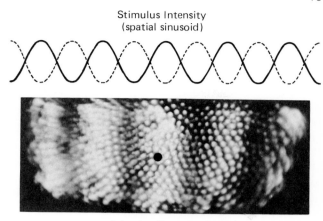

Stimulus Receptor Level
(inner surface of cornea)

Figure 3.15. The photograph shows the stationary spatial sinusoidal distribution of illumination on a *Limulus* eye. It was taken from the rear of the cornea with the retina stripped away. The bright spots are the ends of the crystalline cones, which focus the light into the photoreceptor units. The black dot in the center indicates the position of the receptor unit from which the discharge of impulses was recorded. In the curves above, the solid line shows the spatial sinusoid in the same position as in the photograph of the eye. Note that a peak of the sinusoid is centered on the receptor unit from which impulses were recorded. The dotted line shows the same sinusoid in reversed contrast.

sponse of the network along the temporal dimension, but only for the two spatial patterns (small spot versus large spot) used in the experiment. Because this experiment demonstrates a strong dependence of the response of the network on both the temporal and the spatial characteristics of the stimulus, it is obviously necessary to explore the spatial characteristics more fully. Because we are dealing with a linear system, it is convenient to do this in the frequency domain and to continue to make use of Fourier analysis. To this end, we restrict our attention to sinusoidal stimuli that vary in space only along the x axis (and so at any time t are constant along vertical lines), and we assume that each receptor unit in a given vertical column responds in the same way to such a stimulus. (For justification of this assumption see Brodie et al., 1978a.)

The advantages of Fourier analysis (and synthesis) are as easy to exploit in the spatial domain as they are in the temporal domain. With modern electronics it is easy to generate and to present visual stimuli in the form of spatial sinusoids.[4] Figure 3.15 shows a typical spatial sinusoid focused on the cornea of the *Limulus* eye. (For details of our methods see Brodie et al., 1978a; Shapley & Rossetto, 1976). As indicated, a peak (or trough) of the sinusoid is centered on the receptor unit whose activity is

---

[4] Mach (1866) attempted to construct visual stimuli with sums of spatial sinusoids made out of paper cutouts attached to cylinders or disks but gave up the attempt because of the many practical problems involved. For translations of Mach's papers see Ratliff (1965).

being recorded. The spatial sinusoid is presented in time as a flickering contrast-reversal stimulus. That is, the intensity at any point alternates between the two extremes represented in the figure by the solid line and the dashed line. For example, the intensity at the point at the center shifts alternately from the peak to the trough. Likewise, the intensities at all other points shift back and forth between their extremes. At the nodal points, where the sinusoid crosses the mean, there is no change in intensity at all. Such contrast-reversal stimuli are usually reversed either according to a square-wave signal (that is, changing instantly from one extreme to another) or according to a sinusoidal signal (that is, changing smoothly and continuously from one extreme to another).

Such a flickering contrast-reversal stimulus enables measurements to be made simultaneously in the spatial and temporal domains. To obtain measurements at the point defined by a particular spatial frequency and a particular temporal frequency one simply centers a peak (or trough) of that spatial sinusoid on the photoreceptor unit and modulates it about the mean (reversing peak to trough) with a sinusoidal signal of the chosen temporal frequency. To characterize the network adequately by a combined spatiotemporal transfer function one must devise an experiment that spans all temporal frequencies and all spatial frequencies to which the eye yields significant responses. Because the functions are known to be smooth, one can economize on the number of measurements by sampling a mesh of points and interpolating between them. A barely adequate sample requires at least eight temporal frequencies and at least eight spatial frequencies. This results in a matrix of 64 points. Because several measurements must be made at each point to obtain sufficient data, the total number of measurements required for a rather sparse sample is several times the square of eight. Obviously, some further economies would be desirable.

9 Modulation by a Sum of Sinusoids

The assumption of linearity provides one shortcut for measurements in the temporal domain. It is not necessary to present the separate temporal frequencies of sinusoidal modulation one at a time. Instead, the whole set may be added together and presented all at once (Figure 3.16). If the system is truly linear the output frequencies in the response will all be the same as the input frequencies in the stimulus. (Only amplitude and phase may vary.) Therefore, Fourier analysis of the composite response will yield a set of separate sinusoids with frequencies corresponding to those of the set of separate sinusoidal stimuli that were summed to yield the composite stimulus (cf. Brodie et al., 1978a,b; St. Cyr & Fender, 1969; Victor, Shapley, & Knight, 1977).

This sum of several sinusoids produces a temporal signal that resembles the "white-noise" signal used in classical Wiener analysis of nonlin-

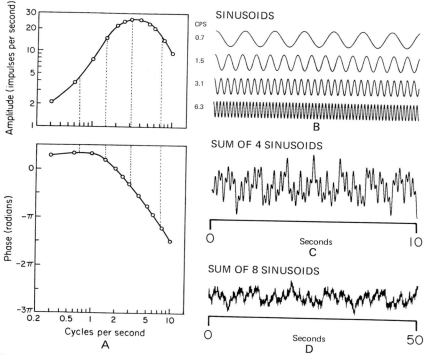

Figure 3.16. (A) A typical temporal transfer function for the *Limulus* retina, measured in the conventional way—one temporal frequency at a time as indicated by the data points. (B) A set of four temporal sinusoids. Note that the frequencies of these four sinusoids alone provide a sparse but nevertheless fair sampling mesh (vertical dotted lines) for the transfer function. Because the system is linear (no "crosstalk" among input frequencies) the four sinusoids may be summed and presented simultaneously as one temporal signal. (C) The corresponding summed response may be separated into the component output frequencies by standard Fourier techniques. (D) The sum of eight sinusoids—the temporal signal actually used to obtain the data in Figures 3.17 and 3.18.

ear systems. The sum of sinusoids is much simpler than the white noise but is still closely related to it, for both are sums of sinusoids. In the case of the sum of sinusoids used here, the signal consists of only a few frequencies; in the case of white noise, all frequencies from zero to infinity (in theory, at least). Another important difference is that the several sinusoids used here are not chosen at random, whereas those in the Wiener white-noise signal are a random set. In spite of these and other differences, the relation to Wiener analysis is an important feature of this new technique, for it permits its extension to the study of nonlinear systems (Victor et al., 1977). We shall consider this application in some detail later.

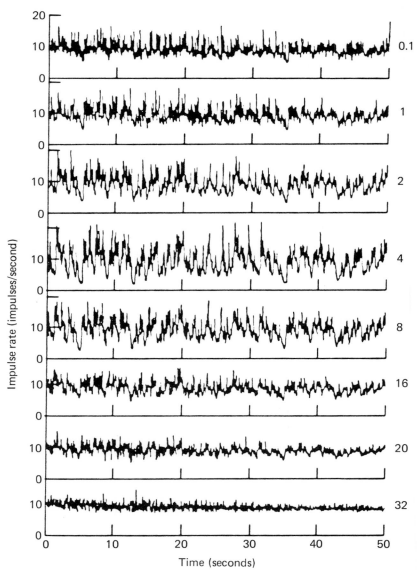

Figure 3.17. Responses of photoreceptor units to contrast reversal of spatial sinusoidal gratings. Each record is the average of 14 repetitions. Each stimulus consisted of a sinusoidal grating with a peak centered over the photoreceptor unit whose discharge of impulses was recorded (as shown in Figure 3.15). This sinusoidal grating was modulated (contrast reversed) by the sum-of-eight-sinusoids waveform shown in Figure 3.16. The sinusoidal gratings were of eight different spatial frequencies as indicated on the right. The same temporal signal from the sum-of-eight-sinusoids was used to modulate all spatial frequencies. (Adapted from Brodie et al., 1978a.)

10   The Spatiotemporal Transfer Function

The response to a particular spatial sinusoid flickered (contrast reversed) by this sum of temporal sinusoids looks like trash at first sight, but it is not. In a set of records taken at several different spatial frequencies (Figure 3.17) two regularities are fairly easy to discern. First, the amplitude of the response varies markedly with spatial frequency. The response is small at very high and at very low spatial frequencies; it is large in the midranges. Second, the time course of the response is similar in all records because the same deterministic sum-of-sinusoids signal was used for the temporal contrast reversal of all of the several spatial sinusoids. Knowing the component frequencies in the input, one can easily extract

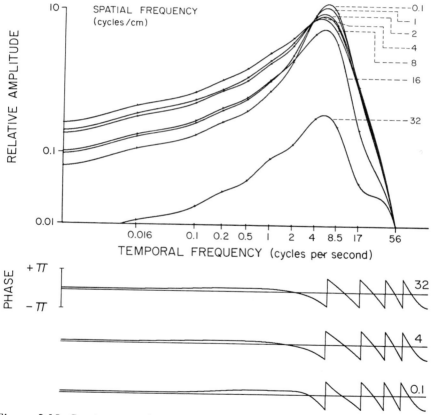

Figure 3.18. Spatiotemporal transfer function obtained from data of Figure 3.17. Above: Relative amplitudes of responses to several different spatial frequencies (in cycles per eye width) at the eight temporal frequencies used in the sum-of-sinusoids signal. (Extrapolations to very low and to very high temporal frequencies were based on other data.) Below: Phase data are shown for spatial frequencies of 0.1, 4, and 32 only. (Redrawn after Brodie et al., 1978a.)

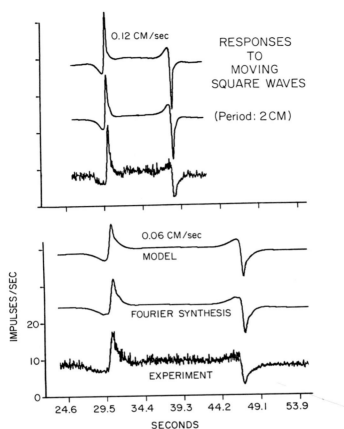

Figure 3.19. Response of optic nerve fiber of *Limulus* retina to two velocities of moving square waves of light imaged on the cornea (eye is about 1 cm wide). Lowest trace in each frame: Observed response. Middle trace (offset upward 15 impulses per second): Prediction by Fourier synthesis based on empirical spatiotemporal transfer function. Upper trace (offset upward an additional 15 impulses per second): Prediction from model of retina. (Redrawn after Brodie et al., 1978a.)

the corresponding sinusoidal variations in the response output and determine their amplitudes and phases. Therefore, the entire temporal transfer function at one spatial frequency can be determined from one such record. From one set of several such records, each taken at a different spatial frequency as shown in Figure 3.17, one can obtain the entire spatiotemporal transfer function for this eye (Figure 3.18). For details see Brodie et al. (1978a,b).

11   Fourier Synthesis of Responses to Arbitrary Stimuli

Once the spatiotemporal transfer function has been determined, one should be able to predict, by Fourier synthesis, the response to any stimulus of any arbitrary form in space and time. (Such predictions, of course, are restricted to the linear range of the eye along the dimensions of space and time represented by the transfer function.) Figure 3.19 shows observed and predicted responses to an arbitrary stimulus—a square wave of intensity moving across the eye at two different velocities. Agreement between the observed responses and the responses predicted by Fourier synthesis is very good. The main discrepancies are truncation errors at very low rates of discharge; negative rates cannot occur in the real network. The agreement between observed responses and predictions of a "physiological" model is equally good (see Section 12).

Certain relations between form and function are clearly evident in these records. One example is the effect of the great breadth of the inhibitory field relative to the narrow excitatory field (Figure 3.5). As the step of excitation moves across the eye, it is preceded by a wave of inhibition. Therefore, the step increase in intensity produces a decrement in the re-

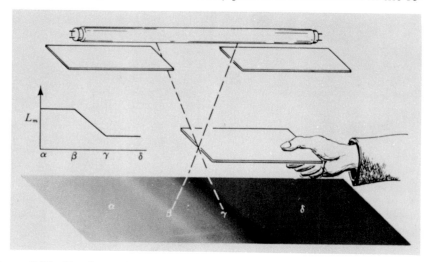

Figure 3.20. Simple method for producing Mach bands. If the light is about 1 ft above the white paper on which the shadow is cast, the card should be held about 1 or 2 in. above the paper. Slight lateral movements of the card may make the bands easier to see at first. The "Mach bands" in the diagram were painted with an air brush and are exaggerated somewhat for illustrative purposes. The light curve (inset at left) shows that there are no physical maxima and minima corresponding to those perceived at the edge of the half-shadow. If a fluorescent desk lamp is used as a source, the effect may be enhanced by masking the (usually) nonuniform ends of the lamp. (From Ratliff, 1965.)

sponse before it produces an increment. Such an effect is somewhat analogous to the so-called Mach bands in human vision (Figures 3.20 and 3.21) and we shall refer to it here as an anticipatory Mach band. Note, however, that the anticipation becomes smaller in width at higher velocities. Here we see another relation between form and function. In the steady state (Figure 3.6) or at a very low velocity, the width of the inhibitory effect is determined solely by the width of the inhibitory field. As velocity increases, the significant delay of the lateral inhibition (resulting from the temporal form of the lateral inhibitory potential) begins to come into play. The excitation produced by the moving step overtakes the delayed inhibition, and as the velocity becomes greater and greater, the anticipatory Mach band becomes narrower and narrower. Indeed, at extremely high velocities there is no anticipatory inhibition at all, and the response to a moving square wave becomes identical to that elicited by a stationary increment and decrement in the intensity of illumination—as was illustrated (open circle data) in Figure 3.8.

Figure 3.21. Breakfast (Le petit déjeuner). Paul Signac, 1886–1887. The Mach bands (e.g., in the shadow of the decanter) and other contrast effects are somewhat exaggerated. Where Signac saw "subjective" contrast he painted some "objective" contrast in addition. Your eyes then add more "subjective" contrast. The Kröller–Müller Museum, Otterlo, The Netherlands. (Photograph courtesy the Solomon R. Guggenheim Museum, New York.) For a colored illustration of this painting see Herbert (1968).

12   Physiological Model

Direct electrophysiological measurements of all of the physiological processes represented in the schema shown in Figure 3.9 and expressed in our static and dynamic equations (see Appendix) have been made either in our laboratory or by other investigators. We have worked out a model for this system that incorporates an excitatory generator potential and the self- and lateral-inhibitory processes (Brodie et al., 1978b). All parameters for the model have been derived from empirical data. Transfer functions calculated from the model show good agreement with laboratory measurements and may be used to predict accurately the response of the eye to arbitrary moving stimuli. (Compare predictions of this model with the

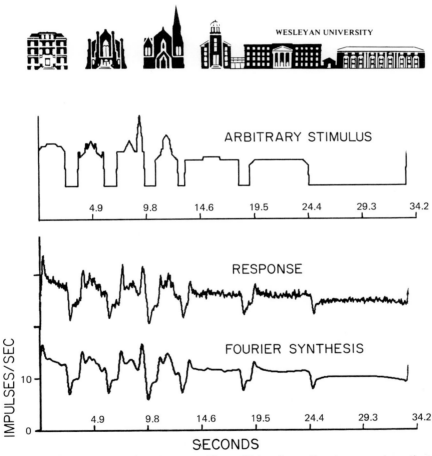

Figure 3.22. Response of optic nerve fiber of *Limulus* retina to a moving stimulus of arbitrary form. Velocity: 0.6 cm/sec. Upper trace: Arbitrary stimulus. Middle trace: Observed response (offset upward 15 impulses per second). Lower trace: Predicted response. (Redrawn from Ratliff, 1978; data from Brodie et al., 1978a.)

predictions by Fourier synthesis in Figure 3.19). The model allows convenient interpretation of complex responses of the network as a whole in terms of directly observable physiological processes that underlie those responses.

Some may complain that an ordinary square wave is not very arbitrary and not a very demanding test stimulus. For a linear system, though, a square-wave stimulus is just as arbitrary as any other. However, to satisfy doubting Thomases (and to go along with the fad for using "natural" stimuli in vision research) we used the profile of a row of buildings for a stimulus (Figure 3.22). Agreement is as good as before. A comprehensive and exact characterization of the network in quantitative terms is much more informative than is a mere classification in some impressionistic terms.

13   Symmetry and Ambiguity

Where there is symmetry there is usually ambiguity. Consider, for example, the peculiar symmetry of the capital letters C, E, H, I, and O about their horizontal axes. When the slogan CHOICE QUALITY, which appears on the side of a pack of Camel cigarettes, is seen along with its horizontal mirror image (Figure 3.23), it is difficult to tell at a glance which is which. Indeed, if the word CHOICE were not immediately adjacent to the word QUALITY (which has only one such symmetrical letter in it) the reversal might not be noticed at all. (By the way, do not overlook the warning from the Surgeon General printed elsewhere on the pack.)

An interesting feature of the network we have been studying in the *Limulus* retina is its (nearly) circular symmetry. In our experiments with

Figure 3.23. Symmetry and ambiguity. (From Ratliff, 1973.)

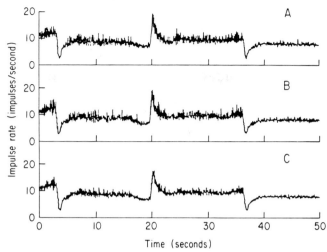

Figure 3.24. Comparison of the responses to mirror-image stimuli, that is, otherwise identical stimuli moving in opposite directions. (A) The average of the responses to 14 square-wave stimuli moving in one direction with a velocity of + 0.06 cm/sec. (B) The average of the responses to 14 square-wave stimuli moving in the opposite direction with a velocity of − 0.06 cm/sec. (C) The average of all 28 responses. (From Brodie et al., 1978a.)

one-dimensional sinusoidal and square-wave stimuli, the network cannot tell the difference between left and right. A square wave moving from one side of the eye to the other produces almost exactly the same response as one moving in the opposite direction (Figure 3.24). These two different stimuli are equivalent, as far as this network is concerned.[5]

To be directionally sensitive—that is, to respond differently to otherwise equivalent stimuli moving in different directions—a neural network must have some intrinsic asymmetry in its form. In the *Limulus* retina a photoreceptor unit at or near the margin of the eye has a natural asymmetry in its inhibitory surround. The surround is complete within the eye but is necessarily truncated at the margin of the eye. This asymmetry shows up clearly in the response (Figure 3.25). A square-wave stimulus

[5] The vertical bilateral symmetry in our own visual system has long been supposed to account for the confusion of vertically symmetrical parts of figures and patterns (cf. Corballis & Beale, 1976; Julesz, 1971; Mach, 1898). For example, the lower case letters "d" and "b" are frequently confused and so are "q" and "p"—presumably because of their symmetry about the vertical axis:

d b

q p

The horizontal symmetry of "d,q" and "b,p" is less troublesome than the vertical symmetry of "d,b" and "q,p". Also, the rotational symmetry of "d,p" and of "b,q" seldom leads to confusion. For some recent experiments on symmetry in human vision see Barlow's chapter in this volume.

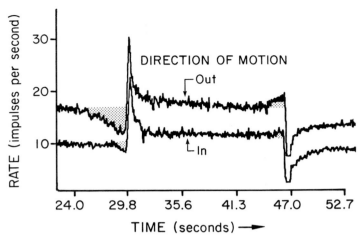

Figure 3.25. Responses of a photoreceptor unit located near the edge of the eye and therefore having an asymmetrical inhibitory field. The anticipatory Mach bands and release from inhibition (stippled) were much more pronounced when the stimulus moved across the large part of the inhibitory field before reaching the photoreceptor unit and then passed out of the visual field of the eye (Out) than when it moved into the visual field from the opposite direction and then across the small part of the inhibitory field before reaching the photoreceptor unit (In). The Out record is offset upward about 7.5 impulses per second. (Redrawn after Brodie et al., 1978a.)

moving from the center of the eye out toward the photoreceptor near the margin will be preceded by a wave of inhibition that will cause an anticipatory Mach band. Similarly, there will be a slight release from inhibition as the end of the square stimulus approaches the edge. A stimulus moving in the opposite direction, however, will produce a different response. There will be little inhibition preceding the stimulus because the inhibitory field on that side is almost completely absent. For the same reason, there will be little release from inhibition. A similar (but more complex) asymmetrical delayed inhibition has been shown by Barlow and Levick (1965) to be the principal mechanism responsible for directionally sensitive cells in the vertebrate visual system.

The difference in the responses to the otherwise equivalent stimuli moving in opposite directions can be greatly enhanced by choosing a photoreceptor unit directly on the margin of the *Limulus* eye so that there is no inhibition at all from that direction. The example in Figure 3.25 is not optimal; it shows the effect of partially, as opposed to completely, eliminating the inhibition on one side. A comprehensive and exact quantitative description of the behavior of these and other asymmetrical networks is more complicated than might be expected. The equations of Wiener and Hopf (1931) have turned out to be well suited to this problem (also see Paley & Wiener, 1934/1960, Chapter 4–17). For theoretical and experimental investigations along these lines see Sirovich (1980) and Sirovich, Brodie, and Knight (1979).

Even when there is a marked asymmetry of one type in the form of a neural network, there is often considerable symmetry of another type. For example, a "directionally sensitive" network may respond quite differently to movements in opposite directions *along* the principal axis of the receptive field, but not respond differently to symmetrical motions of a pair of otherwise identical stimuli moving in opposite directions *across* this principal axis. The experimenter generally plots such responses as different if he is exhibiting them on a map with polar coordinates because the experimenter knows which direction the stimulus has moved across the principal axis. However, the network does not "know" and does not respond differently. As far as the response of the network is concerned, the two symmetrical motions are equivalent. Once one knows the characteristics of a network fairly completely and exactly, one can easily define many classes of stimuli that will yield equivalent responses. That is, one can predict members of "equivalence classes" of visual stimuli in advance of their actual presentation to the eye.

14   Equivalence Classes of Edge Stimuli

In the study of neural networks, if dissimilar stimuli yield similar responses, we generally attribute this to nothing more complicated than a transmission by the network of certain features that the two stimuli have in common and a filtering out or rejection of those features that differ. For example, as was shown in Figure 3.24, a circularly symmetrical network is indifferent to direction of motion of stimuli, but not to the changes in intensity that motion produces. Therefore, the responses of such a network to stimuli that differ only in direction of motion are equal. Similarly, the responses to stationary stimuli that vary differently in time may be equal. For example, responses to a temporal square wave and to a temporal exponential wave (Figure 3.26) are nearly identical. In this case the very high temporal frequencies in the two stimuli—the abrupt step bounded by sharp corners—are nearly identical and are cut off equally by the network. Therefore, effective differences between these two stimuli are primarily in the low temporal frequency range. As illustrated in Figures 3.11, 3.12, 3.16, and 3.18, this is the range in which attenuation by lateral inhibition is strongest. Therefore, information about very low temporal frequencies in the square wave is strongly attenuated by the network. There is little low-frequency information in the exponential wave to begin with. As a result of the strong attenuation of low temporal frequency information in the one stimulus and the absence of low temporal frequency information in the other, the neural responses to the dissimilar stimuli are quite similar.

In human vision, questions about the relation between the form of a neural response in the visual pathway and the form of the corresponding visual appearance frequently have been raised. The question comes up,

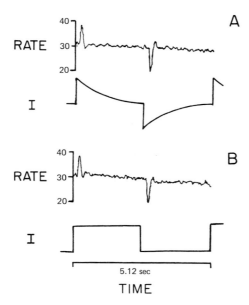

Figure 3.26. Instantaneous rate of discharge of impulses by optic nerve fiber in *Limulus* retina in response to temporal modulation of intensity (*I*) about the mean by exponential waves (A) and by square waves (B). The lateral inhibition was strong; the spot of light illuminated about 50 receptor units. (Redrawn after Ratliff, 1977a.)

for example, in the study of the so-called Craik–O'Brien–Cornsweet effects (Cornsweet, 1970; Craik, 1940, 1966; O'Brien, 1958). These particular edge-dependent effects are very striking (Figure 3.27). For example, a stationary antisymmetrical combination of two gently falling exponentials "looks like" a rectilinear step—this is the familiar "Cornsweet illusion." (Note the similarity to the temporal stimuli in Figure 3.26.) Many persons assume that the neural response and the visual appearance must be isomorphic. Because the Cornsweet stimulus "looks like" a rectilinear step, the suggestion frequently has been made that the usually observed neural response to such a stimulus (pronounced maxima and minima adjacent to the edge) must somehow be "filled in" in order to produce a rectilinear

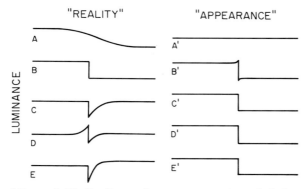

Figure 3.27. Reality and appearance. A graded distribution of luminance (A) such as a "soft" shadow appears uniform (A'). A rectilinear step (B) appears to be a step (B') with (sometimes) slight border-contrast effects. A Craik stimulus pattern (C), a Cornsweet stimulus pattern (D), and an O'Brien stimulus pattern (E)—if properly adjusted—all appear to be rectilinear steps (C', D', and E').

appearance. For this reason, the supposed neural mechanisms underlying these edge-dependent effects frequently have been represented as a "two-stage process" (Fleischer, 1939; Fry, 1948; Gerrits & Vendrick, 1970; Hood & Whiteside, 1968; Ratliff, 1971; Shiffman & Crovitz, 1972; Walls, 1954). In the first stage, lateral inhibition (principally) is supposed to produce the edge effects and, in the second stage, a "filling in" or "homogenization" of the pattern is supposed to take place.

Our intuition may tell us that such a filling-in process is necessary, but logic does not compel us to believe so. A much simpler interpretation based on the concept of *equivalence classes* of visual stimuli is adequate (Ratliff & Sirovich, 1978). For example, in the theoretical calculations shown in Figure 3.28, the rectilinear step stimuli, as well as a wide range of other edge stimuli with curvilinear and rectilinear components (first column), all belong to the same equivalence class of visual stimuli; that is, they all result in effectively the same neural activity (second column). (This figure is discussed in detail in Section 15.) According to this view, the appearance of each and every member of any such equivalence class in human vision would be essentially the same simply because the neural responses are essentially the same. (See, for example, Campbell, Howell, & Robson, 1971; Cornsweet, 1970; Mach, 1865; Ratliff, 1971; Shapley & Tolhurst, 1973; Tolhurst, 1972).

Any question about equivalence is two sided, and so is the answer. For example, we are all struck by the fact that Craik–O'Brien–Cornsweet stimuli (and all other members of that equivalence class of stimuli) look like rectilinear step stimuli, and many find this mysterious. Conversely, however, it is equally true and equally mysterious that rectilinear step stimuli look like Craik–O'Brien–Cornsweet stimuli (and also like all other members of that equivalence class—whatever they may be). In other words, no one of the stimuli in this equivalence class is the "ideal" or "standard" stimulus. Some—it is true—may be more familiar, less complicated, more likely to occur in nature, or may have some rather distinctive physical attribute, but no one is more effective as a visual stimulus than is any other. All belong to the same equivalence class; all appear the same; all supposedly yield the same or similar neural responses.

Logically, nothing more than similarity of neural responses is required to explain the equivalence. Moreover, parsimony demands that any additional stage or process be considered only if neurophysiological evidence for it should appear.

15 Effects of Form on Function

Heggelund and Krekling (1976) found that one of the Craik–O'Brien–Cornsweet effects disappears at low levels of adaptation. They note that their results "might indicate that the Craik effect occurs only under adaptational conditions where the retinal receptive fields have an antagonistic center–surround organization." No such measurements have been made

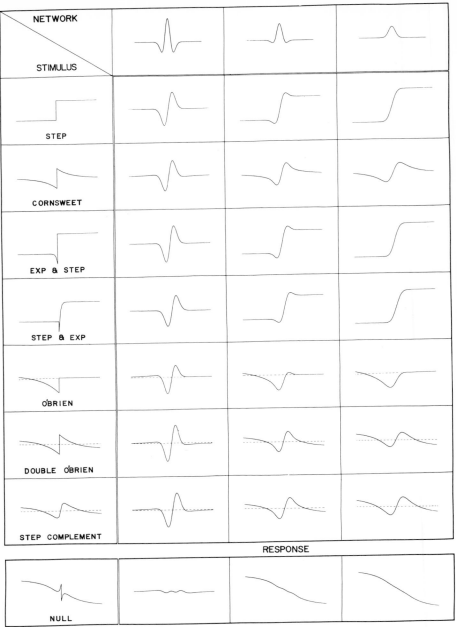

Figure 3.28. Responses of model linear networks to a variety of edge stimuli. The network on the left has a totally compensatory inhibitory surround (inhibition equals excitation); the network in the center has a partially compensatory inhibitory surround (inhibition is weaker than excitation); the network on the right has no inhibitory surround (zero inhibition). To facilitate comparison of responses, the amplitudes of the line-spread functions representing the networks have been adjusted so that the peak-to-peak amplitudes of the responses to the step stimuli are approximately the same for all three model networks. (From Ratliff & Sirovich, 1978.)

on human retinal ganglion cells, but the line-spread function of the human visual system (measured at or near threshold) is known to pass in stages from having a large opponent surround at high light levels to the complete loss of the surround at low light levels (see De Valois, Morgan, & Snodderly, 1974; Kelly, 1972; Patel, 1966). Such a transition is represented in a simplified form by the three (suprathreshold) line-spread functions shown on the top row of Figure 3.28. These represent neural networks with a totally compensatory inhibitory surround, a partially compensatory inhibitory surround, and no inhibitory surround. The first column contains seven different stimulus patterns and the associated rows show how the responses change as the forms of the line-spread functions change—that is, as the amount of surround inhibition changes. (The responses are the convolution product of the stimulus with the various line-spread functions shown.)

Each of the several stimulus patterns can be regarded as a combination of steps and exponentially falling functions. For example, the Cornsweet pattern is the antisymmetrical combination of two gently falling exponentials (each of which can be regarded as a separate Craik pattern); the "exp & step" stimulus is a step function with a sharply falling exponential subtracted on the left. The O'Brien pattern is also of this form but has a left starting point higher than the right and contains a gently falling exponential. The sixth pattern is named "double O'Brien." The "step complement" differs from the "step" the most of all the patterns shown—indeed, as much as possible while still belonging to the same equivalence class.

The next column of this figure shows that all seven stimuli produce very nearly the same response after passing through the network represented by the first of these line-spread functions. They all belong to the same equivalence class of stimuli—for the first line-spread function. This is true even for the O'Brien, double O'Brien, and step complement stimuli which differ from all the others in that they exhibit a relative contrast exchange. That is, although the light intensity at the left is greater than at the right, the response under the first line-spread function is essentially the same as that of a step (first stimulus) with opposite relative intensity. (Note relationship to dotted lines.)

The equivalence class is split under the loss of opponency. The second line-spread function (third column) has half as much inhibition as excitation and is therefore less able to produce pronounced edge effects. The third line-spread function (fourth column) has no inhibitory surround and hence merely results in a "blurred" copy of the stimulus. All three line-spread functions show the same high-frequency suppression. This accounts for the continued equivalence of the step, exp & step, and step & exp stimuli in the transition from one to another of all three line-spread functions. For the same reason the double O'Brien and step complement stimuli also remain equivalent under all three line-spread functions.

For a linear system the difference of any two members of an equivalence class is a "null" stimulus, which gives rise to an effectively null response. This is illustrated in the bottom part of Figure 3.28, where the "null" stimulus is the difference between the step and step complement stimuli in the upper part of the figure. Passage of the null stimulus through the network represented by the first line-spread function yields a nearly uniform (null) response. Actually, by further sculpturing the null pattern, a more nearly zero response can be obtained. This was deliberately avoided here in order to show the location of the vanishing response and to underline the notion that nearly zero responses appear as nulls as they enter the noise. Note that the step and step complement stimuli do not yield equivalent responses under the second and third line-spread functions. Therefore, the stimulus that is a null for the first line-spread function is not a null for the second and third functions.

In summary, stimuli that differ objectively may produce equivalent neural responses (and visual appearances) simply because the visual system "filters" out those features of the stimuli which differ, and transmits some of those features which the stimuli share in common. Such stimuli form an equivalence class. For a linear system, the difference between any two members of the same equivalence class is a null stimulus.

Whatever the causes of these and closely related equivalence phenomena may be, the effects themselves are incontrovertible. Although recently "discovered" by scientists, they have been used by artists for a thousand years or more (see Ratliff, 1971, 1973, 1977a,b). The moon's

Figure 3.29. A Craik-like effect produced by gradient of stippling. Note that the moon's disk at the right of the drawing appears significantly brighter than the open sky at the left of the drawing. (Illustration by Kay Chorao from *The Witch's Egg*, by M. Edmondson. Copyright © 1974 by the illustrator and reprinted by permission of the publisher, Houghton Mifflin/Clarion Books, New York).

disk in Figure 3.29 looks much brighter than the sky, but both are identical expanses of bare paper (in the original). This figure is a variant of the Craik effect. Even more striking is the apparent brightness of the moon's disk on the Korean vase shown in Figure 3.30. Here, the moon is physically darker than the sky about one moon diameter below it, but it appears much brighter. This apparent "contrast reversal" is a variant of the O'Brien effect. These two examples were produced by rather coarse control of the gradient of density adjacent to the moon's disk. With the very fine control that can be obtained in the laboratory, the gradients disappear and a low-contrast Cornsweet type of distribution of illumination, for example, is virtually indistinguishable from a rectangular step distribution (see Cornsweet, 1970; Ratliff, 1965, 1971).

"Explanations" of these and other aspects of human vision in terms of a single linear network or line-spread function have a heuristic value, but

Figure 3.30. Korean vase, Yi Dynasty. The Asia Society, Mr. and Mrs. John D. Rockefeller 3rd Collection. For a color photograph see Griffing (1968).

—even at best—they are not likely to be more than good first approximations to the real physiology. There are many reasons for this. Two main
ones are: (1) The vertebrate visual system is made up of a great many different networks and cell types and (2) many if not most of these are highly
nonlinear. If we are ever to reach a full understanding of the physiology
of the vertebrate visual system we must sooner or later face up to the
problems inherent in this great complexity of form and function. Some
theoretical and experimental work directed to this end is described in the
following sections.

16   Nonlinear Analysis of Neural Networks

The modulation transfer function or its Fourier transform (the line-
spread function in space or the impulse function in time) provides a simple, convenient, and universal characterization for a linear system. The
transfer function is easy to measure (in principle, at least), for if the input
to a linear system is a sinusoid, the output is a sinusoid of the same frequency (only the amplitude and phase may be changed). This holds
whether the input is comprised of one sinusoid or of many sinusoids.
Therefore, if two (or more) sinusoids of different frequencies are input at
the same time there is no "crosstalk" between them in a linear system.
The output to an input signal containing many sinusoids is simply the
sum of the separate output sinusoids that would be obtained if the input
sinusoids were presented singly and separately.

A nonlinear system, in contrast, cannot be completely characterized
by a single modulation transfer function. Sinusoids in the input signal
may appear in the output (just as in a linear system) or they may not appear at all. Also, second harmonics (multiples of two) of the input frequencies may (or may not) appear. In addition, there may (or may not) be
simple second-order combination frequencies in the output—for example, the sum of two input frequencies, or the difference between two
input frequencies. Finally, there may (or may not) be higher order harmonics and combination frequencies—third harmonics, sums of difference frequencies, differences between sum frequencies, etc. Obviously,
nonlinear systems may be very complex, and methods of nonlinear analysis must be able to deal with this complexity.

Consider the time domain. There a linear system can (in principle) be
completely characterized by its response to one brief pulse (the so-called
impulse response). To completely characterize a nonlinear system, however, one must (in principle) observe its response to all possible input signals. Wiener (1958) showed that a dynamic nonlinear system could be
completely characterized by analyzing its output when the input was
Gaussian white noise, for such a signal will eventually come arbitrarily

close to any particular deterministic signal of finite duration. Although Wiener's technique is elegant from a theoretical point of view, the practical problems it poses severely limit its use. One important advance was made by Lee and Schetzen (1965), who developed a simple algorithm (involving cross correlation between input and output signals) for calculating the so-called Wiener kernels. Even so, many practical problems remain in the application of Wiener analysis to biological systems. Most of these problems result from the complexity and long duration of the Gaussian white noise required for the input signal. To circumvent some of these problems, other analytical methods using input signals somewhat less complex than true white noise have been devised (e.g., Krausz & Friesen, 1975; Marmarelis, 1975; Spekreijse & Oosting, 1970). A new method developed by Victor et al. (1977) allows one to use an extremely simple input—namely, the sum of sinusoids referred to in the previous discussion of linear systems—without abandoning the theoretical advantages of Wiener's technique.

With this sum-of-sinusoids input, Fourier analysis can be used to extract quickly the essential information from the experimental data. Fourier analysis also has the advantage that the narrow-band filtering it provides greatly enhances the signal-to-noise ratio. This shortens the time for data collection and aids in discriminating against intrinsic noise (Victor, 1979). Often, the cost of one such advantage gained is the loss of some other advantage. In this case the advantage of use of a small number of separate and distinct frequencies is paid for by loss of direct information about the system in the intervals between those frequencies. Fortunately, responses of the visual system are sufficiently smooth (usually) to allow accurate interpolation between fairly widely separated points. Therefore, the loss of the advantage of continuous measurement provided by white noise is not significant in this instance. Finally, it has been shown (Victor & Knight, 1979) that the kernels obtained with this method are good approximations to the Fourier transform of the classical Wiener kernels. Therefore, the relatively simple sum of sinusoids has several practical advantages (for this particular application) over the classical Wiener white-noise analysis and, at the same time, retains many of the theoretical advantages of the more complex Wiener analysis.

The new method uses a superposition of nearly incommensurate sinusoids. This forms an input signal that is periodic, yet rich enough to provide a useful characterization of a nonlinear system. However, not any set of sinusoids will do; a proper choice of the component frequencies is essential for the procedure to work. Fundamental frequencies must be chosen such that they are not equal to any of their next-order sum, difference, or harmonic frequencies; consider, for example: 0.7, 1.5, 3.1, and 6.3 cps (Figure 3.16). This small sample shows that the fundamental frequencies and the second-order nonlinearities (multiples of two, sums, and differences of the fundamental frequencies) all differ from one another[6] and therefore may be easily identified if they appear in the response:

Fundamental	0.7
Difference	0.8 (1.5 − 0.7)
Harmonic	1.4 (2 × 0.7)
Fundamental	1.5
Difference	1.6 (3.1 − 1.5)
Sum	2.2 (0.7 + 1.5)
Difference	2.4 (3.1 − 0.7)
Harmonic	3.0 (2 × 1.5)
Fundamental	3.1
Difference	3.2 (6.3 − 3.1)
Sum	3.8 (0.7 + 3.1)
Sum	4.6 (1.5 + 3.1)
Difference	4.8 (6.3 − 1.5)
Difference	5.6 (6.3 − 0.7)
Harmonic	6.2 (2 × 3.1)
Fundamental	6.3
Sum	7.0 (6.3 + 0.7)
Sum	7.8 (6.3 + 1.5)
Sum	9.4 (6.3 + 3.1)
Harmonic	12.6 (2 × 6.3).

Victor et al. (1977) have analyzed the responses of cat X and Y ganglion cells to spatial sinusoids that are modulated in time by a sum of sinusoids. The sum of sinusoids used in their experiments spanned a range of about 0.3–30 cps—sufficient to sample the temporal modulation transfer function of such cells. A linear (or nearly linear) network should yield results essentially the same as those obtained from the *Limulus* retina. For example, the so-called X retinal ganglion cell of the cat is nearly linear under certain conditions; in this instance, temporal modulation of a just-resolvable (high-frequency) spatial sine grating. As shown in Figure 3.31, the X cell's response to the sum-of-sinusoids contrast reversal of a spatial sinusoid may be almost completely characterized by a single *Limulus*-like transfer function with a high-frequency cutoff, a strong attenuation at low frequencies, and a prominent peak at intermediate frequencies. As one expects in a (nearly) linear system, there is little or no crosstalk among the several input frequencies. The graph below the transfer function is a plot of the second-order (crosstalk) responses at sum frequencies (upper part) and at difference frequencies (lower part). The few contours indicate that there is practically no response anywhere in this half-plane. What little response there is (two impulses per second

---

[6] It is possible to arrange conditions such that nonlinear responses resulting from interactions up to the eighth order do not contribute to any of the fundamental or second-order response components under consideration (Victor et al., 1977).

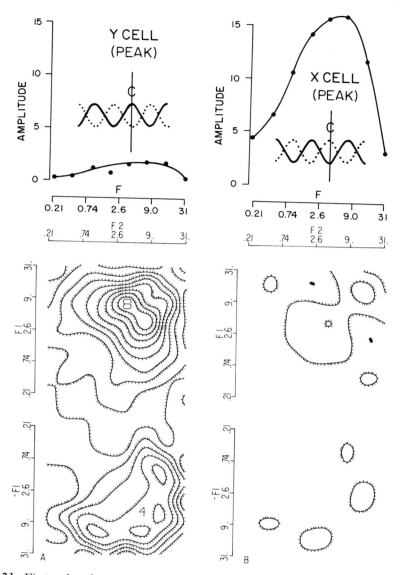

Figure 3.31. First-order (linear) responses (top) and second-order (nonlinear) responses (bottom) from a typical cat retinal ganglion Y cell (left) and a typical X cell (right). The temporal modulation signal was a sum of eight sinusoids (each with a peak contrast of 0.05). The spatial pattern was a sinusoidal grating (0.5 cycles per degree of visual angle) centered (¢) in the position that produced a maximal linear response. The peak linear response of the Y cell (about one impulse per second) is not significant. In the plots of the second-order (nonlinear) frequency kernels each contour line represents one impulse per second, the tick marks point "downhill." Frequency is measured in cycles per second. The second-order (nonlinear) response of the X cell is not significant. The second-order (nonlinear) response of the Y cell reaches a maximum of eight impulses per second in the sum-frequency region and four impulses per second in the difference-frequency region. For details see Fig. 3.32 and Appendix. (Redrawn after Victor et al., 1977.)

maximum) can barely be discriminated from the intrinsic noise of the network.

The so-called Y cells, in contrast, are highly nonlinear under the same stimulus conditions (Figure 3.31). In this particular instance there is virtually no linear response to the temporal input signal. However, there are large amounts of crosstalk among the fundamental components as shown in the contour maps of the second-order responses below. Amplitudes of the sums of input modulation frequencies reach a peak of eight impulses per second in the intermediate ranges. Similarly, the amplitudes of the differences between the input modulation frequencies reach a peak of four impulses per second in the intermediate ranges. Note that the peak response of the sum frequencies (top part) is somewhat sharper than the peak response to the difference frequencies. The form of such responses may be better visualized if the data are plotted as an elevation seen in perspective rather than as a flat contour map. Figure 3.32 shows such a plot for data from another Y cell.

In both X and Y cells the linear components of responses to a contrast-reversal grating (if there are any) vary with the spatial position of the grating. As one would expect for a (nearly) symmetrical network, the maximum response (at all temporal frequencies) is obtained when the point of maximum amplitude of the contrast reversal is centered on the receptive

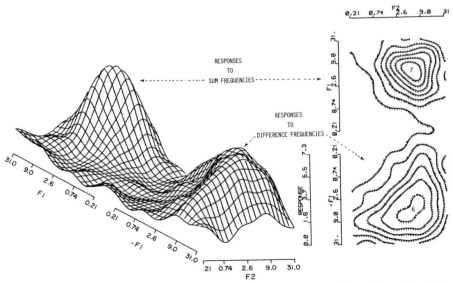

Figure 3.32. Second-order (nonlinear) frequency kernel of another Y cell shown as a contour map and as an elevation in perspective. The nonlinearities resulting from crosstalk among input frequencies appearing in the response as the result of addition are labeled SUM FREQUENCIES. The crosstalk appearing in the response as the result of subtraction are labeled DIFFERENCE FREQUENCIES. See Appendix for further details. (Graphs of data provided by Jonathan Victor.)

field. Also, as one would expect, there is a definite null at a spatial position halfway between optimal spatial positions of the grating.

Therefore, a clear and unequivocal distinction between X and Y cells of the cat retina may be made on the basis of these measurements. At high, just-resolvable spatial frequencies the X cells are essentially linear; their second-order nonlinear responses, if any, are so small that they are practically indistinguishable from the noise. Second-order nonlinearities sometimes (but not always) appear in responses of X cells at lower spatial frequencies. Therefore, a simple linear–nonlinear distinction between X and Y cells holds only at high spatial frequencies. The Y cells, however, do have strong second-order nonlinearities in their responses at all spatial frequencies. Because we have already dealt extensively with linear systems analysis as applied to the *Limulus* retina, let us not consider the X cells further. Instead, let us confine our attention to an analysis of a few significant features of the more complex and highly nonlinear Y cells.

17   Independence of Linear and Nonlinear Responses in Y Cells

At a fairly low spatial frequency of the modulated spatial sine-wave grating, the response of a Y cell exhibits a linear component. The linear component of the Y cell (when there is one) varies sinusoidally with the spatial phase of the grating (Hochstein & Shapley, 1976a). This variation of linear response with position of grating is essentially the same as that observed in the *Limulus* photoreceptor unit and in the X cell. However, at moderate contrasts, the second-order nonlinear reponse of the Y cell is practically independent of spatial phase. It is essentially the same whether the Y cell produces a maximal linear response or none at all. Figure 3.33 shows data collected from an on-center Y cell. When the spatial grating was positioned to produce a peak linear response, the peak amplitudes of the second-order (nonlinear) responses in the sum and difference regions were both large and nearly equal.

When the spatial grating was moved to the null position (at which the linear response was minimal) the peak linear response was reduced by almost a factor of 10. The peak second-order nonlinear responses, on the other hand, remained virtually the same.

18   Dependence of Second-Order Nonlinearities on Spatial Frequency

An on-center Y cell was stimulated in the usual way with temporally modulated gratings at three different spatial frequencies; a coarse grating, a medium grating, and a fine grating. For each spatial frequency the grating was positioned so as to produce a negligible linear response. There-

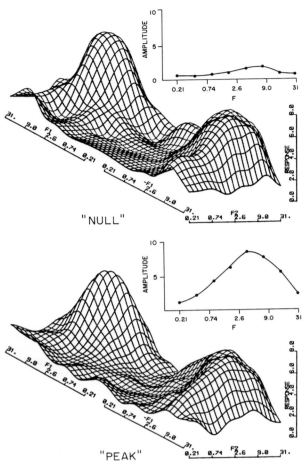

Figure 3.33. Effect of spatial phase on linear and nonlinear responses of a Y cell. The graphs (inset) show the first-order (linear) responses of a Y cell to a sum-of-sinusoids contrast reversal of a spatial sinusoid. Above: A peak of the spatial sinusoid is centered on the receptive field so as to produce the minimum (null) linear response. Below: The sinusoid is positioned so as to produce the maximum (peak) linear response. Note that under these two different conditions there is practically no change at all in the forms of the second-order (nonlinear) responses, which are represented by the grids seen in perspective. (Data from Victor et al., 1977.)

fore, there was no possibility that truncation of a linear response would produce any significant second-order nonlinearities. For ease of comparison (Figure 3.34), only the pure second-harmonic diagonals of the second-order responses are plotted. There is a striking dependence of the response on spatial frequency: as spatial frequency decreased, the temporal frequency of the peak of the second-order (harmonic) response increased.

Figure 3.34. Second-harmonic
responses of a cat retinal ganglion
Y cell as a function of temporal
frequency of contrast reversal of
three spatial frequencies. (Data
from Victor & Shapley, 1979a.)

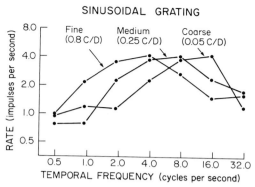

19 Response to a Single Bar versus Response to a Sinusoid

The second-order nonlinearities of Y cells do not depend on the periodicity and great extent of the usual spatial sine-wave grating stimulus. This was shown by comparing the response of such a stimulus with the response produced by a single flickering bar (Figure 3.35). The bar used was about the same width as one half-cycle of the spatial sinusoid. The bar was positioned to produce a maximal linear response; the grating was positioned to produce a minimal linear response. The second-order nonlinearities were nearly the same for the two stimuli.

20 Interpretation

The classical view of the configuration of cat retinal ganglion cells is the now well-known on-center, off-surround (or the converse: off-center, on-surround). Simple linear models have been proposed for these cells (cf. Rodieck & Stone, 1965); they have a form very much like that of the linear network actually observed in *Limulus* (Figure 3.5)—approximately a narrow positive Gaussian superimposed on a broad negative Gaussian. As we have seen, however, only the X cells of the cat retina are actually found to be linear, and these consistently so only at fairly high spatial frequencies. The Y cells, however, are highly nonlinear under all conditions. Indeed, the presence of a spatially widespread nonlinear pathway with high spatial resolution is one feature that characterizes Y cells in the cat retina (and clearly distinguishes them from X cells). Certainly, they cannot adequately be represented by the simple linear addition of opposed excitatory and inhibitory influences. Indeed, the few observations reported here provide strong evidence that the conventional classical view of the center–surround organization of cat retinal ganglion cells must be modified substantially.

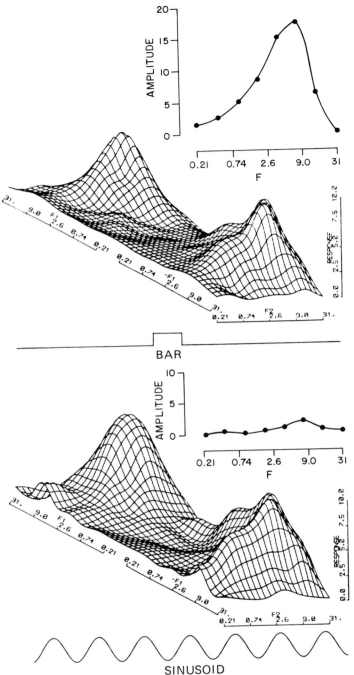

Figure 3.35. Comparison of responses of a Y cell to contrast reversal of a narrow bar (above) and of a spatial sinusoid (below). Note dramatic difference between the first-order (linear) responses (graphs at top) and the near identity of the second-order (nonlinear) responses (elevations of grids below). (Data from Victor & Shapley, 1979b.)

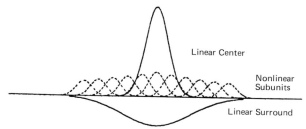

Figure 3.36. One-dimensional spatial model for the Y-cell receptive field. There is a broad linear surround and a narrow linear center (solid lines). Overlapping the entire receptive field is an ensemble of nonlinear subunits (dashed curves), each of which is narrower than the linear center. (Redrawn after Hochstein & Shapley, 1976b.)

A spatial model of the sensitivity profiles of different receptive-field mechanisms in Y cells (Figure 3.36) has been proposed by Hochstein and Shapley (1976b). There are three types of spatial components in their nonlinear model: the conventional, relatively narrow linear center; the conventional, relatively broad antagonistic linear surround (as in Figure 3.5); and a widespread array of very narrow, nonlinear subunits with the same sign as the center mechanism and overlapping both the center and the surround and—to some extent—one another.

Perhaps the strongest support for this nonlinear model presented here is the finding that the second-order nonlinear response of a Y cell is independent of spatial phase (Figure 3.33). If the nonlinear responses were mediated by a single local mechanism, such as the conventional center, then there would have to be a sinusoidal dependence of the second-order response on spatial phase.

Furthermore, if the second-order response were localized in the center, one would expect it to be strongest when stimuli were localized in the center and so produced the maximum first-order (linear) response. The bar versus sine grating experiment (Figure 3.35) shows clearly that this is not the case. Instead, the sine-grating stimulus that is distributed over the entire receptive field, and which produces little first-order response, yields the largest second-order response. Furthermore, experiments not reported here show that a small patch of sine grating located anywhere in the field will generate second-order responses. There must be nonlinear subunits small enough to resolve fine gratings distributed over the whole receptive field—both center and surround; for "like is known only by like."

There is also an indication that these nonlinear subunits may have some opponent structure of their own. For example, if each subunit were to have a small central excitatory region and a larger, slower, inhibitory surround, then the nonlinear response should change with spatial frequency. At low spatial frequencies the hypothetical subunit surround would cancel the hypothetical subunit center response at low temporal frequencies and would reinforce the center subunit response at high temporal frequencies. This is directly analogous to the phenomenon of temporal tuning by lateral inhibition (Figures 3.12 and 3.14) which is well documented in studies on *Limulus*. The net effect of this tuning in nonlinear subunits of the cat Y cell would be to shift the peak of the second-order nonlinear response to higher temporal frequencies as spatial frequency decreases. This is precisely what has been observed (Figure 3.34).

We therefore see that the nonlinear analysis of Y cells has elucidated some new principles of great generality—principles that are akin to, but more complex than, our old ideas about the integrative activity of the retina. Old and fruitful concepts—such as the simple linear summation of opposed center–surround influences—will not have to be abandoned altogether, but in many cases they will have to be greatly modified.

21   Visual Evoked Potentials in Cat and Human

The sum-of-sinusoids method of studying linear and nonlinear systems is not limited to analyses of single cells. It may be applied to the analysis of any signal (whatever its origin) that is adequately sampled by the mesh of input signals. Recently we have carried out some exploratory studies on the highly nonlinear visual evoked potential (which can easily be recorded from cortical or scalp electrodes).

In one study (Shapley, So, & Victor, 1978) visual evoked responses were recorded from the cat (Figure 3.37). The recordings were made from an occipital lead in the midline. The lids of the left eye had been sutured shut since birth. At the age of 9 months (one week prior to the experiment) the eye was opened. The animal was kept in a normal animal house environment at all times (except during the necessary surgery and during the experiment). The stimulus was the same contrast-reversal sinusoidal grating flickered with the same sum of sinusoids that was used in the X- and Y-cell experiments. The second-order nonlinear component of the response for the normal eye has a superficial resemblance to the Y-cell response. There are two principal peaks: one in the low midrange of the sum region and the other in the low midrange of the difference region. The response in the sum region is conical; in the difference region it rises steeply to a small plateau. The peak amplitude is greatest in the difference region. The peak amplitude of the linear component (not shown) was barely visible in the noise. (The corners of the plots, at very high frequencies outside of the range in which the eye can be expected to respond, are very flat, showing that there has been very little noise contributed by nonvisual sources in the preparation or by the recording system.)

The deprived eye, in contrast, yielded a rather bizarre response, with many low-amplitude peaks and valleys in both the sum and difference re-

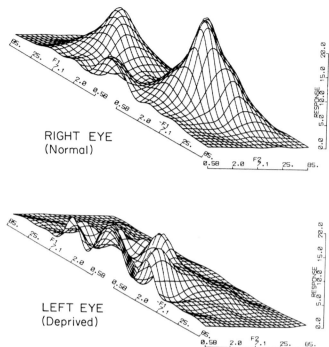

Figure 3.37. Second-order (nonlinear) cat visual evoked potentials resulting from a sum-of-sinusoids temporal contrast reversal of a 0.5 cycle per degree spatial sinusoid. Contrast: 0.10 per sinusoid. Mean: 20 cd/m². Visual field: 20° × 20°. Recorded from occipital lead, midline. The amplitudes of the responses in both graphs are in (equal) arbitrary units. The responses were measured for the normal (right) eye with the deprived (left) eye covered and for the deprived eye with the normal eye covered. (Data from Shapley et al., 1978.)

gions. The most prominent responses were in the very low frequency range.

I emphasize that these are exploratory experiments. No neurophysiological interpretation of the gross differences between the responses of the normal and the deprived eye is possible at this time. Furthermore, no significance should be attached as yet to the superficial resemblance between the second-order nonlinear response of the normal eye and the second-order response of a Y ganglion cell. The only points I wish to make are that the signal-to-noise ratio in these recordings is very good and that there are large, easy to measure differences between the two responses. Also, the "disorderly" appearance of the response of the deprived eye compared with the "orderly" appearance of the response of the normal eye is consistent with a (presumed) visual deficiency resulting from the deprivation.

Records taken from a human subject with normal vision (when corrected for presbyopia!) are shown in Figure 3.38. The recording electrode

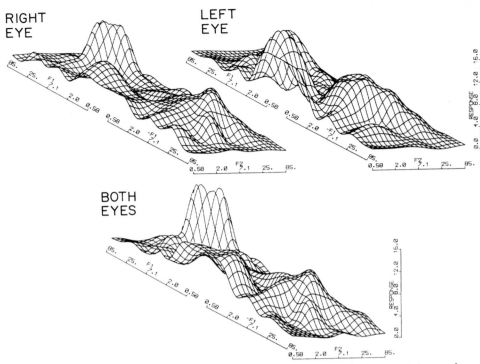

Figure 3.38. Second-order (nonlinear) human visual evoked potentials resulting from a sum-of-sinusoids temporal contrast reversal of a 1.0 cycle per degree spatial sinusoid. Contrast: 0.10 per sinusoid. Mean: 20 cd/m². Visual field: about 10° × 10°. Recorded from midline occipital lead 1 cm above the inion. The amplitudes of the responses in all graphs are expressed in (equal) arbitrary units. Above left: Right eye alone. Above right: Left eye alone. Below: Response to same stimulus viewed by both eyes simultaneously. Subject: Floyd Ratliff. Experimenter: Jonathan Victor.

was placed on the surface of the scalp on the midline of the occipital region about 1 cm above the inion. The stimulus conditions were essentially the same as in the experiment on the cat visual evoked potential, except that the grating stimulus pattern was exposed to each eye separately and then to both eyes simultaneously. In a gross way, all of the second-order nonlinear responses resemble the responses of cat Y cells and the evoked potentials from the normal cat eye in that there are fairly prominent peaks in the midranges of both the sum and difference regions. Also, as in Y cells (usually) the amplitude of the peak in the sum region is slightly larger than the peak in the difference region. The peak amplitude of the linear component of the response to this particular pattern, as expected, rarely exceeded $\frac{2}{10}$ or $\frac{3}{10}$ of the amplitude of the second-order nonlinear component. Considering the background noise, it is doubtful that the linear response is of much significance. There is more nonvisual noise in these data than in the data from the cat, as can be seen by examining the very high frequency corners of the graphs. This is probably because of the different recording techniques: a screw electrode in skull and head fixed by a stereotaxic instrument for the cat and a scalp electrode and head not fixed for the human.

The principal result of interest is the significant increase in amplitude of the peak response in the sum-frequency region when both eyes were exposed. There was essentially no change in amplitude of the peak in the difference region. However, relative phases of the separate responses of the two eyes have not been taken into account in these preliminary observations. Again, little significance can be attached to these results, as yet, except that they demonstrate feasibility of use of the method in studies on human subjects. Indeed, on the basis of these and a few other preliminary results we have confidence that this sum-of-sinusoids method may have considerable utility in the study of visual evoked potentials (Ratliff, Victor, & Shapley, 1978).

22   A Look into the Future

It was a clear day when I decided to comment on future developments in vision research, but a thick fog rolled in when I actually tried to look far ahead. To predict accurately the outcome of a single well-controlled experiment is difficult enough; to predict accurately the course of a large, active, and rapidly evolving field of research is next to impossible. Nevertheless, some trends can be seen here and there, and some goals can be set now—whether they will ever be realized or not. I see several major developments in the making and one major need arising in vision research. They are:

1. The early demise of the concept of retinal ganglion cells as feature detectors
2. The rapid emergence of the concept of parallel processing in the nervous system
3. A more extensive use of applied mathematics in the study of neural networks
4. An increasing need for recognition of and attention to some major problems in organic and holistic aspects of visual perception, which—in turn—may require the development of some new modes of thought.

A   Feature Detectors

Many years ago Mach (1865) carefully examined the most recent anatomical, physiological, and psychophysical researches of his time on the structure and function of the retina. He asked: Considering their similar structure, why should the ganglion cells of the retina behave differently from those of the brain? He raised the question: Why should the retina not have a certain logic of its own? Later (Mach, 1868) he wrote:

> One could say that the retina schematizes and caricatures. The teleological significance of this process is clear in itself. It is an analog of abstraction and of the formation of concepts.

(See Ratliff, 1965, for translation of Mach's papers on the retina.)

These ideas have since been carried much farther. We now know a great deal—by direct experiment—about the integrative action of retinal networks, and we hear a great deal—in unbridled speculation—about "feature detectors" in the retina. What is fact and what is fantasy? It is certainly true that there are several different and clearly distinguishable classes of retinal ganglion cells. Even in the apparently "homogeneous" *Limulus* retina the marginal networks with their truncated asymmetrical inhibitory fields clearly have different forms and different functions from the centrally located networks. Also, it is certainly true that the vertebrate retina is characterized by a multiplicity of "channels"—retinal networks that respond differently, and somewhat selectively, to various temporal, spatial, and spectral distributions of illumination. However, I can say without qualification that in all of the numerous eyes that have been studied in our laboratory over the past 50 years in a wide variety of species (frog, goldfish, eel, alligator, cat, scallop, squid, *Limulus*, and others) no retinal ganglion cell has been found that, in any strict sense of the term, I am willing to call a "feature detector." Distinguishable classes of ganglion cells of all kinds—yes; feature detectors—no. Indeed, a major characteristic of most of these several different classes of cells is that they are broadly rather than sharply "tuned." The three examples shown here— *Limulus* inhibitory network, cat X cell, and cat Y cell—are all sensitive to a very broad range of spatial and temporal frequencies. Therefore, although it is true that they are tuned to be most sensitive in some particular spatiotemporal region, as exact experimental measurements of their transfer functions show, by no stretch of the imagination can those peaks of sensitivity be regarded as feature detectors. Instead, there is every indication that any given response of practically any one of these cells may be elicited by a large equivalence class of visual stimuli.

If what I have said about broadly tuned retinal networks versus sharply tuned feature detectors is true in general, as well as in the specific instances cited in this paper (the reader can judge for himself by taking a critical look at the data—not the speculation—in the original reports on so-called feature detectors), then how is it possible for us to see as well as we obviously do? Color vision provides an instructive model on which to base our thinking about this problem. Consider, for example, the extremely broad spectral tuning of the cones in the retina (in accordance with the Young–Helmholtz theory and supported by direct spectrophotometry and by direct electrophysiological measurements). Consider also the very broad tuning of the opponent interactions among the outputs of these cones (in accordance with the Hering theory and also supported by direct electrophysiological measurements in the retina and at higher levels). There is a certain logic going on in the retina and a definite abstraction of information by various classes of "color-coded" cells with different but widely overlapping sensitivities (but certainly no "feature detection" as such by any one of them). Nevertheless, the information that is abstracted and sent to higher visual centers via these several channels is sufficient to enable us to make color discriminations of only a few millimicrons; it is sufficient for us to perceive in a continuous physical spectrum four distinct and psychologically unique colors, red, green, yellow, and blue; it is sufficient for us to reliably identify and to name these unique colors (as well as many others that are not unique) in practically all cultures with advanced languages—and so on (cf. Ratliff, 1976). However, we look to the retina only for the beginning of these processes in color vision. Color information is abstracted and *partially* analyzed by several separate channels in the retina, but the subtle and fine discriminations are evidently made by comparisons among these several broadly but differently tuned channels at higher levels. I firmly believe that such must also be the case with pattern vision. All necessary information for all aspects of visual perception must be mediated by the retina, but there is no evidence (to my satisfaction) that little more than a separation into a few major parallel channels with different but broad and overlapping sensitivities takes place there. In my opinion, comprehensive mathematical analyses give no indication of the much touted "feature detectors."

B Parallel Processing

There has been much ado in vision research about the convergence of neural activity on single cells at the cortical level, and the notion of hierarchical systems leading to single "pontifical cells" and/or to more numerous "cardinal cells" has been much talked about (cf. Barlow, 1972). It is true that much convergence of activity on single cells is actually observed. Indeed, how could it appear otherwise when we typically record only from single cells? The fact is that visual information does not follow only single serial hierarchical pathways from retina to lateral geniculate to visual cortex. *Convergence* of widespread retinal activity onto single cells at higher levels is a fact of physiology, but so is *divergence* of local retinal activity to several separate cells at higher levels. However, convergence and divergence are in no way contradictory or mutually exclusive. I have pointed out elsewhere (Ratliff, 1965, pp. 93 and 123) that the convolution integral used by Huggins and Licklider (1951) to represent a weighting function (similar to that shown in Figure 3.5) describes influences that arise from many different points on the receptor mosaic and *converge* on a particular second-order neuron. In contrast, the superposition integral used by von Békésy (1960) to represent a similar function (his so-called neural unit) describes influences that arise at a particular point on the receptor mosaic and *diverge* from it to many different second-order neurons. In the special case in which the weighting function in the Huggins–Licklider model and the neural unit in von Békésy's model have the same form, the two equations are mathematically identical. In short, many situations in neurophysiology may be open to apparently different but equally valid interpretations—results obtained depend strongly upon the experimenter's point of view. In the end, however, we must be guided by all of the facts, not just a limited set of them selected by the technique of the experiment or the temperament of the experimenter. As our techniques improve and as our perspectives broaden a much more comprehensive and more enlightening account of information processing by the visual system will gradually emerge. Simplistic theoretical notions may have a heuristic value in the early stages of the study of a complex system, but sooner or later, as we learn more and more, they must be abandoned. As Mach once wrote: "We err if we expect more enlightenment from an hypothesis than from the facts themselves," and the facts are that there is much parallel processing of information in the visual system.

C Applied Mathematics

There is but one good reason to make use of mathematical analyses of neural networks. That one reason is simple and practical: to obtain useful results that lead to further understanding. Consider the application of nonlinear systems analysis to the study of the vertebrate retina. No one can deny the fact that cat retinal ganglion cells and the retinal networks associated with them are, overall, highly nonlinear systems. Moreover, it could be argued that any investigator who presents a visual stimulus to such a network and who measures its response to that stimulus is performing some kind of nonlinear analysis—whether he intends to do so or not, and whether he likes it or not. If so, why not go all the way and apply the most rigorous, most sophisticated, most comprehensive methods of nonlinear analysis that are available?

One can think of many reasons why one should do so and why one should not do so—some personal, some practical. On the personal side, there is the matter of taste, which cannot be disputed; some people simply do not wish to use mathematics in their research, and others do. As far as practical problems are concerned we have seen that the difficulties in the application of nonlinear analysis are numerous and enormous. As Werner Heisenberg (1967) put it in a discussion of nonlinear problems in physics

> it has been argued that every nonlinear problem is really individual, that is, it requires individual methods, usually very complicated and difficult methods, and it is rather improbable that one can learn from one nonlinear problem to solve another nonlinear problem.

However, one thing the history of science teaches us is not to defer to authority. Every nonlinear problem may be individual, but nevertheless it is rather probable that one can learn from one nonlinear problem to solve another related nonlinear problem—which is the situation we face in the comparative study of the neurophysiology of vision.

Another practical problem is that there are many visual systems from which it may not yet be possible to obtain data of the necessary quality to carry out an exact mathematical analysis, even of the relatively simple linear type. In addition, some systems do not lend themselves to currently available techniques of stimulus control, data collection, and data analysis. Finally, the intent of the researcher and the purpose of his experiment may not be best served by, or benefit most from, the application of rigorous mathematical analyses. This is especially true in early phases of exploratory work, where qualitative accounts may be far more informative than a premature quantitative analysis. Moral: Apply mathematical techniques when and where there is some likelihood that they are appropriate and will be productive.

It is my view that once proper techniques have been developed and a sound empirical foundation of quantitative data has been established, the great power and utility of applied mathematics is indispensable in the study of information processing by the visual system. Indeed, in our own experience over the past quarter of a century, a continued interplay between collection of empirical psychophysiological data and formulation of abstract mathematical models has been very productive. I have endeavored to show in this paper that the mathematical model is but one of many experimental tools and techniques, which, in concert, have a synergistic action—each enhances the contributions of all the others. By following this procedure of reciprocal interaction between theory and experiment the mathematical model does not degenerate into a form of mental masturbation that is pursued for its own pleasures and delights, and experimental data are not collected willy-nilly without motivation or purpose. Instead, the model guides the collection of data and the collection of data shapes the model. In my opinion, an understanding of the complex functions of the nervous system can only be achieved by equally complex methods of analysis, some of which are already in use and others of which, although not in use, are readily available in various well-known fields of applied mathematics. Nevertheless, present methods of applied mathematics may very well turn out to be inadequate to achieve a full understanding of information processing by the visual system. This leads to my final point.

D The Organic or Holistic Approach

The currently popular analytic and reductionistic approach to biology in general, and to neurophysiology in particular, has great strengths and numerous accomplishments. Unfortunately, it also has great weaknesses and numerous failures. The major weaknesses and most glaring failures appear to result from an inability to make the transition from a mechanistic approach to an organismic one. For example, in vision we know a

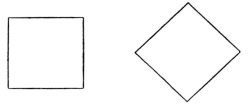

Figure 3.39. Two simple figures that are geometrically congruent appear to be quite different. Few persons immediately recognize the geometrical congruence of these two identical squares without performing some mechanical or intellectual operations. We have no real understanding of the physiological basis of the apparently simple perception of the form of a square or why the forms of these two geometrically congruent squares appear different. (Redrawn after Mach, 1914.)

great deal about the biochemistry of the photoreceptors, about the biophysics of generation and conduction of optic-nerve impulses, and about the interplay of excitation and inhibition over synaptic interconnections among neurons. Furthermore, we even understand much about the form and function of some fairly complex neural networks in the visual system. However, we know next to nothing about organic or holistic problems of vision—such as the perception of form (Figure 3.39).

The difficulty may be, as Elsasser (1975) has put it, that in the physical sciences—broadly defined—theory is almost without exception mathematical theory. There is the widespread idea in science (especially in physics) that theory and application of mathematics are coextensive. Biological theory, however, although essentially abstract, may not be such that it can always be cast into some familiar, already existing mathematical form. This does not mean, however, that biological data cannot be ordered and structured in terms connected by logical operations that may even turn out to be superior to and of a higher form than current systems of mathematics. The problem may simply be that the necessary higher forms of "biological mathematics" and "biological logic" required to deal with the complex problems of organic form and organic function in the brain do not yet exist and remain to be invented.

Such an impasse is not unusual in the history of science. Major developments in mathematics have been made "on demand," as it were, on many occasions. It may be that the intense and increasing interest in the rapidly developing field of the neurosciences will "demand" the development of new forms of mathematics and logic that are better suited to the organic and holistic character of some aspects of this area of research: For "like is known only by like."

Acknowledgment. This research has been supported, in part, by research grants from the National Eye Institute Nos. EY 188, EY 1428, and EY 1472.

Appendix

A   Linear Analysis of *Limulus* Retina[7]

The rate r of discharge of optic-nerve impulses from a particular photore-ceptor unit is a function of several variables, principally, but not exclu-sively, intensity I and wavelength λ. By explicitly representing the influ-ence of these named variables (and implicitly allowing for the inclusion of the influence of many others not named) we may write a simple equation:

$$r = f(I, \lambda, \ldots \ ). \qquad (3.A.1)$$

Because various combinations of these and other variables resulted in equal rates r and so belonged to the same stimulus equivalence class, we concluded (and later proved by experiment) that they all influenced some common excitatory process (ϵ). Therefore, we may rewrite equation (3.A.1) in a simpler and more inclusive form:

$$r = \epsilon. \qquad (3.A.2)$$

We know that illumination of neighboring photoreceptor units dimin-ishes the rate of discharge of the test unit. We call this decrease inhibition (i). To determine the ultimate rate of discharge r we subtract i from ϵ:

$$r = \epsilon - i. \qquad (3.A.3)$$

This apparently simple equation expresses the essence of the interplay of excitation and inhibition in the *Limulus* retina. However, the lumped terms ϵ and i contain (and conceal) a number of complex processes. Con-sider the basic structural and functional organization of the *Limulus* ret-ina summarized in Figure 3.9. Light incident on the retina produces an intracellular voltage change (the generator potential). Changes in the in-tracellular potential also result from self- and lateral inhibition. These voltages sum to produce a net intracellular potential—the input to the impulse-generating mechanism. The trains of nerve impulses generated are conveyed along the optic nerve as the output of the retina and as the input to the brain. These same nerve impulses serve as input to the self- and lateral-inhibitory processes, which feed back into the retina. The steady-state response of this system is summarized by the so-called Hart-line–Ratliff equations (Hartline & Ratliff, 1957, 1958; Knight et al., 1970; Stevens, 1964):

$$r_m = \epsilon_m - K_s r_m - \sum_{n \neq m} k_{m \leftarrow n} \cdot (r_n - t_{m \leftarrow n})_+, \qquad (3.A.4)$$

where r_m is the response of the mth receptor unit, ϵ_m is the "excitation" of the mth receptor unit (a function of the illumination incident on it), K_s is the self-inhibitory coupling constant, $k_{m \leftarrow n}$ is the coupling constant for the inhibitory effect of the nth receptor unit on the mth receptor unit,

---

[7] Adapted from Brodie et al. (1978a,b).

$t_{m \leftarrow n}$ is the threshold for this inhibitory effect, and the notation $(\ )_+$ indicates the piecewise linear operator such that $(x)_+ = x$, $x > 0$; $(x)_+ = 0$, $x < 0$.

The self-inhibitory feedback loop is not accessible to separate analysis in the input–output experiments summarized here. The impulse generator may therefore be combined with the self-inhibition into a single transduction, which we refer to as the "encoder." Therefore, equation (3.A.4) takes on an apparently simpler form:

$$r_m = e_m - \sum_{n \neq m} k_{m \leftarrow n} \cdot (r_n - t_{m \leftarrow n})_+, \qquad (3.A.5)$$

where $e_m = \epsilon_m - K_s r_m$.

In the time-varying situation, the same block diagram in Figure 3.9 applies, but the various quantities in the equations must be reinterpreted. First, we restrict attention to stimuli that cause all the receptor units to fire impulses at a rate that fluctuates about some mean level above their inhibitory thresholds. The input and output variables are redefined to indicate the deviation from the mean value, rather than the absolute magnitude, of the stimulus or response. With these conventions, we may completely ignore the threshold terms (Ratliff et al., 1974). The coupling coefficients are also redefined to consider the response to signals that vary sinusoidally in time (Knight, 1973; Knight et al., 1970). By virtue of the linearity of the system, each portion of the visual transduction (generator potential, encoder, lateral inhibition) will respond to such an input with a sinusoidal output, according to its own transfer function. (See R.B. Barlow & Lange, 1974; Lange, 1965; Ratliff et al., 1974, for a discussion of nonlinearities in the *Limulus* retina.) We treat each stage of the visual transduction in turn. First, consider the excitatory component of the generator potential:

$$\epsilon_m(t) = G(\omega) I_m e^{i\omega t}, \qquad (3.A.6)$$

where $G(\omega)$ is the light-to-generator potential transfer function, and $I_m e^{i\omega t}$ is the illumination incident on the mth ommatidium. The net intracellular potential V_m is the sum of this excitation and the total lateral inhibition:

$$V_m(t) = \epsilon_m(t) - T_L(\omega) \cdot \sum_{n \neq m} k_{m \leftarrow n} r_n(t). \qquad (3.A.7)$$

This equation has been written so as to incorporate the experimental observation (Ratliff, et al., 1974) that all the inhibiting receptor units show the same temporal transfer function for lateral inhibition, which we denote $T_L(\omega)$. [In equation (3.A.7), $V_m(t)$ and $r_n(t)$ are functions of time proportional to $e^{i\omega t}$.] Finally, the impulse-train output is related to the net potential V_m according to the formula

$$r_m(t) = E(\omega) V_m(t), \qquad (3.A.8)$$

where $E(\omega)$ is the transfer function of the encoder, including impulse generation and self-inhibition. Equations (3.A.6)–(3.A.8) can be combined to obtain a dynamic equation analogous to the static equations (3.A.4) and (3.A.5):

$$r_m(t) = E(\omega) \left[G(\omega) \cdot I_m e^{i\omega t} - T_L(\omega) \cdot \sum_{n \neq m} k_{m \leftarrow n} r_n(t) \right]. \qquad (3.A.9)$$

Relation (3.A.9) is an explicit inhomogeneous set of simultaneous linear equations that may be solved for the $r_m(t)$ in terms of the stimulus pattern I_m. Generally it is more convenient to work instead with a continuous version of this system (Kirschfeld & Reichardt, 1964). To this end, we restrict our attention (as in Figure 3.15) to stimuli that vary in space only along the x axis (and so at any time t are constant along any vertical line). Further, we assume that each ommatidium in a given vertical column responds in the same way to such a stimulus. We may now replace the discrete index m with the continuous variable x, the horizontal coordinate along the eye. With this notation, equation (3.A.9) may be replaced by a corresponding integral equation,

$$r(x,t) = E(\omega) \left[G(\omega)I(x)e^{i\omega t} - T_L(\omega) \int k(x - u)r(u,t)du \right], \qquad (3.A.10)$$

where we have incorporated the experimental observation that, at least away from the edges of the eye, the inhibitory coupling between two (vertical strips of) ommatidia depends—to a good approximation—only on the distance between them (Barlow, 1969). In other words, the inhibitory kernel takes the translation-invariant form $k(x,u) = k(x-u)$.

The spatiotemporal transfer function may be obtained from equation (3.A.10) by taking as input a sinusoidal grating $I(x) = e^{i\xi x}$. The response to such a sinusoidal input must be a sinusoidal signal of the form $r(x,t) = F(\xi,\omega)e^{i(\xi x + \omega t)}$, where $F(\xi,\omega)$ is, by definition, the spatiotemporal transfer function of the system. (For reviews and recent experimental and theoretical papers see Brodie et al., 1978a,b; Dodge et al., 1970; Graham, Hartline, & Ratliff, 1972; Knight et al., 1970; Ratliff, 1974; Ratliff et al., 1974).

B Nonlinear Analysis of Neural Networks[8]

This paper has reported on a "sum-of-sinusoids" method of nonlinear analysis. From the neural response to a sinusoidal spatial grating that is amplitude modulated by a sum of several sinusoids one can calculate the first-order frequency response to individual input frequencies and the second-order response to pairs of input frequencies. The first-order frequency response $K_1(f)$ is the transfer function of the linear system that

---

[8] Adapted from Victor et al. (1977).

best approximates the nonlinear system under study. If one is studying a
linear system, then the first-order frequency response (or kernel) is just
the transfer function of that system (*Limulus* eye, Figure 3.18; cat X cell,
Figure 3.31). The second-order frequency response $K_2(f_1,f_2)$ describes the
dynamics of a second-order system that best approximates the system under investigation (e.g., cat Y cell, Figure 3.31). This joint response
(or frequency kernel) $K_2(f_1,f_2)$ is closely related to the Fourier transform
of the second-order Wiener kernel (Wiener, 1958). The frequency kernel
$K_2(f_1,f_2)$ is easy to interpret (see Figures 3.31 and 3.32). The kernel represents the amount of nonlinear response produced by the system because
of the presence of a sinusoid at the frequency f_1 and a sinusoid at the frequency f_2. For a linear system, where there is no "crosstalk" between the
input frequencies, $K_2(f_1, f_2) = 0$.

The temporal modulation signal used in the experiments reported in
this paper is a periodic signal composed of a sum of several sinusoids (as
in Figure 3.16). This modulation signal has been chosen because (1) its
values are distributed approximately as a Gaussian distribution, (2) it has
a power spectrum that spans a broad frequency band, and (3) the discreteness of the input frequencies leads to a corresponding discreteness
in the output frequencies. This latter property allows digital filtering of
frequency-response components. When this modulation signal is used,
one observes the effect of nonlinearities by measuring components in the
response at harmonics and at combination frequencies. Linear transduc-
tions would yield only responses at the input set of frequencies. A qua-
dratic nonlinearity would produce in addition response components at
sums and differences of the input frequencies.

This technique requires a judicious choice of input frequencies so that
the first- and second-order responses can be isolated by Fourier analysis.
If there are N input frequencies, then they must be chosen so that one
can resolve the following N^2 combination frequencies: N second harmonics, $\frac{1}{2}N(N - 1)$ sum frequencies, and $\frac{1}{2}N(N - 1)$ difference frequencies. These frequencies must also be distinct from the N fundamental response frequencies. There are many frequency sets that satisfy this
condition.

If such a set is chosen, all fundamental and second-order response frequencies are distinct. Fourier analysis of the nerve-impulse train suffices
to determine each of the fundamental and second-order response components. The second-order response to each pair of input frequencies f_1 and
f_2 appears at a separate pair of output frequencies $f_1 \pm f_2$. The amplitude
and phase shift measured at each of these output frequencies defines a
single value of the experimentally determined second-order frequency
kernel. The amplitude and phase at $f_1 + f_2$ defines the value of $K_2(f_1,f_2)$;
the amplitude and phase at $f_1 - f_2$ defines the value of $K_2(f_1,-f_2)$.

Contour maps (Figures 3.31 and 3.32) of the amplitude of the second-
order frequency kernel $K_2(f_1,f_2)$ were constructed in the following way.
Cartesian coordinates were chosen that were proportional to the loga-
rithm of the frequencies f_1 and f_2 over the range of the input frequencies.

In the range from zero to the lowest frequency used, the Cartesian coordinates were made linear. The laboratory measurements furnished values of the amplitude of $K_2(f_1,f_2)$ at discrete points within this two-dimensional coordinate system. In principle, the values on the line $f_2 = -f_1$ are not measurable. Therefore, they were approximated by averaging neighboring values. The values of the amplitude at all other points where there was no experimental evaluation were interpolated by a standard two-dimensional cubic spline procedure. On theoretical grounds, the amplitude of $K_2(f_1,f_2)$ remains unchanged if f_1 and f_2 are either interchanged or else are both changed in signature. Because of this symmetry the behavior of the amplitude over the entire plane is determined by its behavior within the wedge between the lines $f_2 = f_1$ and $f_2 = -f_1$. For easier interpretation, the contour maps were plotted on the full right half-plane. Therefore, there are two lines of reflection: One runs diagonally through the upper half of the graph at $f_2 = f_1$ (the second-harmonic diagonal), and the other runs diagonally through the lower half of the graph at $f_2 = -f_1$ (the zero-frequency diagonal).

The second-order frequency kernel is closely related to the Fourier transform of the second-order Wiener kernel. If the system under study has no response components beyond first order (linear) and second order, the correspondence between our frequency kernel and the Wiener frequency kernel is exact. If the system does have higher order response components, then our second-order frequency kernel contains contributions from Wiener frequency kernels of higher order. If the input frequencies were infinite in number and incommensurate, then these higher order contributions would vanish. On theoretical grounds, six or eight is a large enough number of sinusoids of incommensurate frequency to make higher order contributions to the second-order frequency kernel negligible. The fact that we have used sinusoids with commensurate frequencies results in a deviation of another kind: Some higher order combination frequencies of the input frequencies must coincide with the second-order frequencies.

This problem can be countered by presenting the input sinusoids with different relative phases and appropriately averaging the second-order responses. This procedure yields a frequency kernel that is extremely close to the Fourier transform of the second-order Wiener kernel. The lowest order response frequencies whose effects on a second-order response frequency are not canceled are those of order eight.

For mathematical details of the temporal sum-of-sinusoids method and applications in vision research see Brodie et al. (1978a,b); Shapley et al. (1978); Victor (1979); and Victor & Knight (1979); and Victor et al. (1977).

References

Adrian, E.D., & Matthews, R. The action of light on the eye, Part III. The interaction of retinal neurones. *Journal of Physiology* (London) 1928, 65, 273–298.

Barlow, H.B. Summation and inhibition in the frog's retina. *Journal of Physiology* (London) 1953, *119*, 69–88.

Barlow, H.B. Single units and sensation: A neuron doctrine for perceptual psychology. *Perception*, 1972, *1*, 371–394.

Barlow, H.B., & Levick, W.R. The mechanism of directionally selective units in the rabbit's retina. *Journal of Physiology* (London), 1965, *178*, 477–504.

Barlow, R.B., Jr. Inhibitory fields in the *Limulus* lateral eye. *Journal of General Physiology*, 1969, *54*, 383–396.

Barlow, R.B., Jr., & Lange, G.D. A nonlinearity in the inhibitory interactions in the lateral eye of *Limulus*. *Journal of General Physiology*, 1974, *63*, 579–589.

Barlow, R.B., Jr., & Quarles, D.A., Jr. Mach bands in the lateral eye of *Limulus*. Comparison of theory and experiment. *Journal of General Physiology*, 1975, *65*, 709–730.

Békésy, G. von. *Experiments in hearing*. New York: McGraw-Hill, 1960.

Brodie, S.E., Knight, B.W., & Ratliff, F. The responses of the *Limulus* retina to moving stimuli: Prediction by Fourier synthesis. *Journal of General Physiology*, 1978a, *72*, 129–166.

Brodie, S.E., Knight, B.W., & Ratliff, F. The spatio-temporal transfer function of the *Limulus* lateral eye. *Journal of General Physiology*, 1978b, *72*, 167–202.

Campbell, F.W., Howell, E.R., & Robson, J.G. The appearance of gratings with and without the fundamental Fourier component. *Journal of Physiology*, 1971, *217*, 17P–19P.

Colas-Baudelaire, P. Digital picture processing and psychophysics: A study of brightness perception. Thesis, University of Utah, 1973.

Corballis, M.C., & Beale, I.L. *The psychology of left and right*. New York: John Wiley & Sons, 1976.

Cornsweet, T. *Visual perception*. New York: Academic Press, 1970.

Craik, K.J.W. *Visual adaptation*. Thesis, Cambridge University, Cambridge, England, 1940.

Craik, K.J.W. *The nature of psychology: A selection of papers, essays, and other writings* (Ed., S.L. Sherwood). Cambridge: Cambridge University Press, 1966.

De Valois, R.L., Morgan, H., & Snodderly, D.M. Psychophysical studies of monkey vision. III. Spatial luminance contrast sensitivity tests of macaque and human observers. *Vision Research*, 1974, *14*, 75–81.

Dodge, F.A., Jr. Inhibition and excitation in the *Limulus* eye. In W. Reichardt (Ed.), *Processing of optical data by organisms and by machines*. Proceedings of the International School of Physics "Enrico Fermi," Course XLIII. New York: Academic Press, 1969.

Dodge, F.A., Jr., & Kaplan, E. Visual fields in the *Limulus* eye. *Biophysical Journal*, 1975, *15*, 172a.

Dodge, F.A., Jr., Knight, B.W., & Toyoda, J. Voltage noise in *Limulus* visual cells. *Science*, 1968, *160*, 88–90.

Dodge, F.A., Jr., Shapley, R.M., & Knight, B.W. Linear systems analysis of the *Limulus* retina. *Behavioral Science*, 1970, *15*, 24–36.

Edmondson, M. *The witch's egg*. New York: Houghton Mifflin Clarion Books, 1974.

Elsasser, W.M. *The chief abstractions of biology*. Amsterdam: North-Holland, 1975.

Fleischer, E. Zur Physiologie des Flaechensehens. *Zeitschrift der Psychologischen Physiologie der Sinnesorgane*, I, 1939, *145*, 45–111.

Fry, G.A. Mechanisms subserving simultaneous brightness contrast. *American Journal of Optometry and Archives of the American Academy of Optometry*, 1948, Monograph, 45, 1–17.

Gerrits, H.J.M., & Vendrick, A.J.H. Simultaneous contrast, filling-in process and information processing in man's visual system. *Experimental Brain Research*, 1970, *11*, 411–430.

Graham, C.H. The relation of nerve response and retinal potential to number of sense cells illuminated in an eye lacking lateral connections. *Journal of Cellular and Comparative Physiology*, 1932, 2, 295–310.

Graham, N., & Ratliff, F. Quantitative theories of the integrative action of the retina. In R.C. Atkinson, D.H. Krantz, R.D. Luce, & P. Suppes (Eds.), *Contemporary developments in mathematical psychology*. San Francisco: Freeman, 1974.

Griffing, R.P., Jr. *The art of the Korean potter*. New York: The Asia Society, 1968.

Hartline, H.K. Inhibition of activity of visual receptors by illuminating nearby retinal areas in the *Limulus* eye. *Federation Proceedings*, 1949, 8, No. 1, p. 69. (Abstract)

Hartline, H.K., & Graham, C.H. Nerve impulses from single receptors in the eye. *Journal of Cellular and Comparative Physiology*, 1932, *1*, 277–295.

Hartline, H.K., & Ratliff, F. Inhibitory interaction of receptor units in the eye of *Limulus*. *Journal of General Physiology*, 1957, 40, 357–376.

Hartline, H.K., & Ratliff, F. Spatial summation of inhibitory influences in the eye of *Limulus*, and the mutual interaction of receptor units. *Journal of General Physiology*, 1958, *41*, 1049–1066.

Hartline, H.K., & Ratliff, F. Inhibitory interaction in the retina of *Limulus*. In M.G.F. Fuortes (Ed.), *Handbook of sensory physiology* (Vol. VII, part 2). Berlin: Springer-Verlag, 1972.

Hartline, H.K., Ratliff, F., & Miller, W.H. Inhibitory interaction in the retina and its significance in vision. In E. Florey (Ed.), *Nervous inhibition*. New York: Pergamon Press, 1961.

Heggelund, P., & Krekling, S. Edge-dependent lightness distributions at different adaptation levels. *Vision Research*, 1976, *16*, 493–496.

Heisenberg, W. Nonlinear problems in physics. *Physics Today*, 1967, *20*(5), 27–33.

Herbert, R.L. *Neo-impressionism*. New York: The Solomon R. Guggenheim Museum, 1968.

Hochstein, S., & Shapley, R.M. Quantitative analysis of retinal ganglion cell classifications. *Journal of Physiology*, 1976, 262, 237–264. (a)

Hochstein, S., & Shapley, R.M. Linear and nonlinear spatial subunits in Y cat retinal ganglion cells. *Journal of Physiology*, 1976, 262, 265–284. (b)

Hood, D.C., & Whiteside, J.A. Brightness of ramp stimuli as a function of plateau and gradient widths. *Journal of the Optical Society of America*, 1968, 58, 1310–1311.

Huggins, W.H., & Licklider, J.C.R. Place mechanisms of auditory frequency analysis. *Journal of the Acoustical Society of America*, 1951, 23, 290–299.

Julesz, B. *Foundations of cyclopean perception*. Chicago: University of Chicago Press, 1971.

Kelly, D.H. Adaptation effects on spatio-temporal sine-wave thresholds. *Vision Research*, 1972, *12*, 89–101.

Kirschfeld, K., & Reichardt, W. Die Verarbeitung stationärer optischer Nachrichten im Komplexauge von *Limulus*. *Kybernetik*, 1964, 2, 43–61.

Knight, B.W. The horseshoe crab eye: A little nervous system whose dynamics are solvable. In J.B. Cowan (Ed.), *Lectures on mathematics in the life sciences. 6. Some mathematical questions in biology*. Providence: American Mathematical Society, 1973.

Knight, B.W., Toyoda, J., & Dodge, F.A., Jr. A quantitative description of the dynamics of excitation and inhibition in the eye of *Limulus*. *Journal of General Physiology*, 1970. 56, 421–437.

Krausz, H., & Friesen, W.O. Identification of discrete input nonlinear systems using Poisson impulse trains. In G.D. McCann and P.Z. Marmarelis (Ed.), *In Proceedings of the first symposium on testing and identification of nonlinear systems*. Pasadena: California Institute of Technology, 1975.

Kuffler, S.W. Discharge patterns and functional organization of mammalian retina. *Journal of Neurophysiology* (London), 1953, 16, 37–68.

Lange, D. Dynamics of inhibitory interaction in the eye of *Limulus*. Experimental and theoretical studies. Thesis, The Rockefeller University, New York, 1965.

Lee, Y.N., & Schetzen, M. Measurement of the kernels of a nonlinear system by cross-correlation. *International Journal of Control*, 1965, 2, 237–254.

Mach, E. Über die Wirkung der räumlichen Vertheilung des Lichtreizes auf die Netzhaut. *Sitzungsberichte der mathematisch-naturwissenschaftlichen Classe der kaiserlichen Akademie der Wissenschaften*, 1865, 52, 303–322.

Mach, E. Über die physiologische Wirking räumlich vertheilter Lichtreize, III. *Sitzungsberichte der mathematisch-naturwissenschaftlichen Classe der kaiserlichen Akademie der Wisschenschaften*, 1866, 54, 393–408.

Mach, E. Über die physiologische Wirkung der räumlichen Vertheilung des Lichtreizes auf die Netzhaut. IV. *Sitzungsberichte der Wiener Adademie der Wissenschaften*, 1868, 57, 11–19.

Mach, E. *Popular scientific lectures*. Chicago: Open Court Publishing House, 1898.

Mach, E. *The analysis of sensations and the relation of the physical to the psychical* (C.M. Williams, trans.; revised by S. Waterlow). Chicago: Open Court Publishing House, 1914.

Marmarelis, V.Z. Identification of nonlinear systems through multilevel random signals. In G.D. McCann and P.Z. Marmarelis (Eds.), *Proceedings of the first symposium on testing and identification of nonlinear systems*. Pasadena: California Institute of Technology, 1975.

O'Brien, V. Contour perception, illusion and reality. *Journal of the Optical Society of America*, 1958, 48, 112–119.

Patel, A.S. Spatial resolution by the human visual system. The effect of mean retinal illuminance. *Journal of the Optical Society of America*, 1966, 56, 689–694.

Paley, R., & Wiener, N. *Fourier Transforms in the Complex Domain*. Providence: American Mathematical Society, 1934. (Reprinted in 1960.)

Purple, R.L. The integration of excitatory and inhibitory influences in the eccentric cell in the eye of *Limulus*. Thesis, The Rockefeller University, New York, 1964.

Purple, R.L., & Dodge, F.A., Jr. Interaction of excitation and inhibition in the eccentric cell in the eye of *Limulus*. *Cold Spring Harbor Symposia of Quantitative Biology*, 1965, 30, 529–537.

Ratliff, F. Inhibitory interaction and the detection and enhancement of contours. In W.A. Rosenblith (Ed.), *Sensory communication*. Cambridge, Mass.: Massachusetts Institute of Technology Press, 1961.

Ratliff, F. *Mach bands: Quantitative studies on neural networks in the retina*. San Francisco: Holden-Day, 1965.

Ratliff, F. Contour and contrast. *Proceedings of the American Philosophical Society*, 1971, *115*, 151–163.

Ratliff, F. The logic of the retina. In M. Marois (Ed.), *From Theoretical Physics to Biology*. Basel: S. Karger, 1973.

Ratliff, F. (Ed.). *Studies on excitation and inhibition in the retina. A collection of papers from the laboratories of H. Keffer Hartline*. New York: The Rockefeller University Press, 1974.

Ratliff, F. On the psychophysiological bases of universal color terms. *Proceedings of the American Philosophical Society*, 1976, *120*, 311–330.

Ratliff, F. Color, contrast, and contour: Some remarks on relations between the visual arts and the visual sciences. *Neurosciences Research Program Bulletin*, 1977, *15*, 349–357. (a)

Ratliff, F. Remarks on some relations between the visual arts and the visual sciences. In H. Spekreijse and L.H. Van Der Tweel (Eds.), *Spatial contrast: Report of a workshop*. Amsterdam: North-Holland, 1977. (b)

Ratliff, F. A discourse on edges. In J.S. Armington, J. Krauskopf, & B. Wooten (Eds.), *Visual psychophysics: Its physiological basis*. New York: Academic Press, 1978.

Ratliff, F., Hartline, H.K., & Miller, W.H. Spatial and temporal aspects of retinal inhibitory interaction. *Journal of the Optical Society of America*, 1963, *53*, 110–120.

Ratliff, F., Knight, B.W., Dodge, F.A., Jr., & Hartline, H.K. Fourier analysis of dynamics of excitation and inhibition in the eye of *Limulus*: Amplitude, phase, and distance. *Vision Research*, 1974, *14*, 1155–1168.

Ratliff, F., Knight, B.W., & Graham, N. On tuning and amplification by lateral inhibition. *Proceedings of the National Academy of Sciences* (U.S.), 1969, *62*, 733–740.

Ratliff, F., Knight, B.W., & Milkman, N. Superposition of excitatory and inhibitory influences in the retina of *Limulus*: The effect of delayed inhibition. *Proceedings of the National Academy of Sciences* (U.S.), 1970, *67*, 1558–1564.

Ratliff, F., Knight, B.W., Toyoda, J., & Hartline, H.K. Enhancement of flicker by lateral inhibition. *Science*, 1967, *158*, 392–393.

Ratliff, F., & Sirovich, L. Equivalence classes of visual stimuli. *Vision Research*, 1978, *18*, 845–851.

Ratliff, F., Victor, J.D., & Shapley, R.M. Nonlinear analysis of visual evoked potentials in the human. *Journal of the Optical Society of America*, 1978, *68*, 1427.

Rodieck, R.W., & Stone, J. Response of cat retinal ganglion cells to moving patterns. *Journal of Neurophysiology*, 1965, *28*, 819–832.

Shapley, R., & Rossetto, M. An electronic visual stimulator. *Behavior Research Methods and Instrumentation*, 1976, *8*(1), 15–20.

Shapley, R.M., So, Y.T., & Victor, J. Nonlinear systems analysis of retinal ganglion cells and visual evoked potentials in the cat. *Journal of the Optical Society of America*, 1978, *68*, 1427.

Shapley, R., & Tolhurst, D. Edge detectors in human vision. *Journal of Physiology*, 1973, *229*, 165–183.

Shiffman, H., & Crovitz, H.F. A two-stage model of brightness. *Vision Research*, 1972, *12*, 2121–2131.

Sirovich, L. Boundary effects in neural networks. *SIAM Journal of Applied Mathematics*, 1980, *39*/*I*, in press.

Sirovich, L., Brodie, S.E., & Knight, B.W. The effects of boundaries on the responses of a neural network. *Biophysical Journal*, 1979, 28, 423–446.

Spekreijse, H., & Oosting, H. Linearizing: A method for analyzing and synthesizing nonlinear systems. *Kybernetik*, 1970, 7, 22–31.

St. Cyr, G.J., & Fender, D.H. Nonlinearities of the human oculomotor system: Gain. *Vision Research*, 1969, 9, 1235–1246.

Stevens, C.F. A quantitative theory of neural interactions: Theoretical and experimental investigations. Thesis, The Rockefeller University, New York, 1964.

Tolhurst, D.J. On the possible existence of edge detector neurons in the human visual system. *Vision Research*, 1972, 12, 797–804.

Victor, J.D. Nonlinear systems analysis: Comparison of white noise and sum of sinusoids in a biological system. *Proceedings of the National Academy of Sciences* (U.S.), 1979, 76, 996–998.

Victor, J.D., & Knight, B.W. Nonlinear analysis with an arbitrary stimulus ensemble. *Quarterly of Applied Mathematics*, 1979, 37, 113–136.

Victor, J.D., & Shapley, R.M. Receptive field mechanisms of cat X and Y retinal ganglion cells. *Journal of General Physiology*, 1979, 74a, 275–298.

Victor, J.D., & Shapley, R.M. The nonlinear pathway of Y ganglion cells in the cat retina. *Journal of General Physiology*, 1979, 74b, 671–689.

Victor, J.D., Shapley, R.M., & Knight, B.W. Nonlinear analysis of cat retinal ganglion cells in the frequency domain. *Proceedings of the National Academy of Sciences* (U.S.), 1977, 74, 3068–3072.

Walls, G. The filling-in process. *American Journal of Optometry*, 1954, 31, 329–340.

Wiener, N. *Nonlinear problems in random theory*. New York: John Wiley & Sons, 1958.

Wiener, N., & Hopf, E. *Über eine Klasse singulärer Integralgleichungen*. Sitzungsberichte der Preussischen Akademie, Mathematisch-Physikalische Klasse, 1931, pp. 696–706.

Discussion

Dr. McFadden: What is the message in all this for psychologists? Today, and in the past, you have cautioned us that the difference in complexity between the *Limulus* eye and the mammalian eye is extraordinary and that we should be very cautious in rapidly applying what you have documented in the *Limulus* eye to the more complicated eyes. In the face of this caution, you know that psychologists have been eager almost to the point of recklessness to apply the simple lateral-inhibitory networks that you describe to just about everything that comes by. Here today, you show us that if you take as your transfer function the eye of the *Limulus*, and you pass Craik–O'Brien–Cornsweet-type figures through it, what you get out is exactly what's in accord with perception of . . . who? Not of *Limulus*, but of us. So the question is, what is the psychologist to presume from this? He knows that every receptive field in his own visual system, the mammalian visual system, is like the transfer function of the entire eye of the *Limulus*. The fact that you get such good predictions of our perception by passing these stimuli through such a simple transfer function, what does it mean to us? Should we be out looking for stimuli that are equivalent in appearance to our eye even though they differ in their physical fine structure, then work backward to try and deduce what the modulation transfer function that we must be using in that situation is?

Dr. Ratliff: I think one answer is that there is some functional overlap between the very simple visual systems and the more complex ones, and that overlap results because practically all of these visual systems have a local excitatory effect along with some broader reaching opposing inhibitory effect. (They may even be reversed in the vertebrate retina, but you always do have this basic relationship of opposed influences.) It seems to be a very powerful and a very pervasive functional relationship, and it seems to me very likely you're going to find effects that can be interpreted, at least loosely and to a very rough first approximation, in the same general terms. But when you begin to look at the details more carefully, the species differences begin to emerge. What I showed as an equivalence class for *Limulus* was actually not even for the *Limulus* retina, it was for a still simpler model of the real network. One could find other stimuli which would be similar for this network, but which for the human would not look similar at all. I chose these particular stimuli to emphasize the point I wanted to make about the Craik–O'Brien–Cornsweet types of illusions. I think the merit in such comparative studies of human and *Limulus* is the same as it has been since Hartline and Graham worked together 50 years ago. It's largely heuristic. One idea leads to another. One doesn't expect that findings on humans and on *Limulus* have to agree or that what you see in any one species has to explain what's going on in any other species. What you observe in one species aids your interpretation of what you observe in another. Consider, for example, the reciprocity of intensity and time. Psychophysical experiments had been done on that problem long before Hartline did similar experiments on *Limulus*. In the study of quantum fluctuations, the ideas also went back and forth between human studies and *Limulus* studies, but there was no thought at all in anyone's mind that there was any strict one-to-one correspondence between what they were seeing in *Limulus* electrophysiological experiments and what they were seeing in human psychophysical experiments. The parallels between the two served as an idea factory more than anything else. The only thing that turned out to be identical, or nearly so, in the human experiments and in the *Limulus* experiments was the pigment. The measurements that Graham and Hartline made on *Limulus* were later shown by Hubbard and Wald to be characteristic of rhodopsin, and thus there was good reason for Graham and Hartline's 1935 measurements to look almost identical to the human scotopic visibility curve; essentially the same photopigment is involved. That's one of the rare cases where the electrophysiological results on *Limulus* were essentially identical to the psychophysical results on humans.

Dr. McFadden: Is there a class of psychophysical data that is absent from the literature? That is, is there a set of things that you wish you could go look up and find out about when you're examining your mathematical models?

Dr. Ratliff: When we first started doing evoked-potential experiments, we went to the literature to compare our results with psychophysical work on spatial gratings. I was surprised to find how many lines had already been cut across, but even so it didn't seem to make a very tight knit. Each investigator had done a very thorough job in the particular area that he worked on but it cut across here, and somebody else did another job that cut across there, and somehow or other—at least in my limited knowledge of the literature—it didn't seem to coalesce. I wish there were some psychophysical methods that would help us organize all this material in some more systematic way. Maybe there already exist a lot of organizing principles in the work on spatial gratings that I'm just not up to date on.

Dr. Barlow: It may initially seem surprising that *Limulus*, the human, the frog, and the cat should all have Mexican hat-shaped receptive fields, but perhaps this is not so surprising. Obviously the mechanism is very different in the three of them—one has a compound eye, others have simple eyes, and so on. But if there's a common requirement that has to be met, maybe it's not so surprising. I'm thinking of the fact, for example, that if you look across vertebrate eyes you find the independent formation of reflecting tapetum done by a whole host of different actual substances. In one it's collagen, in another it's riboflavin crystals or something extraordinary, and crocodiles are something different again. When you have to do something, there are not many different ways of achieving the same result. In this case, why is it that one has to have a Mexican hat-shaped receptive field in the periphery? Why do you have to have that inhibitory network? Do you want me to give my answer or do you want to give your answer?

Dr. Ratliff: Well, I'll give my answer. I think it's along the lines you've suggested—that there is a requirement for processing certain kinds of information and that most animals share this requirement.

Dr. Barlow: What is that requirement?

Dr. Ratliff: It's largely the detection of changes in time and space. Principally changes, because most animals are not much interested in the steady state. You can think of exceptions, but for the most part, survival depends on knowing that a change is taking place. For example, that here is the edge of an object—a change in space from light to dark—or that something that's stationary has suddenly changed its intensity or color. In short, animals need to know where things are and what they are. Think of excitation and inhibition in a completely abstract sense. If you convolve the Mexican hat function with an edge in either time or space, you are going to obtain maxima and minima in the result. The changes are accentuated relative to the steady states. You see this technique everywhere: physical systems, Xerography, photography, all share it. Astronomers use this technique to sharpen images, and so on. What you're suggesting is the answer. There is a requirement for the animal to get information about changes alone out of more complex information, much of which is not useful; and a Mexican hat type of neural network is a good way of doing it. There are literally thousands of different mechanical, neural, chemical, and other methods for doing something like this. Nature makes use of a good many of them and engineers invent more all the time. But most all of them reduce to a narrow center and broad surround of opposed influences similar to the *Limulus* retina.

Dr. Barlow: That's what I had hoped you would say, except that there's one addition I would make and that is that in both cases, the output channels have a very limited dynamic range. Otherwise this requirement wouldn't be nearly so stringent. It's because of the very limited range nerve fibers have that it's so important.

Dr. Ratliff: There are many obvious economies one can think of that the sense organs might benefit from.

Dr. Barlow: Long time ago, *Limulus* seemed to have two diameters of nerve fiber coming from each ommatidium. Does it still have two diameters of nerve fiber and do they both work?

Dr. Ratliff: At one time you could embarrass me with such questions, but you can't anymore. What I've called a photoreceptor unit here (only to simplify matters, it isn't called that in the technical papers) is actually a cluster of several cells, one eccentric cell, which looks sort of like a fist with one finger sticking up, and then several retinular cells clustered around it. Each one of those retinular cells has an axon and so does the eccentric cell. We record from the eccentric cell axon. No one to my knowledge, and for what reason I don't know, has ever successfully recorded from retinular cell axons. You can record from retinular cell bodies, but not from the axons. Also, one of our former students, Robert Barlow, has recently found fibers that go from the brain out to the eye. I don't think they are the ones that you and I are thinking of because there's only a small number of them. Furthermore, one can record their activity and it has been found that they have something to do with some diurnal changes in sensitivity. Finding neurons one can't record from is a perpetual embarrassment for all electrophysiologists and my only answer is that you can't record from all the cells in the retina or the brain of vertebrates either. But to answer your question about the retinular cell axons—we don't know what they do, and neither does anyone else.

Dr. Boynton: Floyd, I was very surprised, in fact almost shocked, to hear toward the end of your talk that your laboratory is studying visual evoked cortical potentials. This might be telling tales out of school, but it seems to me that I remember your saying with respect to the electroretinogram —and I think you were thinking of human ERGs and some of the literature that was coming out several years back—that there ought to be a hundred-year moratorium on the recording of ERGs, which led me to conclude that you weren't all that enthusiastic about that method. Now, the VECP is certainly more complicated than the human electroretino-gram. Would you say a few words about your assessment of what has been accomplished so far in this area and where it's likely to go, either with or without the techniques that you people have introduced?

Dr. Ratliff: I think the field is changing rapidly and that its possibilities have not yet been completely tested by all of the more powerful new approaches and techniques. I've said, more or less facetiously, that the field of visual evoked cortical potentials is a wilderness to me. Most people who've been working in it for a good many years don't find it to be quite the wilderness that I do. Maybe after we do a few more experiments, and if something systematic doesn't start showing up, I will have to repeat the statement about a moratorium which I made to you a long time ago. Actually, I think the investigation of cortical potentials is soon going to be very productive because the new methods of stimulus control and of data analysis are much more powerful than those which were available a few years ago. Only time will tell.

CHAPTER 4

Cortical Function: A Tentative Theory and Preliminary Tests

Horace B. Barlow

In this paper I am going to pose the question "What does the cortex, and especially visual cortex, do?" The problem is more puzzling than many people realize, and it is especially tantalizing not to be able to answer it in spite of the fact that many laboratories throughout the world routinely record from single cortical neurons. As a tentative answer the hypothesis is advanced here that the sensory cortex does not simply represent sensory information but extracts knowledge from it; this requires the application of statistical tests to the activities of associations of neurons in order to sift out the reliable signals in the representation. Finally, I shall describe some psychophysical measurements we have made of how well, in absolute terms, such decisions are made and shall suggest tentative neural mechanisms.

This work depends on statistical decision theory and gives answers in terms of absolute efficiency. Neither of these is new, and some people will doubtless regard reliance upon them as a pedantic refinement that adds little to commonsense study of perception. However, if I am on the right lines in postulating that the extraction of knowledge is what the cortex does, the only sensible way to measure its performance is by finding how well, in absolute terms, it performs that task. It is only by making such measurements that we can define the true abilities and limitations of that remarkable organ.

1 The Problem of Cortical Function: A Comparison with Retina

There are good reasons why cortical function is proving difficult to comprehend, and these are best brought out by making a comparison. When neurophysiologists first recorded the activity of single retinal ganglion cells it was already known in broad terms what task these cells must perform. The eye gathers information about the environment from the light entering its pupil, and the task of the retina must be to transmit this information from the retinal image that contains it to the parts of the brain that need it. There was, furthermore, a fund of knowledge about how well this task was performed, and this posed a host of good questions that could usefully be answered. We respond visually to a few quantal absorptions: How are these messages transmitted up the optic nerve? We can resolve down to a minute of arc and judge position to within a few seconds: How is this spatial accuracy achieved? Similar questions arise with regard to other visual capacities, such as color discrimination, temporal resolution, incremental sensitivity, dynamic range, and the variations of visual performance with retinal eccentricity. Some of these questions have now been satisfactorily answered, and this has given much deeper insight into what the retina does, as we shall shortly see. However, neurophysiologists who record from cortical neurons are in a radically different position from the retinal neurophysiologists of 30 years ago, because we do not have even the first hint of a sensible theory of cortical function.

There are really two reasons for slow progress. The first is the existence of parallel visual pathways, which makes it difficult to know if the cortex is necessarily involved in a particular visual act. By comparison, the optic nerve is a bottleneck; the eye must pass all its information through the retinal ganglion cells, and everything we see in the world around us is derived from their signals. If we can perform a particular visual task we know with certainty that the messages of retinal ganglion cells enable us to do so, but because of the parallel visual pathways we cannot be sure that the cortex is involved. The other difficulty is our lack of expert guidance in how to measure performance at the kind of task we think the cortex performs; we shall return to this.

The principal parallel pathway is the midbrain system consisting of the optic tectum (also called superior colliculus) with its direct connection from retinal ganglion cells. This is the best developed part of the visual system in lower vertebrates, and it is thought to provide them with optomotor reactions, the ability to identify and localize prey, and perhaps even with their abilities to avoid obstacles and orient themselves in their surroundings. Until recently the role of midbrain vision in mammals, with their well-developed geniculocortical system, was underestimated. However, Sprague and Meikle (1965) showed how serious a defect of vision was caused by destroying the colliculus in cats, and subsequent work has shown that cats with their geniculostriate system destroyed and only their midbrain system intact can perform many of the simpler tests of visual function almost as well as can normal cats (Berkeley & Sprague, 1979). This has led to the doctrine that there are two visual pathways (Held, 1968; Ingle, 1967; Schneider, 1967; Trevarthen, 1968), the midbrain system answering the question "where," and the geniculocortical system the question "what." The doctrine seems to hold true in primates

(Humphrey, 1974; Weiskrantz, 1972), and the visually guided behavior of a monkey with its striate cortex almost totally ablated is, after a lapse of many months, not easy to distinguish from that of a normal monkey by simple observation. The where/what distinction is still upheld, however, for it is not suggested that destriate animals have anything approaching the pattern- and object-recognizing capacities of normal animals; they still cannot distinguish a carrot from a snake.

The reassessment of midbrain vision has been carried through to humans (Pöppel, Held, and Frost, 1973; Weiskrantz, Warrington, Sanders, & Marshall, 1974), and a new aspect of the problem has emerged. A hemianopic patient may be totally unable to "see" test objects or stimuli in a large segment of his visual field; yet though he says he cannot see an object, the patient may be able to point accurately at it with his finger. The fact that without a functional cortex the patient can use visual information, but does not know he has this information, is of course most intriguing for the hypothesis that visual cortex extracts knowledge from the representations it receives. It seems to offer powerful support, but I feel myself that one must be careful not to be misled by words on this point, for it is hard to deny that a person who can point to an object has visual knowledge of it, at least on some definitions of knowledge. However, this striking phenomenon of "blindsight" is certainly fully compatible with the current hypothesis about the cortex, provided we add the qualification that the knowledge that is said to be extracted is what we recognize as ordinary, conscious knowledge, not the kind of "knowledge" that a migrating bird or well-programmed automatic device possesses.

The second reason for slow progress in understanding the cortex is that the best quantitative tests of visual function are aimed at the instrumental capacities of the visual system, not at the interpretive functions we know it also performs. We understand the eye as a physical, image-forming, and transducing device, and such quantitative measures as tests of sensitivity and resolution are aimed at testing these aspects of its function. If we were buying a television camera, these would be the appropriate tests to rate it by, because we simply want to *transmit* a picture. However, the visual system also *interprets* the picture; we no longer have physics to guide us about the limits of such capacities, and a different approach, which will be described later, is required to measure them.

Finally, it needs to be stressed that neurophysiological methods do not allow one to understand function instantly. It has been 50 years since the first recordings were made from the optic nerve (Adrian & Matthews, 1927a,b), and 40 years since the first from single retinal ganglion cells (Granit & Svaetichin, 1939; Hartline, 1938), but in spite of their position at a bottleneck in the informational pathway, and in spite of the firm background of knowledge in optics, photochemistry, and psychophysics, there are still gaps and contradictions in our understanding of retinal function.

Not only has progress been slow, but there have been many quite unforeseen surprises as the story has unfolded. Let us recall a few. No one had foretold that there would be "off" as well as "on" fibers (Adrian & Matthews, 1927a,b; Granit & Svaetichin, 1939; Hartline, 1938). It took two decades for the measured thresholds of neurophysiological preparations to come down to a figure of the same order of magnitude as psychophysical thresholds (Barlow, FitzHugh, & Kuffler, 1957; Pirenne, 1954) and another decade before the spatial resolution of retinal ganglion cells began to be reconciled with that of intact animals (Enroth-Cugell & Robson, 1966). Even now the transmission of color information is most puzzling, for neurophysiologists suggest that complementary colors are linked in opposition very much as Hering suggested (De Valois & Jones, 1961; Svaetichin & MacNichol, 1958), whereas at least one recent account of the perception of colors (Land & McCann, 1971) seems to require that the three color channels be kept well separated up to a very high level. It should also be remembered that the opponent spatial organization of vertebrate receptive fields was pretty much of an empirical discovery (Barlow, 1953; Kuffler, 1953), as was selective sensitivity to direction of movement (Barlow, Hill, & Levick, 1964; Maturana & Frenk, 1963) and also the possibility that the frog's fly detectors attained their selectivity as early as the retina (Barlow, 1953; Lettvin, Maturana, McCulloch, & Pitts, 1959). In addition, it should be recalled that the intercommunication of the cells of the retina by graded potentials, not propagated impulses, was pretty well unsuspected until intracellular recordings were made from identified elements (Dowling & Werblin, 1969; Werblin & Dowling, 1969).

Progress in the retina has been slow, has taken turns in unforeseeable directions, and is still incomplete. We must expect the cortex to be even more difficult, but it seems to me that our inability to answer that very first question—"What does cortex do?"—is a major hindrance; if it could be answered, progress might be rapid, and the main purposes of this essay are to suggest an answer and a way to test it.

2 What the Cortex Does: An Hypothesis

The most obvious function performed by our sensory system is to provide us with a continuous stream of new knowledge about the world around us. Every student nowadays thinks of this process in terms of bursts of nerve impulses arriving in the topographical maps of sensory surfaces in the cerebral cortex. However, these messages do not constitute new knowledge: They represent sensory events and are merely the raw material from which new knowledge can be derived. In the same way a scientist's measurements and meter readings, even when recorded in a notebook, do not constitute new knowledge until they are interpreted. If we want to understand cortical function we cannot be content with the *representation* of sensory events in the cortex; we must look into this process of *interpreting* messages to acquire new knowledge.

That process of interpretation is statistical. R.A. Fisher (1925) said "Inductive inference is the only process known to us by which essentially new knowledge comes into the world." Because our senses undoubtedly provide us with new knowledge, we cannot ignore this process of inductive inference—unless, of course, we can successfully refute Fisher's claim. By induction Fisher meant drawing valid inferences from statistical data, an operation that he did as much as anyone has done to refine and introduce to other scientists. What this implies is that a statistical, decision-making component is interposed between the simple representation of sensory stimuli by volleys of impulses and the creation of new knowledge, which is what sensation and perception are all about. It is a reasonable hypothesis that this interpretive decision-making step occurs in the cerebral cortex.

Before I become more specific about these steps and discuss how they can be measured and may be performed, some general remarks are required. The first is simply to point out that the cortex is a surprisingly uniform anatomical structure (see Braitenberg, 1977; Mountcastle, 1978). It has always been very hard to believe that large parts of this uniform structure, the primary sensory projection areas, simply present sensory information in much the same way that a television screen represents an optical image, whereas other parts of this same structure are responsible for those higher intellectual processes that make humans preeminent. If the cortex is an organ for making statistical decisions, this may go some way toward rectifying the difficulty, for there is a decision-making element in simple sensory awareness, as there is in the exercise of intelligence. The hypothesis postulates that the whole cortex is engaged in one type of task, one that is required in complex judgements as well as simple perception.

However, one must not suppose that everything that goes on in the cortex is automatically specified by such phrases as "statistical decisions" or "extracting knowledge." There is some indication, for instance, that the first step taken in the visual cortex is the creation of a finer grained version of the retinal image by a process of spatial interpolation, and compensation for movement by temporal interpolation (for brief review, see Barlow, 1979). There is also evidence that some form of spatial frequency analysis occurs in visual cortex (Barlow & Sakitt, 1979; Cowan, 1977; Robson, 1975) and it is certain that an important role of the primary visual cortex is to relay information about parts of the image to other parts of the cortex, to the thalamus, and to the midbrain. Interpreting the image is a general task, and much detail needs to be specified before it can be claimed that we know how it is done.

The final remark concerns the relation between the hypothesis being advanced here and signal detection theory as applied to psychology by Swets, Tanner, Birdsall, Green and others (see Swets, 1964). The relation is a close one. Signal detection theory was based on statistical decision theory and came to psychology by way of electrical engineering and the problems encountered in radar (see, for instance, the Introduction to Swets, 1964). I actually came to nearly the same problems by a slightly different route. As an undergraduate I read and was overwhelmingly impressed by Fisher (1925, 1935). Then, as a graduate student I met Woodward in a group that met to discuss information theory, read his work (Woodward, 1953), and was again impressed by the importance of these concepts to sensation, perception, and cognition. As a result, in the early days of signal detection theory I advanced the idea that sensory thresholds should be regarded as our brain's attempt to make a statistical decision of constant fallibility (Barlow, 1957), and the current hypothesis is the direct descendent of that idea.

The present work makes use of signal detection theory, and is partly derived from it, but differs in one respect. The emphasis of much of the research in that area has been simply on the techniques of measuring human performance and I fear some people regard signal detection theory as unnecessary pedantry that adds very little to what can be obtained from a commonsense look at the results. The current hypothesis says that statistical decisions are the main business of the cerebral cortex; the commonsense look at the results only works because the cortex does the same job as the signal detection theorist. On this view statistical decision theory is not just a tool for measurement, but is also a model instructing us on the nature of the task the cortex is performing. I am not using it, in the experiments I shall outline, to obtain greater accuracy or to ward off pedantic critics, but because what I want to measure can only be measured by its use.

One further point. Signal detection theory has been mainly concerned, as its name implies, with the detection process: "Is something present or not?" Statistical decision theory is concerned with the broader question of whether hypotheses are correct or not. Hypotheses often deal with a more complex proposition than the presence or absence of a signal and, in particular, they are often concerned with associative properties of the data being examined. Associative properties of sensory signals, such as motion, collinearity, binocular disparity, and symmetry, are prominent in perception, and statistical decision theory may help us to understand the kind of operations that are necessary to detect them reliably.

The first step is to describe how to measure statistical decision making, then to show examples of its application in perception. If the hypothesis is on the right lines, we expect the statistical efficiency of perception to be high, for nature is not incompetent and it would be foolish to service an effective optical instrument with an inefficient statistical computing system.

A   How To Measure Statistical Decision Making

Fisher (1925) defined the efficiency of the statistics used for a decision as follows. The liability to error of a statistical decision depends on the size of the sample on which it is based: the larger the sample, the greater the reliability and the fewer the errors. However, not all statistical methods are equally good, and a bad method will give more errors than a good one, using the same sized sample. Hence, if one wishes to obtain reliable results using a bad method, one must increase the sample size to compensate, and this leads to Fisher's definition of the efficiency of a method as:

$$F = \frac{\text{minimum sample required}}{\text{sample necessary in method used}} \left.\rule{0cm}{0.9cm}\right\} \text{ for obtaining results of given reliability.}$$

This is the same as the measure of efficiency given by Tanner and Birdsall (1958), and before them it was used by Rose (1942) in the case where the source of statistical variation lay in quantum fluctuations. Hecht, Shlaer, and Pirenne's well-known work (1942) can be regarded in this way, and a number of subsequent workers have made absolute measures of efficiency of detecting and discriminating weak lights (Barlow, 1962a,b; Clark-Jones, 1959; van Meeteren, 1978). Although it has long been known that the performance on simple detection tasks is not too far short of the limit imposed by quantum fluctuations, the best estimate of the fraction of quanta actually absorbed in photoreceptors is now considerably higher than was previously thought. As a result it now appears probable that the central mechanisms are only about 50% efficient (Barlow, 1977).

Thus we already know that on simple signal detection tasks quite high efficiencies can be obtained, but to do this requires little more than good transduction in the periphery and the maintenance of a steady criterion centrally. The hypothesis implies that the cortex makes statistical decisions about complex associative properties of sensory events, and if it is correct, the measured efficiencies in performing such tasks should also be high. Test situations must then be devised such that:

1. Inefficiencies of peripheral transduction are avoided.
2. The decisions are about something more complex than simple detection.

The first of the following experiments shows how problem 1 can be solved, and the second set gives some results on symmetry, which certainly seem to fulfill the second requirement.

B   Experiments on Dot Density

Uttal (1975) has argued that bright dots in an oscilloscope display are efficiently transmitted centrally, so that the detection of regularities in the display depends on intermediate levels of processing in the visual system, which probably means visual cortex. Consider the random dot displays of Figure 4.1. Each black dot is a bright spot on an oscilloscope and it provides easily enough quanta to excite the retinal receptors and cause a message to be transmitted centrally. What makes it difficult to detect the excess of dots in the center, as in Figure 4.1C, is the fluctuation in the number of dots in this central area due to their random positioning and the difficulty of delimiting this area from the remainder. The average number in the central square (Figure 4.1B) is 16, but this is subject to fluctuations with standard deviation $\sigma = 4$. An excess of 80 dots is 20 times σ and is easily detected, whereas an excess of 20 (5 times σ) is harder to see and would be missed in some examples (Figure 4.1C).

To obtain a figure for the efficiency of detecting targets such as those shown in Figure 4.1 we have most often proceeded as follows. The parameters for two populations of targets are chosen: For instance, one population may have zero average excess of dots in the center, the other an average excess of 20; or the first may have an excess of 10, the other an excess of 30. The subject then sits at a keyboard viewing a computer display and calls for samples from the two populations by pressing the appropriate key. He is given every assistance in learning how to distinguish the two populations. After the subject thinks he can distinguish them as well as he is ever likely to be able to, the subject calls for an experimental series of 100 unknowns. These the subject attempts to classify, and from the numbers correct for each population the value of d' is calculated in the normal way. We call this d'_E, the experimental d', and it may be helpful to regard it as an estimate of the signal-to-noise ratio of whatever quantity

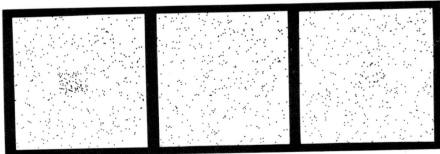

Figure 4.1. Example of a task for which statistical efficiency of perception is readily measured. There are a total of 400 randomly placed dots over the whole area, and the average number in the central square of area 1/25 the whole is 16, with standard deviations ± 4 in a population of examples, such as the middle one. To the left 80 dots ($20 \times \sigma$) have been added to the center square, and this is readily detectable in very nearly every example. To the right 20 dots ($5 \times \sigma$) have been added, and in this case a few errors would be made in classifying examples from such a population and one with zero excess. If the average difference is less, more mistakes are made, and d'_E can be calculated. The ideal d'_I is simply obtained from the ratio of excess dots to standard deviation, and the efficiency F is given by $F = (d'_E/d'_I)^2$.

it is in the nervous system that enables the two populations to be separated.

In the simple situation exemplified here the highest attainable signal-to-noise ratio for distinguishing the two populations is simply $\Delta N/\sigma_N$, where ΔN is the average excess of dots in the target area and σ_N is the standard deviation of the number in this area. Calling this the ideal d'_I, efficiency is simply

$$F = \left(\frac{d'_E}{d'_I}\right)^2. \tag{4.1}$$

This is the same as η defined by Tanner and Birdsall (1958), and the rationale is described more fully in Barlow (1978). Thus, using the methods of signal detection theory, one can readily measure efficiencies of the type defined by Fisher (1925).

My colleagues and I have measured such efficiencies for a good many conditions where the target is simply a region of raised density of randomly placed dots, and the results are easy to summarize. The highest consistently attainable efficiencies are around 50%, except in special circumstances when the number of dots can be counted exactly. This figure can be attained for targets subtending about 1°–5°, and van Meeteren and I have shown that it is also reached for sinusoidal modulations of dot density over a wide range of spatial frequencies. However, in this case efficiency declines if the sinusoid contains more than three to five cycles. Efficiency was no higher for bar-shaped targets than for square ones. Comparable figures were obtained with an experimental setup that produced dynamic noise backgrounds with targets of various shapes and sizes appearing for variable durations. For high efficiencies, target durations of about 1/10 sec were required, and efficiency declined dramatically for long durations. More details of these experiments are given in Barlow (1978).

What does all this mean? Well, in the first place, 50% is quite a high figure, so our suspicion was correct that nature's skill would not desert her in designing a machine for making reliable decisions. What may be involved at a neural level will be discussed later, where it will be shown that these judgements of dot density do not demand an elaborate mechanism. For this reason I moved on to more complex judgements.

C Quantitative Measures of Texture and Pattern Discrimination

The type of task to be considered next is that of detecting the regularities shown in Figure 4.2. A number of dots are placed entirely at random, as in Figure 4.2A; then a pair is placed for each dot according to some regular scheme. In Figure 4.2B it is reflected in the vertical midline; in Figure 4.2C it is displaced a constant distance up and to the right; and in Figure 4.2D it is displaced away from the center and rotated counterclockwise. As

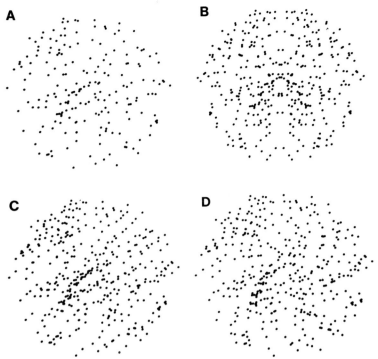

Figure 4.2. Examples of readily perceived patterns among random dots. In (A) 100 dots have been placed entirely at random. In (B) each dot has been repeated at its mirror position about the midline vertical axis. In (C) each dot is repeated at a constant distance up and to the right. In (D) each dot is repeated on an outward, counterclockwise spiral path. The regular feature of each pattern is readily perceived. (From Barlow & Reeves, 1979; see also Glass, 1969.)

Glass (1969) has pointed out, the regular feature of such patterns springs to the eye, whereas the irregularity of Figure 4.2A creates no strong impression; indeed it is such a weak impression that it takes a few moments to confirm that Figure 4.2A is contained twice in each of Figures 4.2B, C, and D.

Everyone will agree that these Glass figures are perceptually salient, but by itself that does not tell one very much about the mechanisms necessary for detecting them; one needs to know how good one is in absolute terms, so the aim of the experiments (done with B. Reeves) that I shall now outline has been to obtain a measure of efficiency similar to those I have described for dot density (for more details see Barlow and Reeves, 1979). The form of symmetry we have investigated most thoroughly is mirror symmetry, as in Figure 4.2B. The reason for that choice was that we were attracted by the global nature of this task; the left edge of Figure 4.2B has to be linked with the extreme right edge of the figure for its symmetry to be recognized, and such global operations seem to require something more than one is accustomed to thinking about in neurophysiological terms. (By the way, I can give no evidence that the cortex is necessary for performing the tasks of either Figure 4.1 or Figure 4.2, but I expect most of you would share my intense surprise if it were ever to be shown that monkeys with area 17 destroyed could reliably detect the symmetry of Figure 4.2B.) We first found out a number of properties of the symmetry-detecting mechanism, of which the most important is its versatility. The axis need not be vertical and need not be in the midline for such figures as Figure 4.2B to be reliably discriminated from random arrays in a brief exposure.

Determining the efficiency requires knowledge of the accuracy with which paired dots can be recognized as symmetrical: Suppose this were very high; then there would only be a very small chance of finding a dot in the symmetrical position, and the detection of one or a few such pairs would be incontrovertible evidence of symmetry. If, in contrast, the accuracy were low, then the probability of finding a pair of dots within the mirror tolerance ranges of each other would be high, even if all dots were placed entirely at random. Furthermore, the statistical variations in the numbers of accidental or spurious pairs puts a theoretical limit to the completeness with which a paired population can be discriminated from a completely random one. What we did experimentally was to generate patterns in which the paired dot was placed in a tolerance range as in Figure 4.3 and to see how the subject's performance was affected. The results are shown in Figure 4.4. Because we know how the symmetrical patterns have been made, we can define a near-optimal method for discriminating them from random patterns and compare the human subject's performance with this optimum for various tolerance ranges.

The results (Figure 4.4) show two points of interest: First that efficiencies as high as 25% can be achieved, and second that this occurs with surprisingly large tolerance ranges—the symmetry-detecting mechanism is

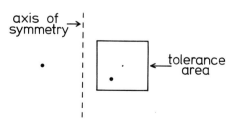

Figure 4.3. Scheme for producing inaccurate symmetry. Instead of the left-hand dot being mirrored at the correct position on the right, it is placed at a randomly chosen position within a tolerance area centered on the correct position. As the tolerance area is increased, "spurious" pairs occur because extra dots are likely to fall by chance within the tolerance areas. These spurious pairs introduce errors in the detection of symmetry, and ideal d_i' values can be determined. Subjects can detect symmetry readily when the tolerance areas are of the order $\frac{1}{2}° \times \frac{1}{2}°$, and efficiency is then about 25%. (From Barlow & Reeves, 1979.)

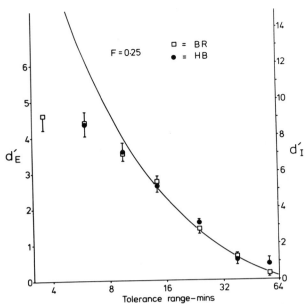

Figure 4.4. Values of d'_E for distinguishing between random displays and ones produced as in Figure 4.3, with tolerance range plus or minus the abscissa value both vertically and horizontally. The continuous line represents the values of d'_I obtained by computer simulation (referred to the ordinate scale at the right). For tolerance ranges above about ±12' this simulation fits the experimental points, and $d'_I = 2 \times d'_E$; hence $F = 25\%$. (From Barlow & Reeves, 1979.)

efficient, but tolerant, or not very precise. With regard to the efficiency, it would be a mistake to regard this as the ultimate performance of the mechanism because we have not tried to carry the optimization of the tolerance range very far; higher figures are likely if elliptical tolerance ranges are used, and it is almost certainly far from optimal to use the same tolerance range close to the axis of symmetry and far from it. To get the best performance, the system of generating the patterns should be matched to the human system for detecting symmetry, and this must surely demand greater accuracy for dots lying close to the axis and hence close together than for dots spaced far apart.

The optimal method for determining symmetry involves searching through the $n(n - 1)/2$ pairs of dots and counting those pairs that qualify for the tolerance range being used. With $n = 100$ or so, this is quite a formidable task, and not one for which it is easy to contemplate a neural mechanism. Do not forget that this type of symmetry is readily detected in a single fixational pause, with no searching eye movements; the 4,950 eye movements required to search all pairs would actually take some time to accomplish!

One clue to how it is done may lie in the lack of precision or, to put it differently, the magnitude of the tolerance range. Instead of taking all

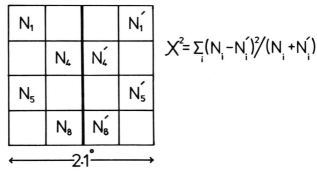

Figure 4.5. Model of scheme for detecting symmetry. The picture area is divided into 16 smaller squares within each of which the numbers of dots are counted. If symmetry about the midline were absent, the difference between mirror-pair- areas $|N_i - N_i'|$ would be distributed with variance $N_i + N_i'$. χ^2 can be formed as indicated, and low values will be indicative of symmetry. This scheme should work well even when the tolerance range (Figure 4.3) for producing symmetry is large, as it is in the human perceptual system.

pairs of dots, suppose the 2.1° square in which the dots are placed is divided up into 16 smaller squares, each of which is $32' \times 32'$ and therefore comparable to the tolerance range for which the eye performs most efficiently. A statistician asked to test whether there was evidence of symmetry about the midline might proceed as follows. If there is no symmetry, then symmetric pairs will show no dependence on each other, and their difference should have a variance equal to twice their mean, which is their sum; therefore, we can do a χ^2 test by summing $(N_i - N_i')^2/(N_i + N_i')$ for all the eight pairs N_1, N_1' to N_8, N_8' (see Figure 4.5). If the dots are placed completely at random, $N_i + N_i'$ is correct for the variance of the difference, and the expected value of χ^2 is 7, the number of degrees of freedom. If pairing were exact, N and N' would necessarily be equal for all pairs of squares, the postulated variance would be much too high, and χ^2 would be zero. With inexact pairing χ^2 will rise, and to discriminate paired from random, one would take a criterion value of χ^2 such that errors of the two kinds were approximately matched.

The dotted curve in Figure 4.6 shows the results of this model, obtained by computer simulation. It gives a surprisingly good fit, but this does not force one to believe that the same details necessarily apply in the nervous system. Before I propose possible neural mechanisms for symmetry detection I shall discuss much simpler tasks.

D Possible Neural Mechanisms of Statistical Decision Making

In order to make a statistical decision one needs a hypothesis and some data or results. The appropriate calculation yields the probability, p, of obtaining the data, or more extreme data, if the hypothesis is correct. All

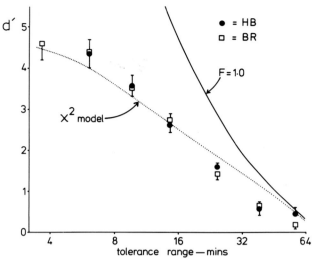

Figure 4.6. Dotted line shows the predictions of the χ^2 model of Figure 4.5. The continuous line shows ideal performance, using the left-hand ordinate.

psychologists are familiar with this process, and if the nervous system is to be thought of as making statistical decisions, the first step is to suggest correspondences for the hypothesis, the data, the probability p, and the criterion.

It is clear that the nervous system must utter a decision by the firing of a neuron, so we are led to regard the firing of a cortical neuron as saying something about the significance of data, given a hypothesis. For a neuron in a primary projection area, "data" must be the sensory messages being received by that particular neuron, and its "hypothesis" would be determined by the particular form of selective sensitivity it possessed—by its trigger feature. The "criterion" would correspond to the threshold of the neuron, but because a graded number of impulses can be emitted, we can regard the cell as signaling some inverse measure of the probability p; for instance, the number of impulses might be approximately proportional to $-\log p$. In this way the selection of the criterion value of p could be deferred to a later element.

Table 4.1 shows the correspondences outlined above. One might summarize the hypothesis by saying it suggests that the vigor with which a sensory neuron fires indicates the certainty of a particular pattern feature being present in the current sensory input.

To illustrate the concept consider Figure 4.7. This shows the results of calculations (Barlow, 1969) of how the impulse frequency would vary with light intensity for a pair of such certainty signalers whose trigger features were an increase, and a decrease, in the illumination of a small patch of visual field. To rephrase these as null hypotheses, for the "on" unit this would be, "There has been no significant increase in the illumi-

Table 1. Hypothetical Correspondences between Statistical Decision Theory and Sensory Neurophysiology

Statistical Decision Theory	Neurophysiology	Ordinary Language
Results to be tested	Synaptic input to a neuron	Sensory stimuli being presented
Null hypothesis	That the trigger feature is *not* present	That the pattern of stimulation required to excite the cell is not being presented
Disproof of null hypothesis	The trigger feature is present	The pattern of stimulation evokes vigorous responses
Significance level (p)	The inverse of the synaptic drive (approximately)	Low values of p show that the trigger feature is present
Criterion value of p	Threshold for cell firing, or firing above a certain rate	Patterns close enough to trigger feature to cause a response
Numerical value of p	Frequency of firing F is inverse monotonic function of p, e.g., $F \doteq -\log p$	Degree of certainty about the presence of pattern

nation"; for the "off" unit, it would be "no significant decrease." In both cases the number of quantal absorptions in the very recent past would be compared with the numbers absorbed over a longer period. It was assumed that the retina was adapted to one of three steady levels, and then the illumination was transiently changed to another level nearby. The ordinates show $-\log p$, where for the "on" type (dashed lines), p is the prob-

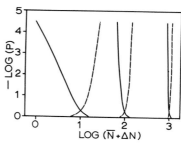

Figure 4.7. Certainty signals from idealized on (dashed lines) and off (solid lines) units. The three sets of intersecting lines refer to the hypothesized conditions that the unit is adapted to the absorption of an average of, from left to right, 10, 100, or 1,000 quanta per unit of time. The light is then assumed to be suddenly changed to values leading to a mean rate of absorption shown on the horizontal axis. The probability (p) of the new rate of quantal absorption occurring if the mean rate did not change is calculated, and $-\log p$ is plotted vertically. This is a measure of the certainty that the light was, in fact, turned on, or off, derived from the sensory events available to the certainty signaling unit. (From Barlow, 1969.)

ability of obtaining as *high* a value of quantum flux as that given by the abscissa value, on the hypothesis that there was really no change in mean quantum flux.[1] For the "off" type (solid line) p is the probability of obtaining as *low* a value if there was no change in mean luminance. Absolute certainty cannot be attained because of quantum fluctuations, so a quantitative measure of the degree of certainty derived from the physical events is the most useful information the retina can provide.

Figure 4.7 therefore shows how one might expect a neuron to behave if its function were to provide the basis for decisions about either an increase, or a decrease, of the light level in a particular part of the visual field. Now the interesting point is that retinal neurons do in fact behave in a similar manner, as shown in Figure 4.8. Both "on" and "off" types occur, they adapt as predicted, and the steepness of their responses increases with adaptation level. It should be added that they saturate, that the increase in slope with adaptation level is much less than it would be if they behaved as ideal certainty-signalers, and that they show surround inhibition which is omitted in the model. However, the similarity between Figures 4.1 and 4.2 is sufficient to encourage one in the notion that neuronal responses are approximations to certainty signals, even before the level of the cortex.

What has just been described would provide an ideal basis for making the simplest type of statistical decision: Does the value of a quantity lie outside the range of its own normal variation? A cortical cell whose task it was to make this decision would merely have to have a threshold so that it responded when the input indicated a significance value beyond criterion. The scheme could readily be extended to any linear function of the spatial pattern of image luminance. For instance, the varying quantity upon which the certainty signal is based could represent a local feature of the visual image, such as a bar or an edge, or a mathematical derivative, such as the coefficient of a particular spatial frequency of the Fourier transform of a domain of the image (Barlow & Sakitt, 1979; Cowan, 1977; Robson, 1975). The manner in which some retinal ganglion cells summate effects over their receptive fields can be described by the integrated product of light intensities with a spatial weighting function, at least to a first approximation (Barlow, 1953; Enroth-Cugell & Robson, 1966; Hartline, 1940) and such an operation could form a wide variety of mathematical derivatives. In particular there is no great difficulty in seeing how simple statistical decisions of the type illustrated in Figure 4.1 can be performed efficiently. First it would be necessary to have elements with receptive fields roughly matched to those sizes of target within which an

---

[1] The signal of certainty postulated here is very similar to what Edwards (1972) defines as "support," but it is based on the log of significance values rather than on the log of likelihoods. His method of support appears to meet logical difficulties of other systems of statistical inference and may provide a preferable basis for a comparison with the nervous system, but I have stuck to Fisherian significance levels because I am more familiar with them, as will be most readers.

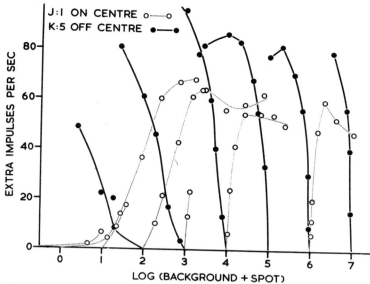

Figure 4.8. Cat retinal ganglion cells as certainty-signalers. The responses of an on- and an off-centre unit were measured for a light turned on and off for 1.28 sec. The luminance was held at an adaptation level indicated by the points where the lines cut the horizontal axis. A spot on the centre was turned on and off, and responses at on or off are plotted in impulses per second above the luminance resulting from spot and background together. These results have some features in common with those calculated in Figure 4.7. for an ideal "certainty-signaler." (From Barlow, 1969.)

excess of random dots can be efficiently detected. The population of dot densities or dot numbers with which a particular sample must be compared is readily available to the cell either by comparison with previous samples in the same area, or by comparison with neighboring samples. Comparisons of a very similar kind undoubtedly occur in the retina and are responsible for adaptation and lateral inhibition. One still requires a large number of parallel elements in order to detect targets of the variety of sizes and shapes that can be detected, but the difficulties do not seem unimaginable, whereas there are other tasks that are very simple to achieve perceptually but for which it is extraordinarily hard to imagine the mechanism. This was the reason we undertook an analysis of symmetry detection.

How might the nervous system achieve the χ^2 analysis suggested in Figure 4.5? Obviously the model depicted there is incorrect in some respects, such as postulating square receptive fields, but these are not essential. I think a plausible neural model would incorporate the following features:

1. Integration over a considerable area (formation of N_1, N_1', etc.). In Fourier terms this would reduce sensitivity to high spatial frequencies

and greatly reduce the number of sample points required to represent the input pattern. Large, summating, receptive fields provide a paradigm.

2. Normalization of integrated quantities in terms of their variability. In the χ^2 model normalization is done for the variance of the difference between paired areas $(N_i + N_i')$, but it would be simpler, and probably equally good, to normalize each area according to the overall average variance, that is, to divide by $2\overline{N}$. Shunting inhibition is a possible mechanism for such normalization, and "gain control," such as is postulated in retinal adaptation, may provide a model. There is actually some evidence that the retinal output is normalized for the *standard deviation* of impulse rate rather than for the *mean* impulse rate, for standard deviation changes less than mean when the adaptation level is changed (Barlow & Levick, 1969). Some such normalization is essential when transmission lines with narrow dynamic ranges are used, a defect from which nerve fibers undoubtedly suffer.

3. Comparing paired areas and combining the results of such comparisons. Subtracting and squaring, as in the χ^2 model [i.e., forming $(N_i - N_i')^2$] is not neurologically implausible, for the interaction of center and surround in retinal ganglion cells is subtractive, and summing the outputs of parallel on-center and off-center paths could provide an analogy to squaring. For the statistician an alternative would be to look at the covariance of N_i and N_i', and compare this with the expected value if they were independent, although it is less easy to find a neural paradigm for this. Whatever sums are done, however, the worrying feature about this step is the necessity of forming quite separate sets of comparisons and combinations for each possible axis of symmetry.

4. Criterion setting. The pattern must be classified as symmetrical or nonsymmetrical according to whether the value obtained in Step 3 causes the firing of more or less than the criterion number of impulses in the neuron or group of neurons concerned.

The difficulty lies in Step 3, for plausible paradigms exist for the other steps. This problem is an anatomical one: How can the quantities that must be compared (N_i and N_i' in Figure 4.5) and summed $[\Sigma(N_i - N_i')^2]$ be brought together in one place? It is a feature of cerebral cortex that the great majority of connections between cells are local ones (Braitenburg, 1977; Fisken, Garey, & Powell, 1975) so it would seem to be necessary to bring close together in one small cortical region all the quantities N_i and N_i' corresponding to a particular orientation and position of the axis of symmetry.

E Cortex as an Associative Organ

At this point let me try to tantalize you with a hypothesis about the cortex that is almost banal in its simplicity and lack of novelty and yet may fit recently acquired neurophysiological knowledge better than is commonly realized. It is that the new function achieved in the cortex is the detection of the statistical association of pairs of events, and that the events must be represented within a millimeter or two of the cortical surface before their association can be so detected. Because there are $N(N - 1)/2$ pairs for every N events it immediately becomes clear why, in order to perform this function, the brain has had to develop its enormous globular skin, the neocortex, with a surface area approaching 0.5 m^2. Let us try to apply the idea to the visual cortex.

Primary Visual Cortex. We understand this better than any other part, thanks largely to Hubel and Wiesel (1977). The associated excitations of a pair of points in the visual field defines a line of a particular *orientation*, and orientational selectivity is the most prominent form of new pattern selectivity found in cortical neurons. Associated excitation of a pair of positions, one in each retina, defines a particular *disparity*, and disparity selectivity is also found. Associated excitation of a pair of points at successive instants defines a *direction of motion*, and cortical neurons show directional selectivity as well. Notice that all these are associations between events whose representations in the cortical map occur very close to each other, as a result of the topographic mapping of visual field on to visual cortex and the interleaving of right eye and left eye maps.

Because of our knowledge of the maturation of area 17 we are in a position to develop the associative hypothesis a little further. It seems that the ability to detect particular associations is impaired if they do not occur within a critical period occurring just after area 17 becomes functional, roughly from birth to 4 months in monkey. It therefore seems that the paired associations that the cortex detects are limited by both developmental and environmental factors (see Barlow, 1975; Hubel, Wiesel, & LeVay, 1977).

According to this view, primary visual cortex is the region where local spatial and temporal associations are detected, and it will be seen that a topographic map of the visual field is necessary for this, because only in a topographic map are neighborhood relations preserved; in a disorderly projection they would be lost. Other types of association exist in visual images, however, and it is crucially important to detect them. Prominent among these are color and movement, and perhaps texture. These are important because objects that move together probably belong together. A set of fragmentary contours edging across the field from right to left may all belong to a tiger slinking behind the bushes, and the two corner patches of blue on my desk represent all that is visible of my telephone directory. The importance of linking characteristics such as these is well known both to Gestalt psychologists, who try to define what is required for foreground–background distinctions, and to those concerned with automatic scene analysis. Symmetry is another such property. In my own mind I have thought of this as the "adjectival" problem. We may understand how the nervous system codes such simple properties as color and motion, and possibly such geometric properties as the orientation and termination of contours. But how can we combine them, how is the fact that an edge is *moving*, or *blue*, coded? Furthermore, if we wish to associate a blue triangle in one region of the visual field with a blue patch in another, how can this be done by a structure that requires the representation of sensory events within 1 mm of each other before it recognizes an association? The answer has to be an anatomical rearrangement of the representation of sensory events. There is scope for this in the relaying of information to peristriate visual areas.

Peristriate Cortex. Surrounding the visual cortex a host of new visual areas have been described by Allman and Kaas (1976) in owl monkey and by Zeki (1978) in rhesus. There is some degree of topographic order in these visual areas, and the dividing lines between one area and another is often marked by a reversal of the sequence of receptive-field positions. However, the receptive fields are characteristically much larger than in primary cortex and the magnification factor less. Consequently one cannot regard these as in any sense exact maps of the visual image.

Hubel and Wiesel have shown that orientation and ocular dominance are represented in a highly orderly manner in the microstructure of area

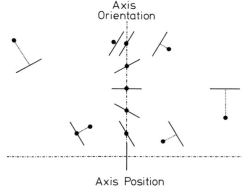

Figure 4.9. One is accustomed to thinking of the cortex mapping topographically the *position* of a feature in the visual field, but other properties could be mapped. In this hypothetical example the two coordinates correspond to position and orientation of an axis of bilateral symmetry in the visual field. For example, at the position in the cortical area corresponding to the line at lower left, all information required to test for symmetry about an axis oriented as shown and positioned down and to the left of the fovea (indicated by dot) would be brought together (see text). For the central line at the same level, the orientation of the axis of symmetry would be the same, but the position would now be central, and for the line to the right, the position of the axis would be up and to the right of the fovea. As the position in the map moves vertically, the orientation of the potential axis of symmetry changes. The scheme requires a formidable complexity and precision of intracortical connections, but we have an indication that a similar complexity can be achieved from Hubel and Wiesel's account of area 17 in the monkey. (From Hubel & Wiesel, 1977.)

17, whereas on a macroscopic scale the orderliness lies in the topographic mapping. It is unlikely that the same features are ordered in the same way in the peristriate regions, but it is surely inconceivable that they entirely lack order, and it will constitute a very important advance when the principles are discovered. Zeki's results may provide the first hint, for he finds that the regions vary in the proportions of units with different types of selectivity. For example, one region has a high proportion of units selective for movement, another a high proportion selective for color, and to these Hubel and Wiesel's neurons selective for disparity in the annectant gyrus may be thought to suggest a third area. The orderliness in these peristriate areas has not yet been discovered, however, and it may illustrate the notion to suggest the type of orderliness of microstructure that could lie behind the detection of symmetry. This is illustrated in Figure 4.9; each position in the map corresponds to a particular orientation and distance of a possible axis of symmetry from the foveal projection.

I am not sure how much value there is in this sort of speculative neurophysiology, but I have set it out all the same. One would hesitate to postulate such an extraordinarily intricate and orderly pattern of connections were it not for the equally intricate and orderly connectivity implied by the account of primary visual cortex given by Hubel and Wiesel (1977). However, there are two positive reasons for putting the scheme forward: First, to exemplify the kind of operation I think one must consider the cortex performing, namely, statistical tests for certain properties of the sensory stimulus; and second, to show that such tests could be performed by appropriately connected elements with the properties we know nerve cells possess.

3   Summary and Conclusions

It is argued that the lack of any overall concept of what cerebral cortex does hinders progress in analyzing its function. Sensory events are certainly represented in the cortex, but to obtain *knowledge* from a representation requires statistical decisions, because it is only by the process of induction that new knowledge can be created (Fisher, 1925).

It is shown that human subjects can make quite complex judgments on random dot patterns with high statistical efficiency; that is, they make use of a high proportion of the information that is available to them in performing the task. This is the case not only for a simple task, such as detecting a region of higher average density of random dots, but also for detecting bilateral symmetry in dot arrays, which requires a more elaborate statistical test.

Finally, some suggestions are put forward to show how nerve cells may perform statistical tests. Nerve cells are capable of making a great variety of specific connections and are capable of varying their response accord-

ing to laws such that their activity would resemble the result of a statistical calculation. Because the brain contains elements that can do the task,
and because we know from psychophysics that it is done, it is not unreasonable to suggest that the main role of the cortex is to extract knowledge
by applying statistical tests to the sensory information that is represented
there.

Acknowledgments. I started thinking seriously about the tasks performed
by the cerebral cortex while working with B. Sakitt on a theory of spatial
frequency filtering in the cortex, supported by NIH grant EY01336. It was
the realization that a specific task of this sort could hardly apply to the
cortex in general that led, in part, to the thoughts developed in this paper.
I am also much indebted to my colleagues Aart van Meeteren, Barney
Reeves, and Pete Mowforth for great help in the experimental (and some
of the theoretical) work reported here.

References

Adrian, E.D., & Matthews, R. The action of light on the eye: Part I. The discharge of impulses on the optic nerve and its relation to the electric changes in
the retina. *Journal of Physiology*, 1927, *63*, 378–414. (a)

Adrian, E.D., & Matthews, R. The action of light on the eye. Part II. The processes involved in retinal excitation. *Journal of Physiology*, 1927, *64*, 279–301. (b)

Allman, J.M., & Kaas, J.H. Representation of the visual field on the medial wall of
occipital-parietal cortex in the owl monkey. *Science*, 1976, *191*, 572–575.

Barlow, H.B. Summation and inhibition in the frog's retina. *Journal of Physiology*,
1953, *119*, 69–88.

Barlow, H.B. Increment thresholds at low intensities considered as signal/noise
discriminations. *Journal of Physiology*, 1957, *136*, 469–488.

Barlow, H.B. A method of determining the overall efficiency of visual discriminations. *Journal of Physiology*, 1962, *160*, 155–168. (a)

Barlow, H.B. Measurements of the quantum efficiency of discrimination in
human scotopic vision. *Journal of Physiology*, 1962, *160*, 169–188. (b)

Barlow, H.B. Pattern recognition and the responses of sensory neurons. *Annals of
the New York Academy of Sciences*, 1969, *156*, 872–881.

Barlow, H.B. Visual experience and cortical development. *Nature*, 1975, *258*, 199–
204.

Barlow, H.B. Retinal and central factors in human vision limited by noise. In H.B.
Barlow and P. Fatt, (Eds.), *Photoreception in vertebrates*. London: Academic
Press, 1977.

Barlow, H.B. The efficiency of detecting changes of density in random dot patterns. *Vision Research*, 1978, *18*, 637–650.

Barlow, H.B. Reconstructing the visual image in space and time. *Nature*, 1979,
279, 189–190.

Barlow, H.B., FitzHugh, R., & Kuffler, S.W. Dark adaptation, absolute threshold
and Purkinje shift in single units of the cat's retina. *Journal of Physiology*, 1957,
137, 327–337.

Barlow, H.B., Hill, R.M., & Levick, W.R. Retinal ganglion cells responding selectively to direction and speed of image motion in the rabbit. *Journal of Physiology*, 1964, *173*, 377–407.

Barlow, H.B., & Levick, W.R. Changes in the maintained discharge with adaptation level in the cat retina. *Journal of Physiology*, 1969, *202*, 699–718.

Barlow, H.B., & Reeves, B.C. The versatility and absolute efficiency of detecting mirror symmetry in random dot displays. *Vision Research*, 1979, *19*, 783–794.

Barlow, H.B., & Sakitt, B. An economical encoding for size and position information. (In preparation December 1975 and thereafter.)

Berkeley, M.A., & Sprague, J.M. Behavioural analysis of the role of the geniculocortical system in form vision. In S. Cool (Ed.), *Frontiers of visual science*. New York: Springer, 1979.

Braitenburg, V. *On the texture of brains*, New York: Springer, 1977.

Clark-Jones, R. Quantum efficiency of human vision. *Journal of the Optical Society of America*, 1959, *49*, 645–653.

Cowan, J.D. Some remarks on channel bandwidths for visual contrast detection. In *Neurosciences research program bulletin*, 1977, *15*, 492–515.

De Valois, R.L., & Jones, A.F. Single cell analysis of the organisation of the primate color-vision system. In R. Jung & H. Kornhuber (Eds.), *The visual system: Neurophysiology and psychophysics*. Berlin: Springer, 1961.

Dowling, J.E., & Werblin, F.S. Organization of the retina of the mud puppy *Necturus maculosus*: I: Synaptic structure. *Journal of Neurophysiology*, 1969, *32*, 315–338.

Edwards, A.W.F. *Likelihood*. Cambridge: Cambridge University Press, 1972.

Enroth-Cugell, C., & Robson, J.G. The contrast sensitivity of retinal ganglion cells of the cat. *Journal of Physiology*, 1966, *187*, 517–552.

Fisher, R.A. *Statistical methods for research workers*. Edinburgh: Oliver and Boyd, 1925.

Fisher, R.A. *The design of experiments*. Edinburgh: Oliver and Boyd, 1935.

Fisken, R. A., Garey, L.J., & Powell, T.P.S. The intrinsic, association, and commissural connections of area 17 of the visual cortex. *Philosophical Transactions of the Royal Society* (London), Ser. B 1975, *272*, 487–536.

Glass, L. Moiré effect from random dots. *Nature*, 1969, *223*, 578–580.

Granit, R., & Svaetichin, G. Principles and technique of the electrophysiological analysis of colour reception with the aid of micro-electrodes. *Upsala läkarenförening Förhandlingar*, 1939, *65*, 161–177.

Hartline, H.K. The response of single optic nerve fibers of the vertebrate eye to illumination of the retina. *American Journal of Physiology*, 1938, *121*, 400–415.

Hartline, H.K. The effects of spatial summation in the retina on the excitation of the fibers of the optic nerve. *American Journal of Physiology*, 1940, *130*, 700–711.

Hecht, S., Shlaer, S., & Pirenne, M. Energy, quanta, and vision. *Journal of General Physiology*, 1942, *25*, 819–840.

Held, R. Dissociation of visual function by deprivation and rearrangement. *Psychologische Forschung*, 1968, *31*, 338–348.

Hubel, D.H., & Wiesel, T.N. Ferrier Lecture: Functional architecture of macaque monkey visual cortex. *Proceedings of the Royal Society* (London), Ser. B., 1977, *198*, 1–59.

Hubel, D.H., Wiesel, T.N., & LeVay, S. Plasticity of ocular dominance columns in monkey striate cortex. *Philosophical Transactions of the Royal Society* (London), Ser. B., 1977, *278*, 377–409.

Humphrey, N.K. Vision in a monkey without striate cortex: A case study. *Perception*, 1974, *3*, 241–255.

Ingle, D. Two visual mechanisms underlying the behaviour of fish. *Psychologische Forschung*, 1967, *31*, 44–57.

Kuffler, S.W. Discharge patterns and functional organization of mammalian retina. *Journal of Neurophysiology*, 1953, *16*, 37–68.

Land, E.H., & McCann, J.J. Lightness and retinex theory. *Journal of the Optical Society of America*, 1971, *61*, 1–11.

Lettvin, J.Y., Maturana, H.R., McCulloch, W.S., & Pitts, W.H. What the frog's eye tells the frog's brain. *Proceedings of the Institute of Radio Engineers*, 1959, *47*, 1940–1951.

Maturana, H.R., & Frenk, S. Directional movement and horizontal edge detectors in pigeon retina. *Science*, 1963, *142*, 977–979.

Mountcastle, V.B. In G.M. Edelman & V.B. Mountcastle (Eds.), *The mindful brain: Cortical organization and the group-selective theory of higher brain function*. Cambridge, Mass.: Massachusetts Institute of Technology Press; 1978.

Pirenne, M.H. Absolute visual thresholds. *Journal of Physiology*, 1954, *123*, 40P.

Pöppel, E., Held, R., & Frost, D. Residual visual function after brain wounds involving the central visual pathways in man. *Nature*, 1973, *243*, 295–296.

Robson, J.G. Receptive fields: Neural representation of the spatial and intensive attributes of the visual image. In E. Carterette & M.P. Friedman (Eds.), *Handbook of perception*, Vol. 5, *Seeing*. New York: Academic Press, 1975.

Rose, A. The relative sensitivities of television pick-up tubes, photographic film, and the human eye. *Proceedings of the Institute of Radio Engineers*, 1942, *30*, 293–300.

Schneider. G.E. Contrasting visuomotor functions of tectum and cortex in the golden hamster. *Psychologische Forschung*, 1967, *31*, 52–62.

Sprague, J.M., & Meikle, T.H. The role of the superior colliculus in visually guided behavior. *Experimental Neurology*, 1965, *11*, 115–146.

Svaetichin, G. & MacNichol E.F., Jr. Retinal mechanisms for chromatic and achromatic vision. *Annals of the New York Academy of Sciences*, 1958, *74*, 385–404.

Swets, J.A. (Ed.) *Signal detection and recognition by human observers*. New York: John Wiley, 1964.

Tanner, W.P., & Birdsall, T.G. Definitions of d' and η as psychophysical measures. *Journal of the Acoustical Society of America*, 1958, *30*, 922–928.

Trevarthen, C.B. Two mechanisms of vision in primates. *Psychologische Forschung*, 1968, *31*, 818–832.

Uttal, W.R. *An autocorrelation theory of form detection*. Hillsdale, N.J.: Lawrence Erlbaum, 1975.

van Meeteren, A. On the detective quantum efficiency of the human eye. *Vision Research*, 1978, *18*, 257–268.

Weiskrantz, L. Behavioral analysis of the monkey's visual system. *Proceedings of the Royal Society* (London), Ser. B., 1972, *182*, 427–455.

Weiskrantz, L., Warrington, E.K., Sanders, M.D., & Marshall, J. Visual capacity in the hemianopic field following a restricted occipital ablation. *Brain*, 1974, *97*, 709–728.

Werblin, F.S., & Dowling, J.E. Organization of the retina of the mud puppy *Necturus maculosus*. II: Intracellular recording. *Journal of Neurophysiology*, 1969, *32*, 339–355.

Woodward, P.M. *Probability and information theory with applications to radar.* New York: Pergamon Press, 1953.

Zeki, S. Functional specialization in the visual cortex of the rhesus monkey. *Nature*, 1978, 274, 423–428.

Discussion

Dr. McFadden: I personally was having a little difficulty squaring your acknowledged commitment to feature detectors and the proposal that you made here. From the way you presented it, you wanted to have a color map, and you wanted to have a velocity map, etc., whereas when I think of features I think of a hierarchical progression where neural elements gradually acquire specificities on a number of different dimensions. What you were saying seems to me to be putting up little cortical areas as color areas, and little areas as velocity areas, and little areas as something else, perhaps, rather than this summing of dimensions and specificities within dimensions which I think of as feature analysis.

Dr. Barlow: I don't think there's a great disagreement. Supposing you did find the unit in the color area which responds when these two particular patches of blue go off caused by my telephone directory. Now that is a very specific type of feature filter, almost bizarrely specific, but of course it's not completely bizarre because the linking characteristic is blueness. You want to know where patches of the same type of blue are in the visual field because they belong to the same object—a clue to something in the environment that has this property—but it is a feature filter.

Dr. McFadden: Yes, I see that, but as you're describing it, some little region of elements would be activated no matter what the, say, geometry of those two little patches of blue. What about three patches of blue being revealed underneath your notes. Would the same area be activated?

Dr. Barlow: There would be activity in the same area but it would be different activity because it would be coming from different regions of the visual field. The way that that was put together, by causing activity of other units, would of course be different so there would be three pairs and so on, but there would still be feature filters. The difference between feature filters and other things is, I think partly, a question of whether you're regarding the activity as indicating a category or whether it is in fact a logical variable you're dealing with—or something like the strength of the Fourier component, which would be a continuous variable and which you would rather hope to be linear because that makes your further analysis very much simpler. I'm not fully committed to feature filters, but I do think that sooner or later one's got to start thinking of what the nervous system does in logical terms and not in terms of linear variables or variables that can be treated as linear.

Dr. Ratliff: This is the sort of thing I had in mind when I came to the end of my talk—that there's a definite limit, it seems to me, of what we can do

with the sort of standard engineering, communication-type of mathematical analysis. It's quite appropriate in some instances, obviously, because
it describes the system well, but we have to go beyond that somehow, and
I see what Horace is trying to do as a good first attempt. I don't want to try
to make an assessment of it on the spot, but it's one of the kinds of things
that I very definitely had in mind when I was speaking about that subject.
I even feel that we may be driven to look for new ways of thinking about
things. It may be that we can't handle some of these things because Boo-
lean logic—or whatever other kind of logic or mode of thinking may
come to mind—just may not be adequate or suitable for the purpose. It's
clear that the way we use ordinary language and the way we run around
and move our arms and legs are very good ways to express what's going on
in the brain, but neither provides a very good scientific way to study it.
We need something between ordinary language and a purely mathematical, engineering type of analysis.

Dr. Rose: Am I correct in assuming that what you are suggesting requires
an anatomical region that should be detectable by using two stimuli
rather than one?

Dr. Barlow: I'm protesting about dependence upon topographic mapping.
To some extent the people who've explored the peristriate areas have
been happy to say, "There's another topographic map there." That can't
be all there is in it. After the Hubel and Wiesel work in the primary cortex
you can no longer believe that the brain is porridge. It's got to have some
fine structure there. So let's look for other ordering principles, as in the
movement map or as in the suggestion about the color map. What are
these organizing principles?

Dr. Rose: It is a requirement—the nice thing about your suggestion is
that it is testable. When you use two stimuli, having (let's say) the same
velocity in one direction, you should be able to discover a whole region
because there must be a region for all movements. What I am asking is
whether I understood you correctly, that you would demand quite a
number of specific maps?

Dr. Barlow: Yes, there are other . . .

Dr. Rose: . . . which I welcome.

Dr. Barlow: You have them in the auditory system?

Dr. Rose: I feel that in the auditory system or in any other system, the
multiple representations are very disquieting because it appears absurd
that there should be multiple representations with the same organizing
principles.

Dr. Barlow: To get back to the question of features or the hierarchical
system again. If you are trying to look for complex feature filters, there
are so many possibilities that one is completely lost. As soon as you look at
the association of three or four variables together, the number of separate
possibilities becomes so enormous that you simply can't handle it. That's
one reason why I think that looking at the binary associations might be a
good idea because that's the simplest thing you can do. And so I am sug-

gesting that that is actually a principle—that you can only in one stage detect binary associations. And there is Bela Julesz's example, and these ones of symmetry here do, so far as they go, seem to provide some support for that.

Dr. Boynton: I would like to ask a simple procedural question as background for a perhaps more profound one that might follow. In your symmetry tests to what extent were the eye movements of the subjects restricted?

Dr. Barlow: They weren't. When detecting the symmetry off axis, for example, we had a fixation point the subject looked at, and then we tried to make sure that he couldn't anticipate the appearance either to the left or right by having it sometimes staying where it was, sometimes appearing to the left, and sometimes to the right. Once the subject knew that this was likely to happen, he didn't try to anticipate; he showed no signs of doing so at any rate.

Dr. Boynton: The best symmetry discrimination occurred when the subjects were looking centrally. The rest of my question may not pertain because it's not possible to be sure what the eyes were doing, but I just wonder whether it bothers you at all that, if the subject were fixating the midline and judging symmetry bilaterally in the horizontal direction, that the projections would be to opposite cerebral hemispheres.

Dr. Barlow: Yes, that does. It seems to imply that to recognize the symmetry you must bring into play the corpus callosum. It would be very nice to do this on somebody with the corpus callosum cut.

Dr. Boynton: Do your results show that to be better than top–bottom symmetry?

Dr. Barlow: Yes, and better than having it displaced. I have very recently, actually, done some tests comparing left hemifield and right hemifield on the off chance that it might be strongly lateralized and you might get different performance in the left and right hemifields. We couldn't find anything at all. We also looked for differences of latency in the left and right hemifields, and again no significant difference.

Dr. Ratliff: I might say that the lower-case letters "d," "b," "p," and "q" show the same results that you described. The confusion children have learning to read "d" and "b," and "p" and "q" is much greater than the confusion about the other axis, and there's practically no confusion of the circular symmetry as when you rotate "p" into "d."

Dr. Barlow: I'm not quite sure about this because I don't think we've done it separately, but you're much better at detecting symmetry about a vertical axis or a horizontal axis than you are if you reflect it through the center—the centric type of symmetry. You do detect that, but it's harder. That of course is the difference between a "d" and a "p."

Dr. Evarts: I would like to expand on Horace Barlow's idea that sooner or later one must start thinking of what the nervous system does in logical terms rather than in terms of linear variables, because the logical detection of combinations of events seems to be a better way of formulating the way in which certain complex somesthetic inputs are integrated in such a way as to regulate motor behavior. The motor output elicited by a given concatenation of sensory inputs occurs by virtue of the fact that the given constellation of afferent inputs has been detected as a set. The notion that Barlow has presented here is certainly one that can be applied to many nonvisual systems. I mentioned to Horace earlier today that there is now abundant evidence that there are in fact multiple topographic representations of the body surface according to different somesthetic submodalities. But these multiple representations of the body surface are not merely separate representations of isolated muscular, cutaneous, and joint afferent inputs. Rather, the re-representations of the body in the areas of SI (areas 3a, 3b, 1, and 2) are actually zones of convergence between corticocortical and thalamocortical projections. For example, the inputs to area 2 conform to Barlow's idea that aggregates within the cortex should detect the "anding" of different inputs. (Area 2 would combine a certain pattern of cutaneous input received by corticocortical fibers from area 1 with joint afferent input received from the ventrobasal complex of the thalamus.) In this sense, the flow of information into these hierarchically organized sensory areas would seem to correspond pretty well to that required of the logical detection model.

Tony Wright (University of Texas Graduate School of Biomedical Sciences, Houston): I have some questions on your efficiency experiments. Measures of performance, and hence your measures of efficiency, are oftentimes dependent upon the subject's criterion; particularly in those experiments where the slope of the receiver-operating characteristic (ROC) is less than unity (and in visual experiments we know that this is often the case). If you have a situation where the subject is more likely to classify displays that are unknown as those with added dots as opposed to those without added dots, then the subject has a response bias. If the ROC is of unit slope, the criterion will not influence your measure of detectability, d'. If it is other than unit slope, it will, and your efficiency measures will be affected. This leads me to a speculation: Your procedure was essentially a yes–no procedure. You could equally well, though, have presented two displays, i.e., a two-alternative forced-choice task, where the subject pointed at the display with the added dots. Now, with a two-alternative forced-choice task there is no theory that I know of, or any data, which indicates that you will get ROC curves of other than unit slope, so that your detectability measures would then be bias free.

Dr. Barlow: Yes. This form of doing the experiment is not the only one we have used. I have tried two-alternative forced-choice; it's a very convenient method of doing these. The subject receives constant reinforcement, that is to say, he's always told whether he's got it right or wrong. He knows that there's a probability of a half of it being from one population or the other, and we've done everything we can to make him use a central criterion that will divide them into roughly equal halves. The possibility of his criterion changing is obviously worrying, and I'm sure that it's because he is unable to keep a completely fixed criterion that in fact his efficiency is not higher than it is. In other words, fluctuations of criterion are, I'm sure, a major cause of inefficiency. I don't like the two-alternative forced-choice paradigm because it's more complicated. For example, if you're interested in location in the visual field, it's obviously inconvenient to have to have two presented simultaneously. We could present them successively, but you get fed up to the teeth looking at these things anyway, and if you have to look at twice as many, that's not so good. I suppose that what one should do is a very thorough study of which method of doing these experiments does give the highest efficiency. I'm afraid I haven't done that very throughly, though in the one or two trials I've done with the two-alternative forced-choice it didn't seem to be any better and it was slower.

CHAPTER 5

The Search for the Engram, II

Richard F. Thompson
in collaboration with Theodore W. Berger,
Stephen D. Berry, and Fred K. Hoehler

At the beginning of the 20th century the prevalent view of brain mechanisms of learning and memory was a specific pathway "switchboard" notion. This view was perhaps most explicitly stated by Karl Lashley (1929), who used the term "engram" to refer to hypothetical, localized memory traces. Several traditions supported this idea. In neurology, localization of function was the dominant view—motor, visual, and auditory regions (and "functions") had been localized on the cerebral cortex. John Watson, developing the behaviorist approach, argued that learning involved the formation of specific stimulus–response connections—complex learned behaviors were concatenations of reflexes. Pavlov (1927) had already developed a similar view, localizing learning to the cerebral cortex, specifically to the cortical projections of the conditioned and unconditioned stimuli and their processes of interaction. All of these developing ideas fit well with the traditional view of human memory as a vast network of specific associations among stimulus representations in the brain. This was derived largely from British associationist philosphers, who argued that when two stimuli occurred simultaneously in time, a specific association, a bond, was formed between them.

Beginning about 1917, Karl Lashley set out to find the engram. His approach was eminently logical, given the historical dominance of localization of function. His work culminated in the classic monograph published in 1929, *Brain Mechanisms and Intelligence*. The outcome of these studies is familiar to everyone—the memory trace, the "engram," could not be localized. In these studies Lashley used mazes of varying difficulty and cortical lesions of varying size and location. He codified his results in two familiar principles: mass action—the more tissue removed the greater the impairment—and equipotentiality—the effect of the lesion on learned behavior is independent of its locus.

In subsequent years he and a great many other investigators employed behavioral tasks ranging from simple conditioning to more complex learning and lesions of subcortical as well as cortical structures. The outcome was essentially the same—the localized engram could not be found. At the end of his career, Lashley reviewed the search for the engram and came to the following rather despairing conclusion:

> I sometimes feel, in reviewing the evidence on the localization of the memory trace, that the necessary conclusion is that learning just is not possible. (Karl S. Lashley, 1950, pp. 477–478)

The above is not meant to discount the very great amount of information that has been obtained about the behavioral functions of various brain regions and systems using the lesion-behavior method. For example, it is possible to characterize the differential functions of frontal and posterior regions of association cortex in primates along several dimensions thanks to the extensive studies by Harlow and associates (Harlow, 1952), Pribram and associates (Pribram, 1971), and others. In a recent series of studies that may be said to exemplify the best of the lesion approach to learning, Robert Thompson and associates (1976) have made discrete lesions throughout the brain of the rat and examined the effects on several forms of learning. Although they did not find the engram, they did find that damage to certain regions had greater effects than damage to other regions. In particular, regions related to certain of the basal ganglia seemed important.

The schematic diagram of Figure 5.1 serves to illustrate the problem for simple conditioned-response learning. It indicates the brainstem reflex level for an unconditioned stimulus (UCS), possible reflex connections of the conditioned stimulus (CS), their ascending projections to higher brain regions, and the descending influences from higher brain regions. If an animal has learned a simple conditioned response, relatively discrete lesions anywhere in higher brain regions have little or no effect. If all higher brain regions above the reflex level are removed, the learning is abolished.

This is not to say that learning cannot be made to occur in reduced

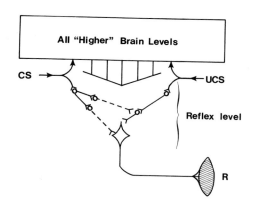

Figure 5.1. Highly schematic diagram of the mammalian CNS in the context of simple learning and conditioning. CS: conditioned stimulus. UCS: unconditioned stimulus. R: behavioral response. Dashed interneurons are hypothetical interconnections at the reflex level.

preparations. The brainstem is capable of some learning (Bard & Macht, 1958; Norman, Buchwald, & Villablanca, 1977). Indeed, even at the level of the spinal cord, conditioning has now been demonstrated clearly in carnivores (Patterson, Cegavske, & Thompson, 1973; Patterson, 1976; Durkovic, 1975) and in humans (N.E. Miller, 1980). Therefore, lower levels of the nervous system can be made to exhibit basic plasticity in the absence of higher structures. Such studies provide valuable models for analysis of possible synaptic mechanisms of plasticity (see e.g., the hypothetical dashed-line interneurons in Figure 5.1). However, such reflex-level learning does not seem to occur in the intact, behaving mammal. For example, if an animal is trained and all higher brain levels above the reflex level removed (see Figure 5.1), the learning is abolished. It may then be possible to retrain the reflex preparation. However, the properties of this reflex learning appear to differ in some regards from normal learning. Brain structures and systems above the reflex level are normally involved.

If the CS pathways are destroyed, learning is permanently abolished— all visual learning is obviously eliminated by section of the optic nerves. However, even at the level of the visual cortex, many learned tasks either remain or can be relearned or recovered. Indeed, recovery of learned functions has become a major area of investigation today relating to brain substrates of learning—see the important recent paper by Meyer and Meyer (1977).

This outcome has forced most workers to abandon the notion of the localized engram; indeed, Lashley had abandoned it by 1929 as a result of his own work. The logic underlying the notion of the localized engram seems to derive from an oversimplified conception of causality. It is an example of what the Soviet psychologist Boris Lomov (1980) terms *linear causality*. The basic idea is a linear or series chain of events from stimulus inputs to final motor output, with a critical change developing at some point in the sequence in the brain. Hence, there would be a direct linear causal chain from this change, the engram, to the learned behavior. Except in very simple systems, it is doubtful that such elementary linear causality ever obtains in the central nervous system.

Perhaps the closest approach to linear causality is found in simplified biological models of habituation, itself the simplest form of behavioral plasticity or learning (Thompson & Spencer, 1966). In Kandel's elegant analysis of habituation in a monosynaptic system of *Aplysia*, the decremental process is localized to the presynaptic terminals of the sensory neurons at their synapses, on the motor neurons (Kandel, 1976). Similarly, in our analysis of a monosynaptic vertebrate model, the lateral column–motoneuron system in the isolated frog spinal cord, the decremental process was localized to the presynaptic terminals of the synapses on the motoneurons. In both cases, the mechanism appears to be a decrease in the probability of release of transmitter as a result of prior iterated stimulation (i.e., habituation training). By inference, similar mechanisms underlie habituation of polysynaptic systems in the mammalian spinal cord (Thompson & Spencer, 1966).

These are clearly examples of linear causality. The decremental process responsible for behavioral habituation occurs within the reflex pathway being repeatedly stimulated, at the one set of synapses interposed between the stimulus and the response. Interneurons also activated by the stimulus do not play a direct role in habituation in either system. However, even in these simple linear systems, if the stimulus intensity is increased or if an effective stimulus is given to another locus, a second process, *sensitization*, intervenes. This process can act on the same synapses that are exhibiting habituation to produce a transient increase in response. This process involves other neurons and systems, different synaptic mechanisms from habituation, and is independent of habituation, in the sense that it does not disrupt the habituation process. Nonetheless, both processes can occur at the same synapses. Even at this very simple level, the net behavioral response is the result of the interaction of at least two processes, both in *Aplysia* and in vertebrate spinal cord (see Groves & Thompson, 1970). Linear causality is insufficient to account for the behavioral outcome to repeated stimulation in even these simplest monosynaptic systems.

Given that a localized engram does not exist and hence that brain mechanisms of learning cannot be accounted for in terms of linear causality, what are the alternatives? Lashley tended toward a general Gestalt approach in later years. Hebb, in his influential *Organization of Behavior* (1949) made a heroic attempt to reconcile the experimental data supporting "mass action" and "equipotentiality" with some form of localized synaptic alterations that might underlie learning. He developed the notion of *cell assemblies*, involving relatively local circuits, and *phase sequences* — interconnected collections of these cell assemblies—which would have widespread representation in the brain. These hypothetical phase sequences can be characterized by temporal as well as spatial organization. Indeed, the temporal organization is critical for learned behaviors varying from "simple" conditioning to mastery of a complex maze.

For Hebb, the brain representation of a learned behavior is no longer a linear causal chain or a single series pathway. Instead, it (the phase sequence) becomes an interconnected set or system of local networks (cell assemblies) having both series and parallel features. Its widespread representation in the brain (cortex) would account both for equipotentiality and for mass action. Insofar as the specific synaptic changes that might result in the formation of cell assemblies are concerned, Hebb, in 1949, favored some form of increased synaptic efficacy as a result of use. However, he later noted that use alone cannot serve—extinction of a conditioned response results from increased use of a learned "pathway" (CS → CR) in the absence of the UCS. A number of studies have since demonstrated that for virtually all neuronal systems tested, increased use at physiological rates leads to decreased synaptic efficacy (e.g., habituation, low-frequency depression, etc.), and decreased use often leads to increased efficacy, as in the case of denervation hypersensitivity. For simple conditioning, at least, a particular temporal combination of the "neutral" CS and the "reinforcing" UCS is clearly necessary. In any event, consideration of synaptic mechanisms is premature.

The major difficulty with Hebb's theory has been that it is not sufficiently specific to be testable, other than in a very general way. He does suggest that the cell assemblies might have some anatomical locus, e.g., for a simple aspect of learned visual perception, neurons in areas 17 and 18 might "interconnect." (Hebb wrote before the discovery of the "feature detector" properties of neurons in sensory systems.) However, there is no specific anatomical substrate for the phase sequence—it is an abstract notion rather than a brain system. It seems to be characterized as diffuse and nonspecific rather than having the properties of an anatomically or physiologically defined neuronal system.

We wish to suggest an alternative view, namely that the memory system of higher animals—mammals—consists of a number of brain systems that play various roles during learning. These systems can be defined, or at least characterized, by anatomical and physiological criteria. Various systems may exist more or less separately, or overlap, or merge. They can have hierarchical organization, as in a sensory "system"; a partly temporal organization, as in certain motor systems; or alternative organizations that have not yet been characterized. The roles these various hypothetical brain systems play in learning and memory may or may not correspond to conceptual categories or terms that now exist. Note that such a multiple-systems theory can also account for results of the lesion studies that give rise to the concepts of equipotentiality and mass action. A discrete lesion might interrupt only a part of one or more systems—the systems could still function, although perhaps not as well. A system, almost by definition, is not localized to one anatomical place. The larger the lesion, the more systems that are damaged, and the greater the damage is to some, yielding greater impairment.

In the cerebral cortex, at least six very general types of "systems" may be defined:

1. Sensory projection systems.
2. Motor systems.
3. The "nonspecific" cortical fields defined by the projections of the intralaminar thalamic nuclei.
4. The cortical projections of the ascending reticular activating system may form a system intersecting with the nonspecific cortical fields; the "limbic" cortical areas, e.g., cingulate gyrus, and their projections via entorhinal cortex to the hippocampus are another system.
5. The dorsomedial nucleus–prefrontal cortex may form still another system, overlapping with the limbic cortex.
6. Still another type of cortical "system" may be defined by the noradrenergic projections from the locus coeruleus, which course through the

prefrontal areas and then distribute in a widespread manner to the neocortex.

Each of these "systems" is very general and may or may not in fact function as a system in learning. There are also many local systems and organizations in the cortex. The point is that these are systems that can be defined by anatomical and/or physiological criteria. Whether or not they play differential roles, or in fact any role, in learning must be determined experimentally. For example, in a recent series of studies, Gabriel and associates (Gabriel, Miller, & Saltwick, 1977) present evidence that limbic cortex and anterior thalamus seem to play different roles in instrumental avoidance learning in the rabbit.

The multiple-systems approach, which we are attempting to make explicit here, is not, of course, original. Many students of brain–behavior relations have emphasized this approach. The work of Pribram (see particularly his stimulating book *The Languages of the Brain*, 1971), Lindsley's (1960) analysis of brain substrates of attention and arousal, the Laceys' analysis of cardiovascular and autonomic activity in humans (Lacey and Lacey, 1977) are examples that come immediately to mind. In the Soviet Union, the systems approach is the dominant conceptualization. Pavlov's notion of the heirarchical organization of the brain has been developed extensively by modern workers in the Pavlovian tradition—Asratyan (1980), Gasanov (1980).

A student of Pavlov, Peter Anokhin, has perhaps developed the systems approach most explicitly in his conception of goal-directed functional systems (Anokhin, 1974). His students, in turn, have continued and extended this approach, e.g., Sudakov (1965) and Shvyrkov (1980). A particularly clear example is Sokolov's (1963) monumental analysis of the orienting response. Indeed, modern experimental psychobiology in the Soviet Union emphasizes the systems approach more than does American psychobiology (see Lomov, 1980).

Modern analysis of the human memory system in psychology provides an analogy. It is characterized as consisting of a number of systems with different properties that interact—as indicated in the diagram of Figure 5.2, taken from Atkinson and Shiffrin (1968). Sensory input is stored accurately but very briefly (up to 200 msec) in the sensory register or iconic memory (Sperling, 1960). It seems to be modality specific. Some of this information is transferred to longer term stores. The short-term memory store has a very limited capacity, about seven items or chunks of information (G.A. Miller, 1956) and decays over a period of about 10-12 sec (Peterson & Peterson, 1959). The search through items in short-term store is linear, requiring about 37 msec per item (Sternberg, 1966). Some information is established in long-term permanent store. The search process through long-term store is of course not linear. It takes something under 200 msec to retrieve a remembered item, independent of the size of the item. For example, the numerical value of π (3.14) and the plot of a novel you have recently read are retrieved from long-term store in the same

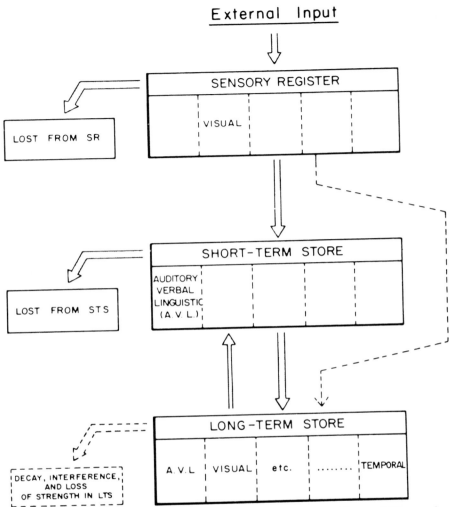

Figure 5.2. A schematic of the human memory system. (From Atkinson & Shiffrin, 1968; reproduced by permission.)

length of time (Wickens, personal communication). However, once in short-term store, such items must be searched linearly. The short-term memory store is in many ways equivalent to immediate consciousness or awareness—it is what you hold continuously in your awareness at a given moment of time, as first pointed out by William James (1890). In addition to the various memory stores, there are a variety of control processes involved in storage and retrieval.

    Granted, this characterization of human memory is hypothetical and not accepted by all workers. Nonetheless, it has heuristic value at least and it serves to illustrate at a behavioral level the notion of various systems playing various roles in learning and memory. Although clearly pre-

mature, it is tempting to speculate about possible physiological substrates. Several lines of indirect evidence suggest that the sensory register
is not limited to receptors, e.g., for vision it is not simply a retinal after-
image, but consists of the primary sensory systems at least up to and including the sensory areas of the cerebral cortex (see Thompson, 1975).
Little can be said about the brain substrates of short-term and long-term
storage processes. Indeed, these behavioral categories may not exist as
particular brain systems. The major point is that the memory system can
be characterized at the behavioral level as a set of interacting systems. By
analogy, and from what we know about the organization of the brain, the
brain substrates of learning and memory undoubtedly consist of sets of
interacting neuronal systems.

The literature on animal learning provides clear analogies to the
human memory system. Consolidation, the well-established fact that a
learning experience is fragile and easily manipulated for a short time after
the experience—it can be impaired by electro-convulsive shock (ECS)
and anesthetics and facilitated by certain drugs and hormones (see Duncan, 1949; Hebb, 1955; Kety, 1976; McGaugh, 1966; McGaugh & Herz,
1972)—provides a close analogy to short-term memory. Long-term memory, in contrast, can be prevented by substances that interfere with protein synthesis (Agranoff, 1967; Flexner, Flexner, & Stellar, 1963). Wagner
and associates have developed paradigms to analyze short-term memory
in rabbits (Terry & Wagner, 1975). The human memory system seems,
except for language, to be the mammalian memory system.

The motor systems of the mammalian brain provide a helpful analogy
for our systems approach to brain substrates of learning. There are a
number of brain structures and systems categorized as "motor." They interact at all levels from the cerebral cortex to the final common path—
the motoneurons that generate the muscle and gland responses we call
behavior. In animal studies, the effects of even large lesions of the motor
structures and systems on motor behavior can range from severe, as with
the cerebellum, to moderate or mild, as with the motor cortex and pyramidal tract, to virtually nondetectable, as with the basal ganglia. Yet
these systems are all characterized as motor. Even a motor structure as
well developed in primates as the pyramidal tract can be ambiguous. The
elegant studies by Evarts (1964) show a precise coding of the force used in
making hand and wrist movements by cells of origin of pyramidal tract
fibers in the motor cortex of the monkey. Towe, in contrast, emphasizes
the minimal nature of motor deficits by monkeys who have had complete
bilateral section of the pyramidal tract:

> Anyone who has watched a healthy pyramidotomized monkey bound-
> ing off the four walls and the ceiling of its enclosure can only stand in
> awe before the concepts that attend such an agile creature (Towe,
> 1973, p. 89).

The first clear demonstration of functional localization of movement
on the cerebral cortex—the motor cortex—was obtained using electrical

stimulation (Fritsch & Hitzig, 1870). Earlier lesion studies had yielded only ambiguous results. Indeed, more recently Woolsey, Travis, Barnard, and Ostinso (1953) demonstrated remarkable recovery of motor function following total bilateral ablation of motor cortex in monkey. In recent years most of the information we have about the roles of various brain structures and systems in movement control, ranging from spinal and cranial motoneurons to motor cortex and the "intentional" units of area 7 (Mountcastle, Lynch, Georgopoulos, Sokoto, & Acura, 1975), has come from recording studies where the electrophysiological signs of neuronal activity are correlated with behavior. Important additional information has come from simultaneous recordings from several systems (Evarts, this volume; Brooks, 1975). The lesion–behavior approach has generally not been too helpful in analyzing the roles of brain structures in behavioral movement. Why, then, should we expect more from the lesion approach with regard to far more complex aspects of behavior, such as learning and memory?

Given that a movement occurs, what is its cause? In a trivial sense the cause is activity of the motoneurons controlling the muscles involved, together with motoneurons acting on synergists, antagonists, and so on. Beyond this, and excluding simple reflexes, most experts in motor systems would probably say it is an impossible question. There is not a unique cause. Movements are not generated by linear causation—by a single series chain of sequential cause and effect relations. Movements are the result of interacting activity among the motor systems.

Analysis of brain systems and mechanisms underlying learning and memory has many parallels with analysis of motor systems. Both are concerned with relating brain events to behavior. The obvious difference is, of course, that learning involves change in behavior as a result of experience. We wish to find the neuronal substrate of the *change* in behavior, as opposed to the substrate of the behavior, per se. This is perhaps just another way of stating the learning vs. performance distinction emphasized in psychology. However, it is a critical distinction from an experimental viewpoint. The paradigms used must permit one to distinguish between neurophysiological substrates of learning and behavioral performance. There must be changes that develop within and/or among the various brain systems involved in learning and memory. This, then, is the engram—not a localized change at one place in the brain, or a diffuse net, but sets of changes in sets of definable, interacting brain systems.

Given the rationale developed above, and by analogy with characterization of motor systems, we have adopted the general approach of recording neuronal unit activity during the course of learning in a simple and discrete conditioned-response situation. The goal is to characterize the activity of various brain systems in learning and memory. Once this is accomplished, the structures and systems that exhibit altered activity with learning will have been identified and analysis of synaptic mechanisms will be feasible. We began by identifying the immediate neuronal substrate of the behavioral conditioned response—the motoneurons—

and characterizing their activity during learning. Results of these studies are indicated briefly below. Having defined the pattern of change of neuronal activity during learning at the final common path, it can be used as a neural "performance" measure against which to compare activity of higher brain structures and systems.

To date, we have focused on the limbic system—the hippocampus and related structures. The mammalian hippocampus has been implicated in learning and memory in a wide variety of experimental and clinical conditions (Isaacson, 1974; Isaacson & Pribram, 1975; O'Keefe & Nadel, 1978; Olds, Disterhoft, Segal, Kornblith, & Hirsh, 1972; Scoville & Milner, 1957). However, the precise role of the hippocampus in learning has not been clear. Our results indicate that the system seems to play a very specific role in learning, at least in the simple classical-conditioning situation we use: Neurons of the hippocampus rapidly develop a temporal model of the behavioral response to be learned, but they develop this model only under conditions where behavioral learning will subsequently occur. This rather surprising discovery will form the major focus of the present contribution. Bear in mind, however, that it is only one of many possible brain systems that act and interact during learning. The many possible brain systems must be characterized and their interactions determined before we can hope to understand the brain substrates of learning and memory.

We selected a preparation developed by Gormezano (Gormezano, Schneiderman, Deaux, & Fuentes, 1962)—classical conditioning of the rabbit nictitating-membrane response to a tone conditioned stimulus (CS) using a corneal airpuff unconditioned stimulus (UCS)—as a simple and discrete model of mammalian learning. This system has a number of advantages, which have been detailed elsewhere (Disterhoft, Kwan, & Lo, 1977; Thompson et al., 1976). The advantages are both practical— the animal is held motionless but not drugged or paralyzed, significant learning occurs within a single 2-hr training session, the airpuff UCS (as opposed to shock) does not give a recording artifact—and conceptual— thanks to the extensive studies of Gormezano *et al.* (1972) the learned response is very well characterized (it is an extremely well-behaved Pavlovian response and shows virtually no pseudoconditioning or sensitization), learning vs. performance substrates can be distinguished at the neuronal level, and the actual amplitude–time course of the behavioral response is easily measured and quantified.

1   Methods

The cartoon of Figure 5.3 shows the general procedures for classical conditioning of the eyelid response in rabbits and in humans. This paradigm has the additional advantage that behavioral data obtained from animals can be compared directly to human data. Both rabbits and humans ex-

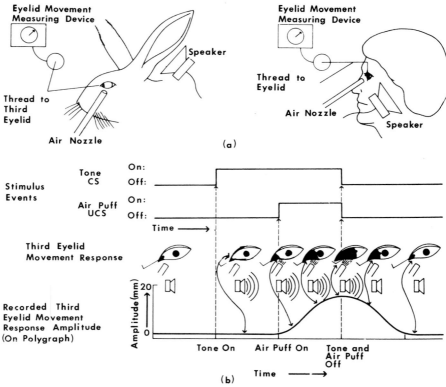

Figure 5.3. (a) Diagram of classical-conditioning methods for the rabbit nictitating-membrane (NM = "3rd eyelid") response and the human eyelid. (b) Reflex
response of rabbit NM to paired tone CS and airpuff UCS at the beginning of
training. There is initially no NM response to tone, only a reflex response to airpuff. As training continues, the NM begins to extend to tone prior to onset of airpuff. (From Lindzey, Hall, & Thompson, 1978; reproduced by permission.)

hibit the same basic phenomena of classical conditioning in this situation.

We have adopted the procedures developed by Gormezano for the rabbit preparation (Gormezano, 1966). A trial early in training for the rabbit
nictitating-membrane (NM) response is shown in Figure 5.3b. In our experiments we have typically used a 250-msec interstimulus interval (ISI)
—it is perhaps the maximally effective interval for conditioning (Gormezano, 1972). At the beginning of training the tone CS (we use an 85-dB,
1-kHz tone) typically does not elicit an NM response—the rabbit shows
no "alpha" responding under these conditions. The airpuff (we use a 100-
msec puff from a source pressurized to 210 g/cm²) elicits a brisk reflex response of the NM. As training continues, the NM response onset begins
to occur before airpuff onset. Similarly, the NM response begins to occur
on tone-alone test trials (we give one paired conditioning trial per minute
and every ninth trial is a tone-alone test trial). As learning proceeds, the

onset latency of the NM response becomes shorter, i.e., closer to onset of the tone. However, the peak of the conditioned NM response tends to remain at about the point in time where the airpuff occurs or would have occurred (Gormezano, 1972). Unpaired control animals in our experiments are given a random sequence of tone CS and airpuff UCS stimuli explicitly unpaired, with a mean interstimulus interval of 30 sec so that the density of stimulation is the same as for paired conditioning animals. In this paradigm, unpaired control animals show virtually no behavioral NM responses to tone—i.e., they do not exhibit sensitization or pseudo-conditioning.

The details of our procedures are given elsewhere and will be indicated only briefly here (Berger, Alger, & Thompson, 1976; Berger & Thompson, 1978a,b,c). A schematic of our recording and analysis procedures for the behavioral NM response is shown in Figure 5.4. The exact amplitude–time course of the NM extension response is measured by a micropotentiometer. Each response is recorded on tape, digitized at 3-msec intervals and stored in the computer. Later analysis involves computation of onset latencies and eight-trial averaged responses, and measurement of the area under the NM response curve. This latter measure provides a useful index of the "amount" of the response in terms of both amplitude and time (Cegavske, Patterson, & Thompson, 1979).

Our general methods of unit analysis are shown in Figure 5.5. Unit spike discharges of neurons (either multiple-unit clusters or isolated single-unit potentials) are recorded on tape. The unit discharges are picked off by a discriminator, converted to standard pulses, and fed into the computer. The basic data collection program counts the number of unit discharges in each 3-msec time bin. Data collection begins 250 msec prior to tone CS onset (the preCS period), continues through the 250 msec of tone (the CS period), and then continues for an additional 250 msec

NM Analysis

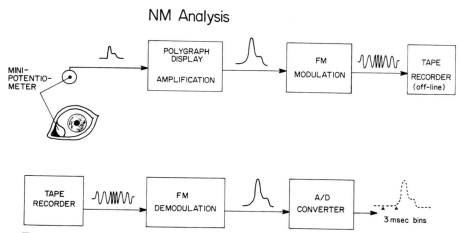

Figure 5.4. Schematic of procedures used for measurement, collection, and analysis of the behavioral nictitating-membrane (NM) response data. A/D, analog to digital.

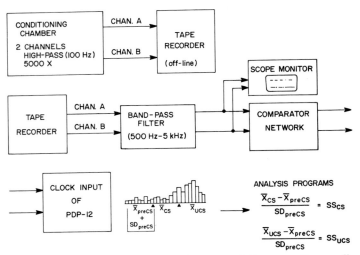

Figure 5.5. Schematic of procedures used for recording, collecting, and analyzing neuronal unit activity.

beginning with airpuff onset (the UCS period). Tone and airpuff terminate together 100 msec after airpuff onset. Airpuff "onset" time is the time at which the airpuff actually arrives at the cornea. Unit counts are cumulated for display, e.g., in eight-paired-trial frequency histograms, all histogram data shown here are cumulated and displayed in 15-msec time bins. Cumulated eight-trial unit count data are also converted to standard scores, relative to background (preCS) activity; e.g., for the CS period the standard score is the mean CS counts minus the mean preCS counts divided by the standard deviation of the preCS activity, the latter computed on an entire day's session (typically 13 blocks, each block consisting of eight paired trials and one tone alone test trial). The unit standard score measure for an eight-trial block for a given time period (e.g., the CS period or the UCS period) can be compared with the area under the averaged NM response curve for that same block of trials.

An example of a typical multiple-unit recording from the hippocampus is shown in Figure 5.6, with the discriminator pickoff level indicated by the arrow. As indicated in Figure 5.6, the pickoff level is well above noise; only unit discharges that can be individually resolved are counted. The multiple-unit microelectrode, of insulated stainless steel with $5-7\mu m$ tip diameter and $40-50\mu m$ exposed shaft, is permanently implanted (while monitoring unit activity for localization) using halothane anesthesia, in the structure to be studied. For single-unit recording, a small chronic microdrive system is implanted in the skull overlying the target structure and single-unit microelectrodes—$3-5\mu m$ tip diameter, insulated to the tip, 0.5-1.0 Megohm resistance–are inserted for each recording session. At least one week is allowed between surgical implantation procedures and the beginning of training–recording sessions.

Figure 5.6. Raw hippocampal unit recordings. (A) Isolated single unit; calibrations equal 80 μV and 5 msec. (B) Multiple-unit record; calibrations equal 80 μV and 10 msec. Arrow in (B) indicates typical comparator level setting relative to raw record. (From Berger & Thompson, 1978a; reproduced by permission.)

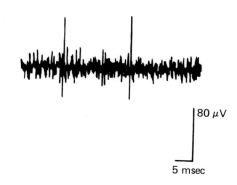

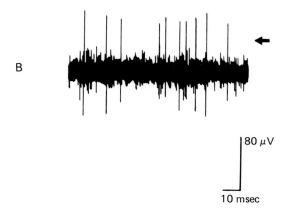

2   The Final Common Path

The highest correlation possible between neuronal and behavioral events should hold for the behavior and its immediate neuronal precedent, the activity of motoneurons in the final common path controlling the behavioral response. In initial studies, we identified the abducens (6th cranial nucleus) motoneurons as the final common path for the NM extension response (the NM extension in the rabbit is a largely passive consequence of eyeball retraction via the retractor bulbus muscle, innervated by the 6th nerve; Cegavske, Thompson, Patterson, & Gormezano, 1976; Young, Cegavske, & Thompson, 1976). We then completed a study comparing eight paired conditioning and eight unpaired control animals with multiple-unit recording electrodes implanted in the abducens nucleus ipsilateral to the eye being conditioned (Cegavske, Patterson, & Thompson, 1979). Examples of eight-trial average NM responses and histograms of abducens unit activity are shown in Figure 5.7 for a conditioning animal before (Figure 5.7A) and after (Figure 5.7B) learning and for a control

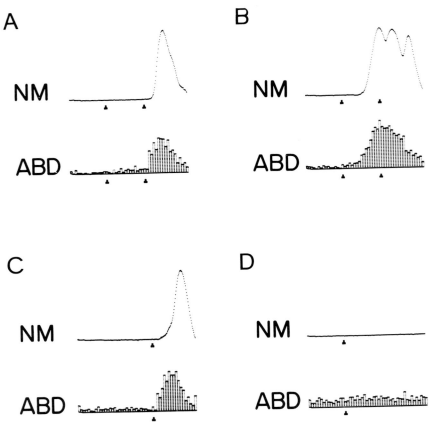

Figure 5.7. Examples of eight-trial averaged behavioral nictitating-membrane (NM) responses and associated multiple-unit histograms of abducens nucleus activity (15-msec time bins) for a conditioning animal at the beginning (A) and end (B) of training and a control animal for the airpuff UCS (C) and the tone CS (D). In this and all subsequent histogram figures, early cursor indicates tone onset, late cursor indicates airpuff onset. Total length equals 750 msec. Note the close correspondence between the histogram of unit activity recorded from the final common path and the temporal form of the behavioral NM response in all cases. (From Cegavske et al., 1979; reproduced by permission.)

animal to airpuff (Figure 5.7C) and to tone (Figure 5.7D). Results are clear—there is a very close coupling between abducens unit activity and the behavioral response, independent of whether the animal has learned or not and whether it is a conditioning or control animal. Whatever the abducens neurons do, so does the nictitating membrane.

Although it hardly seems necessary, a numerical index of the degree of relationship between the neural and behavioral measures of Figure 5.7 can be obtained by shifting the curves so that onsets correspond, i.e., shifting by the latency difference, and computing correlation coefficients for the active period of the response. This was done for the examples shown in Figure 5.7A, B, and C (using 3-msec time bins for computation). The product-moment correlation coefficients for these "time-adjusted" data were: A, $r = 0.94$; B, $r = 0.93$; C, $r = 0.94$; all highly significant ($p < 0.01$). This close correspondence of the amplitude–time course of the NM response and the histogram of unit activity from the motor nucleus is extremely useful. It means that the easily recorded NM response actually portrays the histogram of unit activity in the motor nucleus. It is particularly helpful when studying changes in neuronal activity in higher brain structures during learning. It is necessary to compare the temporal patterns of neural activity in such structures against the pattern of activity in the final common path during acquisition of the conditioned response. Given the present findings (e.g., Figure 5.7), it is not necessary to record activity of abducens motoneurons during acquisition; measurement of the form of the NM response suffices.

The behavioral and neuronal "index" measures—area under NM and unit standard score—are compared for the eight paired-conditioning animals in Figure 5.8. Data are shown for the CS period only. All animals were given two days of acquisition training (13 blocks of eight paired and one tone-alone trials). On Day 3 they were given three blocks of paired trials, then 13 blocks of tone-alone extinction trials, and finally three blocks of paired trials. The major point of this figure is the extraordinarily close correspondence between abducens activity and behavior, particu-

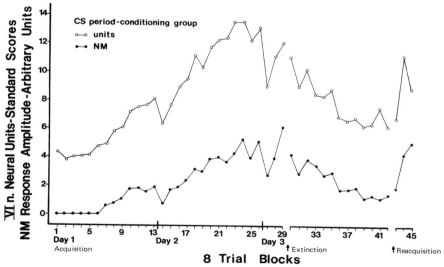

Figure 5.8. Comparison of standard scores of abducens nucleus neural activity and amplitude of the rabbit NM response during acquisition, extinction, and reacquisition phases of classical conditioning. The NM response measure is actually area under the NM response curve in arbitrary units. (From Cegavske et al., 1979; reproduced by permission.)

larly during acquisition. For Day 1, the correlation coefficient between the two groups was 0.99 and for Day 2 it was 0.98. We interpret this virtually perfect correlation between abducens units and the NM during acquisition to mean that activity of abducens neurons is the only causal variable of significance. It is an example of linear causation linking a neuronal and a behavioral event.

Interestingly, the correlation between the neuronal and behavioral measures drops to 0.93 during extinction, significantly lower than the correlation during acquisition. One or more additional variables have come into play—there is no longer a linear causal link between the activity of abducens neurons and the NM. Differential activity of the 3rd nucleus and related structures during extinction is a possibility (see, e.g., Mis, 1977; Moore, 1979). At a more general level, these data suggest that the neuronal mechanisms underlying acquisition and extinction differ, at least to some degree. There is not simply an increase and subsequent decrease in the same given form and/or location of neuronal plasticity during acquisition and extinction.

3   The Hippocampal System

As noted above, we selected the hippocampus as an initial brain system in which to explore possible learning-related changes in this clear-cut classical-conditioning paradigm.

A   Hippocampal EEG

A very simple study of the hippocampal electroencephalogram (EEG) indicated that neuronal activity in the hippocampus is indeed related to learning in this paradigm (Berry & Thompson, 1978, 1979). In brief, 2-min time samples of spontaneous hippocampal EEG were recorded at the beginning and end of each day of training in 16 animals. In the rabbit, the hippocampal EEG is dominated by rhythmic slow activity—a large-amplitude, almost sinusoidal waveform of approximately 3–8 Hz (so-called theta activity), which occurs in the waking state, in response to many forms of stimulation, and during paradoxical sleep (Green & Arduini, 1954; Winson, 1972). It is generally believed to be a good index of behavioral "state"—prominent theta indicates arousal (Lindsley & Wilson, 1975). Examples of hippocampal EEG recorded from the rabbit are shown in Figure 5.9; the upper tracing shows almost pure theta and the lower tracing a more typical mixed waveform.

Initially, we simply compared the frequency spectrum of the 2-min time sample of EEG taken just prior to the beginning of training on the first day of conditioning against number of trials to criterion over the several days of training. Examples of the frequency spectra from two animals are shown in Figure 5.10. Animal (a) has a preponderance of activity in

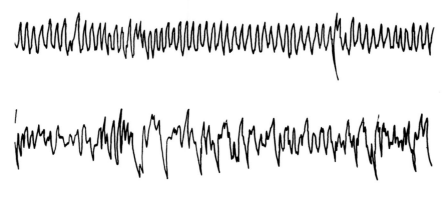

Figure 5.9. Samples of EEG recorded from the dorsal hippocampus of rabbit. Upper tracing shows clear theta rhythm and lower tracing shows a mixture of theta and other frequencies.

the theta range, whereas animal (b) has a more mixed pattern with more higher frequencies. As it happens, (a) is a good learner, and (b) is a poor learner.

In order to characterize the overall (2–22 Hz) EEG in terms of a low/high frequency dichotomy, a ratio was computed: the percentage of 8–22 Hz activity divided by the percentage of 2–8 Hz activity. For example, the ratio for the histogram values in Figure 5.10a was 0.40, whereas

Figure 5.10. Computer histograms showing the number of waves in each indicated frequency category during a 2-min sample of spontaneous EEG activity. (a) An animal with a relatively rapid rate of conditioning. (b) An animal that failed to reach criterion in the 4 days of conditioning. The calibration mark on the ordinate represents 100 waves. (From Berry & Thompson, 1978; reproduced by permission. Copyright 1978 by the American Association for the Advancement of Science.)

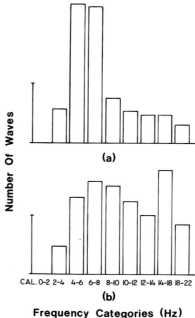

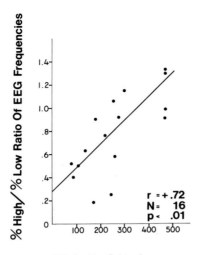

Figure 5.11. Scatter plot and best fitting regression line for the relationship between trials to criterion and the EEG frequency ratio (percentage 8–22 Hz activity divided by percentage 2–8 Hz activity) computed on the 2-min time sample of EEG taken just prior to training. Data from 16 rabbits. (From Berry & Thompson, 1978; reproduced by permission. Copyright 1978 by the American Association for the Advancement of Science.)

Trials To Criterion

that for Figure 5.10b was 1.33. The correlation between this measure and trials to criterion was highly significant ($r = +0.72$, $df = 14$, p < 0.01). Note the clear linear trend of the correlation illustrated by the scatter plot and best fitting linear regression line in Figure 5.11.

Therefore, a brief time sample of hippocampal EEG taken prior to the onset of training is highly predictive of subsequent learning rate, even over a period of days. A higher proportion of hippocampal theta (2–8 Hz) predicts faster rates of learning. To our knowledge, this is the first demonstration that a purely *neurophysiological* measure taken prior to the beginning of training can predict the subsequent *behavioral* rate of learning. This result is nicely consistent with consolidation studies showing a positive relationship between amount of theta in the posttraining EEG and subsequent retention performance (Landfield, McGaugh, & Tusa, 1972) and with studies reporting change in hippocampal EEG frequency and phase relations during training (Adey, 1966; Coleman & Lindsley, 1977; Grastyan, Lissak, Madarasz, & Donhoffer, 1959).

Prokasy (1972) has developed a most interesting mathematical model of behavioral learning for this particular paradigm (i.e., classical conditioning of rabbit NM), based on the general model approach of Bush and Mosteller. Prokasy's analysis indicates that learning occurs in two phases —an initial phase that extends from the beginning of training until the animal begins to give conditioned responses, and a second phase that extends from this point until the response is well learned. Phase one is more variable and more likely to be influenced by "motivation" and other conditions (Prokasy, 1972).

In part to determine whether Prokasy's model could be extended to physiological measures, we compared the number of trials of training required to give the fifth conditioned response against the amount of

Figure 5.12. Scatter plot and regression line showing the relationship between the amount of *change* in the EEG frequency ratio (see text) and the number of trials to the fifth conditioned response (CR) for the 16 animals of Figure 5.11. (From Berry & Thompson, 1980; reproduced by permission.)

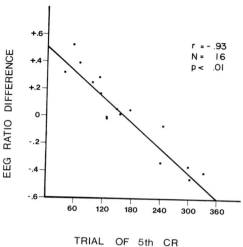

change in the low/high EEG ratio over training for each of the 16 animals described above. The result, shown in Figure 5.12, is striking and seems to provide "physiological" substantiation of Prokasy's model. The correlation between the amount of change in the EEG ratio and the number of trials to the fifth CR is −0.93, a highly significant value. The relationship is such that the greater the shift to higher EEG frequencies, the more rapid the learning. Because more theta is also predictive of fast learning (Figure 5.11), good learners would seem to shift from theta to a desynchronized EEG as they learn. Slow learners, exhibiting a desynchronized EEG initially, would seem to shift more slowly toward theta as they learn. The individual records indicate that this is indeed the case. These results, incidentally, are in complete agreement with the data of Coleman and Lindsley (1977) in their analysis of hippocampal EEG during lever-press learning for reward in cats. The data provide further support for the general notion of an inverted "U" function relating alerting and arousal to learning (Hebb, 1955; Lindsley, 1951). Finally, our data indicate that hippocampal activity is closely related to learning in the rabbit NM paradigm.

B Hippocampal Unit Activity

Our unit analysis of hippocampal activity during learning began with multiple-unit recordings (typically 4–12 units were recorded) from the pyramidal cell layer of CA1-2 and CA3-4 and from the granule cell layer of the dentate gyrus (Berger et al., 1976; Berger & Thompson, 1978a). Essentially the same result was obtained from all these regions. We initially ran a total of 21 conditioning animals and 12 unpaired controls. An example is shown in Figure 5.13. The hippocampal unit poststimulus histogram and averaged NM response for the first block of eight trials are given

PAIRED CONDITIONING

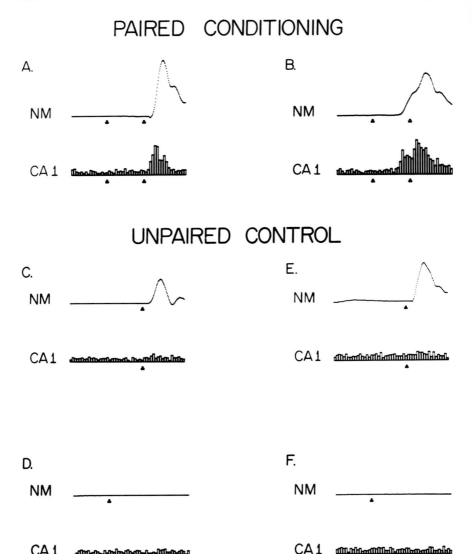

UNPAIRED CONTROL

Figure 5.13. Examples of eight-trial averaged behavioral NM responses and associated multiple-unit histograms of hippocampal activity for a conditioning (A,B) and a control (C–F) animal at the beginning and end of training. Note the very large increase in hippocampal unit activity that develops in the conditioning animal. NM trace: average nictitating membrane response for one block of eight trials. CA1 trace: hippocampal unit poststimulus histogram (15-msec time bins) for one block of eight trials. (A) First block of eight paired conditioning trials, Day 1. (B) Last block of eight paired conditioning trials, Day 1, after conditioning has occurred. (C) First block of eight unpaired UCS-alone trials, Day 1. (E) Last block of eight unpaired UCS-alone trials, Day 2. (D) First block of eight unpaired CS-alone trials, Day 1. (F) Last block of eight unpaired CS-alone trials, Day 2. (From Berger & Thompson, 1978a; reproduced by permission.)

for one animal in Figure 5.13A and for the same animal after learning criterion was reached in Figure 5.13B. Over the first block of eight trials there is a large increase in unit activity in the UCS period that precedes and closely parallels the behavioral NM response form. Over training, this hippocampal unit response increases and moves into the CS period as behavioral learning develops. Indeed, Figure 5.13A and B closely resemble unit activity from the motor nucleus (see Figure 5.7). Actually, the average latency of the hippocampal response is shorter than that for motoneurons (42 msec less than NM onset for hippocampal units and 17 msec less than NM onset for motor units).

In marked contrast, the control-animal hippocampal data are completely different from motoneuron activity. The eight-trial hippocampal unit activity and averaged NM are shown for airpuff-alone trials at the beginning and end of unpaired training for a control animal in Figure 5.13C and E. Although there is a clear reflex NM response, there is little associated unit activity in the hippocampus. There is essentially no NM response or evoked hippocampal activity in tone-alone trials (Figure 5.13D and F).

The hippocampal unit responses illustrated in Figure 5.13 are closely paralleled for all animals in both conditioning and control groups. In Figure 5.14 are shown the standard scores of unit activity for both paired and unpaired groups across all blocks of training trials. For both UCS and CS periods, unit activity in the hippocampus for conditioned animals increases and remains high over all 26 blocks of paired trials (334 trials total, solid lines). In contrast, standard scores for animals given control training remain low across blocks of unpaired trials (broken lines) in both the CS and UCS periods. Although the unpaired standard scores for the UCS period are positive, the differences between paired and unpaired groups are quite dramatic (a difference of about three standard scores is significant). Also, note the clear difference between paired and unpaired UCS scores for the first block of trials. The group data substantiate that the unit increase seen within the first block of paired trials is truly a result of conditioning training.

Behavioral learning curves are not shown. Approximately half the animals learned to criterion on Day 1 and all learned by the end of Day 2 of training. Behavioral learning closely parallels the development of the hippocampal unit response in the CS period. For the average data, this occurred on about Block 6 (see Figure 5.14B). On the average, behavioral conditioned responses began to occur when the hippocampal unit activity in the UCS period had increased to about 12–13 standard scores (see Figure 5.14A). This activity increases linearly over initial blocks of training and begins to decrease its rate of growth at about the time behavioral learning begins to occur.

Because hippocampal unit activity appeared so highly developed at the end of the first block of paired trials (in 17 of the 21 animals), an individual trial analysis for the first eight pairings was completed for all animals. A robust NM response to the airpuff was usually present from the first

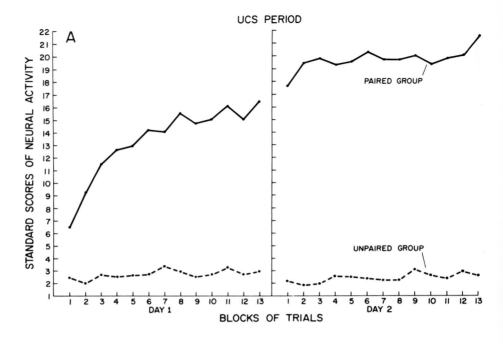

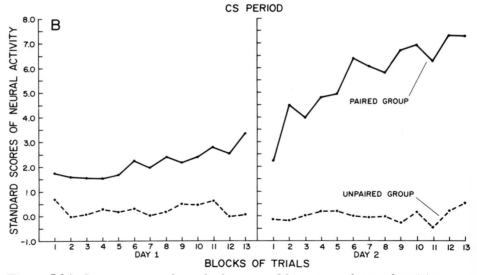

Figure 5.14. Group curves of standard scores of hippocampal neural activity throughout training. (A) Standard scores of unit activity for UCS period, Day 1 and Day 2. (B) Standard scores of unit activity for CS period, Day 1 and Day 2. Solid lines: paired-conditioning group ($n = 21$, Day 1; $n = 14$, Day 2). Broken lines: unpaired control group ($n = 12$, Days 1 and 2). Note expanded y axis and different zero point for CS period graph. (From Berger & Thompson, 1978a; reproduced by permission.)

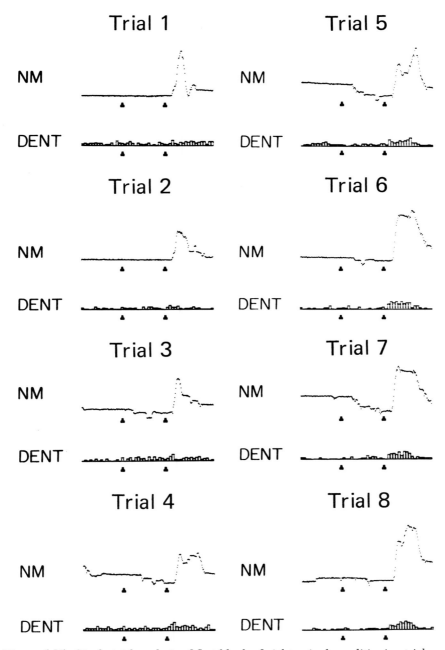

Figure 5.15. Single-trial analysis of first block of eight paired-conditioning trials. NM trace: individual nictitating-membrane response for a paired-conditioning trial. DENT trace: hippocampal unit post stimulus histogram for a paired-conditioning trial. (Adapted from Berger et al., 1976; reproduced by permission. Copyright 1976 by the American Association for the Advancement of Science.)

trial, yet the hippocampal unit response did not appear to develop in conditioned animals until later within the first block. Precisely where within the first block of trials the UCS period unit activity becomes significant relative to preCS levels is difficult to determine for individual animals. (An individual example is shown for the first eight trials in Figure 5.15.) In addition, in some conditioned animals, a small hippocampal unit response was present in the UCS period on the first trial—at levels comparable to that seen in unpaired control animals. The major finding, however, is a definite neuronal enhancement within the initial phase of conditioning. This effect is illustrated in Figure 5.16, which shows the standard scores (see Section 2) of unit activity for the UCS period averaged over the first eight individual CS–UCS presentations for all paired animals versus the first eight individual UCS-alone presentations for all unpaired animals. An analysis of variance showed the paired–unpaired differences within the first block of training trials to be significant at the $p < 0.01$ level. Furthermore, the group data indicate a clear separation between paired and unpaired groups by Trial 2.

The control data shown in Figure 5.13C–F (and in Figure 5.14) argue against the hippocampal response being simply a sensory evoked potential or a "motor" response. There is little increase in hippocampal activity on airpuff-alone trials, even though there is a reflex NM response. Data acquired from animals that occasionally give spontaneous NM responses during trial periods provide further evidence against "motor" or "sensory" interpretation. Examples are shown in Figure 5.17A–C. In Figure 5.17A the animal has not yet learned behaviorally. These are individual paired trials, hence the variability in the NM and the low levels of the hippocampal unit histograms. Note that although there is little or no hippocampal unit activity associated with even large spontaneous NM responses (e.g.,

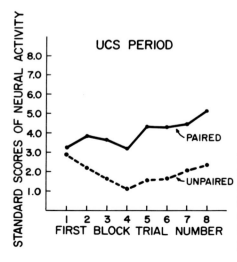

Figure 5.16. Group curves of standard scores of UCS period hippocampal unit activity for first eight paired-conditioning ($n = 21$, solid lines) and unpaired control ($n = 12$, broken lines) trials. (From Berger & Thompson, 1978a; reproduced by permission.)

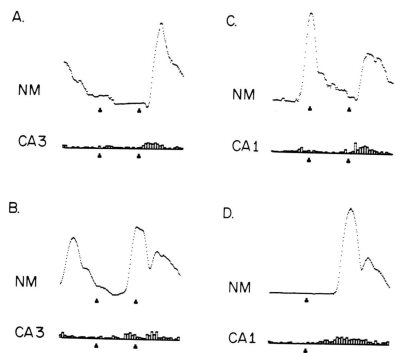

Figure 5.17. Spontaneous, reflex, and conditioned nictitating-membrane responses and associated hippocampal unit activity. NM trace: individual nictitating-membrane response from a single trial. CA1 trace: hippocampal unit post-stimulus histogram from a single trial. (A, B, and C) Paired conditioning trial. (D) Test trial. See text for explanation. Note the virtual absence of hippocampal unit activity associated with spontaneous NM responses and the much larger activity associated with the NM response to paired stimulation. (From Berger & Thompson, 1978a; reproduced by permission.)

Figure 5.17C), there is clear hippocampal unit activity associated with the NM response to the paired stimuli. Figure 5.17D shows an individual test trial for an animal that has learned behaviorally. Although there is no air-puff, there is a clear hippocampal response associated with learned NM response.

To summarize briefly, under conditions of paired training where behavioral learning will occur, unit activity in the hippocampus increases rapidly, initially in the UCS period, forms a temporal "model" of the behavioral response and precedes it in time. As hippocampal activity begins to occur in the CS period, behavioral learning begins to occur. This increased unit activity in the hippocampus does not develop in unpaired control animals. In paired animals the hippocampal activity begins to develop by the second trial of training and may well be the earliest sign of learning in the brain.

C   Generality

It seems likely that these findings have tapped an important functional role of the hippocampus in learning and memory. If this is indeed the case, a number of questions arise. First, it is important to determine the generality of the phenomenon. An obvious issue is the nature of the conditioned stimulus. In a study currently being completed, we used a light (from an LED) as the CS (Coates & Thompson, 1978). Results were essentially the same as for tone (see Figure 5.18). Consequently, the hippocampal response does not seem dependent upon particular characteristics of the conditioned stimulus.

A more critical issue concerns generalization across species. It is possible that the rabbit is somehow unique—the defensive response of eyeball retraction and NM extension is certainly a prominent behavioral response in the rabbit. Patterson and associates have recently developed procedures for classical conditioning of the nictitating-membrane response in the cat (Patterson, Olah, & Clement, 1977). We collaborated in a pilot study of unit activity in the hippocampus in cats run under identical conditions to the rabbit studies (Patterson et al., 1979). The basic finding was the same as in the rabbit (see Figure 5.19). Consequently, the growth in hippocampal unit activity during classical conditioning is not species specific.

Still another aspect of the generality of the hippocampal response relates to the NM paradigm. It would be odd if neurons in the hippocampus became massively engaged only in conditioning of the eyelid. In a pilot study currently in progress, we are running a group of rabbits simply given paired tone and footshock, using the same temporal parameters as with the NM, except that animals are given only 50% reinforcement to permit recording during the UCS period on half the trials (Land, Berger, Patterson, & Thompson, 1980). Although the results are very preliminary at this point, it is clear that unit activity in the hippocampus grows rapidly in the UCS period, almost from the beginning of pairing, just as is true

A   **B**

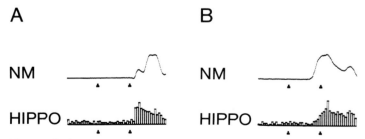

Figure 5.18. Hippocampal unit responses recorded during classical conditioning using a light (LED) CS. NM trace: average nictitating-membrane response for one block of eight trials. HIPPO trace: hippocampal poststimulus histogram for one block of eight trials. (A) One block of trials from early in conditioning. (B) Late in conditioning. (Coates & Thompson, unpublished observations.)

A   B

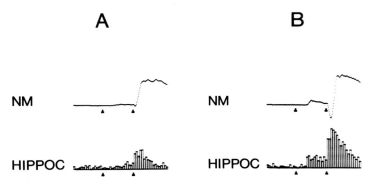

Figure 5.19. Unit responses recorded from cat hippocampus during NM classical conditioning. NM trace average nictitating-membrane response for one block of eight trials. HIPPOC trace: hippocampal poststimulus histogram for same block of trials. (A) Early in conditioning. (B) Late in conditioning after learning has occurred. (From Patterson, Berger, & Thompson, 1979; reproduced by permission.)

for the NM paradigm. There is, however, a major difference—the temporal form of the increased hippocampal unit activity is quite different from that for NM conditioning. Although we have not measured any behavioral response in this pilot study, we would like to suggest that in this situation the hippocampus is forming a model of the behavioral responses to be made—presumably limb movements—which have a temporal form quite different from the NM response.

D   The Interstimulus Interval

Perhaps the single most important and puzzling aspect of classical conditioning is the effect of the temporal relation between the CS and the UCS—the interstimulus interval (ISI) effect. Conditioning does not develop with "backward" presentation (UCS preceding CS) or with simultaneous onset of the two stimuli (in contrast to the classical associationist view). Gormezano (1972) completed an extensive study of the ISI function in the rabbit NM paradigm. His results are shown in Figure 5.20. (A separate group of animals was run for each data point and a trace procedure was used so that durations of the CS and UCS were always the same). There is no conditioning with simultaneous or with a 50-msec forward pairing. Some conditioning develops at a 100-msec ISI, conditioning is maximal between 200 and 400 msec, and it begins to decrease at 800 msec. To the extent tested, this same ISI function holds for a wide range of conditioning situations involving striated muscle responses. Why it occurs is unknown, although it can be assumed to have adaptive value in an evolutionary sense.

   If the hippocampal unit response that develops with conditioning is in fact coding the learning aspect of the situation, then it should show the

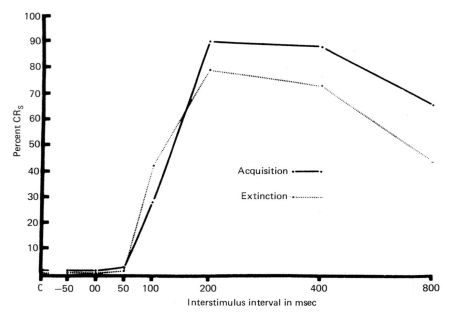

Figure 5.20. Percentage NM responding during test trials of conditioning and extinction as a function of the interstimulus interval (ISI). Data are from a separate group of animals run at each interval, using a trace procedure. (Gormezano, 1972; reproduced by permission of Prentice-Hall, Inc.)

same ISI function as does the learned behavioral response. This is a fairly stringent prediction. With a 50-msec forward pairing, the animal and the hippocampus are receiving the same stimuli as with a 250-msec forward pairing. We have just completed an initial study where groups of rabbits were run at 50-, 150-, and 250-msec forward ISIs (Hoehler & Thompson, 1980). Results are shown in Figures 5.21 and 5.22. The data in Figure 5.21 are eight-paired-trial NM averages and associated histograms of hippocampal multiple-unit activity at the end of training for an animal from each condition. In Figure 5.21A the data are for the 250-msec condition— conditions are exactly the same as for the basic finding described in Section 3,B (see Figure 5.13) and the previous result is exactly replicated.

In Figure 5.21B, the 150-msec ISI is used. Here there is behavioral conditioning and associated increases in hippocampal activity. However, the total amount of increase in hippocampal activity is much less than in Figure 5.21A. Note that it barely has time to begin increasing before airpuff onset. In Figure 5.21C is shown the 50-msec forward condition. Here there is only a reflex NM response (no behavioral conditioning developed) and there is very little increase in hippocampal unit activity.

Data are summed over CS-alone test trials for the last half of the last day of training in Figure 5.22 (the arrow indicates where the airpuff would have occurred on paired trials). Here, any response of the NM or hippo-

Figure 5.21. Averaged nictitating-membrane responses (NM) trace) and hippocampal unit poststimulus histograms (CA1 trace) from the last block of eight paired trials on Day 2. Data are from individual subjects trained with CS–UCS intervals of (A) 250 msec, (B) 150 msec, and (C) 50 msec. First cursor indicates tone onset. Second cursor indicates airpuff onset. (From Hoehler & Thompson, 1980; reproduced by permission.)

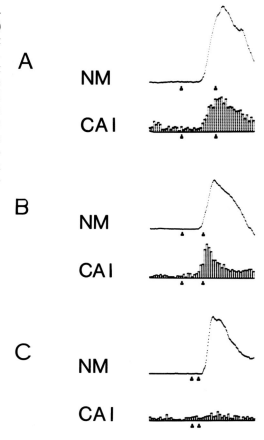

campus would be a conditioned response, because no airpuff is given. For the 250-msec condition (Figure 5.22A) both the NM response and the hippocampal activity are maximally developed, as in Figure 5.21. For the 150-msec ISI (Figure 5.22B), the NM response is much narrower (as reported earlier by Gormezano) and the increase in hippocampal activity is much smaller. At the 50-msec ISI (Figure 5.22C) there is no sign of behavioral NM learning, or of increased hippocampal activity.

In brief, whatever effects the stimulus and training conditions have on learning, they have the same effect on hippocampal unit activity. To put it another way, the degree to which behavioral learning will occur can be predicted from the extent to which the hippocampal unit response develops. In looking at the data of Figures 5.21 and 5.22, one has the compelling impression that the hippocampal unit response must have time to at least begin to develop before learning can occur. At the 50-msec ISI, there is simply not enough time for hippocampal activity to grow after tone onset before the airpuff occurs. Hence, learning does not develop. This, in fact, may be the basic explanation for the ISI effect in behavioral

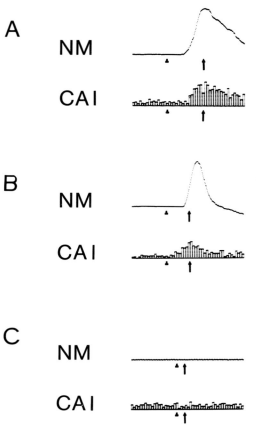

A

NM

CAI

B

NM

CAI

C

NM

CAI

Figure 5.22. Averaged nicti-tating-membrane responses (NM trace) and hippocampal unit poststimulus histograms (CA1 trace) from CS-alone test trials given during the last half of Day 2 (six trials). Data are from individual subjects trained with CS–UCS intervals of (A) 250 msec, (B) 150 msec, and (C) 50 msec. Cursor indicates tone onset. Arrow indicates when the airpuff would have occurred on paired trials. (From Hoehler & Thompson, 1980; reproduced by permission.)

learning. In terms of earlier behavioral theories of learning, the increased unit activity in the hippocampus seems to have many of the properties of Hull's "stimulus trace." However, it forms not a model of the stimulus, but a temporal model of the behavioral response.

E Hippocampal Projections

If the large, learning-dependent response that develops in the hippo-campus is to exert an influence on other brain structures and systems and ultimately on the activity of motoneurons in the final common path for the behavioral conditioned response—the abducens nucleus—then it must be projected out of the hippocampus to other structures. A classical diagram of the major efferent projections of the hippocampus is shown in Figure 5.23.

The projection fibers, the axons from hippocampal pyramidal cells, course out through the fimbria and fornix. There are two major systems, the precommissural fornix, projecting to the septal nuclei, and the post-

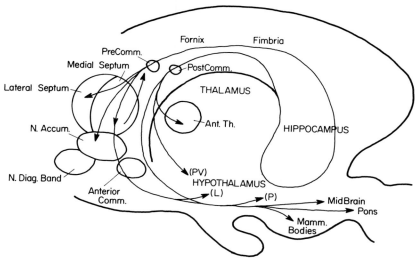

Figure 5.23. Highly schematic diagram of the classically described fornix projections with respect to the hippocampus. The precommissural fornix (Pre-Comm.) was thought to contain efferent projections from the hippocampus to the lateral septum and to the hypothalamus and brainstem, and afferent projections to the hippocampus from the medial septum. The postcommissural fornix (Post-Comm.) was thought to project efferents from the hippocampus to the anterior thalamus (Ant. Th.) and the hypothalamus. Recent anatomical studies agree in general on the sites of termination of the fornix fibers but not on a hippocampal origin for projections to the anterior thalamus, the hypothalamus, and the brainstem. See text for details. (Isaacson, 1974; reproduced by permission.)

commissural fornix, projecting to the mammillary nuclei of the hypothalamus and other structures. We have examined the lateral and medial septal nuclei and the mammillary nuclei in a series of studies using multiple-unit recordings, with a comparison microelectrode always in the hippocampus (Berger & Thompson, 1978c).

Recent anatomical data indicate that the majority of fibers projecting from the hippocampus to the septal nuclei project to the lateral septal nucleus (Meibach & Siegel, 1977; Nauta, 1956; Raisman, Cowan, & Powell, 1966; Swanson & Cowan, 1977). The medial septal nucleus, in contrast, is predominantly a source of fibers projecting to the hippocampus (Andersen, Bruland, & Kaada, 1961; Mosko, Lynch, & Cotman, 1973; Segal & Landis, 1974; Storm-Mathisen, 1970). Examples of simultaneous recordings from the lateral septal nucleus and the hippocampus are shown in Figure 5.24. As is clearly seen, the same growth in unit activity occurs in the lateral septum as in the hippocampus, and only under paired training, not in unpaired controls. Group data comparing unit standard scores for the lateral septum and hippocampus recorded simultaneously during the course of training (seven animals) are shown in Figure 5.25. Note that initial growth of activity is faster in the hippocampus than in the lateral

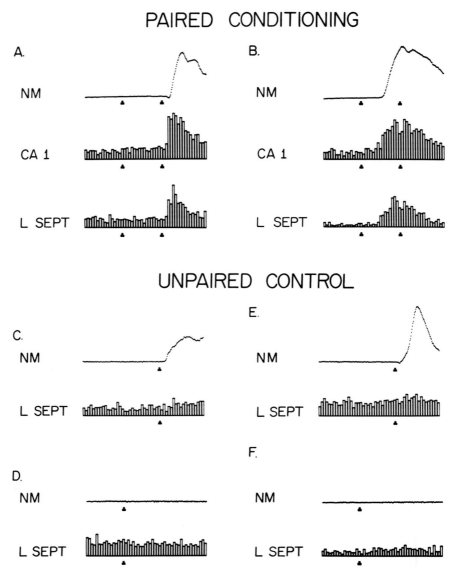

Figure 5.24. (A,B) Simultaneously recorded hippocampal and lateral septal unit responses for one paired conditioning animal. NM trace: average nictitating-membrane response for one block of eight trials. CA1 trace: hippocampal unit poststimulus histogram for one block of eight trials. L SEPT trace: lateral septal unit poststimulus histogram for one block of eight trials. (A) One block of paired trials early on Day 1. (B) One block of conditioning trials late on Day 1. (C–F) Results for one unpaired control animal– (C) and (E), UCS-alone trials from early and late in unpaired training, respectively; (D) and (F), CS-alone trials from early and late in unpaired training, respectively. (From Berger & Thompson, 1978c; reproduced by permission.)

Figure 5.25. Linear regression analysis of unit responses recorded simultaneously from hippocampus and lateral septum during paired conditioning: (A) UCS period standard scores of unit activity. (B) CS period standard scores of unit activity. Solid lines: hippocampus. Broken lines: lateral septum. Note expanded y axis and different zero point for CS period graph. (From Berger & Thompson, 1978c; reproduced by permission.)

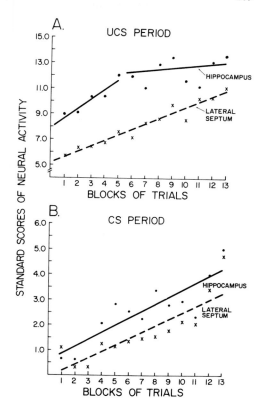

septal nucleus in the UCS period but that lateral septal activity eventually catches up. The growth of activity during the CS period is the same in both structures. It is as though the increasing activity in the hippocampus induces a similar plasticity in the lateral septal nucleus, but it takes a bit more time to develop initially.

Results from the medial septal nucleus are quite different. An example is shown in Figure 5.26. Here there is evoked unit activity to the onset of the stimuli. However, this activity does not grow over training. Instead it decreases or habituates, at the same time that unit activity is growing in the hippocampus and the lateral septum. The medial septum does not exhibit the learning-dependent plasticity—the increase in unit activity that models the behavioral response. Instead, it appears to be providing the hippocampus with information about the occurrence of stimuli. Results for both lateral and medial septal nuclei are in complete accord with current anatomical data and appear to show a functional projection of learning-dependent increases in unit activity over a defined anatomical pathway (hippocampus → lateral septum).

Results for the mammillary nuclei were initially quite disappointing. Activity there resembled somewhat the data for the medial septum—there was a diffuse increase in activity in response to the stimuli (but not

PAIRED CONDITIONING

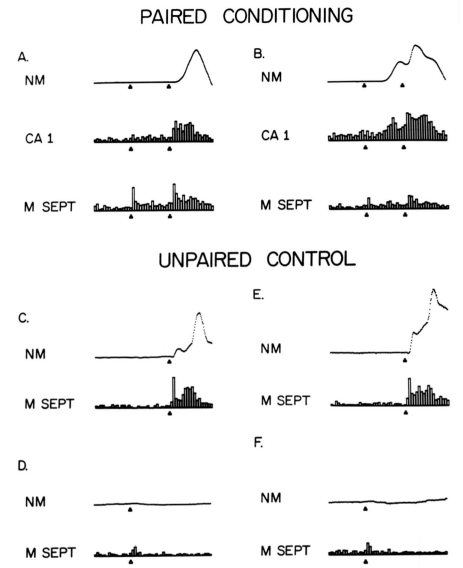

Figure 5.26. Simultaneously recorded hippocampal and medial septal unit responses from a paired-conditioning animal. NM trace: average nictitating-membrane response for one block of eight trials. CA1 trace: hippocampal unit poststimulus histogram for one block of eight trials. M SEPT trace: medial septal unit poststimulus histogram for one block of eight trials. (A) and (B), results for one paired-conditioning animal–(A) One block of paired trials early on Day 1. (B) One block of conditioning trials late on Day 1. (C–F) Results for one unpaired control animal–(C) and (E), UCS-alone trials from early and late in unpaired training, respectively; (D) and (F), CS-alone trials from early and late in unpaired training, respectively. (From Berger & Thompson, 1978c; reproduced by permission.)

sharply evoked activity to stimulus onsets), which did not increase over the period of training. During the course of completing this study, new anatomical data were published (Swanson & Cowan, 1975, 1977) indicating that there are, in fact, no projections from the hippocampus to the mammillary bodies. The earlier defined pathway was based on lesion–terminal degeneration methods, the new data on autoradiographic techniques. Presumably the hippocampal lesions interrupted fibers of passage from the subiculum and other structures coursing through the hippocampus. Consequently, our data indicating no learning-dependent increase in unit activity in the mammillary nuclei are in complete accord with current anatomical findings.

The other major input–output system of the hippocampus involves the entorhinal cortex. Indeed, the perforant path from entorhinal cortex is the largest fiber projection system to the hippocampus. We are currently exploring this sytem, but the data are as yet too preliminary to discuss.

F   Single-Unit Analysis

All of the hippocampal data discussed so far involved multiple-unit recording—measurement of the activity of small clusters of units. The fact that this unit response grows to such a large extent over the course of training (an average increase of 20 standard scores—see Figure 5.14) implies that a substantial number of units in the hippocampus are involved. However, more detailed information about unit activity requires isolated single-unit recording. A related issue of great importance concerns analysis of the synaptic mechanisms underlying the increase in neuronal activity. It is first necessary to identify the classes of neurons involved.

In our initial single-unit studies (Berger & Thompson, 1978a), we did not identify the neurons. It quickly became evident that there were at least two functional classes of neurons (Figure 5.27). One group generated a response closely resembling the multiple-unit measure. The other class showed decreased activity or no changes in firing rates during trial periods. Therefore, not all units participated in generating the large, learning-dependent increase in multiunit activity in the hippocampus.

The anatomy of the hippocampus provides a convenient method for identifying at least one class of neurons, the pyramidal cells. As Spencer and Kandel (1961) showed, pyramidal cells can be antidromically activated by electrical stimulation of the fornix (Figure 5.28). We utilized this method with a chronically implanted bipolar stimulating electrode in the fornix. Actually, the fimbria–fornix system has both efferent axons from pyramidal cells and afferent fibers projecting to the hippocampus. Electrical stimulation of the fornix can produce antidromic (backward nonsynaptic) firing of pyramidal cells (determined by short latency, low variability of latency, and ability to follow at high frequencies) or orthodromic mono- or polysynaptic activation of hippocampal neurons. The

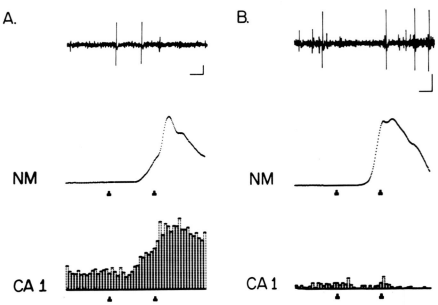

Figure 5.27. Averaged NM responses and hippocampal single-unit poststimulus histograms generated over the course of one day (13 blocks) of paired-conditioning trials. Upper trace: raw data record of single unit recorded in each case. (A) Single-unit data showing same characteristics as hippocampal multiple-unit responses (third paired day). (B) Single-unit data showing no correlation to hippocampal multiple-unit responses (second paired day). Both units were recorded from the CA1 pyramidal layer. Unit calibrations equal 160 μV and 10 msec. (From Berger & Thompson, 1978a; reproduced by permission.)

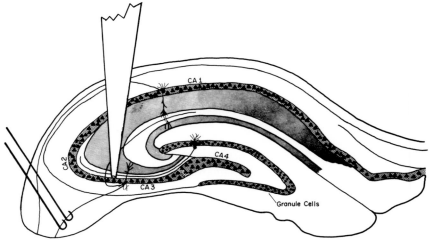

Figure 5.28. Schematic of procedure used for antidromically identifying hippocampal pyramidal cells. Stimulating electrode in fornix, recording microelectrode in hippocampus.

latter could be interneurons or pyramidal cells. Certainty of identification exists only for pyramidal cells activated antidromically.

We recently completed an initial study of 36 hippocampal neurons using this identification technique (Berger & Thompson, 1978b). The procedure involved lowering the microelectrode with the chronically implanted microdrive until a spontaneously active neuron was isolated. It was then tested with fornix stimulation and then studied in the conditioning paradigm. With single-unit recording, it is necessary to collect data for at least three to five blocks of eight-paired trials to build up a histogram (as opposed to one block for multiple-unit recording). Because an animal only learns the behavioral response once and thereafter is trained, and because most animals learn by the beginning of the second day, most of our single-unit data are from already trained animals.

There were three categories of units in terms of reponse to fornix stimulation: antidromically activated pyramidal neurons, orthodromically activated neurons (otherwise unidentifiable), and some neurons that could not be activated at all by fornix stimulation. This last class of neurons tended to have very low spontaneous activity rates. Results were unexpectedly clear (Figure 5.29). The majority of neurons identified as pyramidal cells (16 of the 20) generated the typical "multiple-unit" histogram (Figure 5.29A). The majority of orthodromically activated neurons showed inhibition during the trial period (Figure 5.29B). The third class —cells that did not respond to fornix stimulation—showed no apparent changes in activity over the trial periods (Figure 5.29C).

We were able to hold one identified pyramidal cell over the course of initial training until the animal showed behavioral learning. The growth in activity of this cell is shown in Figure 5.30. There is a clear increase from the beginning of training in the UCS period. Activity in the CS period increases above background PreCS levels at about the time (seventh block of four trials) that the animal began to show behavioral conditioned responses. The growth in activity of this identified pyramidal cell parallels closely the growth of the multiple-unit response.

Consequently, it seems that the growth in unit activity in the hippocampus during learning is primarily the result of increased activity of pyramidal cells. (We are not yet certain whether the inhibition shown by orthodromically activated neurons develops over training.) Once we have identified the pyramidal cells as the major class of neurons generating the learning-dependent hippocampal response, it becomes possible for us to test hypothetical mechanisms. One likely candidate is the process of low-frequency, long-term potentiation (LTP) (Alger & Teyler, 1976; Andersen, Sundberg, Sveen, & Wigström, 1977; Bliss & Lømo, 1973; Chung, 1977; Douglas & Goddard, 1975; Lynch, Dunwiddie, & Gribkoff, 1977; Schwartzkroin & Wester, 1975). It could be that the specific patterns of overlapping conditioned and unconditioned stimulus activation of the hippocampal circuits established conditions much like the brief trains of electrical stimuli that are used to induce LTP. This possibility is, of course, only speculation now but can be subjected to experimental test.

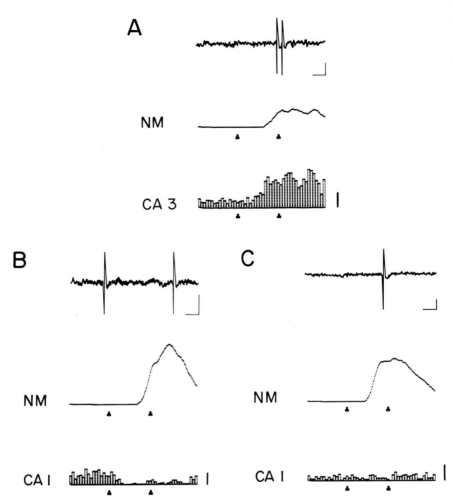

Figure 5.29. Middle traces show average NM response and bottom traces show poststimulus histograms generated by isolated single hippocampal units recorded during paired conditioning. Top traces show examples of spontaneous activity from the single cells that generated the respective poststimulus histograms. Calibrations for upper raw data trace equal 5 μV and 5 msec. (A) Data collected from an antidromically activated unit (pyramidal cell). Vertical histogram calibration is equivalent to 25 unit counts per 15-msec time bin. (B) Data collected from an orthodromically activated unit. Calibration equals 21 counts per 15-msec time bin. (C) Data collected from a hippocampal cell not activated by fornix stimulation. Calibration equals 28 counts per 15-msec time bin. (From Berger & Thompson, 1978b; reproduced by permission.)

Figure 5.30. Mean number of unit spikes over the course of conditioning for a pyramidal cell recorded from the CA3 region of hippocampus. Data are averaged in successive four-trial blocks for paired-conditioning trials: (A) UCS period (solid line) and preCS period (broken line); (B) CS period (solid line) and preCS period (broken line). (From Berger & Thompson, 1978b; reproduced by permission.)

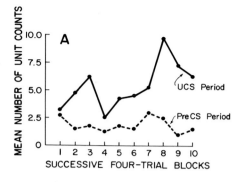

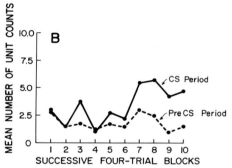

4   Conclusions

The data presented here represent our initial efforts at a systems analysis of one brain system—the hippocampus and related structures. The basic finding was surprising. For animals given conditioning training, the unit activity that develops in the hippocampus closely resembles the activity in the motor nucleus. However, it is not a "motor" potential—it does not develop in unpaired control animals, even though they show a clear behavioral reflex response; it does not occur with spontaneous responding; and most important, it does not develop in animals given a 50-msec forward ISI—these animals show well-developed reflex behavioral responses but do not learn.

Perhaps the most surprising aspect of the hippocampal response is that it actually forms a temporal model of the behavioral response (see Figure 5.13). To determine how good a model it is, we completed a correlation analysis (Berger, Laham, & Thompson, 1980). The analysis consisted of computing a "real-time" correlation coefficient for each eight-trial block for each of 21 conditioning animals between the NM response amplitude and the number of unit discharges of hippocampal neurons. In the example shown in Figure 5.13A, for instance, the two measures were taken every 3 msec from the beginning of the preCS period to the end of the

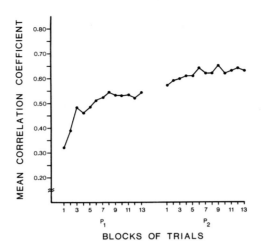

MEAN CORRELATION COEFFICIENT

0.80
0.70
0.60
0.50
0.40
0.30
0.20

1 3 5 7 9 11 13   1 3 5 7 9 11 13
P_1 P_2

BLOCKS OF TRIALS

Figure 5.31. Mean correlation ($N = 21$, $P_1 = $ Day 1; $N = 14$, $P_2 = $ Day 2) between block hippocampal poststimulus histogram and average NM response throughout conditioning training. (From Berger, Laham, & Thompson, 1980; reproduced by permission.)

UCS period and a product-moment correlation coefficient was compiled. This was done for each block for each animal and then averaged across animals. The result—the mean correlation between brain and behavior over the blocks of training—is plotted in Figure 5.31. As can be seen, the correlation is initially modest but grows over training as the unit activity comes to form a very good model of the behavior ($r = 0.63$). Note that this real-time correlation could not be perfect because the hippocampal response occurred earlier in time than the behavioral response (mean onset latency of hippocampal activity was 42 msec less than mean onset of NM). To determine the maximum possible correlation we time shifted the hippocampal response so it and the NM had the same onset point and compared only the active phases of the response. At the end of training this time-shifted correlation was $r = 0.88$, a very good model indeed.

We began with an attempt to characterize the hippocampal system in a simple learning situation. Our results have suggested a new and important role or function of the hippocampus—to form a temporal model of behavior in learning. This is not the place to review the vast hippocampal literature; our findings appear to be consistent with certain theories of hippocampal function (Routtenberg, 1975; Vanderwolf, 1969; Vanderwolf, Kramis, Gillespie, & Bland, 1976) and inconsistent with certain other views (O'Keefe, 1976; O'Keefe and Nadel, 1978).

All of our results can be summed up in the following rather simple statement: In the learning paradigm we employ, the growth of the hippocampal unit response is completely predictive of subsequent behavioral learning. If the hippocampal response does not develop, the animal will not learn. If it develops rapidly, the animal will learn rapidly. If it develops slowly, the animal will learn slowly. Further, the temporal form of the hippocampal response predicts the temporal form of the behavioral response. The only thing more that could be asked of any brain system in relation to learning would be to find the engram there.

Acknowledgments. This research was supported by research grants from NIMH (MH26530), NIH (NS12268), NSF (BMS 7500453), and the McKnight Foundation. We thank Fe Glanzman and Carol Cooper for histology; Craig Cegavske, Richard Roemer, and William Whipple for illustrations; Juta Kiethe for photography; and Carol Hibbert and Sharon Phillips for typing the manuscript. This paper was brought to completion while the first author was a Fellow of the Center for Advanced Study in the Behavioral Sciences, Stanford, California, with the support of Center funds and funds from the NIMH (5 T 32 14581-03) and the NSF (BNS 76-22943 A02).

References

Adey, W.R. Neurophysiological correlates of information transaction and storage in brain tissue. In E. Stellar & J.M. Sprague (Eds.), *Progress in physiological psychology* (Vol. 1). New York: Academic Press, 1966.

Agranoff, B.W. Agents that block memory. In G.C. Quarton, T. Melnechuck, & F.O. Schmitt (Eds.), *The neurosciences.* New York: Rockefeller University Press, 1967.

Alger, B.E., & Teyler, T.J. Long-term plasticity in the CA1, CA3, and dentate regions of the rat hippocampal slice. *Brain Research*, 1976, *110*, 463–480.

Andersen, P., Bruland, P.H., and Kaada, B.R. Activation of field CA1 of the hippocampus by septal stimulation. *Acta Physiologica Scandinavia*, 1961, *51*, 29–40.

Andersen, P., Sundberg, S.H., Sveen, O., & Wigström, H. Specific long-lasting potentiation of synaptic transmission in hippocampal slices. *Nature*, 1977, *266*, 736–737.

Anokhin, P.K. *Biology and neurophysiology of the conditioned reflex and its role in adaptive behavior.* New York: Pergamon Press, 1974. (Russian edition published by Meditsina, Moskow, 1968).

Asratyan, E.A. Reflex mechanisms of motivated behavior. In R.F. Thompson, L.H. Hicks, & V.B. Shvyrkov (Eds.), *Neural mechanisms of goal-directed behavior and learning.* New York: Academic Press, 1980.

Atkinson, R.C., & Shiffrin, R. Human memory: A proposed system and its control processes. In K.W. Spence & J.T. Spence (Eds.), *Psychology of learning and motivation* (Vol. II). New York: Academic Press, 1968.

Bard, P., & Macht, M.B. The behavior of chronically decerebrate cats. In *Ciba Foundation symposium, neurological basis of behavior.* London: Churchill, 1958, 55–71.

Berger, T.W., Alger, B.E., & Thompson, R.F. Neuronal substrates of classical conditioning in the hippocampus. *Science*, 1976, *192*, 483–485.

Berger, T.W., Laham, R.I., & Thompson, R.F. Hippocampal unit-behavior correlations during classical conditioning. *Brain Research*, 1980, (in press).

Berger, T.W., & Thompson, R.F. Neuronal plasticity in the limbic system during classical conditioning of the rabbit nictitating membrane response. I. The hippocampus. *Brain Research*, 1978, *145*, 323–346. (a)

Berger, T.W., & Thompson, R.F. Identification of pyramidal cells as the critical elements in hippocampal neuronal plasticity during learning. *Proceedings of the National Academy of Sciences* (U.S), 1978, *75*(3), 1572–1576. (b)

Berger, T.W., & Thompson, R.F. Neuronal plasticity in the limbic system during classical conditioning of the rabbit nictitating membrane response. II. Septum and mammillary bodies. *Brain Research*, 1978, *156*, 293–314. (c)

Berry, S.D., & Thompson, R.F. Prediction of learning rate from the hippocampal electroencephalogram. *Science*, 1978, *200*, 1298–1300.

Berry, S.D., & Thompson, R.F. EEG–multiple unit relationships during classical conditioning of the NM response in rabbits. *Science*, 1979, *205*, 209–210.

Berry, S.D., & Thompson, R.F. Interrelations among hippocampal EEG activity, hippocampal unit activity and medial septal nuclei in classical conditioning of the rabbit nictitating membrane response. 1980. (In preparation.)

Bliss, T.V.P., & Lømo, T. Long-lasting potentiation of synaptic transmission in the dentate area of the anaesthetized rabbit following stimulation of the perforant path. *Journal of Physiology* (London), 1973, *232*, 331–356.

Brooks, V.B. Roles of cerebellum and basal ganglia in initiation and control of movements. *Le Journal Canadien des Sciences Neurologiques*, 1975, 265–277.

Cegavske, C.F., Thompson, R.F., Patterson, M.M., & Gormezano, I. Mechanisms of efferent neuronal control of the reflex nictitating membrane response in rabbit. *Journal of Comparative Physiological Psychology*, 1976, *90*, 411–423.

Cegavske, C.F., Patterson, M.M., & Thompson, R.F. Activity of units in the abducens nucleus (the final common path) during classical conditioning of the rabbit nictitating membrane response. *Journal of Comparative and Physiological Psychology*, 1979, *93*, 595–609.

Chung, Shin-Ho. Synaptic memory in the hippocampus. *Nature*, 1977, *266*, 677–678.

Coates, S.R., & Thompson, R.F. Comparing neural plasticity in the hippocampus during classical conditioning of the rabbit nictitating membrane response to light and tone. *Society for Neuroscience Abstracts*, 1978, *4*, 256.

Coleman, J.R., & Lindsley, D.B. Behavioral and hippocampal electrical changes during operant learning in cats and effects of stimulating two hypothalamic–hippocampal systems. *Electroencephalography and Clinical Neurophysiology*, 1977, *42*, 309–331.

Disterhoft, J.F., Kwan, H.H., & Lo, W.D. Nictitating membrane conditioning to tone in the immobilized albino rabbit. *Brain Research*, 1977, *137*, 127–143.

Douglas, R.M., & Goddard, G.V. Long-term potentiation of the perforant path granule cell synapse in the rat hippocampus. *Brain Research*, 1975, *86*, 205–215.

Duncan, C.P. The retroactive effect of electroshock on learning. *Journal of Comparative and Physiological Psychology*, 1949, *42*, 34–44.

Durkovic, R.G. Classical conditioning, sensitization, and habituation of the flexion reflex of the spinal cat. *Physiology and Behavior*, 1975, *14*, 297–304.

Evarts, E.V. Temporal patterns of discharge of pyramidal tract neurons during sleep and waking in the monkey. *Journal of Neurophysiology*, 1964, *27*, 152–171.

Flexner, J.B., Flexner, L.B., & Stellar, E. Memory in mice as affected by intracerebral puromycin. *Science*, 1963, *141*, 57–59.

Fritsch, G., & Hitzig, E. Über die elektrische Erregbarkeit des Grosshirns. *Archiv für Anatomiz Physiologie und Wissenschaftliche Medicin*, 1870, *37*, 300–332.

Gabriel, M., Miller, J.D., & Saltwick, S.E. Unit activity in cingulate cortex and anteroventral thalamus of the rabbit during differential conditioning and reversal. *Journal of Comparative Physiological Psychology*, 1977, *91*, 423–433.

Gasanov, U.G. The plasticity of interneuronal relations in learning. In R.F.

Thompson, L.H. Hicks, & V.B. Shvyrkov (Eds.), *Neural mechanisms of goal-directed behavior and learning*. New York: Academic Press, 1980.

Gormezano, I. Classical conditioning. In J.B. Sidowski (Ed.), *Experimental methods and instrumentation in psychology*. New York: McGraw-Hill, 1966.

Gormezano, I. Investigations of defense and reward conditioning in the rabbit. In A.H. Black and W.F. Prokasy (Eds.), *Classical conditioning (Vol. II) Current research and theory*. New York: Appleton-Century-Crofts, 1972.

Gormezano, I., Schneiderman, N., Deaux, E.B. & Fuentes, I. Nictitating membrane: Classical conditioning and extinction in the albino cat. *Science*, 1962, *138*, 33–34.

Grastyan, E., Lissak, K., Madarasz, L., & Donhoffer, H. Hippocampal electrical activity during the development of conditioned reflexes. *Electroencephalography and Clinical Neurophysiology*, 1959, *11*, 409–430.

Green, J.D., & Arduini, A. Hippocampal electrical activity and arousal. *Journal of Neurophysiology*, 1954, *17*, 533–557.

Groves, P.M., & Thompson, R. F. Habituation: A dual process theory. *Psychological Review*, 1970, *77*, 419–450.

Harlow, H.F. Functional organization of the brain in relation to motivation and behavior. In *The biology of mental health and disease*. New York: Hoeber, 1952.

Hebb, D.O. *The organization of behavior*. New York: Wiley, 1949.

Hebb, D.O. Drives and the C.N.S. (Conceptual Nervous System). *Psychological Review*, 1955, *62*, 243–254.

Hoehler, F.K., & Thompson, R.F. Effect of the interstimulus (CS-UCS) interval on hippocampal unit activity during classical conditioning of the nictitating membrane response of the rabbit, *Oryctolagus cuniculus. Journal of Comparative and Physiological Psychology*, 1980 (in press).

Isaacson, R.L. *The limbic system*. New York: Plenum Press, 1974.

Isaacson, R.L., & Pribram, K.H. (Eds.) *The hippocampus* (Vols. 1 & 2). New York: Plenum Press, 1975.

James, W. *Principles of psychology*. New York: Dover, 1890.

Kandel, E.R. *The cellular basis of behavior*. San Francisco: Freeman, 1976.

Kety, S. Biological concomitants of affective states and their possible role in memory processes. In M.R. Rosenzweig & E.L. Bennett (Eds.), *Neural mechanisms of learning and memory*. Cambridge, Mass.: Massachusetts Institute of Technology Press, 1976.

Lacey, J.I., & Lacey, B.C. Change in heart period: A function of sensorimotor event timing within the cardiac cycle. *Physiological Psychology*, 1977, *5*, 383–393.

Land, T., Berger, T.W., Patterson, M.M., & Thompson, R.F. Growth in hippocampal unit activity in a classical conditioning leg shock paradigm. 1980. (In preparation.)

Landfield, P.W., McGaugh, J.L., & Tusa, R.J. Theta rhythm: A temporal correlate of memory storage processes in the rat. *Science*, 1972, *175*, 87–89.

Lashley, K.S. *Brain mechanisms and intelligence*. Chicago: University of Chicago Press, 1929.

Lashley, K.S. In search of the engram. In *Symposium of the society for experimental biology* (Vol. 4). New York: Cambridge University Press, 1950.

Lindsley, D.B. Emotion. In S.S. Stevens (Ed.), *Handbook of experimental psychology*. New York: Wiley, 1951.

Lindsley, D.B. Attention, consciousness, sleep and wakefulness. In J. Field (Ed.),

Handbook of physiology: Neurophysiology (Vol. III). Washington, D.C.: American Physiological Society, 1960.

Lindsley, D.M., & Wilson, C.L. Brainstem-hypothalamic systems influencing hippocampal activity and behavior. In R.L. Isaacson and K.H. Pribram (Eds.), *The hippocampus* (Vol. 2). New York: Plenum Press, 1975.

Lindzey, G., Hall, C.S., & Thompson, R.F. *Psychology* (2nd ed.). New York: Worth, 1978.

Lomov, B.F. Introductory remarks to the Soviet–American symposium on neurophysiological mechanisms of goal-directed behavior. In R.F. Thompson, L.H. Hicks, & V.B. Shvyrkov (Eds.), *Neural mechanisms of goal-directed behavior and learning*. New York: Academic Press, 1980.

Lynch, G.S., Dunwiddie, T., & Gribkoff, V. Heterosynaptic depression: A postsynaptic correlate of long-term potentiation. *Nature*, 1977, *266*, 737–738.

McGaugh, J.L. Time dependent processes in memory storage. *Science*, 1966, *153*, 1351–1358.

McGaugh, J.L., & Herz, M.J. *Memory consolidation*. San Francisco: Albion, 1972.

Meibach, R.C., & Siegel, A. Efferent connections of the septal area of the rat: An analysis utilizing retrograde and anterograde transport methods. *Brain Research*, 1977, *119*, 1–20.

Meyer, D.R., & Meyer, P.M. Dynamics and bases of recoveries of function after injuries to the cerebral cortex. *Physiological Psychology*, 1977, *5*, 133–165.

Miller, G.A. The magic number seven plus or minus two: Some limits on our capacity for processing information. *Psychological Review*, 1956, *63*, 81–97.

Miller, N.E. Homeostasis as goal-directed behavior. In R.F. Thompson, L.H. Hicks, & V.B. Shvyrkov (Eds.), *Neural mechanisms of goal-directed behavior and learning*. New York: Academic Press, 1980.

Mis, F.W. A midbrain-brain stem circuit for conditioned inhibition of the rabbit's (*Oryctolagus cuniculus*) nictitating membrane response. *Journal of Comparative and Physiological Psychology*, 1977, *91*, 975–988.

Moore, J.W. Brain processes and conditioning. In A. Dickinson & R.A. Boakes (Eds.), *Mechanisms of learning and memory: A memorial to Jerzy Konorski*. Hillsdale, N.J.: Lawrence Erlbaum, 1979.

Mosko, S., Lynch, G., & Cotman, C.W. The distribution of septal projections to the hippocampus of the rat. *Journal of Comparative Neurology*, 1973, *152*, 163–174.

Mountcastle, V.B., Lynch, J.C., Georgopoulos, A., Sokoto, H., & Acuna, C. Posterior parietal association cortex of the monkey: Command functions for operations within extrapersonal space. *Journal of Neurophysiology*, 1975, *38*, 871–909.

Nauta, W.J.H. An experimental study of the fornix in the rat. *Journal of Comparative Neurology*, 1956, *104*, 247–272.

Norman, R.J., Buchwald, J.S., & Villablanca, J.R. Classical conditioning with auditory discrimination of the eye blink in decerebrate cats. *Science*, 1977, *196*, 551–553.

O'Keefe, J. Place units in the hippocampus. *Experimental Neurology*, 1976, *51*, 78–109.

O'Keefe, J., & Nadel, L. *The hippocampus as a cognitive map*. Oxford: Oxford University Press, 1978.

Olds, J., Disterhoft, J.F., Segal, M., Kornblith, C.L., & Hirsh, R. Learning centers of rat brain mapped by measuring latencies of conditioned unit responses. *Journal of Neurophysiology*, 1972, 35, 202–219.

Patterson, M.M. Mechanisms of classical conditioning and fixation in spinal mammals. In A.H. Riesen & R.F. Thompson (Eds.), *Advances in psychobiology* (Vol. 3). New York: John Wiley and Sons, 1976.

Patterson, M.M., Berger, T.W., & Thompson, R.F. Neuronal plasticity recorded from cat hippocampus during classical conditioning. *Brain Research*, 1979, 163, 339–343.

Patterson, M.M., Cegavske, C.R., & Thompson, R.F. Effects of a classical conditioning paradigm on hind-limb flexor nerve response in immobilized spinal cat. *Journal of Comparative and Physiological Psychology*, 1973, 84, 88–97.

Patterson, M.M., Olah, J., & Clement, J. Classical nictitating membrane conditioning in the awake, normal, restrained cat. *Science*, 1977, 196, 1124–1126.

Pavlov, I. *Conditioned reflexes*. New York: Oxford University Press, 1927.

Peterson, L.R., & Peterson, M.J. Short-term retention of individual verbal items. *Journal of Experimental Psychology*, 1959, 58, 193–198.

Pribram, K.H. *Languages of the brain: Experimental paradoxes and principles in neuropsychology*. Englewood Cliffs, N.J.: Prentice Hall, 1971.

Prokasy, W.F. Developments with the two-phase model applied to human eyelid conditioning. In A.H. Black & W.F. Prokasy (Eds.), *Classical conditioning* (Vol. II) *Current research and theory*. New York: Appleton-Century-Crofts, 1972.

Raisman, G., Cowan, W.M., & Powell, T.P.S. An experimental analysis of the efferent projection of the hippocampus. *Brain*, 1966, 89, 83–108.

Routtenberg, A. Significance of intracranial self-stimulation pathways for memory consolidation. In P.B. Bradly (Ed.), *Methods in brain research*. New York: Wiley, 1975.

Schwartzkroin, P.A., & Wester, K. Long-lasting facilitation of a synaptic potential following tetanization in the *in vitro* hippocampal slice. *Brain Research*, 1975, 89, 107–119.

Scoville, W.B., & Milner, B. Loss of recent memory after bilateral hippocampal lesions. *Journal of Neurological Psychiatry*, 1975, 20, 11–21.

Segal, M., & Landis, S. Afferents to the hippocampus of the rat studied with the method of retrograde transport of horseradish peroxidase. *Brain Research*, 1974, 78, 1–15.

Shvyrkov, V.B. Goal as a neuronal system-creating factor in behavior and learning. In R.F. Thompson, L.H. Hicks, & V.B. Shvyrkov (Eds.), *Neural mechanisms of goal-directed behavior and learning*. New York: Academic Press, 1980.

Sokolov, E.N. *Perception and the conditioned reflex*. Oxford: Pergamon Press, 1963.

Spencer, W.A., & Kandel, E.R. Hippocampal neuron responses to selective activation of recurrent collaterals of hippocampal axons. *Experimental Neurology*, 1961, 4, 149–161.

Sperling, G. The information available in brief visual presentations. *Psychological Monographs*, 1960, 74, whole No. 496.

Sternberg, S. High speed scanning in human memory. *Science*, 1966, 153, 652–654.

Storm-Mathisen, J. Quantitative histochemistry of acetylcholinesterase in rat hippocampal region correlated to histochemical staining. *Journal of Neurochemistry*, 1970, 17, 739–750.

Sudakov, K.V. The interaction of the hypothalamus, midbrain reticular formation, and thalamus in the mechanism of selective ascending cortical activation during physiological hunger. *Fiziologicheskii Zhurnal SSSR*. 1965, *51*, 449–456.

Swanson, L.W., & Cowan, W.M. Hippocampo–hypothalamic connections: Origin in subicular cortex, not Ammon's horn. *Science*, 1975, *189*, 303–304.

Swanson, L.W., & Cowan, W.M. An autoradiographic study of the organization of efferent connections of the hippocampal formation in the rat. *Journal of Comparative Neurology*, 1977, *172*, 49–84.

Terry, W.S., & Wagner, A.R. Short-term memory for "surprising" versus "expected" unconditioned stimuli in Pavlovian conditioning. *Journal of Experimental Psychology: Animal Behavior Processes*, 1975, *104*, 122–133.

Thompson, Robert. Stereotaxic mapping of brainstem areas critical for memory of visual discrimination habits in the rat. *Physiological Psychology*, 1976, *4*, 1–10.

Thompson, R.F. *Introduction to physiological psychology*. New York: Harper & Row, 1975.

Thompson, R.F., Berger, T.W., Cegavske, C.F., Patterson, M.M., Roemer, R.A., Teyler, T.J., & Young, R.A. The search for the engram. *American Psychologist*, 1976, *31*, 209–227.

Thompson, R.F., & Spencer, W.A. Habituation: A model for the study of neuronal substrates of behavior. *Psychological Review*, 1966, *173*, 16–43.

Towe, A.L. Motor cortex and the pyramidal system. In J.D. Maser (Ed.), *Efferent organization and the integration of behavior*. New York: Academic Press, 1973.

Vanderwolf, C.H. Hippocampal electrical activity and voluntary movement in the rat. *Electroencephalography and Clinical Neurophysiology*, 1969, *26*, 407–418.

Vanderwolf, C.H., Kramis, R., Gillespie, L.A., & Bland, B.H. Hippocampal rhythmic slow activity and neocrotical low-voltage fast activity: Relations to behavior. In R.L. Isaacson & K.H. Pribram (Eds.), *The hippocampus* (Vol. 2). New York: Plenum Press, 1976.

Winson, J. Interspecies differences in the occurrence of theta. *Behavioral Biology*, 1972, *7*, 479–487.

Woolsey, C.N., Travis, A.M., Barnard, J.W., & Ostinso, R.S. Motor representation in the postcentral and supplementary motor areas. *Federation Proceedings*, 1953, *12*, 160.

Young, R.A., Cegavske, C.F., & Thompson, R.F. Tone-induced changes in excitability of abducens motoneurons in the reflex path of the rabbit nictitating membranes response. *Journal of Comparative and Physiological Psychology*, 1976, *90*, 424–434.

Discussion

Dr. Kandel: I'm wondering to what degree Lashley's coming to the conclusion that he did about distribution of memory was not in part based on the task that he used, a much more complicated task than you used, and in some ways an unsatisfactory one for the neural analysis.

Dr. Thompson: I agree with that completely. As you know, in his initial classical studies, Lashley used maze learning with a series of mazes varying in complexity. He only got substantial deficits with the most complicated maze. Additional problems with maze learning include the fact that we can't identify the stimuli, and the response systems are very hard to identify neuronally. As you know, if you injure the animal's legs he'll roll through the maze; it you put water in the maze, he'll swim through it. The behavioral "movements" are very difficult to analyze neuronally.

Dr. Kandel: So that if you would make a lesion, the animal might use completely new cues to relearn it. It wasn't the fact that the system involved was not critical for the learning, it's the fact that the learning had changed.

Dr. Thompson: Or could use many cues indeed. You remember Hunter suggested that in his analysis of Lashley's work.

Dr. Kandel: The other question I have is how compelling you really find the evidence for different memory systems in the brain—whether the same kinds of experiments aren't quite compatible with the notion of a single memory system, at least anatomically?

Dr. Thompson: What we've seen so far is just one kind of process occurring in the hippocampus that seems to be projected to other systems. We think it is a part of the memory system in the brain. I was really arguing by analogy with the human information-processing model, which is appealing to me.

Dr. Kandel: You can take exactly the same data, as a number of people like Wickelgren and others have done, and interpret them in terms of a single memory trace that changes in character. In fact, although Hebb speaks about two memory systems—a reverberating one and sort of a plastic, morphological one—the fact is that the location for the two in space is the same. He presumes that by the repeated bombardment of this specific set of synapses, it undergoes a morphological change.

Dr. Thompson: Indeed, many of you will recall that Art Melton argued for years against the notion of more than one memory trace. He said simply that the memory process occurs over a time course with properties that change, but it's the same trace. Yes. I think the evidence is not compelling but I find the possibility of a multitude of systems interacting—by analogy with motor systems—to be an attractive one.

Dr. Kandel: One final point on that is that if one looks at the data on motor systems, like the analysis of Hans Kypers, one does not get the impression that pyramidal and extrapyramidal motor systems are redundant, that is, identical. They actually seem to carry out different processes, the pyramidal system being involved in small delicate movements of the distal extremities, while the extrapyramidal system is involved in grosser movements and in postural adjustments. I would think it's only when the task is ambiguous that a lesion in one system would be so readily compensated for by the other system.

Dr. Thompson: But see, that's the analogy I like because I would conceive of similar kinds of systems in the brain doing different things in relation to memory.

Dr. Kandel: Oh, I see.

Dr. Barlow: May I ask you a question about something that puzzles me? If I understand you correctly, every single pyramidal cell—or 18 out of 20 —responds in this extremely trivial learning situation. Now that seems to me very extrordinary. Where does all the important learning take place?

Dr. Thompson: Well, the situation may seem trivial to us, perhaps, but not to the rabbit. [*Note added in proof:* We have now examined about 60 identified pyramidal neurons, mostly from CA3 (R.F. Thompson & T.W. Berger, *Society for Neuroscience Abstracts*, 1979, 5, 325). Approximately 80% of them show the marked learning-dependent increase in activity that models the actual amplitude–time course of the behavioral NM response. Consequently, it seems a reasonable inference that the majority of pyramidal neurons in the hippocampus participate in the response. I would emphasize again that the NM response is a most important defensive reflex for the rabbit. Hippocampal neurons become engaged not simply in the reflex response, but when the warning tone (the CS) predicts the close temporal continuity of the threat to the eye (the corneal airpuff UCS). In other terms, the hippocampus becomes involved in learning situations that are biologically meaningful to the animal.]

Dr. Rose: Do you have any knowledge from putting the electrodes somewhere else in the hippocampus region, particularly in the subiculum, presubicular area, entorhinal cortex, and what not?

Dr. Thompson: We are now looking in the entorhinal cortex and the story seems complicated. There appear to be some regions of the entorhinal cortex that show changes that are similar to those in the hippocampus but not as large. However, they do not show much increase over learning. There is activity in the entorhinal cortex but little change over learning. Anatomically, there are certain regions of entorhinal cortex that receive projections from the hippocampus, other regions that do not. It would be very nice if these anatomical differences corresponded to functional differences in our paradigm, but we don't know that yet. Entorhinal cortex is the source of the major input system to the hippocampus through the perforant path. So, a very real possibility, which Dr. Rose raised, is that the activity is in fact initially developing elsewhere in the brain and then being projected in to hippocampus. [*Note added in proof:* We have now completed our initial study of entorhinal cortex (G.A. Clark, T.W. Berger, & R.F. Thompson, *Society for Neuroscience Abstracts*, 1978, 4, 217). In general, we have found that there is an increase in neuronal activity within trials that may provide a model or template of the behavioral response (i.e., NM response) to be learned, which could be projected to the hippocampus. However, this pattern of unit activity in entorhinal cortex does not appear to increase over the course of learning as occurs in the hippocampus.]

Dr. Barlow: Supposing you had any other two stimuli paired together: Are we to suppose the same pyramidal cells in hippocampus would also respond to that pairing?

Dr. Thompson: I would say that if it's a pairing of stimuli that are of biological significance or importance to the animal, yes. The airpuff is aversive to the rabbit. It is a very important situation in his life at this point.
Dr. Barlow: I don't mean to say that this is not an important type of learning to investigate or anything like that, but what puzzles me is the fact that you arbitrarily take one pairing and arbitrarily select one pyramidal cell and you find that it detects it. There are so many possible pairings that that surprises me. I would expect that some pyramidal cells would respond to one pairing, others to another, but that doesn't seem to be the case. It's astonishing.
Dr. Thompson: Another astonishing thing is that we get the same growth in activity in CA1 and CA3. There's not a regional segregation of the development of the response.
Dr. Kandel: I don't quite see why one should or should not be astonished. You're talking as if this were a motor nucleus and we knew exactly what it is doing. We don't know what the hippocampus is doing. This is the kind of information that might clarify what it is doing. It is possible that the whole hippocampus has to be involved in a sort of arousal process in order for the animal to learn effectively. I don't see how one can have a preconceived notion as to how the system works because we haven't any notion of what it does.
Dr. Barlow: I should have thought that hippocampus would get confused with all these paired things.
Dr. Kandel: The other thing is that there could be timing differences that you are clearly not analyzing so it isn't that every cell fires at exactly the same . . .
Dr. Thompson: For example, we haven't even done interspike interval analysis yet to look at that. [Note *added in proof:* As noted in my contribution to this volume, we get the marked increase in hippocampal unit activity when a light CS is paired with corneal airpuff and when a tone is paired with hindpaw shock. The increased hippocampal unit response does indeed appear to develop with pairing of any "neutral" CS with any reinforcing stimulus (at least of an aversive nature) *that will result in behavioral learning*. Furthermore, the temporal pattern of increased unit firing appears to "model" the amplitude–time course of the *behavioral response being learned*. We now think that this temporal neuronal model of the learned behavioral response may in fact be the "engram," or at least the neurophysiological trace of the engram for simple learning situations. The fact that the hippocampal pyramidal neurons appear to become massively engaged whenever biologically meaningful pairings of neutral and potentially harmful stimuli occur implies, as Dr. Barlow notes, that the engram itself is not permanently stored in the hippocampus. Instead, the hippocampus may function in the storage and retrieval of the memory trace.]
Terry M. Mikiten (University of Texas Health Sciences Center, San Antonio): I couldn't help but wonder whether the phenomena you were

looking at were in fact present not only in the hippocampus but in other cortical areas as well. Have you looked at some other cortical area, such as an association area, a specific projection area, or even a motor section of cortex, to demonstrate that the phenomenon is not a widespread one? You happen to be focusing your attention on the hippocampus because it's the thing to do these days, but could this activity be present elsewhere? And might it not reflect the activity of the cortex generally?

Dr. Thompson: Actually, I had no special love for the hippocampus when I started this project, and we did not look at it simply because it is the "thing to do." Our research program involves a systematic examination of all major brain systems and regions during learning. It happens that the hippocampus shows an extraordinary result, which we felt should be pursued. We have not systematically examined cerebral cortex yet. It's something that we have to do. We've done a few control recordings with the movable microelectrodes in the cortical region just above the hippocampus. That region turns out not to show any change in activity with learning, but we haven't searched systematically in the cortex.

Charles Wood (Applied Research Labs, University of Texas, Austin): Do the inhibitory neurons show the same sort of conditioning?

Dr. Thompson: We had only one single cell that we were able to hold from the beginning of training until the animal learned, and that turned out to be an identified pyramidal cell. It was very nice in that its activity started increasing within a couple of trials and built up steadily. We have not yet succeeded in holding one of these inhibitory type of interneurons —inhibitory in terms of what it does—over the course of training. My guess would be that it does build up; it would be very nice if it did, but I honestly can't say yet. It's technically difficult. You only have one shot at the initial learning. Once it occurs the animal is permanently changed.

Dr. McFadden: Relative to Dr. Barlow's question, am I correct in presuming that you think of the hippocampus as a kind of control center that during the course of learning is doing things elsewhere in the brain? That is to say, are you thinking about an engram being located elsewhere and that the hippocampus is working to establish it and/or to carry out its bidding? Might not such a view act to reduce the surprise that Dr. Barlow has over so many of the pyramidal cells being activated by what seem to be simple pairings?

Dr. Thompson: I like that conceptualization. It's a very real possibility. We can't be certain yet but that's certainly one way to look at it. I do not think that the engrams are being laid down permanently just in the hippocampus. Beyond that it's very hard to say, but one possibility would be that it is part of a control system that is involved in the establishment of engrams. In our current thinking we find the computer analogy of an "index" helpful—the hippocampus seems to be critically involved in the storage and/or retrieval of learned information.

Chapter 6

Brain Mechanisms in Voluntary Movement

Edward V. Evarts

1 Introduction

Thirty years ago, shortly following the Hixon Symposium on which the present meeting is patterned, Karl Lashley was kind enough to take me on as a postdoctoral fellow at the Yerkes Laboratories of Primate Biology in Orange Park, Florida. It therefore brings back many memories today as I speak on movement, for it was with movement that Lashley was concerned in his Hixon Symposium paper, "The Problem of Serial Order in Behavior." Furthermore, it was in association with Lashley that my work on monkeys began—with studies on brain mechanisms underlying auditory–visual association. At the time of these early studies (Evarts, 1952), much of the work on the cerebral cortex in general and the motor cortex in particular utilized the technique of cerebral ablation and/or electrical stimulation, but in the intervening years a third technique has been developed, one that allows observations of neuronal activity in the brain of the intact animal, and it is with the use of this third technique that I am concerned in this discussion of brain mechanisms in voluntary movement. The pioneering work in this area was done by Herbert Jasper (1958), who studied activity of single brain cells in association with acquisition of conditioned responses. Jasper was interested in the events occurring in association with the learning process, but when I entered the field I devoted attention primarily to the somewhat simpler task of observing the neurophysiological correlates of well-established volitional movements. In these studies operant conditioning techniques were employed to establish reliable motor performance, and it was only after learning had been well established that activity of single brain cells was recorded. The essential features of the simple reaction-time paradigm that was employed in my early work (Evarts, 1966) are illustrated in Figure 6.1. Here we see a schematic representation of a simple visual reaction-time setup where the monkey depresses a manipulandum and awaits a visual stimu-

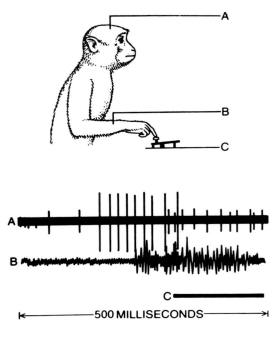

Figure 6.1. Temporal relation between the discharge of a nerve cell in the motor cortex and a simple hand movement. A monkey was trained to depress a telegraph key and then to release it within 350 msec after a light came on. The upper trace (A) shows the activity of a single nerve cell in the arm region of the motor cortex, which was recorded by a microelectrode. The traces start at the onset of the light signal. In a series of trials, the nerve cell became active first, usually within 150 msec of the signal. There followed a contraction of arm muscles (B), which was detected by an electromyograph. Trace (C) shows when the telegraph key opened. (Reprinted from Evarts, 1973b.)

A
B
C
500 MILLISECONDS

lus. If reaction time from visual stimulus to movement was sufficiently brief, a reward was delivered. When the operantly conditioned limb movement was well-established, a microelectrode recorded activity of single brain cells and electromyogram (EMG) electrodes recorded the muscle activity associated with the learned motor response. It is with data obtained in paradigms such as this that I will deal in my discussions today.

2   The Pyramidal Tract Neuron: A Final Common Pathway

In initiating studies on the activity of the brain in relation to volitional movement, it seemed reasonable to start by examining the output of the cerebral cortex—investigating those neurons which send their axons to the spinal cord. Pyramidal tract neurons (PTNs) of the cerebral cortex seemed a reasonable starting point not only because they subserve this output function, but also because of their especially important role in the primate. The pyramidal tract and the motor cortex have undergone a remarkable increase with phylogenetic development. Not only is the pyramidal tract restricted to mammals, but it shows remarkable enhancement even within the primate order, and the motor cortex and pyramidal tract are especially critical for those aspects of motor behavior that are

most especially human. The bulk of the precentral motor cortex is devoted to control of body parts important for manipulation and for speech.
Phillips and Porter (1977) point out that there is a particularly rich termination of PTNs in relation to motoneurons controlling intercostal muscles. It might at first seem odd that the phylogenetically new motor cortex
should be devoted to control of phylogenetically old respiratory muscles.
However, respiratory muscles are critical in production of speech, and
Phillips and Porter point out that the PTN termination on thoracic motoneurons is for speech and song rather than for breathing: Lesions of the
dominant hemisphere's motor cortex can eliminate control of the respiratory muscles in the context of speech while leaving respiration per se unimpaired. The same is true for muscles of the hand, whose use in precisely controlled fine movements is eliminated by destruction of the
pyramidal tract, whereas coarser movements involving these same muscles remain intact. It would seem from the evolutionary standpoint, then,
that PTNs provide a pathway that parallels earlier pathways controlling
the motoneuron, adding certain special features to a motor system that
was already present in lower forms.

3   When Do PTNs Discharge in Relation to Movement?

One of the first questions that arose in connection with the relation of
PTN discharge to movement was one of timing, and it was to get information on this point that the simple visual reaction-time paradigm was employed. Results obtained in connection with such a paradigm are illustrated in Figure 6.2. Figure 6.2 shows activity picked up from a PTN in
the precentral motor cortex in association with performance of a visually
triggered movement. This figure shows data for 12 trials. It may be seen
that there is considerable variation in the interval between the visual
stimulus (the traces of the figure begin with this stimulus) and the occurrence of the single unit discharge. Variability such as this requires that
these data be subjected to statistical analysis and that many trials be taken
for each cell that is investigated. Analysis and display of data such as these
may be facilitated by use of the "raster," as illustrated in Figure 6.3, where
each of the rows corresponds to one trial that an animal has made, and
each dot in the row corresponds to one action potential of a single nerve
cell. The vertical line in each row corresponds to the detection of the
motor response. A further advantage of the computer display is shown in
Figure 6.4, indicating realignment of raster rows so that neuronal activity
can be timed in relation to the occurrence of the motor response as well
as in relation to occurrence of the stimulus. In the bottom raster of Figure 6.4 the rows of dots are aligned with respect to the stimulus; the time
of occurrence of the stimulus is shown by the solid line at the center of

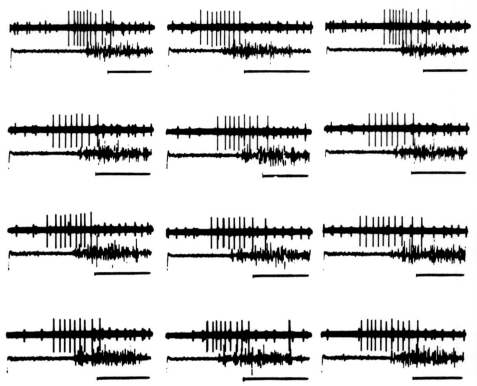

Figure 6.2. The PTN and extensor electromyogram (EMG) response to a visual stimulus. This is a series of 12 trials for a PTN that was silent during flexion and that consistently discharged prior to visually triggered extension of the contralateral wrist. All tracings start at the onset of the light. The minimum response latency for this PTN was about 120 msec. This latency of PTN response was associated with an EMG latency of 170 msec. In general, the shortest latency PTN responses were associated with the shortest latency EMG responses. Sweep duration is 500 msec. (Reprinted from Evarts, 1966.)

the lower raster. In the right half of this raster the heavy dots (one in each row) show when the motor response was detected. After these heavy dots (i.e., after each motor response) there is an increase of discharge in the neuron. If the rows of dots in the lower raster are realigned so that each row moves to the left until the point of response detection reaches the center of the raster, one derives a display of neuronal activity aligned with respect to response (R) instead of stimulus (S). This is shown in the upper raster of Figure 6.4, which again shows an increase of neuronal activity following R, but which in addition reveals a decrease of discharge prior to response detection, as seen in the histogram labeled R. When activity of this neuron is aligned with respect to S, the decrease fails to appear (histogram labeled S). This failure results from the variable latency between the S and R. It is clear that for neuronal activity that is related in time to R rather than S, it is useful to align discharges in relation to R.

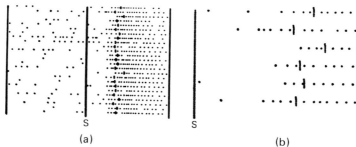

(a)   (b)

Figure 6.3. (a) A raster with 25 rows corresponding to 25 trials; in the center of this 25-row display is a vertical line indicating the time of occurrence of the stimulus (S); the dots to the left of this central line represent neuronal activity occurring 500 msec prior to the stimulus. Each heavy dot to the right of the central line represents the time at which the response was detected. (b) An enlarged view of the poststimulus activity for the first six trials of the display at the left. (Reprinted from Evarts, 1974.)

Not only is PTN activity related in time to R (rather than S), but it is related to the nature of R rather than the nature of S. Therefore, motor-cortex activity prior to a given movement is the same regardless of whether the movement is triggered by an auditory or a visual stimulus, whereas a change in the operant response intervening between visual stimulus and reward will be associated with a change in PTN activity. Re-

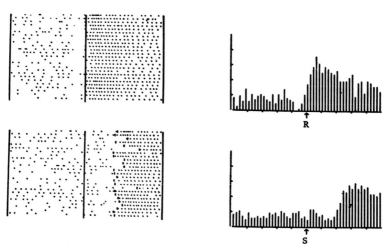

Figure 6.4. Rasters may be aligned with respect to either the stimulus (S) or the response (R). In the lower raster the central vertical line represents S, and the single heavy dot in each row to the right of S represents R. The histogram corresponding to this dot display (lower right) is centered on S, whose time of occurrence is indicated by the arrow. In the upper raster each row of dots has been shifted to the left until R reaches the center of the display. The corresponding histogram (upper right) is therefore centered about R, whose time of occurrence is indicated by the arrow. (Reprinted from Evarts, 1974.)

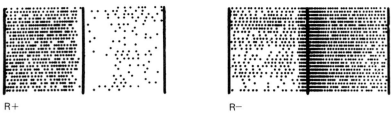

R+   R−

Figure 6.5. Computer analysis allows separation of two sorts of movements that may have occurred alternately. In the display shown here, R + means flexion and R − means extension. During the actual experiment these two movements occurred alternately, and the neuron whose activity is represented in this figure showed a decrease of activity prior to R + and an increase of activity to R −. (Reprinted from Evarts, 1974.)

sults for different operant responses are illustrated in Figure 6.5, where there are two rasters, one corresponding to 25 flexions of the wrist and the other corresponding to 25 extensions. Monkeys had been trained to maintain wrist flexion and abruptly extend and then to maintain extension and abruptly flex in response to the same visual stimulus. Therefore, for each neuron, two sorts of motor responses were alternately obtained, and for each of these motor responses neuronal activity was observed. For the neuron shown in Figure 6.5, flexion of the wrist was associated with a decrease of activity prior to the motor response. This decrease is shown at the left of Figure 6.5, where the raster reveals a reduction of neuronal discharge in association with the movement. For the raster at the right, there is an increase of activity for this same neuron in association with wrist extension. Therefore, for this neuron there is an opposite change in discharge for the two oppositely directed movements of the wrist.

Using methods such as those which have been discussed, it was possible to sample many precentral motor cortex PTNs, and within the region of motor cortex involved in control of movements of the contralateral wrist, there was an intermingling of reciprocally related PTNs, some of which would become active with extension and inactive with flexion, whereas others would become active with wrist flexion and inactive with extension. The PTN illustrated in Figure 6.5 became active with wrist extension and inactive with wrist flexion, and immediately adjacent to it may have been a PTN with opposite relations to wrist movement. Later in this report I will return to a discussion of the significance of the interrelationship between PTNs that are so close to one another that their action potentials are picked up simultaneously with the same microelectrode. For the moment, however, it is sufficient to point out that adjacent PTNs do not necessarily show the same relationship to a particular movement: Two PTNs recorded simultaneously with the same microelectrode may show opposite changes of discharge frequency for the same movement.

However, the major goal of the studies utilizing the visual reaction-time paradigm was to obtain information on timing, and this information showed that many precentral PTNs as well as precentral non-PTNs become active prior to movement. Analyses in which motor-cortex discharges were aligned first with respect to the triggering visual stimulus and then with respect to the onset of the motor response showed that the time of change of motor-cortex discharge was linked with the time of occurrence of the motor response. Therefore, variations in the latency of movement were reflected in corresponding variations in the latency of PTN discharge. However, there was an additional feature of PTN discharge that was also related to movement latency. This is illustrated in the individual trials shown in the "raw data" of Figure 6.2. Note that in addition to variations in the delay from the visual stimulus to the first PTN impulse, there are also variations of impulse frequency within the "burst" of spikes that occurs with each trial. We may infer that burst frequencies on successive trials for this particular PTN are highly correlated with burst frequencies of synergistic PTNs, and that when PTNs have high burst frequencies there will be a shorter latency between onset of motor-cortex output and onset of EMG discharge. In summary, then, studies using the visual reaction-time paradigm reveal that overall reaction time depends on both latency and frequency of motor-cortex discharge.

4   Hand Outputs Triggered by Hand Inputs

In the visual reaction-time (VRT) paradigm the monkey's "set" determined the properties of motor-cortex responses to the visual stimulus. Depending on the monkey's "set" to flex or to extend, a given PTN could be turned on or turned off by an identical visual stimulus. Furthermore, when the monkey became satiated and was no longer motivated to acquire additional reward, this same visual stimulus would evoke no motor-cortex discharge at all.

For one modality, however—somesthesis—this total dependence of motor-cortex discharge on set was lost, and results to be presented now deal with this special case. The differences between the VRT paradigm and a new somesthetic reaction-time (SRT) paradigm are illustrated in Figure 6.6. At the time these experiments were begun, it was already well known that somesthetic inputs to a given zone of motor cortex from the corresponding body part were prominent and of relatively short latency (Albe-Fessard & Liebeskind, 1966; Brooks & Stoney, 1971; Oscarsson & Rosén, 1963, 1966; Rosén & Asanuma, 1972; Towe, 1968). In contrast, there are no such strong visual inputs to motor cortex. For the SRT experiments, hand movements were initiated by an input to the hand. In these experiments the monkey held the handle in the correct position (a light indicated when the handle was in the correct position) for a variable length of time (2–5 sec) awaiting a kinesthetic trigger, which, like the vi-

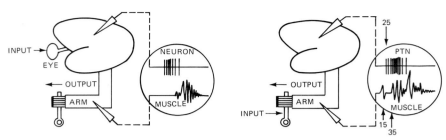

Figure 6.6. When input is visual (left), PTN activity occurs at a latency of about 100 msec, and muscle response occurs even later. For inputs via the responding hand, the muscle and PTN responses occur much earlier, at the times indicated in the right-hand section of the figure. (Reprinted from Evarts, 1974.)

sual stimulus in the VRT paradigm, was the signal to move. The trigger moved the handle forward or backward, and the monkey was rewarded for returning the handle to the correct position.

Whereas motor-cortex activity in the VRT paradigm occurred approximately 100 msec after the visual stimulus, discharges for the somatosensory stimulus occurred in motor-cortex PTNs in as short a time as 25 msec following the stimulus (Figure 6.7). Activity in the postcentral somatic receiving area occurred even sooner, the interval from stimulus to neuronal discharge being as short as 10 msec. Therefore, when the input initiating a hand movement enters via the hand, discharge in the postcentral area occurs *prior* to discharge in the precentral area, whereas the reverse order occurs for movement initiated by a visual stimulus. Finally, it should be pointed out that there are latency differences between pyramidal and nonpyramidal tract neurons in the motor area. For the visually elicited movement, no difference was found between onset times of PTNs and non-PTNs in the precentral motor cortex. However, for the movement elicited by the input to the hand, differences were found in motor cortex for PTNs and non-PTNs. The differences were slight but clearly significant; motor-cortex non-PTNs were found to discharge at latencies of less than 20 msec from the stimulus to the hand. The difference between PTNs and non-PTNs is slight (about 5 msec), and such difference might easily have been missed because of variability in the case of the visually triggered movements, where the onset times of neuronal discharge were less tightly locked to the stimulus.

The results for the movement triggered by the somesthetic stimulus therefore reveal three classes of neurons discharging at successively greater delays from the stimulus. The earliest discharge occurs in neurons of the postcentral gyrus; presumably these are classical sensory responses to the inputs that are delivered to the tactile, pressure, joint, and muscle receptors of the hand and arm when the handle is abruptly deflected by the external power source. The second set of neurons to discharge are non-PTNs in the precentral motor cortex. Finally, at an interval of about 25 msec following the stimulus, PTNs of the motor cortex begin to discharge.

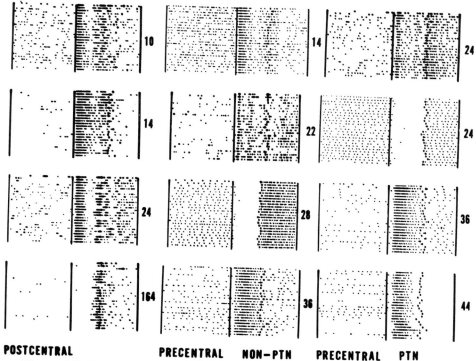

POSTCENTRAL   **PRECENTRAL   NON-PTN   PRECENTRAL   PTN**

Figure 6.7. Each of the 12 rasters shows neuronal activity for 500 msec before and 500 msec after the abrupt handle movement, whose time of occurrence is indicated by the vertical line at the center of the raster. In each raster there are 25 rows of dots, corresponding to 25 successive trials. The individual dots in each row correspond to individual neuronal impulses. Neuronal response latency from handle perturbation to first change in neuronal discharge frequency (either increase or decrease) was computed for each neuron on the basis of 25 trials, and this latency is shown at the right of each raster. In the right half of each raster a single heavy dot on each line of dots indicates the time at which the handle was returned to the correct zone by the monkey's motor response. This heavy dot may be seen most clearly in the PTN raster at the lower right. Rasters in columns at left, center, and right correspond to postcentral neurons, precentral non-PTNs, and precentral PTNs, respectively. The latency values for one non-PTN (28) and one PTN (24) refer to decreases of activity; remaining latencies refer to increases of neuronal activity. (Reprinted from Evarts, 1973a.) (Copyright 1973 by the American Association for the Advancement of Science.)

5   The PTN in a Transcortical Servoloop

What might be the functional role of these strong short-latency inputs from limb receptors to motor-cortex PTNs controlling limb movements? A formulation as to this functional role was made by Phillips in his discussion of my finding that discharge of some PTNs varied with load in tasks requiring either fixed-velocity movements (Evarts, 1968) or maintained posture (Evarts, 1969). My own early formulations concerning the significance of this finding on the relation of PTN discharge frequency to load involved the assumption that the PTN was providing a central program or command specifying some peripheral event. I had given little attention to the altered feedback that might have been reaching the PTN with different loads until Phillips proposed that changes in corticomotoneuronal (CM) activity with changed loads might be the result of a mismatch between actual and intended movement. In his Ferrier lecture, Phillips (1969) stated that:

> One may hazard the speculation that the increased discharge of the PT cell . . . was in response to a signal of mismatch between "intended" and actual displacement. Whether this signal is a crude one from the muscle spindles, or whether the mismatch has been computed by the cerebellum is still unknown; nor, in this experiment, can the contributions of joints, skin and vision be assessed. But however "instructed," the CM projection would transfer the "instruction" for increased force to the α motoneurons with maximum directness. If the CM projection is indeed part of a control loop, new sense is made of the old observation that "voluntary" movements of a monkey's arm are grossly impaired by deafferentation (Knapp et al., 1963), when responses to cortical stimulation are unaffected (Mott and Sherrington, 1895; Denny-Brown and Sherrington in Sherrington, 1913). It may well be that the most important function of fusimotor co-activation in the case of the hand is to maintain the inflow of information of muscle length to the cortex and cerebellum.

Figure 6.8 illustrates an experimental paradigm (Evarts & Fromm, 1978) used in demonstrating the relationship between centrally programmed volitional movement and the feedback reaching the motor cortex via the receptors of the moving part. The monkey illustrated in Figure 6.8 was trained to position a handle within a small zone and rotate it by pronation–supination movements. The monkey viewed two horizontal rows of lamps (track and target lamps), each lamp in the track row being directly above a corresponding lamp in the target row. At all times only one lamp in each row was on. Output from a position transducer coupled to the handle selected which of the track lamps was illuminated. Although the track display informed the monkey of the actual handle orientation, the location of the target lamp was programmed by the experimenter and indicated how the handle should be positioned. The behavioral sequence established by operant-conditioning methods involved:

1. A *holding period* of continuous correct alignment varying in duration from 1.5 to 2.5 sec. The monkey held the handle vertically to align the central track with the central target lamp. In the figures that follow, a horizontal position (i.e., potentiometer) trace indicates steady holding, and the thickness of the horizontal line in superimposed position traces reflects the width of the hold zone (1.5°).
2. *Small error-correcting supination–pronation movements of* 1°–2°

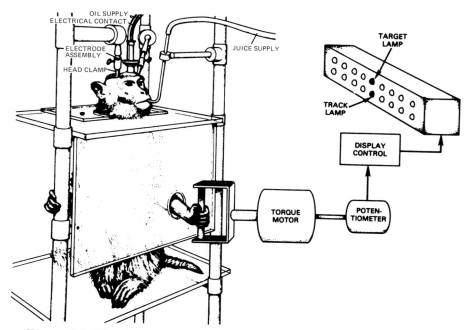

Figure 6.8. Visual pursuit-tracking paradigm. The movements of the handle grasped by the monkey changed a potentiometer output that controlled the position of the track lamp. Displacements of the hand could be produced by the torque motor. The monkey was required to maintain alignment between track lamp and target lamp.

occurred when a misalignment of track and target lamps was caused by the monkey's failure to keep the handle within the narrow hold zone. Figure 6.9 shows a series of pronation (top) and supination (bottom) corrective movements carried out by the monkey in order to realign the track with the fixed target lamp. The same type of small corrective movements could also be triggered by a shift of the track display resulting from an error signal added to the output of the position transducer that controlled the track display. In Figure 6.9 the small corrective movements resulting from the monkey's errors are marked "small (1)," whereas the small corrections triggered by addition of an artifical error signal are marked "small (2)." Addition or removal of this artifical error is seen as abrupt deflection in the position trace of the corrections marked "small (2)" in Figure 6.9, although there has been no actual movement of the handle. This artificial error resulted in a shift of the track display from the center lamp to the one on its right or left, therefore requiring of the monkey a corrective movement in the opposite direction to realign track with the fixed target at the center.

3. *Fast supination–pronation movements of large amplitude* (20°) (marked "ballistic" in Figure 6.9) were triggered by a jump of the target to the extreme right or left of the panel. The monkey was rewarded

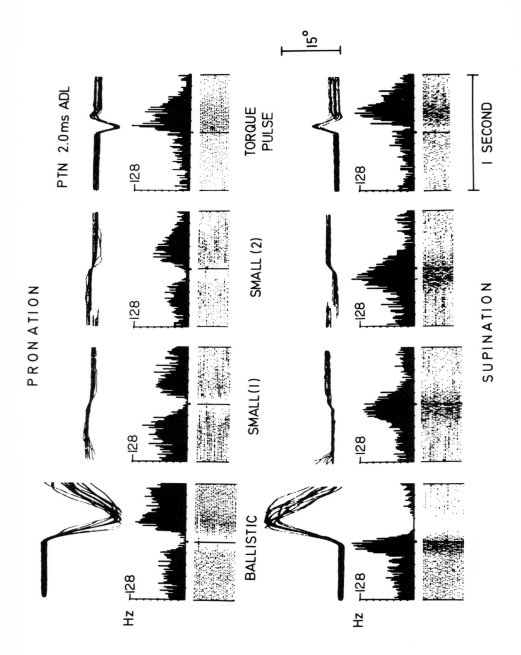

with a drop of juice after the handle had been rapidly rotated in the direction of the target jump; movement time had to be less than 150 msec for reward to be delivered. The monkey's ballistic movements were not precisely controlled as to termination, because target zones at both extreme positions were bounded by a physical barrier. These movements commonly reached velocities that were 20–30 times greater than the peak velocities occurring for the small controlled movements.

4. Immediately after a ballistic movement, the target jumped back to the center and the monkey returned the handle to the central hold zone to initiate a new cycle (Step 1).
5. The handle was coupled to the axle of a DC torque motor (Colburn & Evarts, 1978), which produced a constant torque during steady holding. This torque required either steady supinator or pronator force and resulted in an effective force of 90 g applied to the monkey's hand. Units were usually tested under both load conditions. In addition, 50-msec rectangular *torque pulses* could be delivered to the handle via the motor to study unit sensitivity to peripheral inputs. Randomly alternated pronating and supinating torque pulses were applied (a) after 700 msec of steady holding; (b) at a fixed delay of 120 msec after a target jump, and so immediately preceding the ballistic movement; (c) at the start of a ballistic movement; and (d) at the start of a small movement. The latter pulses (c and d) were triggered at the time the handle left the central hold zone.

For successive cycles of the paradigm, directions of target jumps, "artifical errors," torque pulses, and perturbed and unperturbed movements were varied in a pseudorandom order.

One of the major points that Fromm and I sought to clarify using this paradigm concerned the relationship between motor-cortex discharge and very small precisely controlled movements. The fineness of motor output possible for the human hand is truly remarkable. In their recent book, Phillips and Porter (1977) comment upon the fineness of movement possible as follows:

> In man, very small and accurate movements of the fingers are possible, guided by vision under the microscope. With a little practice, a person is able to position a slide accurately on the stage of a micro-

---

◀ **Figure 6.9.** Each set of three sorts of records consists of a series of superimposed position traces (top), a histogram of associated unit discharge (middle), and rasters of unit discharge corresponding to the histogram (bottom). At left are records for ballistic pronation (top) and ballistic supination (bottom). Records marked "small (1)" show data for small corrections resulting from the monkey's errors, whereas records marked "small (2)" show small movements triggered by the "artificial error" described in the text. At right is shown activity evoked by torque pulses. For further details, see text. (Reprinted from Evarts & Fromm, 1978.)

scope using only his hand and visual control. A technician will soon find it possible to focus first on the centre of a single red blood cell viewed under high magnification, and then to move the slide so that the centre of focus is on the rim of that same erythrocyte. A delicate, controlled movement of only 3 or 4 μm has been executed with the musculature of the arms, hand and fingers. Accuracy requires external, visual feedback and the accomplishment of the precise movement performance is intimately linked with and dependent upon the sensory experience. We can also do fairly fine dissections under a dissecting microscope without recourse to a micromanipulator.

In considering the mechanisms underlying the capacity of the human hand to exercise such precise control, it is useful to recall "Craik's ratio rule," which states that for all but the very smallest movements the magnitude of the error is proportional to the magnitude of the movement. How can the error become smaller as the intended movement becomes smaller? Motor-cortex discharge frequencies rarely exceed 150 pulses per second even for large arm movements. If motor-cortex output is to precisely control fine movements, however, then there would have to be marked modulation of motor-cortex output even for very small changes in muscular contraction. Therefore, it seemed a priori that in order to control the finest, most precise movements, motor-cortex discharge would have to be very strongly modulated for even the most minute fluctuations in activity of peripheral musculature. Furthermore, as pointed out in the statement by Phillips and Porter, precise movement performance is intimately linked with and dependent upon sensory input. Therefore, in the paradigm illustrated in Figure 6.8, we sought to examine motor-cortex activity in relation to the fine, precisely controlled movements used by the monkey in positioning the handle and then to observe the consequences of sensory inputs occurring in the course of such movements.

6   Enhanced PTN Somesthetic Responses during Fine Movement

Results obtained in the paradigm described above have been reported in several papers (Evarts & Fromm, 1977, 1978; Fromm & Evarts, 1977). A major focus of attention in these reports was motor-cortex responses to kinesthetic inputs during precise fine movement. These responses during precisely controlled movement were compared with responses to kinesthetic inputs during postural stability (when the monkey was seeking to maintain the handle steadily in one position) and during ballistic movement (when the monkey was seeking to make a rapid large displacement). In these studies over 700 neurons were analyzed. In about 30% of these neurons significant changes of activity were detected for both small and large movements, whereas another 30% changed exclusively in relation to the large fast ballistic movements. All units discharging with small movements also discharged with larger movements, but with the larger movements many additional PTNs that had been inactive with the small movements were recruited. Those PTNs which became active even with the smallest movements were also the most sensitive to peripheral inputs arising from limb receptors. Almost invariably, there was intense reflex activation of those units (especially the tonically discharging PTNs) most involved in control of precise small movements. A particularly striking result obtained in this experiment was a heightened sensitivity to kinesthetic inputs during precise fine movement. Figure 6.10 illustrates this enhancement. In Figure 6.10, the column marked "small + torque" shows enhanced responses when compared to the control responses, marked "torque pulse holding." Heightened sensitivity to disturbance of fine movements—particularly obvious for the excitatory reflex—is reflected not only in the increased magnitude and duration of discharge but also by a discharge pattern showing fluctuations that are tightly time locked to the torque pulse. Moreover, it should be noted that both the inhibitory and excitatory sensory inputs during precise movement had to override the oppositely directed change of unit activity called for by the "movement program." This result indicated that different PTN excitability (membrane polarization) at the time the somesthetic input reaches motor cortex during a perturbed movement can hardly account for the differential responsiveness to disturbances during fine movements as compared to postural stability.

The foregoing has shown the existence of a highly sensitive transcortical loop during precisely controlled movement. However, does this loop have properties consistent with servocontrol? To answer this question, let us begin by considering some of the a priori expectations that we may have for PTN discharge in relation to movement, assuming that the PTNs are summing points in a transcortical servoloop. For PTNs that are summing points in such a loop, realization of the action resulting from discharge of the PTNs should tend to reduce (i.e., to inhibit) discharge, whereas failure of realization should tend to increase (i.e., to excite) discharge. This is merely a restatement of the Phillips hypothesis as to the effect of "match" and "mismatch" on PTN discharge. A familiar circuit exhibiting such negative feedback is the loop involving muscle receptors and alpha motoneurons (αMNs). Within this loop, the consequences of αMN discharge (decreased muscle length and/or increased muscle tension) feedback onto the αMN so as to reduce αMN discharge:

$\downarrow$ muscle length $\rightarrow$ $\downarrow$ muscle spindle discharge $\rightarrow$ $\downarrow$ αMN discharge
$\uparrow$ muscle tension $\rightarrow$ $\uparrow$ Golgi tendon organ discharge $\rightarrow$ $\downarrow$ αMN discharge

The motor-cortex PTN shown in Figure 6.10 appears to be in a loop analogous to the one impinging on spinal cord αMNs, a loop carrying information such that externally induced (i.e., passive) movement corre-

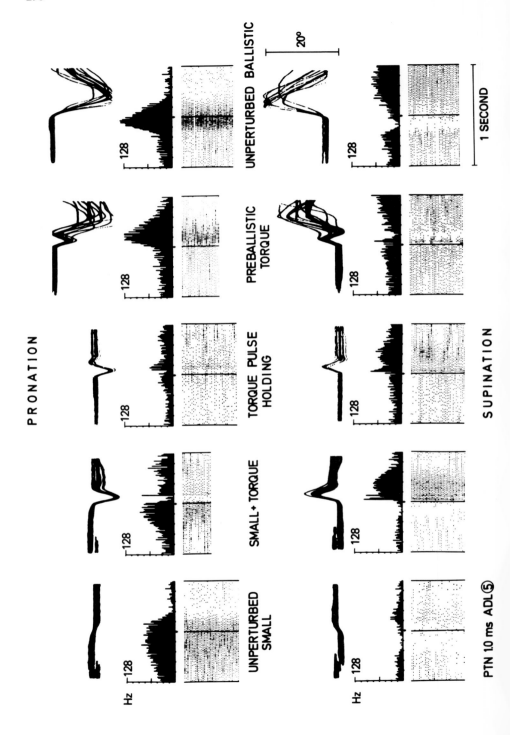

sponding to the active movement called for by the PTN inhibits the PTN's discharge. By analogy with the model of negative feedback presented for the αMN, an external "assist" that helps to realize the movement "commanded" by the discharge of the PTN will inhibit its discharge, whereas application of a force that opposes this movement will excite the PTN.

7   Central Programs Can Override Servocontrol

The neuronal discharge illustrated in Figures 6.9 and 6.10 underlies the operation of an automatic system that is of critical importance in stabilizing our finest, most precise movements. What happens, however, when a subject wishes to carry out a movement requiring muscular activity opposite to that which would be called for by the servocontrols underlying stability? What happens when we wish to make a movement that contradicts the reflex inputs that are "hard wired" to elements of our motor control system? How does a subject execute an instruction calling for a motor act that runs counter to reflex drives? In order to get information on this point, Tanji and I (Evarts & Tanji, 1976; Tanji & Evarts, 1976) studied PTN responses in monkeys trained to react to a limb displacement according to a prior instruction and regardless of the direction in which the perturbation displaced the limb. A key goal in the design of this experiment was dissociation of the reflex from the intended components of motor activity. It was in this respect that this study in monkeys differed from previous experiments in monkey (Evarts, 1973a) or in man (Hagbarth, 1967; Hammond, 1956). To achieve this dissociation, either of the two possible instructions (ins-pull and ins-push) was followed by either of the two possible directions of perturbation (per-pull and per-push). For example, when a monkey was given an instruction to push (ins-push) in response to a subsequent perturbation of its arm, the perturbing trigger could move the arm in either of two possible directions: either toward the monkey (per-pull) or away from the monkey (per-push). When ins-push was followed by per-pull (a perturbation that stretched triceps and op-

◄ **Figure 6.10.** Three sorts of displays are shown: superimposed position traces, histograms of unit discharge, and rasters of unit discharge. Attention is directed to several points: unperturbed small pronation (top left) is preceded by more prolonged unit discharge than is the case for unperturbed ballistic movement (top right); the inhibitory effect of the torque pulse is greater when it is delivered during a small pronation (top row marked "small + torque") than when it is delivered during holding (top, marked "torque pulse holding"); there is a corresponding accentuation of the excitatory effects of the supinating torque pulse when this is delivered during small movement (bottom, marked "small + torque") as compared to holding (bottom, marked "torque pulse holding"). For further details, see text. (Reprinted from Evarts & Fromm, 1978.)

posed the intended push movement), the segmental reflex response in the stretched triceps muscle was of the same sign (+) as the intended response (+), and there was association of the reflex and intended components of the muscle response. When ins-push was followed by per-push, however, a triggering perturbation which shortened triceps and assisted the intended push movement, the segmental reflex response (−) in the shortened triceps muscle was opposite to the intended response (+): now the segmental reflex response of triceps (to becoming shorter while its antagonist was being stretched) was to become less active, and the triceps discharge that occurred when the monkey carried out the intended push movement was in spite of, rather than because of, segmental inputs.

This dissociation of reflex from intended response components by the combination of two sorts of instructions with two sorts of triggering perturbations was seen in motor-cortex PTNs as well as in muscle, as illustrated in Figure 6.11. This figure shows the change of perturbation-evoked activity in a PTN as a result of a change of the prior instruction. This PTN was reciprocally related to push–pull movements, becoming active with push and silent with pull. The per-pull perturbation (which moved the handle toward the monkey, opposing the intended push movement in association with which the neuron discharged) excited the PTN at short latency. Although this excitation was evoked by the perturbation regardless of the prior instruction, the magnitude and the duration of the excitation were greater when the perturbation followed the ins-push instruction than when it followed the ins-pull instruction. The ef-

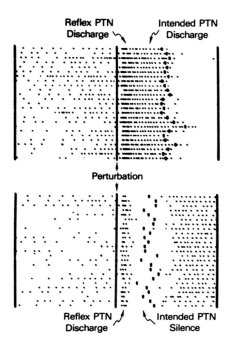

Reflex PTN Discharge   **Intended PTN Discharge**

Perturbation

Reflex PTN Discharge   **Intended PTN Silence**

Figure 6.11. Raster displays of PTN activity show activity occurring 500 msec before and 500 msec after a perturbation that occurred at the center line of the display. The single heavy dot in each row following the perturbation shows when the handle reached the intended push or pull zone. This PTN was one that discharged with intended push movement and fell silent with intended pull movement. In the raster at the top, the heavy dots marking completion of the push movement are followed by PTN silence as the monkey pulls back into the "hold zone" to initiate a new trial. In the lower raster the heavy dots occur during PTN silence as the monkey pulls; the PTN then becomes active as the monkey pushes back to the hold zone to start a new trial. For further details, see text. (Reprinted from Evarts & Tanji, 1976.)

fect here is analogous to the enhanced triceps tendon jerk when triceps stretch follows ins-push. Comparison of the perturbation-evoked responses of this PTN for the two different instructions (Figure 6.11) reveals that the two responses had the same initial onset latency but very different magnitudes and durations. When the prior instruction was ins-pull, the excitation was very brief, terminating after about 10 msec.

Arm area PTN discharge associated with a contralateral arm movement triggered by an input to the responding arm was found to have two components: (1) a relatively short-latency reflex component that depended on the nature of the input to the arm, and (2) a longer latency component that depended on the movement that the subject intended to perform. The first component of discharge appears comparable to discharges that a number of previous investigators have described for motor-cortex neurons in response to stimulation of cutaneous, muscle, or joint receptors (Albe-Fessard & Liebeskind, 1966; Albe-Fessard, Liebeskind, & Lamarre, 1965; Brooks & Stoney, 1971; Oscarsson, 1966; Porter, 1973; Rosén and Asanuma, 1972; Towe, Patton, & Kennedy, 1964; Wiesendanger, 1973). The second component of PTN discharge is related to the nature of the intended output and seems to depend on a central program rather than on the nature of the input that triggers this program. When an excitatory perturbation triggers a movement involving quiescence of the PTN, only the first (or reflex) component of discharge occurs. Conversely, when a movement involving discharge of the PTN is triggered by a perturbation that suppresses activity of the PTN, only the second (or intended) component of PTN discharge occurs.

8 Significance of Trigger Modality in Reaction-Time Paradigms

Intended arm-muscle discharge occurs at shorter latency when the trigger is a disturbance of the arm that is to respond than when the trigger is an auditory or a visual stimulus (Evarts & Vaughn, 1978). This shorter reaction time is seen even when the initial reflex effect of the kinesthetic trigger is inhibitory. For example, intended muscle discharge in the present experiment occurred at 80-msec latencies even when the initial effect of the perturbation was inhibitory. If an auditory or visual stimulus replaces the arm perturbation in such a paradigm, reaction times are prolonged to at least 120 msec. Comparable observations have been made in humans (Evarts & Granit, 1976) using the same paradigm as the one for the present experiment in monkeys. In studies with human subjects instructed to respond as quickly as possible, intended biceps discharge could be triggered at latencies of 70 msec even by a perturbation that unloaded biceps and was initially inhibitory. In these same human subjects, auditory and visual reaction times exceeded 110 msec, and perturbations of the arm opposite to the one that was to respond also failed to evoke short-latency responses. Therefore, the short-latency intended responses depend on triggers delivered to the responding arm. Information as to the receptors that may be involved in mediating this short-latency response in humans is provided by observations of Hammond (1956) and of Marsden Merton, and Morton (1972). Hammond found that the short-latency (50 msec) responses were not evoked by a tap on the wrist, and Marsden *et al*. found that the short-latency (50 msec) "servoresponse" was abolished by blockade of cutaneous and joint inputs from the moving part, even though function of muscle receptors remained unimpaired. Taken together, these studies point to the importance of the combined inputs from a number of different receptors, because muscle afferents alone or cutaneous afferents alone fail to evoke the response.

9   Classes of Inputs to Motor Cortex

Phillips and Porter divide inputs to motor cortex into two main classes (Phillips & Porter, 1977, p. 205):

> Those descending from higher functional levels and those ascending from lower levels. The sources of the former would include the whole of the neocortex, the lateral cerebellum, the basal ganglia and the ventrolateral thalamus. These can be loosely described as sources of "command" derived from "programmes for movement," both inborn and learned, whose nature and location still elude us, as their engrams eluded Lashley (1950), and whose activities are believed to be subject to continuous or intermittent correction by sensory information of progress towards the attainment of the overriding behavioural goals.

The broad features of brain organization underlying the sources of what Phillips and Porter have referred to as "command" have been illustrated by Kemp and Powell (1971) in Figure 6.12, which shows the pathways whereby signals from basal ganglia and cerebellum reach the motor cortex via the thalamus. In Figure 6.12 the motor cortex (M) is crosshatched, and is shown in relation to thalamus, basal ganglia, and cerebellum. It was once thought that the pyramidal system (including motor cortex and the pyramidal tract fibers descending from it to the spinal cord) controlled higher level, voluntary movements, and that an extrapyramidal system (including cerebellum and basal ganglia) controlled lower level, automatic movements, but anatomical and physiological studies now make it clear that pyramidal and extrapyramidal systems are *not* separate. As Kemp and Powell point out, fibers from the dentate nucleus of the cerebellum

> terminate in the ventrolateral and ventroanterior principal nuclei and certain of the intralaminar group. The inner segment of the globus pallidus also projects upon the same principal nuclei of the thalamus and upon the centromedian nucleus of the intralaminar group. As

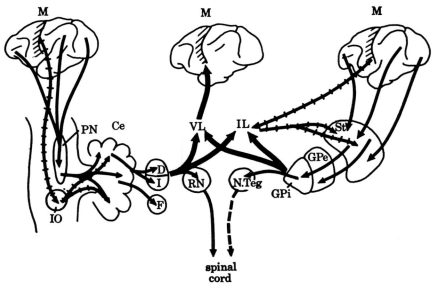

Figure 6.12. Similarity in organization of the cerebral connections of the cerebellum and basal ganglia. Presumed equivalent pathways in the two systems are shown by the same kinds of symbols. Interrupted lines indicate possible connections. Ce, cerebellar cortex; D, dentate nucleus; F, fastigial nucleus; GPe, globus pallidus, external segment; GPi, globus pallidus, internal segment; I, nucleus interpositus; IL, intralaminar nuclei of the thalamus; IO, inferior olive; M, motor cortex; N.Teg., tegmental nuclei; PN, pontine nuclei; RN, red nucleus; St, striatum; VL, ventrolateral nucleus of the thalamus. (Reprinted from Kemp & Powell, 1971.)

> these ventral nuclei project upon the motor cortex, the major cerebral influence of *both* the cerebellum and the basal ganglia is upon the motor area of the cortex.

Given the fact that both basal ganglia and cerebellum (once viewed as extrapyramidal) have a critical role in controlling pyramidal output, the objective of much current research has become the elucidation of how these interconnected parts of the brain—the motor cortex, thalamus, cerebellum, and basal ganglia—act together to control movement. Studies along these lines were carried out by Thach (1970a,b), who discovered that changes in cerebellar activity occurred prior to movement. Then De-Long (1974) extended studies to the basal ganglia and found that nerve cells in that region also become active in advance of muscular contraction. The discovery that cerebellum, basal ganglia, and thalamus as well (Evarts, 1971) discharge prior to movement supports the notion of the functional relations put forth by Kemp and Powell (1971). The entire cerebral cortex sends fibers to both the basal ganglia and the cerebellum, and these two structures in turn send massive connections back to the motor cortex by way of the thalamus. Therefore, the basal ganglia and the cerebellum receive information from all regions of the cerebral cortex, transform this information, and then send a new pattern of signals to the motor cortex. Whereas the traditional view held that the cerebral motor cortex was at the highest level of motor integration and that the subcortical structures were at a lower level, that is, closer to the muscle, it now appears that the situation is quite the reverse. The inputs going into the cerebellum and into the basal ganglia may be coded in a more abstract and complex manner than the outputs leaving the motor cortex. In addition, the motor cortex is more directly connected to spinal cord motoneurons than either the cerebellum or the basal ganglia. All of this is consistent with Phillips' view that motor cortex should be thought of in relation to the middle level of Jackson's hierarchical organization.

10   Definitions of Volitional Movement

Writing in 1875, Hughlings Jackson (1958) quoted Laycock as follows:

> Four years have elapsed since I published my opinion, supported by such facts as I could then state, that the *brain*, although the organ of consciousness, *is subject to the laws of reflex action; and that in this respect it does not differ from the other ganglia of the nervous system.* I was led to this conclusion by the general principle that the ganglia within the cranium, being a continuation of the spinal cord, *must necessarily be regulated as to their reaction on external agencies by laws identical with those governing the spinal ganglia and their analogues in the lower animals.* And I was confirmed in this opinion by finding, after the investigation and collocation of known facts, that observations and arguments like those satisfactorily adduced in proof of the existence of the reflex function of the spinal ganglia may be brought forward in proof that the cerebral ganglia have similar endowments.

The point made here by Laycock, accepted by Hughlings Jackson, and clearly supported by the results obtained with studies of single-neuron discharge in the monkey is that the processes underlying volitional movement are "subject to the laws of reflex action." Reflexes and volitional movements are not opposites. In the past there has been a tendency to dichotomize reflex and volitional movements and to assume that if a movement is voluntary it cannot at the same time be reflex. Such an assumption is fallacious. However, if we cannot define volitional movement by exclusion (i.e., if we cannot define volitional movement as something that is not reflex), then how can we define voluntary movement? The approach taken by Bernstein (1967), and one to which I subscribe, is given in the following quotation from his book, *The Coordination and Regulation of Movements:*

> If the program of motor act is discussed, as a whole, in macroscopic terms we cannot discover any other determining factor than the

image or representation of the result of the action (final or intermediate) in terms of which this action is directed and which leads towards
the comprehension of the corresponding motor problem.

This notion of voluntary movement has also been put forth by Granit.
In his recent book, *The Purposive Brain*, Granit (1977, p. 175) states:
"What is volitional in voluntary movement is its purpose." By combining
the statements of Laycock, Granit, and Bernstein, we arrive at a proposition that the volitional features of a voluntary motor act are to be thought
of in terms of the goal or result toward which this act is directed, but with
the actual events underlying acquisition of the goal built up from a variety of reflex processes.

I recently discussed the matter of voluntary movement with Viktor
Gurfinkel, a colleague of the late Nicholas Bernstein. Gurfinkel's definition of volitional movement corresponds rather closely to that of Granit,
for he too defined volitional movement in relation to the goal. As an example of the sorts of processes underlying volitional movement, Gurfinkel told me of some kinesiological studies he had carried out with the aim
of assessing motor control characteristics in the "best pistol shots in the
Red Army." An essential characteristic of a marksman is the capacity to
maintain stability of the pistol. In studies of the electromyographic and
kinematic characteristics of expert marksmen, Gurfinkel found that the
pistol was virtually immobile in spite of the fact that many parts of the
body exhibited movement. The key to pistol stability was that for each
movement of the trunk or limbs, there was a corresponding counterbal-
ancing movement that stabilized the position of the pistol in space. All
sorts of reflex systems were involved in achieving this goal of pistol stability—the vestibuloocular, vestibulospinal, and many other reflex systems
—all of which could, in their integrated action, maintain stability and so
contribute to acquisition of the goal.

Gurfinkel's selection of the motor behavior of a marksman in his discussions of voluntary movement recalls the views of William James, who,
writing almost a century ago, took a similar position in relation to the essence of volitional movement. As James (1890/1950, p. 497) put it:

> The marksman ends by thinking only of the exact position of the goal,
> the singer only of the perfect sound, the balancer only of the point of
> the pole whose oscillations he must counteract. The associated mech-
> anism has become so perfect in all these persons that each variation in
> the thought of the end is functionally correlated with the one move-
> ment fitted to bring the latter about. Whilst they were tyros, they
> thought of their means as well as their end: the marksman of the posi-
> tion of his gun or bow, or the weight of his stone; the pianist of the
> visible position of the note on the keyboard; the singer of his throat or
> breathing; the balancer of his feet on the rope, or his hand or chin
> under the pole. But little by little they succeeded in dropping all this
> supernumerary consciousness, and they became secure in their move-
> ments exactly in proportion as they did so.

Discussing this matter of consciousness somewhat later in the same chapter, "Will," James (1890/1950 p. 519) wrote as follows:

> What we are *interested* in is what sticks in our consciousness; everything else we get rid of as quickly as we can. Our resident feelings of movement have no substantive interest for us at all, as a rule. What interest us are the ends which the movement is to attain. Such an end is generally an outer impression on the eye or ear, or sometimes on the skin, nose, or palate. Now let the idea of the end associate itself definitely with the right motor innervation, and the thought of the innervation's *resident* effects will become as great an encumbrance as we formerly concluded that the feeling of the innervation itself would be. The mind does not need it; the end alone is enough.
>
> The idea of the end, then, tends more and more to make itself all-sufficient. Or, at any rate, if the kinaesthetic ideas are called up at all, they are so swamped in the vivid kinaesthetic feelings by which they are immediately overtaken that we have no time to be aware of their separate existence. As I write, I have no anticipation, as a thing distinct from my sensation, of either the look or the digital feel of the letters which flow from my pen. The words chime on my mental *ear*, as it were, before I write them, but not on my mental eye or hand. This comes from the rapidity with which often-repeated movements follow on their mental cue. An end consented to as soon as conceived innervates directly the centre of the first movement of the chain which leads to its accomplishment, and then the whole chain rattles off *quasi*-reflexly.

Here, then, one finds a remarkable degree of agreement between individuals of widely differing backgrounds and disciplines: Granit believes that what is volitional about a voluntary movement is its goal, and in his view Granit shares an opinion with James, Bernstein, and Gurfinkel, all of whom accept the Sherringtonian notion that purposive movements are built upon a base of reflex processes. Such a view is also shared by clinical neurologists generally. Kinnier Wilson, for example, has stated (1928, p. 143) that "A large part of every voluntary movement is both involuntary and outside consciousness." Of course, this was the view of James, who had long before asserted that consciousness was irrelevant to the performance of volitional movement.

What, however, are the features that differentiate voluntary from involuntary movements? A number of these features have been brought out clearly in Kinnier Wilson's (1928) chapter entitled "The Voluntary Motor System in Striatal Disease." Several forms of striatal disease are associated with marked impairment of voluntary movement—either by virtue of the failure of movements to occur when they are desirable or on account of the presence of movements that are unwanted. The unwanted movements are commonly referred to as choreiform. Wilson points out that the movements occurring in patients with chorea resemble those "executed at the bidding of volition. Each fresh movement appears to be directed to an end—which is never attained." The point is that the movements of chorea are aimless. The actual muscular events associated with the movements may closely resemble the muscular events associated with volitional movements in healthy individuals.

Wilson's studies of voluntary movement and disorders thereof led him to the view that

> The spontaneous activity of choreo-athetosis, thus conceived, is nought else than a succession of cortical reflexes, high-grade movements largely comparable to those called voluntary except that the patient's volition neither initiates nor inhibits them.

Further ideas as to the nature of volitional movement come from observations of patients with Parkinsonism. These patients are almost at the opposite pole from patients with chorea, for the Parkinsonian patient exhibits paucity of movement. Patients with Parkinsonism may remain relatively immobile for long periods, and when questioned concerning this immobility they may often state that during the period of immobility they did not feel any strong impulse to move. It is difficult for them to summon sufficient "effort of the will" to move, yet under conditions of stress or emergency, patients with Parkinsonism who have found it very difficult to move may for a brief period at least overcome their bradykinesia. Of course, pharmacological agents too may overcome bradykinesia – as has been well known since the introduction of L-DOPA.

Conditions associated with excessive rather than insufficient movement include Gilles de la Tourette's syndrome, choreatic disorders such as Huntington's disease, and tardive dyskinesia, a disturbance that may follow administration of drugs that are dopamine antagonists. Here one has a picture quite opposite to the reduced tendency to move in patients with Parkinsonism. It is perhaps in the condition Gilles de la Tourette's syndrome that one has some of the most striking involuntary movements. These are the explosive profane utterances of the individuals affected with this disease. Patients with Gilles de la Tourette's syndrome may gradually feel building up within them the impulse to utter certain unacceptable words. They are quite well aware that the words are offensive and make every effort to suppress them. At times the patient may realize that the pressure to emit unacceptable words has reached the bursting point and will dash out of the room to allow the pressure to be vented in a series of foul and unprintable epithets. Thus relieved, the patient may return to resume normal conversation. The utterances in these cases occur in spite of the wishes of the subject, and there are specific pharmacological agents that reduce the tendency of this explosive production of language. However, the words themselves and the muscular events producing them are similar to those which occur with volitional utterances regardless of the fact that the Gilles de la Tourette's utterances are neither volitional nor goal directed.

In the utterances of patients with Gilles de la Tourette's syndrome, one has the example par excellence of the involuntary movement—one that is in many respects identical to a volitional movement but that differs in two essential respects: (1) the involuntary movement has no goal, and (2) the subject has limited capacity to prevent and/or terminate the movement. An essential characteristic of volitional movement is the possibility of its being terminated by the subject.

11   Summary and Conclusions

In this discussion of brain mechanisms in voluntary movement we have considered the characteristics of neuronal discharge during motor performance in the primate. It has been shown that the laws of reflex action, long known to operate at the level of the spinal cord motoneuron, also operate at the level of the cerebral cortex. Motor-cortex PTNs are impinged upon by afferent inputs that constitute the incoming limb of a transcortical servoloop. Thus, the phylogenetically new pyramidal tract system of the mammal is subject to the same laws of reflex action that characterize phylogenetically older components of motor control systems. However, in addition to being driven by a servosystem that stabilizes movement and posture, PTNs are driven by a second major set of inputs, and it is this second set of inputs that underlies internally generated motor programs. These programs, reaching the motor cortex from the thalamus, are themselves a product of activity in basal ganglia and cerebellum.

Some of the keenest insights into the nature of voluntary and involuntary movements have come from the disorders of movement associated with diseases of the basal ganglia. It is in patients with such disorders that one clearly sees the contrast between voluntary and involuntary movement. The patterns of muscular activity occurring in association with the involuntary movements of certain basal ganglia disorders may be similar to the patterns associated with normal voluntary movement. The difference between the voluntary movements of the healthy individual and the involuntary movements of patients with Gilles de la Tourette's syndrome or Huntington's disease are twofold: (1) The involuntary movements in the neurological disorders are purposeless, and (2) the patients exhibiting these involuntary movements are unable to prevent them.

Of the two major classes of inputs impinging upon the cerebral motor cortex and generating the stream of impulses passing via the pyramidal tract of the spinal cord, that class of inputs which operates automatically and constitutes the afferent limb of the transcortical servosystem seems the simplest to understand. This transcortical servosystem operates according to Sherringtonian principles of reflex action. The second set of inputs passing via the thalamus to the motor cortex depends upon the basal ganglia and cerebellum and is much more complicated. In order to understand voluntary movement, therefore, we need to comprehend the sorts of information processed by cerebellum and basal ganglia and to discover the way in which the outputs of cerebellum and basal ganglia interact in the thalamus. An understanding of the significance of all of these structures will depend on what Karl Lashley (1941) referred to as a "coalescence of neurology and psychology." Indeed, it would seem fitting to end this discussion with some remarks of Lashley made at a symposium on "Recent Advances in Psychology." What Lashley said in this address concerned mental processes in relation to the activity of the brain:

> Perhaps the most important contribution of psychologists to this problem has been the realization that the characteristics of the mental can be stated meaningfully only as a structure or organization of elements which are themselves as purely conceptual as is the energy of physics. Such a notion was foreshadowed by the growth of behaviorism (Holt, 1914; Lashley, 1923), but it remained for the logical positivists to develop a critique of scientific thinking which gives it rigorous formulation (Stevens, 1935). When the supposed characteristics of the mental are tried in the fire of operational definition, the most imposing of them evaporate. Mind, when analyzed to its definable constituents, has no discernible properties other than organization or integration of processes which differ through a range of complexities as wide as the structural differences between the virus and the human body.

References

Albe-Fessard, D., & Liebeskind, J. Origine des messages somato-sensitifs activant les cellules du cortex moteur chèz le singe. *Experimental Brain Research*, 1966, 1, 127–146.

Albe-Fessard, D., Liebeskind, J., & Lamarre, Y. Projection au niveau du cortex somato-moteur du singe d'afferences provenant des recepteurs musculaires. *Comptes Rendus des Séances de la Societé de Biologie*, 1965, 261, 3891–3894.

Bernstein, N. *The co-ordination and regulation of movements*. Oxford: Pergamon Press, 1967.

Brooks, V.B., & Stoney, S.R., Jr. Motor mechanisms: The role of the pyramidal system in motor control. *Annual Review of Physiology*, 1971, 33, 337–392.

Colburn, T.R., & Evarts, E.V. Use of brushless DC torque motors in studies of neuromuscular function. In J.E. Desmedt (Ed.), *Cerebral motor control in man: Long loop mechanisms, Progress in clinical neurophysiology* (Vol. 4). Basel: Karger, 1978

DeLong, M.R. Motor functions of the basal ganglia: single-unit activity during movement. In F.O. Schmitt & F.G. Worden (Eds.), *The neurosciences*. Cambridge, Mass.: Massachusetts Institue of Technology Press, 1974.

Evarts, E.V. Effect of ablation of prestriate cortex on auditory-visual association in monkey. *Journal of Neurophysiology*, 1952, 15, 191–200.

Evarts, E.V. Pyramidal tract activity associated with a conditioned hand movement in the monkey. *Journal of Neurophysiology*, 1966, 29, 1011–1027.

Evarts, E.V. Relation of pyramidal tract activity to force exerted during voluntary movement. *Journal of Neurophysiology*, 1968, 31, 14–27.

Evarts, E.V. Activity of pyramidal tract neurons during postural fixation. *Journal of Neurophysiology*, 1969, 32, 375–385.

Evarts, E.V. Activity of thalamic and cortical neurons in relation to learned movement in the monkey. *International Journal of Neurology*, 1971, 8, 321–326.

Evarts, E.V. Motor cortex reflexes associated with learned movement. *Science*, 1973, *179*, 501–503. (a)

Evarts, E.V. Brain mechanisms in movement. *Scientific American*, 1973, *229*, 96–103. (b)

Evarts, E.V. Sensorimotor cortex activity associated with movements triggered by visual as compared to somesthetic inputs. In F.O. Schmitt & F.G. Worden (Eds.), *The neurosciences*. Cambridge, Mass.: Massachusetts Institute of Technology Press, 1974.

Evarts, E.V., & Fromm, C. Sensory responses in motor cortex neurons during precise motor control. *Neuroscience Letters*, 1977, *5*, 267–272.

Evarts, E.V., & Fromm, C. The pyramidal tract neuron as summing point in a closed-loop control system in the monkey. In J.E. Desmedt (Ed.), *Cerebral motor control in man: Long loop mechanisms, Progress in clinical neurophysiology* (Vol. 4). Basel: Karger, 1978.

Evarts, E.V., & Granit, R. Relations of reflexes and intended movements. In S. Homma (Ed.), *Progress in brain research* (Vol. 44). Amsterdam: Elsevier, 1976.

Evarts, E.V., & Tanji, J. Reflex and intended responses in motor cortex pyramidal tract neurons of monkey. *Journal of Neurophysiology*, 1976, 39, 1069–1080.

Evarts, E.V., & Vaughn, W.J. Intended arm movements in response to externally produced arm displacement in man. In J.E. Desmedt (Ed.), *Cerebral motor control in man: Long loop mechanisms, Progress in clinical neurophysiology* (Vol. 4). Basel: Karger, 1978.

Fromm, C., & Evarts, E.V. Relation of motor cortex neurons to precisely controlled and ballistic movements. *Neuroscience Letters*, 1977, *5*, 259–265.

Granit, R. *The purposive brain*. Cambridge, Mass.: Massachusetts Institute of Technology Press, 1977.

Hagbarth, K.-E. EMG studies of stretch reflexes in man. In L. Widén (Ed.), *Recent advances in clinical neurophysiology, electroencephalography and clinical neurophysiology* (Suppl. 25). Amsterdam: Elsevier, 1967.

Hammond, P.H. The influence of prior instruction to the subject on an apparently involuntary neuromuscular response. *Journal of Physiology* (London), 1956, *132*, 17P-18P.

Holt, E.G. *The concept of consciousness*. London: G. Allen & Co., 1914.

Jackson, J.H. On the anatomical and physiological localisation of movements in the brain. In J. Taylor (Ed.), *Selected writings of John Hughlings Jackson* (Vol. 1). London: Staples Press, 1958.

James, W. *The principles of psychology* (Vol. 2). New York: Dover, 1950. (Originally published in 1890.)

Jasper, H.H. Recent advances in our understanding of ascending activities of the reticular system. In H.H. Jasper, L.D. Proctor, R.S. Knighton, W.C. Noshay, & R.T. Costello (Eds.), *Reticular formation of the brain*. Boston: Little, Brown, 1958.

Kemp, J.M., & Powell, T.P.S. The connexions of the striatum and globus pallidus: Synthesis and speculation. *Philosophical Transactions of the Royal Society* (London), Ser. B, 1971, *262*, 441–457.

Knapp, H.D., Taub, E., & Berman, A.J. Movements in monkeys with deafferented forelimbs. *Experimental Neurology*, 1963, *7*, 305–315.

Lashley, K.S. The behavioristic interpretation of consciousness. *Psychological Review*, 1923, *30*, 237–272; 329–353.

Lashley, K.S. Coalescence of neurology and psychology. *Proceedings of the American Philosophical Society*, 1941, *84*, 461–470.

Lashley, K.S. In search of the engram. In *Symposia of the Society for Experimental Biology* (No. 4). Cambridge: Cambridge University Press, 1950.

Marsden, C.D., Merton, P.A., & Morton, H.B. Servo action in human voluntary movement. *Nature*, 1972, *238*, 140–143.

Mott, F.W., & Sherrington, C.S. Experiments upon the influence of sensory nerves upon movement and nutrition of the limbs. Preliminary communication. *Proceedings of the Royal Society* (London), 1895, *57*, 481–488.

Oscarsson, O. The projection of group I muscle afferents to the cat cerebral cortex. In R. Granit (Ed.), *Muscular afferents and motor control*. New York: Wiley, 1966.

Oscarsson, O., & Rosén, I. Projection to cerebral cortex of large muscle spindle afferents in forelimb nerves of the cat. *Journal of Physiology* (London), 1963, *169*, 924–945.

Oscarsson, O., & Rosén, I. Short latency projections to the cat's cerebral cortex from skin and muscle afferents in the contralateral forelimb. *Journal of Physiology* (London), 1966, *182*, 164–184.

Phillips, C.G. Motor apparatus of the baboon's hand. *Proceedings of the Royal Society* (London), Ser. B, 1969, *173*, 141–174.

Phillips, C.G., & Porter, R. *Corticospinal neurones: Their role in movement*. New York: Academic Press, 1977.

Porter, R. Functions of the mammalian cerebral cortex in movement. In G.A. Kerkut & J.W. Phillis (Eds.), *Progress in neurobiology* (Vol. 1). Oxford: Pergamon Press, 1973.

Rosén, I., & Asanuma, H. Peripheral afferent inputs to the forelimb area of the monkey motor cortex: Input-output relations. *Experimental Brain Research*, 1972, *14*, 257–273.

Sherrington, C.S. Quantitative management of contraction in lowest-level coordination. *Brain*, 1913, *54*, 1–28.

Stevens, S.S. The operational definition of psychological concepts. *Psychological Review*, 1935, *42*, 517–527.

Tanji, J., & Evarts, E.V. Anticipatory activity of motor cortex neurons in relation to direction of an intended movement. *Journal of Neurophysiology*, 1976, *39*, 1062–1068.

Thach, W.T. Discharge of cerebellar neurons related to two postures and movements. I. Nuclear cell output. *Journal of Neurophysiology*, 1970, *33*, 527–536. (a)

Thach, W.T. Discharge of cerebellar neurons related to two postures and movements. II. Purkinje cell output and input. *Journal of Neurophysiology*, 1970, *33*, 537–547. (b)

Towe, A.L. Neuronal population behavior in the somato-sensory systems. In D.R. Kenshalo (Ed.), *The skin senses*. Springfield, Ill.: Charles C Thomas, 1968.

Towe, A.L., Patton, H.D., & Kennedy, T.T. Response properties of neurons in the pericruciate cortex of the cat following electrical stimulation of the appendages. *Experimental Neurology*, 1964, *10*, 325–344.

Wiesendanger, M. Input from muscle and cutaneous nerves of the hand and forearm to neurones of the precentral gyrus of baboons and monkeys. *Journal of Physiology* (London), 1973, *228*, 203–219.

Wilson, K. Disorders of motility and of muscle tone, with special reference to the
    corpus striatum. I. The voluntary motor system in striatal disease. In *Modern
    problems in neurology*. New York: William Wood, 1928.

Discussion

Dr. McFadden: In the experiments you mentioned near the end with the
magnifying and telescoping lenses, did I understand that demonstration
correctly to show that at the neural level there was no adaptation and, if
so, is that also true at the behavioral level?

Dr. Evarts: No, there is adaptation. What I showed in one of Fred Miles'
slides was that after the monkey had worn the enlarging prisms, a given
head velocity evoked a much larger eye velocity, thus implying adaptation at the neural level. Masao Ito (1974) has proposed that this neural
adaptation involves a modified signal from the Purkinje cells whose axons
end on the vestibular neurons that constitute the second stage in the
three-neuron chain of the vestibuloocular reflex (VOR). Ito's hypothesis
implies that in the adapted state (with high or low VOR gain), there will
be modulation of the Purkinje cell output—modulation that is not present in the nonadapted state. You'll recall that for the normal VOR with
equal and opposite head and eye velocities, the eye-velocity and the head-
velocity signals going to the cerebellum are also equal and opposite, and
that as a result they cancel each other out in their summation, which
takes place on the Purkinje cell membrane. So, with the normal VOR
having unity gain, the Purkinje cell output is not modulated at all. Ito's
hypothesis would have it that during the adapted state, when VOR gain is
higher or lower than one, the cerebellar Purkinje output cell will exhibit
modulation. The idea is that for a gain change to be present, the synaptic
relationships between the collaterals of vestibular afferents that branch
off to end on Purkinje cells must have been modified by a number of
coincidences between arrival of this collateral vestibular afferent input
and a second input to the Purkinje cell, a climbing fiber input from the
inferior olive. Fred Miles (Miles & Braitman, 1978) has recorded from
cerebellar flocculus Purkinje cells in the adapted state and found that
even with marked alterations of VOR gain, there continued to be little if
any modulation. These negative findings for the Purkinje cells of the flocculus suggested that there might have been a change in the synaptic interaction between primary vestibular afferents and the cells that they im-
pinge upon in the vestibular nuclei. Although the cerebellum does not
generate a corrective signal underlying adaptation *after* it has taken place,
it is likely that the cerebellum is necessary for the adaptation *to* take
place. Therefore, it may be that the slip of the retinal image has effects on
the cerebellar Purkinje cells such that synapses outside the cerebellum
undergo important changes. However, once these extracerebellar
changes have taken place, it is possible that the Purkinje cells can drop

back to a condition in which no modulation occurs if there is no retinal slip. These proposals are not inconsistent with the findings of David A. Robinson (1976) at Johns Hopkins that animals with lesions of the flocculus do not exhibit VOR adaptation.

Dr. Kandel: Then I would think that one of the critical experiments would be to see what happens during the acquisition of the learning task.

Dr. Evarts: That's exactly what Lisberger and Miles (1979) are hoping to do. They have found that inputs to the vestibular nuclei via the vestibular nerve are unaltered during changed VOR gain. They have also completed a series of experiments in which they recorded from the vestibular nucleus and looked at a population of cells in high-gain and low-gain animals. Unfortunately, all sorts of problems arise when one compares two populations of neurons in two different states. The ideal experiment would be one in which one could record from the same individual neuron long enough to determine its properties in both high- and low-gain conditions.

Dr. Barlow: If I understood you correctly, you said that if you took out the flocculus in an animal that had already adapted to a high-gain situation, it would make no difference.

Dr. Evarts: The problem is that removal of the flocculus will itself tend to elevate the gain of the reflex.

Dr. Barlow: Then if you do it in a low-gain animal?

Dr. Evarts: To my knowledge, that experiment has not yet been done. According to this hypothesis, cerebellar removal should "freeze" the VOR gain at whatever level it had prior to the lesion.

Dr. Kandel: That actually is a very attractive idea. Let's take the simplest case. Let's assume that the cerebellum is involved in facilitating a synaptic connection between a particular set of neurons. It is quite likely that that would only be necessary during the acquisition of the learning task. After that, the memory essentially would be stored in the connection that is modified, and the priming pathway would no longer be essential for it to be maintained.

Dr. Evarts: That's the idea. I think there may be some pretty serious problems with interpreting the effects of the cerebellar lesions, however. As Horace Barlow says, it would be very nice to show that if you knocked the VOR gain down to zero and took out the cerebellum, the gain would be locked at zero. Unfortunately, it hasn't been shown that this happens.

Dr. Ratliff: In some of the experiments using sinusoidal motion where you get exact cancellation or exact reinforcement—if I understand the experiment correctly—this implies no phase shift or else a phase shift of 180 degrees. This, of course, is not impossible at some frequency but it would be remarkable if it held at all frequencies.

Dr. Evarts: This has been done only at rather low frequencies, and the question of the phase shifts at higher frequencies is one that I am not competent to discuss.

Dr. Ratliff: Typically, in most physiological systems the phase shift at a very low frequency is either a very slight lead or so small that you might not be able to detect it as different from the noise.

Harvey Sussman (University of Texas, Austin): I'm very much in favor of any kind of notion that talks about afferent driving of a motor system, but one thing in your talk that puzzled me was the fact that you speculated on postcentral area as being the source of the afferent driving but yet the ventrolateral thalamic nuclei showed no correspondence in terms of latency. Do you think other thalamic sensory relay nuclei are the source of the afferents projecting up to the cortex, or exactly where are the afferents coming from?

Dr. Evarts: One pathway for sensory input to motor cortex might involve a projection from the nucleus ventralis posterolateralis of the thalamus to the somatosensory receiving areas of the postcentral gyrus, from which second-order fibers project into the precentral motor cortex. This afferent pathway activating motor cortex is not from the thalamus to the motor cortex directly, but from the thalamus to the postcentral gyrus, and then to the motor cortex. In contrast, the nucleus ventralis lateralis, which projects directly to the motor cortex, relays signals from cerebellum and basal ganglia rather than from primary afferent systems.

Dr. Sussman: Have there to your knowledge been any degeneration or staining techniques showing the course of fibers across from postcentral to precentral?

Dr. Evarts: Absolutely. The pattern of this connection is really quite interesting in terms of the sort of ideas that Horace Barlow was talking about yesterday. First, let us note the existence of four separate regions of the postcentral gyrus—regions that are distinguished on the basis of cytoarchitectonics as well as type of afferent inputs: area 3a receives muscle afferent information, areas 3b and 1 receive cutaneous inputs, and area 2 receives inputs from joint receptors and other deep afferents. These inputs to the various SI subsectors of the postcentral gyrus are relayed via the ventrobasal complex of the thalamus. Next let us consider the interconnections between these four subsectors of the postcentral gyrus. Vogt and Pandya (1978) studied corticocortical connections of somatosensory cortex (areas 3b, 1, and 2) in the rhesus monkey using ablation–degeneration techniques. In commenting on the finding of Jones and Powell (1970) and Jones (1975), of a heavy projection from thalamus to area 3b and weaker thalamic projection to areas 1 and 2, Vogt and Pandya point out that conversely, area 3 receives a relatively small projection from areas 1 and 2, whereas outgoing connections from areas 3 to 1 and 1 to 2 are quite strong. The authors go on to interpret these findings as follows:

> The relative influence of thalamic and SI afferents on each of these areas, therefore, is quite different. Thus, cellular activity in area 3b may be dominated by peripheral stimulation entering via the thalamus while areas 1 and 2 which also respond to peripheral stimulation may be influenced to a greater degree by cortically processed somatic information which is mediated via cortical connections.

   One negative finding in the study of Vogt and Pandya is of particular significance: area 3b did not project forward into MI. Although it had strong projections caudally, into area 1 and to a lesser extent into area 2, area 3b failed to project to the motor cortex. Thus, the somatosensory information reaching area 3b (skin mechanoreceptor information) is further processed in areas 1 and 2 before it influences activity in the motor cortex. In an overall sense, the Vogt and Pandya findings provided strong support for a hierarchical sequential system of information processing from receipt of afferent input to control of motor output. Vogt and Pandya concluded that:

> Thus, the projections of these three subdivisions of the postcentral gyrus indicate that there is a strong and sequential outflow of connections from area 3 to areas 1 and 2, then from area 1 to area 2, and finally from area 2 to area 5 and rostral area 7. Each of these connections originates to a large extent from the suprangranular layers. In contrast, connections of these areas in the opposite direction toward the central sulcus are less pronounced.

Marc Lewis (University of Texas, Austin): You mentioned that the overlap in colonies has important implications for the organism, but the slide that you showed seemed to imply that the overlap was essentially random. It can be shown mathematically that a random overlap is the least likely to be advantageous for the organism. So I'm predicting that these are not random; I'm wondering if indeed that is the case.

Dr. Evarts: The techniques that are available really don't provide a fine-grain picture at this level. Furthermore, the pyramidal tract neurons in the motor cortex are distributed in clumps. One of the few parts of the cortex that has a feature of this sort which can be seen in a Nissl stain is the motor cortex. Columns in other regions have to be delineated anatomically by some special technique as Hubel, Wiesel, and LeVay (1977) have done, but in motor cortex there are clumps of large pyramidal tract neurons and if one does a horizontal section through the fifth layer one can see a clump here, a clump here, etc. What these sorts of elementary blocks are, nobody knows yet.

Dr. Lewis: Would it be useful to have a technique that adjusts for that sort of clumping?

Dr. Evarts: It would be very, very useful to know what characterizes one of these clumps. No one knows as yet. You say that these colonies should not be random. I think that probably is true because Ted Jones in St. Louis has recently done work in which he put horseradish peroxidase into a region of the spinal cord and then looked at the uptake of this in pyramidal tract neurons in motor cortex. Elements of a particular clump tended to be labeled or not labeled. Thus, one clump of pyramidal tract neurons and an adjacent clump may be viewed as labeled–unlabeled. Then you move a bit further and now you find a clump that is labeled again, so that there seem to be relatively segregated clumps of 8 or 10 cells that are projecting to a particular part of the spinal cord, then a clump that isn't projecting, then a clump that is projecting, and so forth.

Dr. Boynton: What I'm going to ask might be characterized as one of these irritating kinds of questions that undergraduates ask and that you're blissfully insulated from there at NIMH, but I'll go ahead with it anyway. Would you be willing to make any speculations about the sort of thing that might be going on as an athlete, let's say a professional golfer, over a very protracted period of time develops the, what is to me, almost incredibly high level of motor skill necessary for him to succeed at that occupation?

Dr. Evarts: The problem of how skills such as golf are acquired illustrates a problem which arises to some extent in all motor learning—when there is a motor output whose consequences (i.e., success or failure) are fed back at a long delay following the emission of the motor output. It's very difficult to propose any simple mechanism for the adaptations that take place in golf or the many other analogous situations. In the case of the vestibuloocular reflex, one can imagine that the detection of retinal slip will get back into the cerebellum within 100 msec and that there can be some residuum of the patterns of activity that were occurring in the flocculus prior to this. But other forms of acquisition—like golf—I haven't heard any notions that can explain them mechanistically as has been done for the vestibuloocular reflex.

Michael Wolf (University of Texas, Austin): In your closing statement, discussing the similarity between voluntary and involuntary movements, such as the choreatic movements, you seem to me to imply that there is no neuronal location of the intent to move. Do you hypothesize where or what the intent to move is, and if there is one, how can you say that involuntary and voluntary movements are that similar?

Dr. Evarts: I believe that voluntary movements have a goal. In contrast, there are purposeless movements that are similar to voluntary movements to the extent that for both sorts of movements the patterns of activity in motor cortex, spinal cord, and many parts of the nervous system utilize the same neural mechanisms. As to the sites from which volitional and purposeless movements arise, let us consider Parkinson's disease, where in addition to the presence of purposeless movements (e.g., tremors) there is an impairment of volition. It is not merely that given a certain volitional state patients have difficulty moving (which they do), but that in many cases they may have a reduced desire to move. At the other extreme, in certain drug-induced basal ganglia disturbances (diseases involving excessive dopamine rather than too little), there can be excessive desire to move. Thus, there is a localized—in the sense of a chemically specifiable—system that will either reduce or elevate volition, but the involuntary movements in disorders of dopaminergic systems utilize the same pathways and mechanisms as are utilized by the voluntary movements in these same patients. Involuntary and voluntary movements utilize the same machinery. But where volition is, is very hard to say. It's much like the search for the engram.

Peter MacNeilage (University of Texas, Austin): Could you clarify for me your views about motor-cortex neurons? Are you saying that there's a population of relatively large motor-cortex neurons that are relatively immune from sensory feedback, and if so, is the implication that we can make relatively less use of feedback control in movement sequences involving high force levels?

Dr. Evarts: Within a particular focus—let's say the one where there are many, many neurons all reciprocally related to a particular act—the neurons whose axons are smallest have the highest probability of being involved with the finest movements and being most intensely driven by afferent input. In that sense there's a parallel between the functional correlates of neuronal size in motor cortex and in spinal cord. But a difference between motor cortex PTNs and spinal cord motoneurons is in the proportion of neurons relatively undriven by afferent input: Within the motor cortex focus, the proportion of PTNs unresponsive to afferent input is somewhat less than in the spinal cord. In the spinal cord there is a rather larger group of the phasic motor neurons, which are weakly, if at all, influenced by afferent input.

Dr. Barlow: I'm trying to formulate a question about how the goal of a set of movement control systems is determined. What you were saying about the person holding the pistol still, but everything else moving. Supposing he changed that to his other hand, or supposing he got another goal in his mind, like holding a glass of water and not spilling it. He would have to set up a whole set of different connections in his set of muscles. This is very nicely shown by some experiments that I'm sure you know about by Merton, Marsdon, and Morton, where they measure the muscle action potentials in different muscles while the person is doing movements that are interrupted in different ways. They initially concentrated on the muscles that were executing the movements and they got a comparison of what happened when the movement was executed uninterruptedly, when it was interrupted by increasing the resistance, and when it was interrupted by decreasing the resistance. They got characteristic differences with quite short latency, which they argued—quite correctly as I think it now turns out—must be mediated by the cortex. If you now do the same thing with almost any other muscle in the body, you find that there's a similar pattern of changes, which means that the whole of the motor cortex must have been reset in some very specific way. I would like to ask your views about how many different ways it can be reset, and how in the world this can be organized.

Dr. Evarts: In response to your question, I would like to discuss some ideas of Nicholas Bernstein as derived from his book, *The Coordination and Regulation of Movements*. In this book (written 30 or 40 years ago and translated in 1967), Bernstein discusses the issue which you raise. I'm going to read what he has written on this matter:

> There is the deeply seated inherent indifference of the motor control centre to the scale and position of the movement effected, as we have

discussed above. It is clear that each of the variations of a movement (for example, drawing a circle large or small, directly in front of one-self or to one side, on a horizontal piece of paper or on a vertical blackboard, etc.) demands a quite different muscular formula; and even more than this, involves a completely different set of muscles in the action. The almost equal facility and accuracy with which all these variations can be performed is evidence for the fact that they are ulti-mately determined by one and the same higher directional engram in relation to which dimensions and position play a secondary role.

Bernstein then goes on to say that the features of a movement which are localized are not, in any elementary sense, the muscles. The features sig-nificant for the motor cortex seem to be movements at a particular joint and the return of afferent information via the cutaneous, muscular, and joint afferents relevant to this movement. Furthermore, the fact that goal-oriented movements can be carried out, independent of the particu-lar joint movement that has to be effected, presumably means that the goal-setting region has to be located somewhere outside the motor cortex.

Jack Morelli (University of Texas, Austin): It occurred to me that in the push–pull situation, the animal could be controlling one of six variables, all of which could achieve the same result. For example, position or force in any of its first and second derivatives and, additionally, for the control of each of those variables there are probably an unlimited number of con-trol configurations that could accomplish that task in the time you speci-fied. Do you have a set of rules or operations you employ to try and deter-mine what the goal is—the actual control variable—and to satisfy yourself that you actually have it?

Dr. Evarts: One approach that we have been thinking about which might allow us to separate the different feedback variables would involve observ-ing the activity of motor-cortex neurons during isometric as compared to isotonic performances. In the isometric case (where the monkey grasped an immovable object), the task would involve controlling force—and feedback would be primarily via tension receptors, since muscle length and joint position would be relatively fixed. In contrast, the isotonic case would require that the monkey control the position of a handle with the force requirements being constant and with feedback coming from mus-cle length and joint position receptors rather than tension receptors. Just as we have thought about trying to dissect the feedback pathways, we have thought about trying to get paradigms in which we can pull these things apart. We haven't done any of these things yet, but I think a lot of them are possible.

Discussion References

Bernstein, N. *The co-ordination and regulation of movements.* Oxford: Pergamon Press, 1967.

Hubel, D.H., Wiesel, T.N., & LeVay, S. Plasticity of ocular dominance columns in monkey striate cortex. *Philosophical Transactions of the Royal Society* (London), Ser. B, 1977, *278*, 377–409.

Ito, M. The control mechanisms of cerebellar motor systems. In F.O. Schmitt & F.G. Worden (Eds.), *The neurosciences. Third study program.* Cambridge, Mass.: Massachusetts Institute of Technology, 1974.

Jones, E.G. Lamination and differential distribution of thalamic afferents within the sensory-motor cortex of the squirrel monkey. *Journal of Comparative Neurology*, 1975, *160*, 167–204.

Jones, E.G., & Powell, T.P.S. Connexions of the somatic sensory cortex of the rhesus monkey. III. Thalamic connexions. *Brain*, 1970, *93*, 37–56.

Lisberger, S.G., & Miles, F.A. Modifications underlying adaptive plasticity of the primate vestibulo-ocular reflex are post-synaptic to the medial vestibular nucleus. *Society for Neuroscience Abstracts*, 1979, *5*, 376.

Miles, F.A., & Braitman, D.J. Effect of prolonged optical reversal of vision on the vestibulo-ocular reflex: Some neurophysiological observations. *Society for Neuroscience Abstracts*, 1978, *4*, 167.

Robinson, D.A. Adaptive gain control of vestibuloocular reflex by the cerebellum. *Journal of Neurophysiology*, 1976, *39*, 954–969.

Vogt, B.A., & Pandya, D.N. Cortico-cortical connections of somatic sensory cortex (areas 3, 1 and 2) in the rhesus monkey. *Journal of Comparative Neurology*, 1978, *177*, 179–192.

CHAPTER 7

Cellular Insights into
the Multivariant Nature of Arousal

Eric R. Kandel

1 Historical Considerations on the Concept of Arousal

The concept of arousal initially developed from the well-known observation that most stimuli, particularly weak or familiar ones, have a restricted influence and only affect a very limited range of behaviors; however, some stimuli—particularly novel, aversive, or appetitive ones—have more general effects. In addition to producing a direct action, these broadly effective stimuli are able to modulate a widespread family of responses by altering an animal's responsiveness to other stimuli (Figure 7.1). The heightened responsiveness that results is called sensitization. Moreover, inasmuch as the modulating effect of a single stimulus may persist for minutes and even hours, sensitization resembles the memory of a learning process. However, unlike associative learning, sensitization does not require a specific temporal relationship between the test stimulus and the sensitizing stimulus.

That novel, aversive, and appetitive stimuli have a wide sphere of influence has been interpreted by a number of theorists, such as Elizabeth Duffy (1941), Donald Hebb (1949), and R.B. Malmo (1959), to indicate that these stimuli have an arousing or activating capability. Most of the early theorists who invoked the concept of arousal assumed it to represent a single behavioral system that varied along a continuum ranging from states of sleep through wakefulness, to states of high excitement. The idea of unitary arousal systems developed by Malmo and by Hebb seemed initially to be supported by the finding, by Moruzzi and Magoun (1949), of what appeared to be a single, diffusely acting, arousal system in the reticular formation of the brainstem. From their observation that this area was capable of producing desynchronization of the electrical activity recorded from the surface of the cortex, it seemed tempting to assume

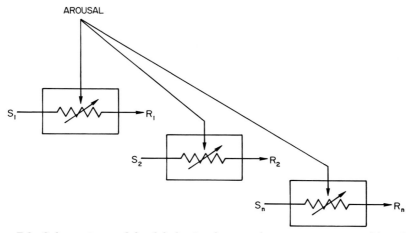

Figure 7.1. Schematic model of behavioral arousal as a process capable of modulating a variety of different behavioral responses. Several responses (R_1, R_2, R_n) are triggered by their appropriate eliciting stimuli (S_1, S_2, S_n). The ability of these constant stimuli to trigger a response is variable (as indicated by the variable resistors). Arousal can modulate the gain of the response by changing the setting of the resistor. (From Kandel, Krasne, Strumwasser, & Truman, 1979.)

that this neural system mediated behavioral arousal (for review see Magoun, 1954).

Even a rapid reading of the literature of the last 10 years makes it clear that our understanding of the relation of the reticular formation to behavioral arousal has not been significantly advanced. In particular, it has not proved possible to determine whether arousal is unitary or multivariant. The problems have been of two sorts. First, recent anatomical and physiological studies have revealed that different parts of the reticular system have distinct biochemical and functional properties (Jouvet, 1972; Ungerstedt, 1971). Each of these parts presumably has its own effects on behavior. Which one or several of these regions, if any, is related to behavioral arousal has not yet been determined.

Second, the concept of arousal has been used in a variety of different ways. In the best of cases different investigators simply used different paradigms to study arousal. In the worst of cases the term was not operationally defined and therefore not related to any paradigm (for review see Andrews & Little, 1971).

However, most of the paradigms that try to alter the level of behavioral arousal use stimuli that are novel, aversive, or appetitive. As such, these behavioral paradigms share a number of features with a simple and well-known process called *behavioral sensitization*. Sensitization refers to an enhancement of the response to a stimulus as a result of the presentation of another (usually strong) stimulus, where the enhancement does not depend on pairing of stimuli.

While studying extinction of a classically conditioned response, Pavlov

(1927) first found that a strong, novel stimulus enhanced an animal's responsiveness to a previously ineffective conditioned stimulus. This phenomenon was later studied in detail by Grether (1938) and came to be known as sensitization. Sensitization has now been shown to be extremely widespread; it is found in humans as well as in all higher animals (Figure 7.2; Hagbarth & Kugelberg, 1958; Kandel, 1976, 1979).

The novel, noxious, or appetitive stimuli used to produce arousal are similar to those commonly used to produce behavioral sensitization. Thus, the theoretical construct of arousal shares features with the observed behavioral phenomenon of sensitization. Although sensitization typically refers primarily to a nonassociative enhancement of a response, arousal stimuli may also produce nonassociative depressions of responses. For example, a noxious stimulus can cause a rat to freeze,

A

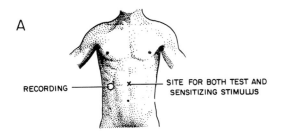

B

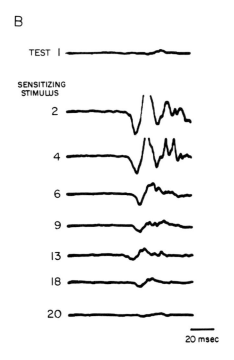

Figure 7.2. Sensitization of human abdominal reflex. (A) Experimental arrangement. Recordings obtained from right external oblique muscles. Both the test stimulus (a weak mechanical stimulus) and the sensitizing stimulus (a strong blow) were applied to the epigastrium. (B) Sensitization. Repeated weak test (mechanical) stimuli to the epigastrium (interstimulus interval, 5–10 sec) produced habituation of reflex (trace 1). Three sensitizing stimuli (blows to epigastrium) were then applied. These produced sensitization of the previously depressed response that lasted for the next 17 trials, and the response returned to control by the 20th trial. (After Hagbarth & Kugelberg, 1958.)

thereby reducing locomotor behavior. It therefore seems useful to extend the term sensitization to include all nonassociative modulation of the behavioral response to one stimulus by another, enhancement (positive sensitization) as well as depression (negative sensitization).

I would emphasize that although the consequences of sensitization are included in the construct "arousal," the two terms are not fully equivalent. Arousal is commonly defined as consisting of three components: general activity, somatic responsiveness, and autonomic activity. Sensitization often pertains only to the last two components. In addition, whereas arousal can be produced by internal as well as external stimuli, sensitization refers only to changes produced by external stimuli, but this distinction does not seem very fundamental.

Nonetheless, there are considerable advantages in reducing the examination of arousal to that of reflex sensitization. The sensitization paradigm is simple and well-defined (Grether, 1938) and can therefore be readily applied even to simple invertebrate preparations, such as lobsters, leeches, crayfish, and snails. These invertebrates offer four technical advantages over vertebrate experimental preparations for studying behavioral processes at the cellular level:

1. Invertebrates have nervous systems that consist of fewer cells—typically 10,000–100,000—and are relatively simpler than those of vertebrates.
2. Many of the nerve cells are large and identifiable in every member of the species.
3. The individual behaviors are often simpler than those of vertebrates and therefore easier to analyze.
4. The total behavioral repertoire is limited.

I would like to illustrate these points by considering some recent studies by my colleagues and myself designed to clarify the concept of behavioral arousal. In these simple preparations one can examine the effects of different appetitive and noxious stimuli on different response systems and determine, on both a behavioral and a cellular level, whether sensitization of different behavioral responses involves a unitary process with a single cellular locus or whether different response systems use independent neural systems for sensitization. These are the questions that I would like to consider by reviewing some of our recent work on sensitization in *Aplysia*. These studies have examined the consequences of different sensitizing stimuli (food and shock) on different response systems (biting and defensive reflexes). We have attempted in these studies to answer two related questions: (1) Do aversive and appetitive stimuli have different modulating consequences for different response systems? and (2) How are the loci and mechanisms that subserve sensitization of feeding related to the loci and mechanisms subserving defensive gill withdrawal.

I will begin by briefly reviewing data on the locus and mechanism of sensitization of defensive reflexes.

2 Positive Sensitization of Defensive Behavior by Noxious Stimuli

The responses I will consider first are components of a family of defensive withdrawal reflexes of the external organs of the mantle cavity (Figure 7.3A). The mantle cavity of molluscs is a respiratory chamber that houses the gill. This chamber is covered by a protective sheet, the mantle shelf, which terminates in a fleshy spout, the siphon. When the siphon or the mantle shelf is stimulated with a weak tactile stimulus, the siphon, mantle shelf, and gill all contract and withdraw into the mantle cavity. This reflex is analogous to defensive escape and withdrawal responses found in almost all higher invertebrates as well as vertebrates. The defensive withdrawal response can be habituated—that is, diminished and eventually extinguished for a period of time—by repeated presentations of the eliciting stimulus. It can also be readily sensitized by a strong, noxious stimulus (Figure 7.3B).

Sensitization has two interesting behavioral features: (1) its relation to habituation, and (2) its time course. The relationship of sensitization to habituation is revealed in a behavioral comparison of the two processes. As I have indicated, gill withdrawal can be produced by stimulating two independent pathways, the siphon or the mantle shelf. The response habituates with stimulation of either of these pathways, but habituation is restricted to the activated pathway. By contrast, sensitization is more widespread and will enhance both the siphon and the mantle shelf pathway, as well as other closely related defensive reflexes. Moreover, sensitization will enhance both habituated and nonhabituated responses (Fig-

Figure 7.3. Short-term sensitization of the gill-withdrawal reflex in *Aplysia*. ▶ (A1) Experimental arrangement for behavioral studies in the intact animal. A gill-withdrawal reflex is elicited by a water jet (tactile) stimulus to the siphon. The sensitizing stimulus is a noxious mechanical or electrical stimulus to the head or neck. (A2) The contracted gill. Dotted lines indicate the position of the gill when relaxed. (B) Photocell records showing sensitization of a habituated response. Habituating stimuli were presented to the siphon at 1-min intervals (I.S.I.). A noxious mechanical stimulus was applied to the neck. Following this sensitizing stimulus, the response was facilitated for several minutes. (C) Widespread nature of sensitization. Sensitization of habituated and nonhabituated responses following presentation of a single strong stimulus to the neck. After a single test stimulus to the purple gland (time 0'0"), repeated stimuli were delivered to the siphon every 30 sec, producing habituation of gill withdrawal. A second test to the purple gland (time 2'20") indicated that no generalization of habituation had occurred. A strong stimulus was then applied to the neck region, producing prolonged gill contraction. Subsequent stimulation of the purple gland produced a facilitated nonhabituated response (sensitization); stimulation of the siphon produced a facilitated habituated response (dishabituation). (A from Pinsker, Kandel, Castellucci, & Kupfermann, 1970; B from Kandel, Brunelli, Byrne, & Castellucci, 1976.)

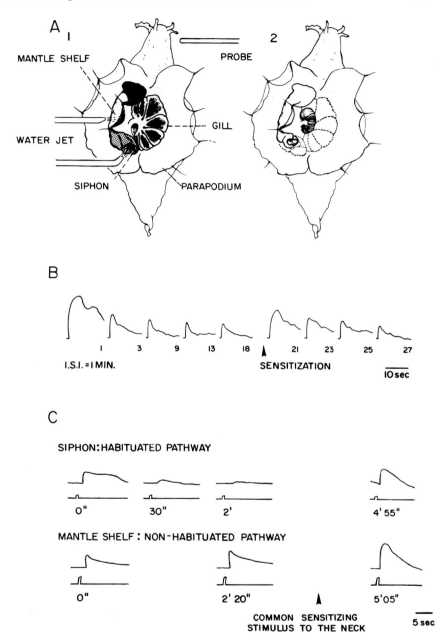

Figure 7.3

ure 7.3C). Studies first carried out by Spencer, Thompson, and Neilson (1966) in the cat, and subsequently by Carew, Castellucci, and Kandel (1971) in *Aplysia*, have shown that dishabituation is really only a special form of sensitization. Therefore, dishabituation is not a removal of habituation but a sensitization superimposed upon habituation. These experiments also provide a nice illustration of the fact that weak and familiar stimuli of the sort that produce habituation have a restricted sphere of influence, whereas strong or noxious stimuli of the sort that produce sensitization have a broad sphere of influence (Figure 7.3C).

The second interesting aspect of sensitization is its time course. Whereas a single noxious stimulus produces short-term sensitization lasting minutes and hours, repeated noxious stimuli have long-term effects and produce sensitization that lasts days and weeks (Figure 7.4).

In earlier work we delineated what we believe to be the virtually complete neural circuit of the gill- and siphon-withdrawal reflex to siphon stimulation. There are 13 identified central motor cells: five for the gill, seven for the siphon, and one for both gill and siphon. There are also about 30 peripheral motor cells for the siphon. These motor cells are activated by two populations of sensory neurons, each containing about 24 cells. One of these populations innervates the siphon skin; the other innervates the mantle shelf. Finally there are several interneurons, of which one producing inhibition and two producing excitation are illustrated in Figure 7.5. The sensory neurons make direct connections to the interneurons and to the motor cells. The motor cells connect directly to muscle.

By examining the various sites within the circuit during habituation and sensitization in the intact animal, we found that the critical change underlying both types of behavioral modification occurred at the synapses made by the sensory neurons. With repeated sensory stimulation, at rates that produce habituation in the intact animal (once every 10 sec to once every 3 min), the monosynaptic excitatory connection between the sensory neurons and the motor neurons undergoes a homosynaptic depression because of a decrease in the number of transmitter quanta released by each impulse in the sensory neurons. A sensitizing stimulus produces rapid presynaptic facilitation of the connection because of an increase in the amount of transmitter (the number of transmitter quanta) released per impulse (Figure 7.6).

As is reflected in the behavioral response, the synaptic depression accompanying habituation is restricted to the stimulated synapses (Carew, Castellucci, & Kandel, 1971). Similarly, the presynaptic facilitation resembles behavioral arousal in its widespread action: It acts on both habituated and nonhabituated pathways (Figure 7.7).

Recently, Hawkins, Castellucci, and Kandel (1976) have searched for and found two cell groups that mediate sensitization. These cells (L28 and the cluster of L29 cells) are higher order excitatory interneurons in the neural circuit for gill withdrawal. Preliminary morphological work, based

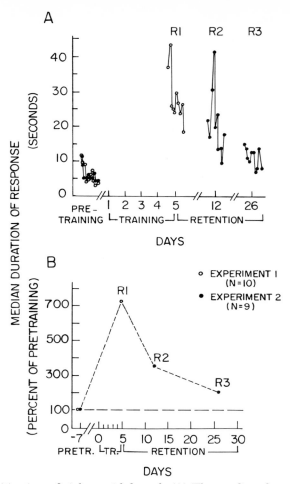

Figure 7.4. Long-term sensitization of siphon withdrawal. (A) The median duration of siphon withdrawal is shown for each trial of a 10-trial block (minimum
intertrial interval was 30 sec). The results of two independent experiments are
shown. Experimental animals were given four electrical shocks a day for 4 days;
the controls received no shocks. In Experiment 1 retention of dishabituation was
tested one day (R1) after the last shock. In Experiment 2 retention was tested one
week (R2) and three weeks (R3) after the last shock. Significant sensitization was
evident in the 1-day and 1-week retention tests, whereas there was almost complete recovery in the 3-week retention test. (B) Time course of sensitization (data
from A). Responses for each daily session have been summed and expressed as a
single (median) score. Twenty-four hours and one week after the end of training
the experimental animals showed significantly longer siphon withdrawal compared to their own pretraining score and the score of the controls, both of which
are expressed in the graph as 100% (Mann–Whitney U tests used for intergroup
comparisons). In the 3-week retention test there was no longer a significant difference between the experimental and control groups, but the responses of the experimental animals were still significantly prolonged compared to their own pretraining levels (Wilcoxon matched pairs signed-ranks test; $p < 0.005$); the control
animals were unchanged. (From Kandel, 1978.)

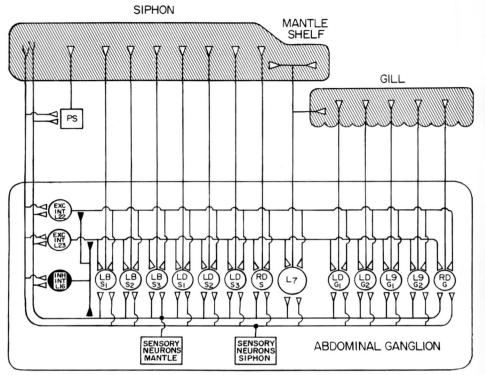

Figure 7.5. Schematic neural circuit of the defensive-withdrawal reflex, indicating the sensory, interneuronal, and motor-neuronal components of the total reflex. There are two populations of sensory neurons consisting of about 24 cells each. One population innervates the siphon skin, the other innervates the mantle shelf (purple gland). These neurons have direct connections to the motor neurons and indirect connections via two excitatory and one inhibitory interneuron. The three interneurons and the 13 central motor cells in the abdominal ganglion are all unique, identified cells. The peripheral siphon motor cells (PS) are not uniquely identified. The same population of sensory neurons activates both the siphon and gill motor neurons. This accounts for the fact that the two acts of the reflex pattern occur simultaneously. (From Kupfermann, Carew, & Kandel, 1974.)

upon intracellular injections of a marker substance into L29, suggests that these cells are serotonergic or use a closely related biogenic amine (Bailey, Hawkins, Chen, & Kandel, 1980). The vesicle types located near active sites resemble those found by Shkolnik and Schwartz (1980) in identified serotonergic neurons. Moreover, serotonin applied to these cells simulates presynaptic facilitation (Figure 7.8A; Brunelli, Castellucci, & Kandel, 1976), whereas a large number of other putative transmitter substances do not (Tomosky-Sykes, 1978). Furthermore, the presynaptic facilitation produced by a sensitizing stimulus is blocked by the serotonin antagonist cinanserin.

We next addressed the question: What is the molecular mechanism for

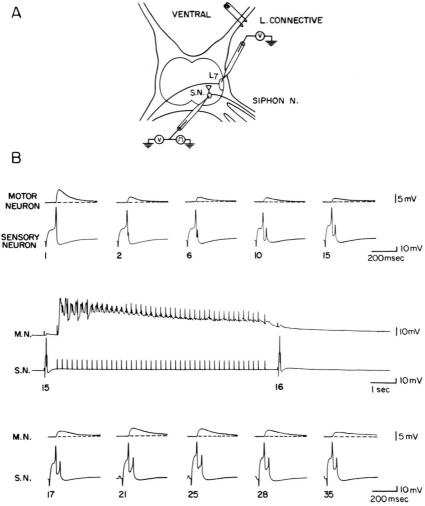

Figure 7.6. Depression and facilitation of monosynaptic EPSP (excitatory post-synaptic potential) produced in the motor neuron by stimulating a single sensory neuron. (A) Experimental arrangement. (B) Synaptic depression and facilitation. Top set of traces: Selected records of depression during a series of 15 consecutive stimuli to the sensory neuron, one every 10 sec. Middle set of traces: The left connective was stimulated between the 15th and 16th stimulus to the sensory neuron. Connective stimulation did not fire the sensory neuron. (Vertical lines in the sensory neuron trace between spike number 15 and 16 are shock artifacts.) Bottom set of traces: Selected records of the synaptic facilitation of the response to the 17th stimulus and the next 18 responses following connective stimulation. Facilitation lasted several minutes. Interneuronal activity was reduced by using a solution with high Mg^{++} and Ca^{++} concentrations. (From Kandel et al., 1976.)

sensitization? The first possibility is that sensitization involves the synthesis of a new protein. However, inhibiting protein synthesis by up to 95%
does not interfere with the acquisition and retention of either short-term
habituation or sensitization (Schwartz, Castellucci, & Kandel, 1971).
These findings suggested to us that sensitization did not involve a change
in macromolecular synthesis but might result from a change in the levels
of a small molecule—perhaps an intracellular second messenger, such as
cyclic adenosine monophosphate (cAMP)—that alters the distribution
of the transmitter from one compartment in the presynaptic terminal to
another.

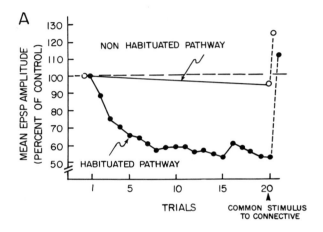

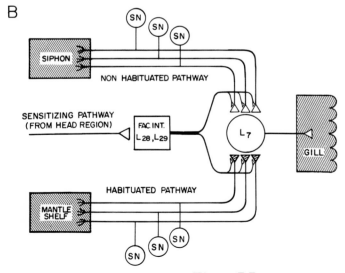

Figure 7.7

To test this idea, Cedar, Kandel, and Schwartz (1972) examined the effects on the level of cAMP of connective stimulation that produces the facilitation accompanying sensitization. We found that strong stimulation produced a twofold increase in cAMP. The increase seemed to be synaptically mediated; it was blocked by high concentrations of Mg^{++} and was simulated by serotonin, dopamine, and octopamine (Cedar & Schwartz, 1972).

These several findings suggested that the interneurons mediating sensitization might release serotonin. These neurons might then act on the terminals of the sensory neurons to increase cAMP and thereby enhance a transmitter release. We therefore exposed the ganglion to dibuteryl cAMP and found that it increased the synaptic facilitation at the sensory-to-motor neuron synapse (but not at two other synapses examined). Moreover, intracellular injection of cAMP into the sensory neurons also simulated the facilitation (Figure 7.8B).

These data suggested a preliminary model of how presynaptic facilitation might work (Figure 7.9). The facilitation might be mediated by the terminals of serotonergic neurons. We posit that these neurons end on or near the terminals of the sensory neurons and act there to increase the concentration of cAMP in the terminals.

How might cAMP enhance transmitter release? The critical ion for transmitter release is Ca^{++}, which is thought to be responsible for allowing transmitter vesicles to bind to discharge sites—a critical precursor step in exocytotic release. Calcium ion influx into the terminal is triggered by the depolarizing action of the action potential. Cyclic AMP

◀ **Figure 7.7.** Cellular changes caused by sensitization are not restricted to one reflex pathway. (A) Pooled data from nine experiments. A single test EPSP was produced by stimulation of the control nerve ($N = 9$). The experimental nerve ($N = 9$) was then repeatedly stimulated (I.S.I. = 10 sec), producing significant ($p < 0.005$) depression of the EPSP in the motor neuron. A second stimulus was then applied to the control nerve, producing a test EPSP that was not significantly different from the first test EPSP. This demonstrated that depression had not generalized to the test nerve. After a train of stimuli to the connective (six per second for 6 sec), both depressed and nondepressed EPSPs were significantly facilitated ($p < 0.005$ and $p < 0.025$, respectively). (B) Schematic comparison of sensitization and habituation of the gill-withdrawal reflex. Habituation is selective and quite restricted in its action. Following stimulation of either the mantle shelf or the siphon, only the stimulated pathway is habituated; the homosynaptic (self-generated) depression is limited to synapses (hatched triangles) between the activated sensory neurons (SN) and motor neuron L7. By contrast, a strong stimulus from the head sensitizes both the habituated and nonhabituated pathways. This results from the fact that presynaptic facilitation acts on all the synapses made by primary sensory neurons on the motor neuron L7. The difference in the spatial distribution of the pathways mediating habituation and sensitization explains the restricted nature of habituation and the widespread action of sensitization. (From Carew et al., 1971.)

might work by enhancing Ca^{++} influx into the terminals, much as it does in the heart in response to the excitatory transmitter, norepinephrine (Tsien, 1977).

Marc Klein, a graduate student in my laboratory, and I have obtained some evidence in support of this scheme (Klein & Kandel, 1978). We have found that the presynaptic facilitation activates a voltage-dependent Ca^{++} conductance, which is then brought into its effective voltage range by the depolarizing action of the spike that invades the terminals.

The best way to examine the action of cAMP on the terminals would obviously be to record from the terminals themselves. We have not been able to do this. However, the terminals are sufficiently close to the cell body so that some of the electrical changes in them are reflected by

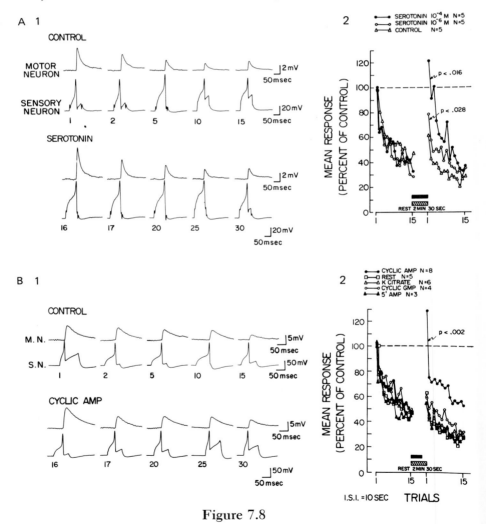

Figure 7.8

◀ **Figure 7.8.** Facilitation of a monosynaptic EPSP by serotonin and cyclic adenosine monophosphate (cAMP). (A) Effect of serotonin on monosynaptic EPSP. (A1) A sensory neuron was stimulated once every 10 sec and produced a monosynaptic EPSP in a gill or siphon motor neuron. Between the 15th and 16th action potential there was a 2.5-min rest, during which the ganglion was bathed with 10^{-4} M serotonin. (A2) A sensory neuron was stimulated and produced a monosynaptic EPSP in a gill or siphon motor neuron; the interstimulus interval (I.S.I.) was 10 sec. In each experiment, the EPSP amplitudes were normalized with respect to an initial control EPSP ($N = 5$ in all cases). In the control group (open triangles), 15 stimuli produced synaptic depression. After a rest of 2.5-min (hatched bar) and a slight recovery of EPSP, a second group of 15 stimuli was applied to the sensory neuron, producing further depression. In the two experimental groups, the 15 initial stimuli produced similar synaptic depression. During the 2.5-min rest period (black bar), serotonin (2×10^{-4} M, closed circles; or 2×10^{-6} M, open circles) was introduced into the perfusing solution. During the initial EPSP depression, the control and experimental curves overlapped completely. After treatment with serotonin, however, both experimental curves were significantly higher than the control curve (triangles) ($p < 0.016$ for 2×10^{-4} M and $p < 0.028$ for 2×10^{-6} M; one-tailed Mann–Whitney U test). To determine the statistical differences between the experimental and the control curves, the amplitudes of the responses to each of the 15 stimuli of a run were summed to obtain a single score. (B) Effect of cAMP on monosynaptic EPSP. (B1) A sensory neuron was first stimulated once every 10 sec for 15 stimuli (1–15). During a 2.5 min rest cAMP was introduced by iontophoresis into the cell body of the sensory neuron. Hyperpolarizing current pulses (1 sec long) of 3×10^{-7} to 4.5×10^{-7} A were applied every 2 sec for 2 min from one barrel of a double electrode filled with 1.5 M cAMP; the second (recording) barrel was filled with 3 M potassium citrate. Thirty seconds after the end of the injection a second series of 15 stimuli was given (16–30). The amplitudes of the evoked EPSPs of the second series are higher than the amplitudes of comparable EPSPs evoked in control experiments. (B2) The experimental group (closed circles; $N = 8$) is compared with a first control group, in which the test (2.5 min; indicated with hatched bar) was simply followed by 15 additional stimuli without any current injection (open squares; $N = 5$). In a second control group, a hyperpolarizing current pulse, comparable to that used to inject cAMP, was injected into the sensory neuron but the pulses were applied through an electrode filled with 3 M potassium citrate (open triangles, $N = 6$). In a third group, cyclic guanosine monophosphate (cGMP) (1.5 M) was injected intracellularly (open circles, $N = 4$). In a fourth group, 5'-AMP (closed triangles, $N = 3$) was injected. Black bar indicates 2-min period of injection used in all experiments. The five curves generated during the initial EPSP depression produced by the first 15 stimuli overlap completely. After injection of cAMP (filled circles), however, the experimental group was significantly higher than either the first control group ($p < 0.002$, one-tailed Mann–Whitney U test) or the three other control groups (for potassium citrate, $p < 0.001$; for cGMP, $p < 0.14$; for 5'-AMP, $p < 0.12$). (From Brunelli et al., 1976.)

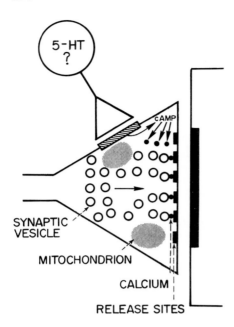

Figure 7.9. A preliminary model of sensitization. The presynaptic terminal of a sensory neuron is schematically illustrated with its complement of synaptic vesicles (small circles), mitochondria (shaded ovals), and active sites (small black rectangles). The subsynaptic region of the postsynaptic neuron is also shown (long black bar). The terminal of the postulated presynaptic neuron that releases serotonin is indicated. The serotonin acts on a membrane-bound adenylate cyclase (cross-hatched bar) to increase cAMP in the terminals of the sensory neurons, which leads to an increase in transmitter release, perhaps by means of an increase in free Ca^{++}. (From Kandel, 1978.)

changes in the cell body. In addition, the properties of the Ca^{++} channels of the cell body seem to resemble those of the terminals. This also had previously been suggested by the work of Stinnakre and Tauc (1973). We therefore set about to examine the changes in the membrane properties of the cell body that accompanied the presynaptic facilitation and found that synaptic action altered the currents underlying the action potential. A first clue that a voltage-sensitive Ca^{++} conductance might be increased

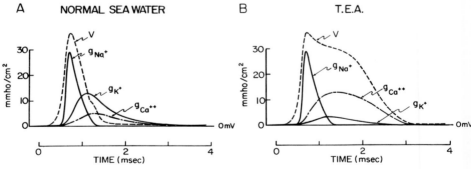

Figure 7.10. Schematic diagram of the action potential (V) and the sodium, potassium, and calcium conductances, g_{Na}, g_K, and g_{Ca} (A) in normal sea water and (B) in tetraethylammonium (TEA). These conductance changes give rise to the currents that produce the action potential. The TEA blocks g_K, which results in a slowed repolarization that unmasks and enhances the Ca^{++} current. (From Kandel, 1978.)

was that the connective stimulation that leads to presynaptic facilitation often produced a small change in the configuration of the spike.

As is well known from the work of Katz and Miledi (1969), the Ca^{++} current in the terminals is normally masked by the much larger Na^+ and K^+ currents. In particular, the K^+ current overlaps much of the duration of the Ca^{++} current (Figure 7.10A). That a change in Ca^{++} current may produce only a small change in the action potential is therefore not surprising. We therefore incubated the ganglion with tetraethylammonium (TEA), an agent that selectively blocks one of the delayed K^+ channels. The TEA produces a significant prolongation of the spike because it blocks the repolarizing action of the K^+ current (Figure 7.10B). Much of this prolongation results from the unopposed action of the Ca^{++} current (see also Horn & Miller, 1977). This current is now sufficiently unmasked so that it can itself produce a depolarization of the membrane, which in turn can further prolong and enhance the Ca^{++} conductance increase. The prolongation in the sensory neuron spike is almost totally prevented by cobalt ion, which blocks the Ca^{++} channel. Moreover, in TEA, the late phase of the plateau has the properties of a Nernst calcium electrode. A 10-fold change in Ca^{++} concentration produces a 28-mV change in the

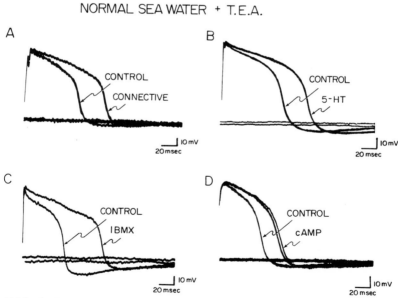

NORMAL SEA WATER + T.E.A.

Figure 7.11. Spike broadening may be obtained by intervention at several steps in the proposed mechanism for presynaptic facilitation of the sensory neuron-to-motor neuron synapse. (A) Connective stimulation. (B) Incubation with 10^{-4} M serotonin (5-HT). (C) Incubation with the phosphodiesterase inhibitor, IBMX, which reduces cAMP hydrolysis, leading to increased intracellular levels of cAMP. (D) Intracellular injection of cAMP. (From Klein & Kandel, 1978.)

amplitude of the late phase of the plateau. In addition, the prolongation produced by TEA occurs in the absence of external Na^+.

As Katz and Miledi (1969) pointed out, in the presence of TEA the duration of the spike is very sensitive to slight changes in Ca^{++} current. The prolonged TEA-treated spike therefore is a good assay for changes in Ca^{++} current, although the assay does not distinguish, as I will indicate below, whether the action is on the Ca^{++} channel directly or whether that channel is affected indirectly by the inactivation of a K^+ conductance.

Klein and I were now in a position to see how the Ca^{++} current was altered by: (1) connective stimulation; (2) serotonin, the putative mediating transmitter; (3) cAMP, the possible second messenger; and (4) IBMX, a phosphodiesterase inhibitor that enhances the action of endogenous cAMP. All four procedures prolong the TEA-treated spike, further indicating that all of these prolong the Ca^{++} current, directly or indirectly (Figure 7.11). Tomosky-Sykes (1978) has now also used this assay system to examine 24 possible candidates for transmitters mediating presynaptic facilitation, including various amino acids, histamine, octopamine, and dopamine. Of these, only serotonin produced significant broadening of the action potential, and the broadening was blocked by cinanserin. In addition, Hawkins (1980) has found that firing a single facilitator neuron

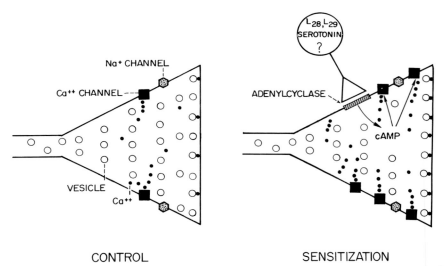

CONTROL   SENSITIZATION

Figure 7.12. A model for sensitization. In the control state, an action potential in the terminal membranes of the sensory neurons opens up a number of Ca^{++} channels (squares) in parallel with the Na^+ channels of the membrane (hexagons). Sensitization is produced by cells L28 and L29 (and perhaps by some other cells); these cells are thought to be serotonergic. Serotonin acts on an adenylate cyclase in the terminals, which stimulates the synthesis of cAMP. Cyclic AMP in turn increases the availability of Ca^{++} channels, leading to an increase in g_{Ca}, a greater influx of Ca^{++}, and greater binding of vesicles to release sites, and therefore to an increased probability of release. (From Klein & Kandel, 1978.)

also produces broadening of the TEA-treated sensory neuron action potential.

The finding that presynaptic facilitation produces a prolonged activation of a voltage-sensitive Ca^{++} conductance is interesting because it provides a powerful and efficient mechanism for controlling synaptic effectiveness. This mechanism may work in both directions and thereby allow synaptic transmission to be depressed as well as enhanced. Indeed, Klein and I have now found that habituation produces a progressive decrease in Ca^{++} conductance as a result of the repeated invasion of the terminals by action potentials. We have looked at the action potential of the sensory neurons in TEA during repeated stimulation at rates that produce habituation and found that the spike narrowed progressively, indicating a progressive decrease in the Ca^{++} current. This decrease in the duration of the action potential parallels the decrease in the amplitude of the EPSP.

Figure 7.12 summarizes our speculations about how cAMP may produce its actions. In the resting state the depolarization produced by each action potential opens up a certain number of Ca^{++} channels. The Ca^{++} flows in and binds the vesicles to the membrane, allowing their release. We posit that sensitization is mediated by serotonergic cells. These act to increase cAMP, which we postulate to operate for prolonged periods of time to enhance transmitter release by incresing the Ca^{++} current directly. Cyclic AMP could act on the Ca^{++} channels directly in one of four ways: (1) by making new Ca^{++} channels available, (2) by increasing the conductance of preexisting Ca^{++} channels, (3) by reducing the activation

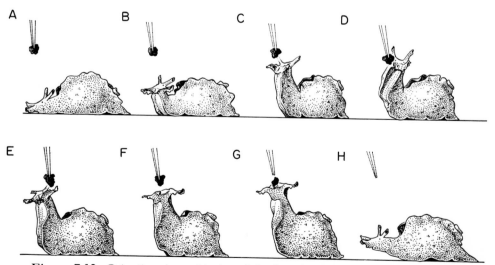

Figure 7.13. Orienting (appetitive) and feeding (consummatory) responses of *Aplysia*. (A–F) The orienting component of feeding behavior, a reflex pattern. (G) The ingestive component, a fixed-action pattern. (H) Return to resting state. (From Kandel, 1976.)

threshold of each Ca^{++} channel, or (4) by increasing the open time of each Ca^{++} channel that is activated. In addition, it could act on the Ca^{++} channel indirectly by depressing the action of the opposing K^+ current.

3 Positive Sensitization of Consummatory Behavior by Appetitive Stimuli

Kupfermann and his colleagues have studied feeding behavior in *Aplysia* and found that food stimuli arouse hungry animals (for review see Kupfermann, 1974). Exposure of an *Aplysia* to food produces sensitization of the consummatory (biting) response (Figure 7.13). After the presentation of the arousing stimulus the amplitude of successive biting responses increases and the latency for biting decreases (Figure 7.14). Food stimuli also increase heart rate (Dieringer, Koester, & Weiss, 1978).

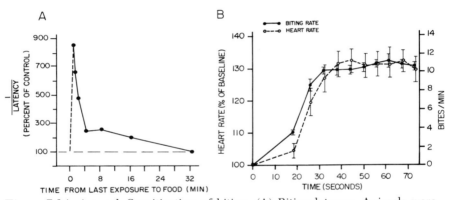

Figure 7.14. Arousal: Sensitization of biting. (A) Biting latency. Animals were presented with pieces of seaweed to the rhinophores (the pair of tentacles on the back of the head that function as chemosensory organs) until they oriented so that the lips were visible. The lips were then stimulated until animals performed four biting responses. The time from the onset of stimulation of the rhinophore and lips until the first biting response was noted. Seven groups of animals were tested, with six animals in each group. Each was allowed a different period of nonstimulation (0.5, 1, 2, 4, 8, 16, and 32 min) and times needed for rhinophore and lip stimulation to elicit biting were again noted. Decline of sensitization is evident in the gradual increase in latency of biting over the time since the animals were last exposed to food. The control level (100%) is the mean latency of the initial response of all experimental animals together with a control group (dashed line) that was tested after a piece of seaweed was placed in the cage without touching it to the animal. (B) Comparison of time courses for increase in heart rate and biting rate in response to appetitive stimuli. Starting at time zero a small piece of seaweed, held with a forceps, was kept in continuous contact with the lips. (A after Susswein, Kupfermann, & Weiss, 1976, and unpublished; B after Dieringer, Koester, & Weiss, 1978, and Kupfermann, unpublished.)

The neural circuit controlling feeding in *Aplysia* is now partially understood (Cohen, Weiss, & Kupfermann, 1978; Weiss, Cohen, & Kupfermann, 1978a). A number of motor neurons control protraction and retraction of the buccal muscle, the feeding organ. The motor cells are activated by two groups of command elements and the command cells are in turn activated by a modulatory command element (Figure 7.15).

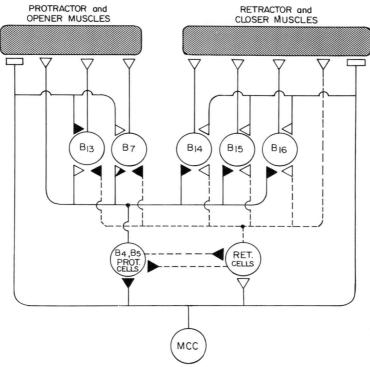

Figure 7.15. The postulated neural circuit controlling feeding in *Aplysia*. The muscles that protract the radula and open its two halves are innervated by motor cells that are not interconnected. The motor cells are innervated by command cells. The two command cells for protraction are identified multi-action cells (B_4 and B_5). The retractor command cells are not yet identified but are postulated to be dual-action cells as well. The protractor and retractor command cells make mutually inhibitory connections. The command cells are innervated by one or more receptors that excite the protractors and inhibit the retractors. The dual-action protractor and retractor command cells are innervated by higher order dual-action metacerebral cells (MCC). These excite the retractor command cells and motor cells and inhibit the protractor command cells and some of the protractor motor cells. The metacerebral cells also innervate the buccal musculature, causing a facilitation of motor neuron action by means of direct enhancement of contraction as well as by acting on the connections between the motor neurons and the muscle. Unidentified cells and their connections are drawn as dashed lines. (From Kandel, 1979.)

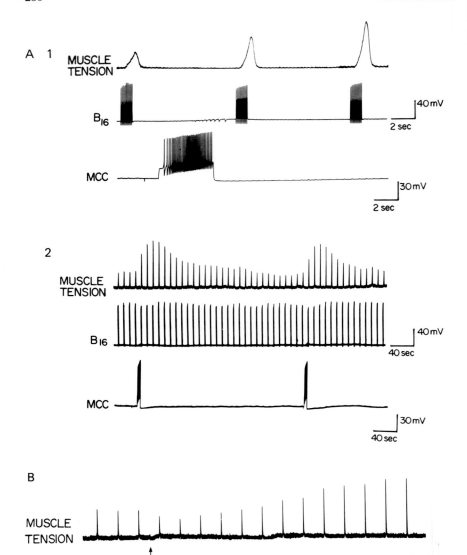

Figure 7.16. Role of the metacerebral cells in the sensitization of biting in *Aplysia*. (A) Potentiation of buccal muscle contraction produced by an identified buccal motor neuron, B_{16}. (A1) Fast-sweep record showing muscle contractions produced by a fixed number and frequency of motor neuron spikes before and after stimulation of a metacerebral cell (MCC). (A2) Slow-sweep record showing the time course of MCC potentiation. The MCC was stimulated twice to show the reproducibility of the effect. (B) Potentiation of muscle contraction by an analog of cAMP. Muscle contractions were produced by a constant burst of motor neuron spikes every 10 sec. At the arrow the preparation was perfused with 5×10^{-4} M 8-benzylthio-cAMP. (A from Weiss et al., 1978a.)

The modulating command cell, the metacerebral cell, has a particularly important role in feeding. It acts on both the buccal muscle and the motor cells to the buccal muscle to increase contractility (Weiss & Kupfermann, 1976). The metacerebral cell is also critically involved in mediating sensitization of biting. The cell is normally silent, but brief exposure of the animal to food activates the cell and causes it to fire as long as the animal remains aroused by food. Activity of the metacerebral cells in turn seems to affect the presynaptic terminals of the motor neurons, enhancing the size of the excitatory junctional potential they produce in muscle (perhaps by presynaptic facilitation). In addition, the metacerebral cells act on the muscle directly to enhance its strength of contraction (Figure 7.16).

As seems to be the case for cell L29, which produces sensitization of gill withdrawal, the metacerebral cells are serotonergic. Moreover, the metacerebral cells also appear to mediate their sensitizing action to the buccal muscle by means of cAMP. Serotonin, applied to the intact muscle or to cell-free homogenates, increases the synthesis of cAMP, and analogs of cAMP simulate the enhanced contraction produced by the metacerebral cells. Moreover, stimulating a single metacerebral cell increases

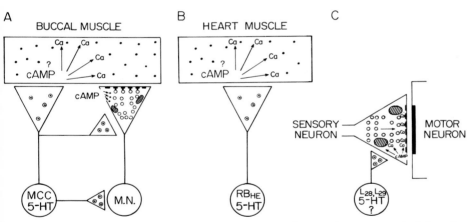

Figure 7.17. Common features of the molecular mechanisms underlying the sensitization of biting, heart rate, and gill withdrawal. (A) Biting. The metacerebral cells (MCC) act on the terminals of the motor neurons (M.N.) and on the muscle to increase the level of cAMP. The cAMP level in turn determines the level of free Ca^{++}. In the terminals the increase in free Ca^{++} enhances transmitter release; in the muscle it enhances excitation–contraction coupling. (B) Heart rate. The serotonergic heart excitor produces a prolonged increase in heart rate by increasing the level of cAMP, which in turn is proposed to act on the level of free Ca^{++} to produce a rate change. (C) Gill withdrawal. The presumed serotonergic interneurons produce presynaptic facilitation of the sensory neuron terminal to enhance gill withdrawal by increasing cAMP, which enhances Ca^{++} influx. (From Kandel, 1979.)

the level of cAMP in the buccal muscle (Weiss, Schonberg, Mandel-baum, & Kupfermann, 1978b).

A similar situation seems to apply to the sensitization of heart rate following the presentation of food. This increase in heart rate is largely mediated through the pericardial nerve, which carries the axon of RB_{HE}, the major heart excitor (Mayeri, Koester, Kupfermann, Liebeswar, & Kandel, 1974). This cell is serotonergic (Liebeswar, Goldman, Koester, & Mayeri, 1975) and produces a prolonged speeding up of heart rate by means of an intracellular increase in cAMP (Mandelbaum, Koester, Schonberg, & Weiss, 1979).

Therefore, sensitization of gill withdrawal, biting, and heart rate in *Aplysia* appears to utilize a common molecular mechanism. It is tempting to speculate that in each case serotonin may act by means of cAMP to control the intracellular level of free Ca^{++}. In the case of gill withdrawal, the control is exerted in the presynaptic terminals, where Ca^{++} may enhance transmitter release. In the case of heart rate the action is on the muscle directly, where Ca^{++} may control the strength and frequency of contraction. In the case of biting, the control is exerted at three points: (1) on the muscle, (2) on the motor neuron terminals, and (3) centrally in an as yet unspecified manner on the central program. Each of these actions again may be mediated by means of Ca^{++} (Figure 7.17).

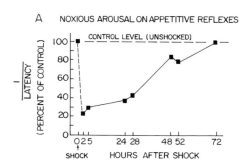

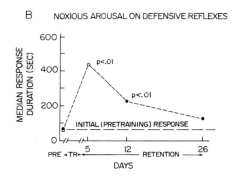

Figure 7.18. Effect of noxious stimuli on defensive and appetitive responses. (A) Negative sensitization of biting. The data are mean latencies of the feeding response of shocked and unshocked (control) animals. The control level is the average latency for all unshocked trials in both experiments. (B) Positive sensitization of siphon withdrawal. (A after Kupfermann & Pinsker, 1968.)

Equally relevant for this discussion is that the neurons that mediate sensitization of the two types of behavioral systems are an intrinsic part of the neural circuit of the systems themselves, acting as interneurons or premotor neurons for the respective behaviors. This anatomical arrangement is required by the nonunitary nature of arousal in *Aplysia* and suggests that each set of behavioral responses may have its own arousal system. That the neurons mediating arousal are an intrinsic part of the neural circuit of the behavior is another example of the parsimony in structure that has previously been emphasized in invertebrates, whereby single cells can mediate a variety of functions depending upon how they are activated.

Having examined the separate effects of noxious stimuli on defensive reflexes and of appetitive stimuli on feeding, we began to compare the effects of each type of stimulus on the other type of behavior. First, we examined the effects of noxious stimuli on biting.

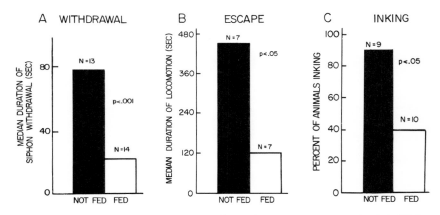

Figure 7.19. Depression of defensive reflexes by appetitive stimuli. (A) Withdrawal. Median duration of siphon withdrawal to 10 water jet stimuli (interstimulus interval = 30 sec) in two groups of animals. One group (fed) was examined immediately after eating, the other (unfed) was examined 24 hr after its last meal. Animals that were tested without prior stimulation exhibited significantly greater reflex responsiveness than those tested after ingestion. (B) Locomotion (escape). The effect of feeding on locomotion elicited by an aversive stimulus (salt crystals applied to the base of the siphon). The effect was determined by comparing the duration of locomotion (number of seconds elapsing until the animal remained stationary for a period of 60 sec) of animals who had just been fed and those who had not been fed for 24 hr. Fed animals crawled significantly less after the aversive stimulus. (C) Inking. Inking to a noxious stimulus (shock) in two groups of animals. One group (unfed) received shock 24 hr after a daily meal; the other group (fed) received shock immediately following a meal. The unfed animals showed a greater tendency to ink than fed animals. These results demonstrate that prior feeding depresses responsiveness to noxious stimulation. (From Kandel, 1979.)

4   Negative Sensitization of Consummatory Behavior by Noxious Stimuli and of Defensive Behavior by Appetitive Stimuli

As we have seen, noxious stimuli produce positive sensitization of defensive siphon withdrawal. By contrast, noxious stimuli depress the biting reflex. Kupfermann and Pinsker (1968) found that a strong electric shock to the head increases the latency for the biting reflex for at least 24 hours (Figure 7.18).

Similarly, whereas arousal produced by food stimuli leads to positive sensitization of biting, food arousal depresses a variety of defensive reflexes—siphon withdrawal, gill withdrawal, inking, and escape galloping (Figure 7.19; Advokat, 1980; Advokat, Carew, & Kandel, 1977).

5   Perspective

The selective effects of food and noxious stimuli suggest that arousal in *Aplysia* is not a unitary process. Sensitization produced by noxious or appetitive stimuli has opposite effects on different response systems (feeding

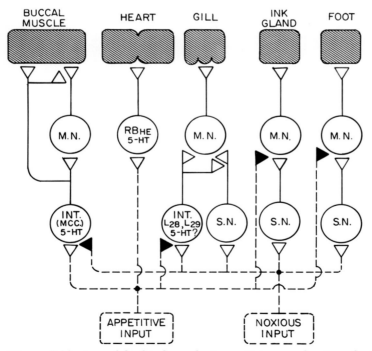

Figure 7.20. A model of independent sensitizing mechanisms for biting, heart rate, gill withdrawal, inking, and escape walking. M.N., motor neuron; S.N., sensory neuron; MCC, metacerebral cell. (From Kandel, 1979.)

and defensive withdrawal) and each of the sensitizing stimuli has opposite effects on the same system (Figure 7.20). For example, noxious stimuli that enhance siphon withdrawal depress biting (Kupfermann & Pinsker, 1968), whereas food stimuli that depress siphon withdrawal enhance biting (Susswein & Kupfermann, 1975). Moreover, noxious stimuli produce long-lasting effects (be they positive or negative), whereas appetitive stimuli produce short-lasting ones (be they positive or negative). These results are consistent with the physiological findings that separate cells located in different ganglia mediate sensitization of biting and of gill withdrawal.

These findings are particularly interesting in view of the evidence that sensitization of biting and heart rate resembles sensitization of gill withdrawal in being mediated by serotonergic neurons that produce their sensitizing actions by increasing cAMP in the target organ (Brunelli et al., 1976; Weiss et al., 1978b). Therefore, even though the neurons mediating sensitization of the two behavioral responses are different, the molecular mechanism for sensitization seems in each case to be the same.

References

Advokat, C. Modulation of defensive reflexes in *Aplysia californica* by appetitive stimulation. *Behavioral and Neural Biology*, 1980, 28, 253–265.

Advokat, C., Carew T., & Kandel, E.R. Modulation of a single reflex in *Aplysia californica* by arousal with food stimuli. *Society for Neuroscience Abstracts*, 1977, 2, 313.

Andrews, E., & Little, C. Ultrafiltration in the gastropod heart. *Nature* (London), 1971, 234, 411–412.

Bailey, C., Hawkins, R.D., Chen, M., & Kandel, E.R. Interneurons involved in mediation and modulation of the gill-withdrawal reflex in *Aplysia*. IV. The morphological basis of presynaptic facilitation. *Journal of Neurophysiology*, 1980 (in press).

Brunelli, M., Castellucci, V., & Kandel, E.R. Synaptic facilitation and behavioral sensitization in *Aplysia*: Possible role of serotonin and cyclic cAMP. *Science*, 1976, 194, 1178–1181.

Carew, T.J., Castellucci, V.F., & Kandel, E.R. An analysis of dishabituation and sensitization of the gill-withdrawal reflex in *Aplysia*. *International Journal of Neuroscience*, 1971, 2, 79–98.

Carew, T.J., Castellucci, V.F., & Kandel, E.R. Sensitization in *Aplysia*: Restoration of transmission in synapses inactivated by long-term habituation. *Science*, 1979, 205, 417–419.

Cedar, H., Kandel, E.R., & Schwartz, J.H. Cyclic adenosine monophosphate in the nervous system of *Aplysia californica*. I: Increased synthesis in response to synaptic stimulation. *Journal of General Physiology*, 1972, 60, 558–569.

Cedar, H., & Schwartz, J.H. Cyclic adenosine monophosphate in the nervous system of *Aplysia californica*. II: Effect of serotonin and dopamine. *Journal of General Physiology*, 1972, 60, 570–587.

Cohen, J., Weiss, K., & Kupfermann, I. Motor control of buccal muscles in *Aplysia*. *Journal of Neurophysiology*, 1978, 41, 157–180.

Dieringer, N., Koester, J., & Weiss, K. Adaptive changes in heart rate of *Aplysia californica*. *Journal of Comparative Physiology*, 1978, 123, 11–21.

Duffy, E. The conceptual categories of psychology: A suggestion for revision. *Psychological Review*, 1941, *48*, 177–203.

Grether, W.F. Pseudo-conditioning without paired stimulation encountered in attempted backward conditioning. *Journal of Comparative Psychology*, 1938, *25*, 91.

Hagbarth, K.E., & Kugelberg, E. Plasticity of the human abdominal skin reflex. *Brain*, 1958, *81*, 305–318.

Hawkins, R., Castellucci, V., & Kandel, E.R. Identification of individual neurons mediating the heterosynaptic facilitation underlying behavioral sensitization in *Aplysia*. *Society for Neuroscience Abstracts*, 1976, *2*, 325.

Hawkins, R. Interneurons involved in mediation and modulation of the gill-withdrawal reflex in *Aplysia*. III. Identified facilitating neurons increase the Ca^{++} current in sensory neurons. *Journal of Neurophysiology*, 1980 (in press).

Hebb, D.O. *The organization of behavior: A neuropsychological theory*. New York: Wiley, 1949.

Horn, R., & Miller, J.J. A prolonged, voltage-dependent calcium permeability revealed by tetraethylammonium in the soma and axon of *Aplysia* giant neuron. *Journal of Neurobiology*, 1977, *8*, 399–415.

Jouvet, M. The role of monoamines and acetylcholine containing neurons in the regulation of the sleep-walking cycle. *Ergebnisse der Physiologie Biologischen Chemie und Experimenteller Pharmakologie*, 1972, *64*, 166–307.

Kandel, E.R. *A cell-biological approach to learning*. Bethesda: Society for Neuroscience, 1978.

Kandel, E.R. *Cellular basis of behavior: An introduction to behavioral neurobiology*. San Francisco: Freeman, 1976.

Kandel, E.R. *Behavioral biology of Aplysia*. San Francisco: Freeman, 1979.

Kandel, E.R., Brunelli, M., Byrne, J., & Castellucci, V. A common presynaptic locus for the synaptic changes underlying short-term habituation and sensitization of the gill-withdrawal reflex in *Aplysia*. *Cold Spring Harbor Symposium on Quantitative Biology: The Synapse*, 1976, *40*, 465–482.

Kandel, E.R., Krasne, F.B., Strumwasser, F., & Truman, J., eds. Cellular mechanisms in the modulation of behavior. *Neurosciences Research Program Bulletin*, *17*, 1979.

Katz, B., & Miledi, R. Tetrodotoxin-resistant electric activity in presynaptic terminals. *Journal of Physiology* (London), 1969, *203*, 459–487.

Klein, M., & Kandel, E.R. Presynaptic modulation of voltage dependent Ca^{++} current: Mechanism for behavioral sensitization in *Aplysia californica*. *Proceedings of the National Academy of Sciences* (U.S.), 1978, *78*, 3512–3516.

Kupfermann, I. Feeding behavior in *Aplysia*: A simple system for the study of motivation. *Behavioral Biology*, 1974, *10*, 1–26.

Kupfermann, I., Carew, T.J., & Kandel, E.R. Local, reflex, and central commands controlling gill and siphon movements in *Aplysia*. *Journal of Neurophysiology*, 1974, *37*, 996–1019.

Kupfermann, I., & Pinsker H. A behavioral modification of the feeding reflex in *Aplysia californica*. *Communications on Behavioral Biology*, 1968, *2*, 13–17.

Liebeswar, G., Goldman, J.E., Koester, J., & Mayeri, E. Neural control of circulation in *Aplysia*. III: Neurotransmitters. *Journal of Neurophysiology*, 1975, *38*, 767–779.

Magoun, H.W. The ascending reticular system and wakefulness. In J.F. Delafresnaye (Ed.), *Brain mechanisms and consciousness*. Oxford: Blackwell, 1954.

Malmo, R.B. Activation: A neuropsychological dimension. *Psychological Review*, 1959, *66*, 367–386.

Mandelbaum, D.E., Koester, J., Schonberg, M., & Weiss, K.R. Cyclic AMP mediation of the excitatory effect of serotonin in the heart of *Aplysia*. *Brain Research*, 1979, *177*, 388–394.

Mayeri, E., Koester, J., Kupfermann, I., Liebeswar, G., & Kandel, E.R. Neural control of circulation in *Aplysia*. I: Motorneurons. *Journal of Neurophysiology*, 1974, *37*, 458–475.

Moruzzi, G., & Magoun, H.W. Brain stem reticular formation and activation of the EEG. *EEG Clinical Neurophysiology*, 1949, *1*, 455–473.

Pavlov, I.P. *Conditioned reflexes: An investigation of the physiological activity of the cerebral cortex.* (G.V. Anrep, Trans. and ed.) London: Oxford University Press, 1927.

Pinsker, H., Kandel, E.R., Castellucci, V., & Kupfermann, I. Analysis of habituation and dishabituation in *Aplysia*. In E. Costa, (Ed.), *Biochemistry of simple neuronal models* (Vol. 2). New York: Raven Press, 1970.

Pinsker, H.M., Hening, W.A., Carew, T.J., & Kandel, E.R. Long-term sensitization of a defensive withdrawal reflex in *Aplysia*. *Science*, 1973, *182*, 1039–1042.

Schwartz, J.H., Castellucci, V.F., & Kandel, E.R. Functioning of identified neurons and synapses in abdominal ganglion of *Aplysia* in absence of protein synthesis. *Journal of Neurophysiology*, 1971, *34*, 939–953.

Shkolnik, L., & Schwartz, J.H. Genesis and maturation of serotonergic vesicles in the identified giant cerebral neuron of *Aplysia*. *Journal of Neurophysiology*, 1980 (in press).

Spencer, W.A., Thompson, R.F., & Neilson, D.R., Jr. Response decrement of the flexion reflex in the acute spinal cat and transient restoration by strong stimuli. *Journal of Neurophysiology*, 1966, *29*, 221–239.

Stinnakre, J., & Tauc, L. Calcium influx in active *Aplysia* neurons detected by injected aequorin. *Nature New Biology*, 1973, *242*, 113–115.

Susswein, A.J., & Kupfermann, I. Bulk as a stimulus for satiation in *Aplysia*. *Behavioral Biology*, 1975, *13*, 203–209.

Susswein, A.J., Kupfermann, I., & Weiss, K.R. Arousal of feeding behavior of *Aplysia*. *Society for Neuroscience Abstracts*, 1976, *2*, 468.

Tomosky-Sykes, T. Pharmacology of presynaptic facilitation of the gill-withdrawal reflex in *Aplysia*. *Society for Neuroscience Abstracts*, 1978, *4*, 208.

Tsien, R.W. Cyclic AMP and contractile activity in heart. In P. Greengard & G.A. Robinson (Eds.), *Advances in cyclic nucleotide research* (Vol. 8). New York: Raven Press, 1977.

Ungerstedt, U. Stereotaxis mapping of the monoamine pathways in the rat brain. *Acta Physiology Scandinavia* (Suppl. 367), 1971, *82*, 1–48.

Weiss, K.R. Cohen, J.L., & Kupfermann, I. Modulatory control of buccal musculature by a serotonergic neuron (metacerebral cell) in *Aplysia*. *Journal of Neurophysiology*, 1978, *41*, 181–203. (a)

Weiss, K.R., & Kupfermann, I. Homology of the giant serotonergic neurons (metacerebral cells) in *Aplysia* and pulmonate molluscs. *Brain Research*, 1976, *117*, 33–49.

Weiss, K.R., Schonberg, M., Mandelbaum, D.E., & Kupfermann, I. Activity of an individual serotonergic neurone in *Aplysia* enhances synthesis of cyclic adenosine monophosphate. *Nature*, 1978, *272*, 727–728. (b)

Discussion

Dr. McFadden: While I fear that most psychologists do not have the necessary biochemical knowledge to fully appreciate all the implications and subtleties of your beautiful experimental manipulations and your results, it is nevertheless impressive and thought-provoking for us to see you attacking at a molecular level concepts such as sensitization and habituation which were recognized and studied initially in classical-conditioning experiments. I again find myself wondering how the participants in the Hixon Symposium might have reacted to this.

In regard to your comment about serotonin and its role in the mammalian brain, am I not correct that serotonin has been identified as being important in regulating the states of sleep and isn't it some kind of offshoot of the basic arousal system when an animal moves in and out of the rapid eye movement (REM) state?

Dr. Kandel: Yes. What the function of serotonin in the mammalian brain is, is not at all worked out; in the sleep system it seems to have sort of an antiarousal function. That is, it's actually involved in generating phases of sleep. The best data on the cellular level in mammals are those of George Aghajanian who has found that serotonin can produce enhancement of neuronal discharge in the facial nerve nucleus and the parallel behavioral studies of Davis that demonstrate an enhanced responsiveness of the brainstem and spinal reflexes to startle stimuli. Whether serotonin is the actual (natural) transmitter for the sensitization of these reflexes one doesn't know yet; the analysis of it is just beginning. I pointed it out only to indicate that the complete analysis of something like sensitization for defensive tasks is really a hierarchy of processes in which the invertebrate studies can suggest certain models that can be seriously entertained. It then becomes important to try to see the generality of these models by developing relatively simple systems in mammals in which this can be studied.

Dr. Evarts: I was just going to comment on the point that Eric ended with —this interesting fact that there are certain sorts of changes in responsiveness which are brief; for instance, the effect of the appetitive stimulus on the escape response. As Eric pointed out, the noxious stimulus tends to have a longer term effect on the appetitive response. In looking at the cellular mechanisms underlying these changes, one wonders if they're the same mechanism or different. The problem of trying to think about these rapid switching processes and the longer term plasticity processes also arises in the case of the vestibuloocular reflex, where one has the remarkable fact that plasticity takes quite a while (several hours) to be acquired and furthermore that the plastic changes remain for quite a while. In contrast, there appear to be other situations in which it is possible for an animal to turn off the vestibuloocular reflex for a very short time and then turn it right back on again. There clearly appear to be two different mechanisms operating here.

Dr. Kandel: Yes. Actually, there's a whole family of processes. For example, conventional postsynaptic inhibition could shut a process off for a brief period of time. What is interesting is that there is a whole range of processes ranging from minutes to hours, in addition to those that last for days and weeks. Some of these may be related. Thus, an appetitive stimulus produces only a brief enhancement of the biting response and yet the mechanism for that enhancement in terms of serotonin and cAMP seems to be formally quite similar to the longer duration effects produced by noxious stimuli in defensive responses. That is, both enhancements seem to involve serotonin and cAMP, although in one case it's a question of a minute or two and in the other case it can go on for an hour.

Dr. Evarts: One further thing, right at the beginning you showed the Kugelberg slide on the abdominal reflexes. An interesting feature that occurs with the abdominal reflex is that if a person is asked to touch the surface of *his own* abdomen there is no abdominal reflex. One does not evoke these reflexes in one's self, though the receptor stimulation is the same.

Dr. Kandel: It's constantly under control of some kind of a central arousal process. I did mention that when he startled the subject, the response would be much larger, and he can get the response by just suggesting to startle the subject.

Dr. Evarts: But I think the point is, what happens in the *Aplysia*, for instance, when in the animal's own movements it delivers a stimulus to itself?

Dr. Kandel: We have not analyzed that but Frank Krasne has done that analysis in the crayfish. The crayfish shows an escape swimming response that can be elicited. The tail-flip response that is involved in escape swimming can also be elicited by tactile stimulation of the abdomen. In earlier work Krasne and Zucker worked out the neural circuit of the behavior and they've shown that the habituation of that reflex to tactile stimulation of the abdomen is exactly as in *Aplysia*. The snyapses made by the sensory neuron on the interneurons become tremendously depressed. So Krasne asked the question, what happens when the animal flips its own tail; that should stimulate the mechanoreceptors and lead to depression of the reflex. Krasne found that those same synapses are presynaptically inhibited when the animal moves itself. As a result of the presynaptic inhibition the synapse is not used, there's no transmitter released, and therefore there is no depletion of transmitter. One way this might work is by means of some kind of system like an efference copy that allows the animal to distinguish its own movement from movement elicited from the outside.

Dr. Barlow: I wondered if you have any comments on the mechanism of presynaptic inhibition?

Dr. Kandel: Before we encountered presynaptic facilitation, presynaptic inhibition had been known for a number of years. As a matter of fact it was described at the NIH by Fuortes and Frank and later analyzed by

Dudel and Kuffler and then by Eccles. When Tauc and I encountered presynaptic facilitation we were struck by the fact that it was not the mirror-image process to presynaptic inhibition. Presynaptic facilitation lasts minutes and hours and presynaptic inhibition lasts only seconds. Presynaptic inhibition was thought to be a conventional chloride-inhibition mechanism acting on the terminals that essentially shunts the presynaptic action potential so that the depolarization produced by the spike is smaller; therefore less calcium comes in and less transmitter comes out. Recently a second type of presynaptic inhibition has been discovered that is mediated by peptide hormones. It seems to be particularly important in pain systems where enkephalin is thought to act on neurons mediating pain and to prevent transmitter release. Certain dorsal root ganglion neurons in the pain systems are thought to use substance P as their transmitter. The cells have receptors on their terminals to various opioid peptides like enkephalin. Iversen and Snyder have shown that those peptides cause a depression of transmitter release that lasts for fairly long periods of time. Recently Gerald Fischbach and his colleagues have examined this problem in dissociated cell cultures. Fischbach and Dichter had earlier found that the dorsal root ganglion cells have a calcium component to the spike. He has now, in collaboration with Mudge, looked at that component when enkephalin was applied, and he's found that the duration of the action potential decreases when he adds enkephalin. When they add TEA to the cells, the action potential duration decreases even more. So the model Fischbach and his colleagues are developing for that form of presynaptic inhibition is in fact the mirror image to the model that we find useful for presynaptic facilitation.

Dr. Mikiten (University of Texas Health Sciences Center, San Antonio): You've been very eloquent in your description of presynaptic mechanisms involved in plasticity. How about postsynaptic change?

Dr. Kandel: My own feeling is that plasticity is going to be like synaptic transmission. There is going to be a whole family of different processes involved. I by no means have the illusion that there is going to be just one very general mechanism for all forms of plasticity. There is already ample evidence for the fact that postsynaptic processes of the neuron can be affected for long periods of time, and I think it's just a question of time before one hooks that up to a specific behaviorally relevant paradigm. For example, one can find that certain cells that are silent can be turned on so they become endogenously active for minutes and occasionally hours. That can be done by peptide hormones as Earl Mayeri has shown and sometimes by just conventional synaptic stimulation. The threshold of neurons can change. So there are a number of mechanisms for postsynaptic plasticity and there is no question that it's very likely that some of these are going to be tied into specific instances of behavioral modifications. The fact is that very, very few instances of behavioral modifications have been worked out. People have tended to work on the simplest forms, such as habituation or on sensitization. That is, they have worked on offshoots of the classical-conditioning paradigm. Changes in postsynaptic processes, such as changes in endogenous activity, are much more likely to be involved in operant conditioning, where you're dealing with an ongoing behavior whose frequency of emission is altered. If one studies a form of operant conditioning one will, I think, optimize the circumstances for finding postsynaptic changes. But operant paradigms are somewhat more difficult to work with from a cellular point of view. The only person who has really made some headway with that is Graham Hoyle, who has been working on leg lifting in the insect with operant reinforcement, and he does in fact find changes in the endogenous rhythm of a particular motor neuron that seems to be causally involved in the learning.

Dr. Evarts: You mentioned that you had used serotonin antagonists in these studies; did you use LSD?

Dr. Kandel: Yes. LSD has not been effective in blocking presynaptic facilitation. We have used cinanserin which turned out to be the most effective agent that Gunter Liebeswar found when studying the serotonergic action on the heart. The situation with serotonin antagonists is not as nice as with the cholinergic system. Practically none of the serotonin antagonists are highly specific. First of all, there are a number of different serotonin receptors, and LSD only acts on some of these. In addition, LSD acts on some dopaminergic receptors. Cinanserin, which blocked this particular response, also partially blocks the cholinergic response. So this is why I'm not completely comfortable with serotonin attribution even though it's all consistent with it. If one had something relatively specific like the various channel blockers, TEA, TTX, or cobalt, I think one would feel much more comfortable with the blocking story that we have.

General Discussion

Dr. McFadden: What I would appreciate hearing are the comments of a couple of you about a development that has been particularly interesting to me in recent years, namely, the discovery that certain cells in what were regarded to be primary sensory areas are in fact sensitive to more than one sensory modality. I think the first inkling of this came with the Horn and Hill demonstration in the late 1960s (*Ed. Note:* G. Horn and R.M. Hill, *Nature*, 1969, *221*, 186–188.) that various visual cells seem to have some vestibular input to them, and then in more recent years there have been several reports of visual cells with auditory sensitivity as well —both in the cortex and in the superior colliculus.

Dr. Barlow: As far as nonvisual input to the visual area is concerned, I'm very dubious about many of the claims that are being made about this, and I'm not sure how well they've stood up. Even apart from that, it's been a sufficiently difficult job to work out what everybody has agreed is the main input to the visual area. My own attitude is that until we understand in even greater detail what the visual input does, it's premature to pay too much attention to the other inputs to that area. Nobody seriously suggests that the auditory input, if there is any, to area 17 is as important as the main input from lateral geniculate nucleus, so let's try and understand that first. There was a very nice example Ed Evarts gave of a visual input to the motor cortex and that seems to be just about the kind of thing one would expect, but it's not a very specific effect and until we understand the specific functions, it may be premature to pay too much attention to something which resulted from a visual input but would not really be called a visual input to the motor cortex.

Dr. Kandel: If I remember those studies, I think there are two kinds of problems with them. One is I'm not sure they were in area 17; they might have been in a higher visual area. The other thing—particularly in Gabriel Horn's experiments, in which the animals are awake—is that one has to take arousal into consideration. One needs to demonstrate the specificity of the other modality. The effect might be general; you are drawing the animal's attention to a particular stimulus and that might be a very nonspecific kind of response. One knows from Bob Wurtz's work that if the animal attends to a visual stimulus it will give a somewhat brisker response than if it does not.

Dr. Evarts: Additional evidence along these lines is the presence of visual inputs to nonvisual areas, such as the vestibular system. There is now very well-documented evidence of visual inputs to neurons in the vestibular nuclei. An example of nonvisual inputs to a visual structure would be the inputs that go to the lateral geniculate nucleus from the region of the pons that is important in eye movements. Much remains to be learned of the significance of these nonvisual inputs to the lateral geniculate. They don't really seem to drive major outputs from lateral geniculate to striate cortex, but they may be important in terms of long-term plasticity, and in fact it may be abnormalities of the inputs from oculomotor centers to the lateral geniculate that are important in giving rise to some of the changes in the geniculate that occur with strabismus, for instance. So perhaps some of the nonprimary inputs—let us say visual inputs to the vestibular system and eye movement inputs to the lateral geniculate—may be important not in instant-to-instant regulation but in long-term changes, adaptation, etc.

Dr. Barlow: It was originally thought that Horn and Hill had discovered a mechanism whereby the orientational selectivity of cortical neurons could be modified by the vestibular input. The initial results did suggest that, but I think if you read their second and more lengthy paper, you get a very much hazier picture of what's happening than you did from the first paper. When they tilted the animal, they had to wait half an hour or so before the orientation of the unit changed. Someone in Baumgartner's lab in Zurich has repeated that experiment with the same result.

Dr. Ratliff: I interpret your question more as a question of philosophy or logic rather than one of physiology itself. We know certainly that the input from any sensory system can interact with and influence the input from practically any other sensory system. A touch on my hand can affect what I hear, in the sense that I will respond differently to what I hear if you tell me to do so when you touch my finger. It really just boils down to an empirical question of whether these interactions occur early in the system or somewhat later, and I don't attach any great significance to whether they occur early or late. We know that they occur and it's just a matter of finding out where they occur and to what extent one influences the other.

Jerry Lame (University of Texas, Austin): Doctor Rose, you suggested that there may be a connection between phase locking and consonance, which raises the question whether above 4,000 Hz—where phase locking doesn't seem to be a factor—consonance might have different properties or could be assumed to be operating on different principles.

Dr. Rose: This is purely a speculation that depends on two assumptions.

First, that the cadence of neural discharges or interspike intervals are really significant for perception tones. We do not know that they are. The second is that the discharge cadence is relevant for consonance judgement of a musical interval. Since the larger the denominator in the frequency ratio, the greater the irregularity of the cadence, it would follow that the larger the denominator, the more dissonant the musical interval. If this were so, there would be a simple way to account for the correlation between the scale of consonances and the frequency ratio. Since both premises are hypothetical it is difficult to speculate. The prevalent theory is that consonance is due to beats between harmonics. This is the Helmholtz explanation, and I think many people support this idea. Now the trouble with Helmholtz's explanation, for which he was criticized very severely by a number of Germans who played violin, is that if you take out harmonics, the degree of consonance of an interval is not changed. Observations to this effect were in turn criticized, the argument being that a trained observer who knows about music will recognize as consonant any ratio that he expects to be consonant. I am not very convinced as to the soundness of this argument, but many reliable observers accept it. I think it is true in the history of music—and I am sorry to say that I know very little about it, so I do not speak with any authority—that once an interval had been admitted as consonant, such an admission had a great effect on the further development of the art. The question to be considered is: Is the consonance of a musical interval naturally determined by the way the cochlea works, or is it the result of cultural experience altogether?

Clayton Lewis (University of Texas, Austin): I feel a need of hearing some more of the interesting speculations of Dr. Barlow about the color and motion areas that he was outlining and, in particular, I'm curious to know something about the nature of the communication between the area with the retinotopic mapping and the areas with the nonretinotopic mapping —say, the color-mapping one, to be concrete. I was puzzling over what a unit in the color-mapping area does when it receives signals from, say, the two patches of the blue telephone directory. What's the content of these signals? Do they contain, for instance, some description of the shape of the patches? If not, at what stage in the detection of the telephone book does the information about the shape of the color patches come together with the coincidence of color that the color area is detecting?

Dr. Barlow: What I'm going to say now is going to be mainly more speculation. I originally thought that maybe the peristriate areas feed back to the main striate areas. What one wants is some way of highlighting those objects in the original picture which have the common property, so that you make the blue corners blink, as it were, and somehow tell whatever is dealing with area 17 in the most important way, "Look, these two regions have this in common." I originally thought, by my reading of some of the anatomy, that there was a rich connection from the peristriate areas back to the striate areas. Discussing this with some anatomists in Cambridge and Semir Zeki in London, it now appears that that is not so. There's a rich connection from area 17 out to the peristriate areas but the connection back is very sparse. Therefore it won't do the job that I wanted it to do. So, the answer is I don't know what happens after that. There are connections from those areas down to the thalamus and the input through the thalamus is accessible to influences from the peristriate areas down there or it could, alternatively, feed on to yet more visually connected areas. So the answer is really I just don't know, but the first stage in trying to understand how something is done is to postulate that there is a mechanism for detecting the particular characteristic which you're interested in, and that's really the basis for my proposal. You need to detect where two different regions of the visual field have some property in common, like color or movement. You've got to be able to detect that. After you have detected it we'll go ahead, and we can figure out what to do with it next, but the first thing is to bring those two pieces of information together on one neuron so that it can respond when the two regions have this common property and not respond when they don't.

Dr. Lewis: This may not be productive but if I could try to pursue that one step further, it seems that the simple detection of the coincidence will not get you very far. Suppose for the moment that you could imagine projections going back to the visual area so that you do get them to blink. Now you have these two places blinking, you need some further mechanism that will detect, as it were, the coincidence of blinking. That is, it seems that what you need to do is detect not only the coincidence of color but also extract on the basis of that coincidence the attributes of the things that are showing the coincident color. It suggests that one needs to be sending information around not just about the sameness of color but the sameness of color packaged with some more elaborate description of the stimulus.

Dr. Barlow: If I'm looking for my telephone directory I've got to feed into the system somehow that my telephone directory is blue, and therefore I'm interested in blue patches in front of me. Quite clearly there are many more things to feed in here. Take the other example of a tiger slinking around behind the bushes. Before you've brought it all together and started blinking out this outline of "object moving in one direction," there's no tiger shape there. It's only by virtue of the fact that it has this common property that you have a tiger-shaped object in your visual field at all. Otherwise it's confused. There's no signal of something with the characteristic shape of a tiger. So you do win a little bit by linking together all the regions that have this one common property. Similarly with texture discrimination. If you can bring together all the things that have a textural property in common, that does win you something.

Dr. McFadden: In our off-camera conversation I believe you indicated that you are thinking about these maps as being rather like parallel channels with the hierarchical progression scheme of Hubel and Wiesel. That is, as I understand it you're not proposing this as a substitute for a hierarchical scheme that builds precise responsivity to particular shapes, etc., but rather that, in parallel with such a scheme, there may be some abstraction along some other dimensions.

Dr. Barlow: I don't really see that there's an enormous conflict between parallel systems and hierarchical systems. There could be a parallel system for extracting information about specific links, which could then be fed back to a later stage of a hierarchcial system. I think it's perfectly possible that there's both parallel and serial hierarchical arrangement.

Dr. Kandel: I just wonder if Drs. Barlow and Ratliff would comment on the notion that visual perception might work without requiring an enormously complicated hierarchical system. It seems to me intuitively, as a number of the critics of the scheme have pointed out, that it is difficult in the limit to think of the notion of grandmother and pontifical cells for each particular percept. Might then the system simply work by having parallel processing going on of the kind that Zeki has been finding? According to such a scheme we would perceive a particular thing when concomitant neurons concerned with color detection fire, and those neurons concerned with shape detection, and with movement, fire. Those three groups of neurons may not even communicate with each other. The perception might simply arise when those three groups of neurons are active simultaneously. They don't need to converge in order to have the percept. They can be acting independently.

Dr. Barlow: But how many such neurons are you going to have? I would very much agree with this—the idea that each of our percepts corresponds to a different pontifical cell going off is ludicrous in many ways because then none of our perceptions would have anything in common with each other. It seems to me that it must be represented by more than one single neuron to account for the fact that what I'm seeing now has something in common with what I saw a minute or two ago, and I would assume that what it has in common is that some of the cells representing it are firing in both circumstances and others are not, and those which are firing are what it has in common. So I think I would very much agree with your suggestion. If you're going to subscribe to a scheme like that, you have to pay a very great deal of attention to the kind of neurons you are going to use to represent the visual scene. You can't just choose any old neurons and hope that you will get an adequate representation. My view is that though there may be many cells representing any given scene, it's not as large as the number of cells which, for example, are activated in the retina when you look at a visual scene. In other words, there is a great reduction in the number of elements that you react to.

Dr. Kandel: I wasn't trying to imply some kind of a random scheme. I think there's a kind of specificity that could be built in there, but that the neurons that dissect the percept—that deal with the different aspects of the stimulus—need not necessarily be in communication with each other for the percept to arise. The percept might be some particular elements in population A, B, C being active in some sequence.

Dr. Boynton: I'd like to comment on Eric's comment and begin by saying how delighted I am to hear him say it because I was about to bring up a similar proposal, with some fear and trepidation because the last time I did it, which was about 10 years ago at a symposium in Buffalo, the neurophysiologists in the crowd were about to ride me out of town on a rail. I've talked to a number of psychologists and neurophysiologists about this and among the physiological group, before now anyway, I think there has only been one person who was ever willing to even consider the idea seriously. To take a specific example, we know that it's possible to make a judgment about which of two events occurred first, whether or not these two events are in the same sensory modality. Within an interval of 50–75 msec, or something like that, it's very difficult to make such a discrimination, but beyond that it becomes relatively easy. A real-life example of this would be what a first-base umpire has to do in a baseball game where he watches the foot of the runner hit the bag while listening to the ball hit the first baseman's glove—he makes his decision on the basis of an intersensory comparison. Systematic psychophysical experiments of this sort can be done. Now the question is, is it absolutely necessary to suppose that the neurophysiological representation of these two different classes of events must, absolutely *must*, be brought together at some *point* for comparison? I think the necessity for this has been an implicit, if not an explicit, assumption in neurophysiology for a long time, although I think that some of the things Sherrington said a long time ago could be considered otherwise. Time and time again in this symposium things have gone along rather well up to a point, and then you have to ask, "How are things brought together and synthesized in order to make sense out of the whole?" I think the alternative possibility that Eric raises needs to be considered very seriously.

Dr. Kandel: I think that the main problem is that I'm really the inappropriate person to talk about this. It's hard to know what the readout for a percept is in the nervous system. We don't know where it occurs and exactly what form it takes. As a result, people struggling with this notion came up with the simplest initial idea of an immense amount of convergence to a sort of a grandmother cell. This idea had a certain appeal; it predicted that you would ultimately get to the point where the cell recognizes and responds to the configuration of the grandmother's face, but not to other things. But certainly the findings that are beginning to emerge do not suggest that that's what happens. You more or less get the feeling from Zeki's work that different aspects of the stimulus are analyzed by different areas of the visual system. One area analyzes color, another movement or shape. From that, one could easily be led to the conclusion that you don't have to bring them back together again. As you have indicated for intersensory modalities, one could have parallel processing all the way.

Dr. Barlow: I think the example of yellowness that Bob Boynton produced is rather nice in this respect because you make the yellowness fit the contour even though you know that by itself there's nothing like resolution in that system to enable you to say to which side of the contour line it goes. Here you seem to have a very nice example of a property of the stimulus that is gotten with a lower resolution being added to something visible at a higher resolution.

Dr. McFadden: If I understand Dr. Kandel's proposal that there is this neural sheet somewhere, and that different stimuli lead to different patterns of activity across this neural sheet, and that the infinitude of possible percepts simply results from the infinitude of possible patterns that can exist on this sheet, then it is the case that I don't understand it. It seems to me that the beauty of the hierarchical scheme, with all of its acknowledged flaws, is that one can understand the process. You eventually converge upon a single cell, but in this sheet thing, *what* is it that's detecting this infinitude of possible patterns? What is the homoculus looking back down on this sheet?

Dr. Kandel: There is no homoculus. The assumption we have carried with us is that there is a little cell in the brain that acts like a man, that does average-response detection on all the activity of neurons to tell us what we see or feel or hear at a particular time. I think that an alternate way, by no means original, is that the readout, the percept *is* cells firing in distributed areas in the brain. Your saying "sheet" is quite correct, but the implication when you state it that way is that we're back to the random nerve net model, which is not at all implicit in what I would like to argue for. There is in fact tremendous specificity of connections and there are, in principle, a huge number of unique cells in the brain. But within that very specificity of connections, cells only respond to particular aspects of the configuration and ultimately the percept is not achieved by cells just hooking up and firing some further cell. Why can't the mind, the mental event, simply be five populations of cells firing at particular points in the space of the brain? That is the readout. That's what the little man sees.

Dr. McFadden: I certainly acknowledge that you as an electrophysiologist standing on the outside could say, "Ah, it's that set of five neurons or it's this set of five neurons," but I do not understand how the mind can do it. What I lack is insight into the detection and identification mechanism.

Dr. Kandel: But the mind *is* those neurons doing it. That is the mind.

Dr. Evarts: Let's think of the baseball analogy here and the problem of the umpire who is very quick to say "safe" or "out." Let's assume that the umpire has no mind, and try to explain his being able to say "safe" or "out." In trying to imagine the linkages between these sensory inputs and his behavior, can we think of a pontifical "safe" neuron and a pontifical "out" neuron? Or is it easier to think of overlapping neuronal sets that give rise to these different forms of behavior? This is a simpler case to understand than "mind," but one which may give us insights into the sort of processes that would underlie "mind." I believe that some of Hughlings Jackson's ideas are relevant to this matter:

But of what "substance" can the organ of mind be composed, unless of processes representing movements and impressions; and how can the convolutions differ from the inferior centres, except as parts representing more intricate co-ordinations of impressions and movements in time and space than they do? Are we to believe that the hemisphere is built on a plan *fundamentally* different from that of the motor tract? What can [the anatomical substratum of] an "idea"— say a ball—be, except a process representing certain impressions of surface and particular *muscular adjustments?* What is recollection but a revivification of such processes, which, in the past, have become part of the organism itself? What is delirium, except the *disorderly* revival of sensori-*motor* processes received in the past? What is a mistake in a word, but a wrong *movement*—a chorea? Giddiness can be but the temporary loss or disorder of certain relations in space, chiefly made up of muscular feelings. Surely the conclusion is irresistible, that "mental" symptoms from disease of the hemisphere are fundamentally like hemiplegia, chorea, and convulsions, however specially different. They must all be due to lack, or to disorderly development, of sensori-*motor* processes. [*Ed. note:* quoted from J. Taylor, *Selected Writings of John Hughlings Jackson* (Vol. 1). London: Staples Press, p. 123, 1958.]

A movement can never be thought of as involving a pontifical single element on which everything ultimately converges. There are different neuronal mixtures that represent different movements, and there is no reason to believe that the organs of mind and the mechanisms underlying them have to be fundamentally different from this. Just as a particular movement is simply a mix of a certain pattern of motoneuronal discharge, and this we can easily understand as giving rise to such and such a movement, I think we're going to be driven to the belief that such and such a pattern of activity in the brain *is* a certain perception. We might sometimes like to think that there is a unique element that gives rise to what we believe to be a unique thought, but that may not be the case.

Dr. Ratliff: I can't conceive from any physiological or psychological or philosophical or religious view that everything that I perceive and experience, however you want to describe it, can be handled by a single neuron. Once you admit that it takes more than one, then you've got two, and, if you're willing to accept two, then why not three, or 3,000,000. The idea that it can be done with one cell seems to me so absurd that you are driven to accept the idea that more than one is required, and once you're driven that far, why, you can go the limit.

Dr. Barlow: I think there's another side of this. We talked about whether it's one or two or how many it is, but what we should be discussing is whether it's one selected from say five or six, or one selected from 10 million, or five selected from 10 million, or whatever. The number from which you select the active ones is just as important as the number that are actually active, and the way it looks to me that the representation of sensory events is going to turn out is that a given sensory scene is going to be represented by a rather small number active, selected from an extremely large number. How many it's selected from is the point I'm trying to direct your attention to.

Dr. Boynton: This particular comment I think should be referenced in the record to Dr. Barlow's very provocative and interesting paper in the journal *Perception* in which he goes into this in some detail. I personally find it a very attractive idea. (*Ed note:* H.B. Barlow, *Perception*, 1972, 1, 371–394.)

Dr. Barlow: I think it's rather similar to what Eric Kandel was saying.

Dr. McFadden: Perhaps we ought to move to another topic.

Don Foss (University of Texas, Austin): This is on the same topic, I think. What you've been speaking about in the last 5 minutes stimulates me to ask a question that's been troubling me since noon. I couldn't decide whether it was trivial or profound, but since it's on the table now I guess it doesn't matter. Most of you are working on problems of single cells or small groups of cells, and now you are all more or less agreeing that percepts arise from the activity of potentially huge aggregates of neurons. Yet most of you seem to be working on what I would call signal transmission into the nervous system. That is, you're not, to my mind, concerned with how the signals get translated into what we might call symbols. Dr. Evarts said in his talk that when we move what we're trying to do is to reach a goal or to get our bodies into some location, and the way we do it is tremendously variable. You can think of the actual movements of the muscles in programming that as a very low level of machine language operation—that's what I mean by a signal. It seems to me that what you need to worry about is some language for the nervous system that organizes concepts like space and concepts like objects. One of the talks I found extremely stimulating was Dr. Barlow's about symmetry perception. Something I mentioned to him yesterday off the record was: Imagine that I have two rectangles, one of them perpendicular to the angle of regard and the other tilted. It's my opinion that I could detect symmetry on the latter— as long as the angle off the perpendicular wasn't too bad—I could detect symmetry very rapidly as long as I interpreted that set of dots as lying on a plane. That means that the way I have coded the information in my nervous system depends upon my interpreting it as on a plane tilted away. Is anybody going to worry about what codes at higher levels handle such perceptions?

Dr. Barlow: What you say about symmetry detection rings a bell because Barnie Reeves and I were trying to find some pictures to illustrate an article we were writing about symmetry detection, and we knew that there were lots of symmetrical kinds of objects like buildings, airplanes, and things like that, and that it ought to be easy to find nice pictures of them. But all the pictures we found had the symmetrical object placed obliquely or with some perspective transformation, and the only conclusion I could come to from this was that in fact we don't very often see symmetrical objects exactly with proper symmetry. There is always some perspective distortion of the symmetrical object, yet we still recognize it. It would of course not be too difficult to try putting perspective transformations into the symmetrical arrays of dots, and seeing how well we recognize that, but I haven't done it yet.

Dr. Kandel: I think there are two points to your question. The first is that you are posing a tremendously sophisticated question for neurophysiology. Imagine us as being the psychiatrists of the brain, we really know practically nothing. Don't have any illusions about the level of understanding that we have. We are really very much at the beginning. What we have at the moment, what our generation has an illusion about, is that we are on the right track. The reason we feel we are on the right track is implicit in the other comment that you made—that we have an aggregate view of the brain, which I think may in part miss the mark. When we say populations of neurons are active, we do not have the aggregate view of the brain that people had 20 or 30 years ago when some people thought it was like the liver or like a bowl of Jello and it really didn't matter which cells popped off as long as a certain number popped off. The application of single-unit techniques to the brain made it clear that there is just enormous diversity in the brain, that different cells respond differently to certain kinds of stimuli, and that it is absolutely essential to analyze even group processes at the cellular level. That simple idea is one of the most profound about higher order function. That is, that even though perception is an aggregate property, it cannot at the moment be studied as an aggregate because we don't have good readouts of aggregate function. The only good readout we have in most cases is single-cell function, and then somehow through ingenuity or computation you have to divine how the appropriate aggregate will respond to a particular stimulus. That's why the task is so difficult. At the moment we are just really at the beginning of the sensory systems and at the tail end of the motor systems. What happens in the areas in between, where the kinds of processes that you are talking about are, one doesn't really know. I think one of the ultimate attractions of invertebrates is that one might be able to work out the bridge there more simply because the neural language is likely to be much simpler. As a result one might be able to get clues about how certain kinds of transformations could occur.

Dr. Ratliff: I think some of the difficulty of the problem can be illustrated by looking at the work in the machine pattern-recognition field and seeing how very little real progress has been made in that area. There are a lot of very sophisticated devices for recognizing simple patterns with templates and so on, if the stimuli are precast in a certain form and if not too much is demanded of the device, but anything approaching real pattern recognition, insofar as I've kept up with the literature, has been a dismal failure up to this point. Many practical problems in pattern recognition have been solved, but most of the progress that has been made has depended on the great speed, power, and memory of modern computers.

Very few, if any, basic principles about pattern recognition have actually been elucidated. You're asking us to accomplish what professionals working full time in the field have not been able to do very well thus far.

Dr. Foss: One other thing in response to that. If you look at some of the people who've worked on some pattern-recognition problems—the ones that I know a little bit about are word recognition in the auditory system —there are programs around that with a limited vocabulary, say maybe 100 words spoken by one speaker, can in just about real time do 99.8% correct when the words are spoken in isolation, but if you take those words and make sentences out of them, the probability correct goes plummeting and even to the extent they do well, it takes them 20 to 30 times real time in machines which do 40 million operations per second. So they're not really doing very well. The point is that you might think that the people doing pattern recognition have taken some interesting steps, but to my view they've gone in the wrong direction when they've tried to do things just in isolation. So, when you say you're going to work on simple preparations and work out their operations, I'm concerned just how generalizable that's going to be until you have some idea that the symbol code in those nervous systems is like that possessed by complicated beings like us.

Dr. Kandel: I agree. I was just giving you a personal bias that for certain kinds of things, for example strategies used in the control of movement, I think invertebrates might be very useful even if it turns out that the mechanisms they use are not fully generalizable. You can see how specific solutions are achieved, and that's tremendously helpful. Once you know how something works, you can test it in a more complex system with a specific idea in mind even if you're going to falsify it. As it turns out, there have been—Ed Evarts can speak to this much better than I— several ideas that have come out of invertebrate neurobiology that have proved to be very powerful. Don Wilson's work on locomotor sequences is a good example. You know, Sherrington at one point had the notion that locomotor sequences are a series of reflexes, that each phase of the action depends upon feedback from the periphery which initiates the next component of the movement. Don Wilson, looking at insect flight, was the first to show that in fact complex motor sequences in invertebrates can be centrally programmed, and that the whole sequence of the movement does not require sensory input but is based upon a pattern generator in the nervous system. Random input will drive that pattern generator. The purpose of proprioceptive feedback is to correct for asymmetries that might exist in the wingspan or turbulence in the air—that is, to correct for incidental genetic or environmental variations. Now people have reexamined the Sherringtonian evidence and analyzed vertebrate motor sequences in much greater detail and found that locomotor patterns in the cat and monkey are also centrally generated. They also do not require proprioceptive feedback for the sequence of movement. So, on a very crude level, in terms of simple strategies for studying perception and motor coordination, I think that analyses of invertebrates might be able to help.

Lee Willerman (University of Texas, Austin): I have been marvelously impressed with the pretuning of the sensitivity of the sensory systems, particularly in the case of Dr. Rose's work, where a lot of the processing is going on peripherally, and Dr. Evart's work, which is concerned with the output end. One of the things that has struck me, however, is that in the area in which I work—the nature of intelligence—one is struck with the finding that there are many individuals, such as Lord Bridgeman or Helen Keller, who have been blind as well as deaf, and other individuals who have had congenital motor paralyses, and yet these people with really severe deficits seem to be able to abstract the essential features of intelligence. I think none of us would argue that Bridgeman and Keller were certainly intelligent individuals, despite the fact that they suffered extreme sensory losses. I'm wondering whether there are any comments about what is going on in the black box that could permit them to extract the relevant information using their remaining senses. Is there so much redundancy in the environment that it permits them to develop a conceptual framework that is at least a semblance of what those of us who have most of our organs intact can extract?

Dr. Ratliff: I would like to make one comment, and that is that Bridgeman and Keller lived in a society of people who could see, hear, smell, touch, and speak, and they could communicate with them. So they had the use of the eyes, ears, and other senses of this community of people with whom they lived. That in itself was a tremendous advantage. Had they been on their own on a desert island I think they wouldn't have made quite as much progress. You can get essentially the same information, if you code it correctly, through any sensory channel. In fact, this has something to do with the nature of scientific objectivity. We try to devise instruments that do not require us to depend on any particular sensory system. One can convert weight into sound, if one wants to go to this trouble; one can convert all kinds of chemical analyses into mechanical taps on one's finger, and so on. So long as there is a single channel available for getting the information in to the brain and somebody around to code it in the proper form, then the situation is not hopeless.

Dr. Willerman: I agree, but that suggests that the black box is really a lot more complicated and has many more abstracting qualities than I think it has been given credit for. Take the case of recognizing the letter "t" from proprioceptive movement, which is fairly easy with the right hand and the left hand as Dr. Evarts was talking about—obviously different populations of neurons are involved, but it is even more complicated than that because I can recognize the letter "t" when it's written on my back. To have a device that is capable of doing all of this integration, and I think Sherrington was right about the increasing intersensory integration, it seems to me that it is far beyond the complexity that has been speculated about.

Dr. Barlow: During the last half hour, we've been talking as if perception occurred perhaps not *at* area 17, but not very far behind it, and I'm sure that that must be wrong. The thing which intrigues people, of course, is the conscious aspect of perception, but I've been involved fairly recently trying to argue that anything one is conscious of is something that one is just about to communicate to somebody else. It's very near not just the output in terms of walking or anything like that but, specifically, the linguistic output. If you take that into account, then one is clearly miles from the sensory parts of the cerebral hemispheres. The other thing one also has to bear in mind is how much goes on in the brain of which one has no conscious awareness at all. What we're consciously aware of, whether it's perception or anything else, is only a very small fraction of everything that's going on up there.

Dr. Evarts: I have a comment on this matter of how we emit motor behavior. Consider the case of emitting the same output when we visualize the symbol "t" and when we hear the sound "t"—both of these can make us emit the sound "t." Now there are a whole class of inputs which tend to generate outputs where there is some sort of proportionality between input eliciting the output and the actual output. A well-studied case in higher systems would be the vestibuloocular reflex, where there's a proportionality between the labyrinthine input and the magnitude of the eye movement. The VOR is an unconscious process and seems to utilize the cerebellum in its calibration. But there are other sorts of afferent inputs that have to generate outputs where there is no isomorphism or proportionality whatever between input and output, and that's the case with many of these things that you're bringing up. I can vocalize the sound "t" when I see a form "t," or if I can read other alphabets I could see some very different forms that would also lead me to vocalize the sound "t." A part of the brain we've talked rather little about, and which seems to have the inputs that would enable it to make the transformation and ultimately link up motor ouputs with such symbolic inputs, is the striatum. It's a part of the brain that neurophysiologists have studied relatively little. It has none of the lovely architectural features of the cerebral cortex or the cerebellum; in fact, it's almost totally without architecture. Yet it's a part of the brain which, in terms of its mass, has grown in parallel with the cerebral cortex. Every part of the cerebral cortex has a link into the striatum. Even the primary visual cortex has an input to the striatum. The striatum may have a role in feature detection as far as motor behavior is concerned. What happens in terms of motor behavior when a particular feature is detected? Let's focus on the motor output that is generated— and forget about impressions and perceptions for the moment—thinking only of the sort of action which is generated when the feature is detected. It is obvious that this action is not simply a slavish result of the feature we've detected. Instead, the action consists of what we are going to do on the basis of this feature, and this action has no isomorphism whatever with the feature. There must be some pathway whereby this arbitrary feature, if it's a Chinese character or whatever, is able to link up with some sort of behavior—and the linkage is often absolutely arbitrary. There is no innate connection between the pattern we see and the motor behavior which this pattern evokes. The reason for my belief that the striatum must provide the linkage is that for certain systems it seems to be the only part of the brain that has the necessary inputs (from cortical associative areas) and the proper outputs, which ultimately funnel into brain structures that generate motor behavior.

Dr. McFadden: I am afraid that time has caught up with us, and that we must end our discussion with this intriguing suggestion by Dr. Evarts. It will indeed be interesting to see if thirty years from now Dr. Evarts' prediction about the striatum has been confirmed. Thank you, gentlemen, for a most interesting symposium.

Index